Politics,
Policy,
and the
Constitution

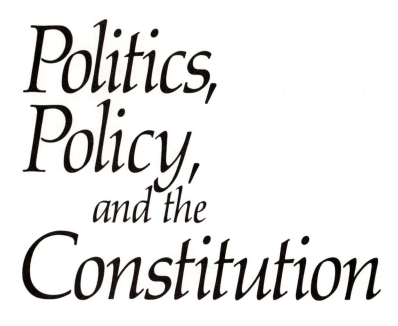

Politics, Policy, and the Constitution

FRANK M. COLEMAN

University of Colorado, Boulder

St. Martin's Press　New York

To Sarah Daniell Coleman

Library of Congress Catalog Card Number: 80-52138
Copyright © 1982 by St. Martin's Press, Inc.
All Rights Reserved.
Manufactured in the United States of America.
65432
fedcba
For information, write St. Martin's Press, Inc.,
175 Fifth Avenue, New York, N.Y. 10010

cover design: Myrna Sharp

typography: RFS Graphics

cloth ISBN: 0–312–62941–9
paper ISBN: 0–312–62942–7

Contents

10   The Federal Bureaucracy   238

11   Justice in America   261

12   City Politics   288

13   The Terms of Political Conflict   312

14   The Constitutional System: In Dreams, Equilibrium, and Crisis   325

Preface

Politics, Policy, and the Constitution explores the ways in which the Constitution shapes political discourse and decision making in the United States. The impact of the Constitution on the political life of the nation is pervasive. My hope is that this book will help the student of American government to understand that impact better and to think more deeply about the problems and possibilities of American politics and their social and economic ramifications.

Our analysis begins with a definition of politics and a review of conflicting interpretations of American politics. I suggest that the Constitution, properly speaking, is more than the written document of 1787. It is also a set of practical political arrangements that shape political institutions and the political process in visible and important ways. In addition I maintain that the Constitution is a tradition of ideas: the ideas of the liberal tradition in politics. Although expressions of this tradition —such as John Locke's *Second Treatise*, the Declaration of Independence, and the *Federalist Papers*—do not have the legal force of the written document, they are frequently invoked as a guide to the practice of politics in America. Of course, to say that the Constitution has several forms is not to say that America has several constitutions. America has only one constitution, but it finds expression in a variety of forms.

To understand the American Constitution we must delve into some history and philosophy. I attempt to show that the origin of our present constitution lies in the constitutional conflicts of seventeenth-century English history; that the liberal tradition of ideas comes to us from Thomas Hobbes by way of John Locke; and that the founding fathers, notably James Madison, created our constitutional system on the basis of that history and those ideas. I further argue that the predicament of American politics today is that the practical arrangements of the Madisonian system cannot cope with the realities of the late twentieth century; that, in fact, the Madisonian system has been undermined by the power of modern oligopoly. *Politics, Policy, and the Constitution* is thus a discussion of the period of crisis which America, with its eighteenth-century constitution, is now entering.

In the course of our analysis we will touch on many of the topics of the American government course: the three branches of government, the federal system, political parties, interest groups, and so on. In so doing we will cover many of the issues that bedevil America today—problems such as urban decay, energy matters, political corruption, and economic stagnation.

Some of the main themes of this book, especially those in chapter three (which concerns the ancestry of America's political ideas), were first published in an essay of mine, *Hobbes and America*, by the University of Toronto Press. The influence of C. B. Macpherson and H. Mark Roelofs upon the main lines of argument in this earlier work is evident, and that influence continues in the present book. I am particularly indebted to Mark Roelofs for inspiring my interest in the origins of modern liberalism and for his patient criticism of some of my more extravagant views. His friendship goes well beyond the conventional boundaries of scholarship and is one of the most cherished, unexpected rewards of my academic life.

This book originated with a prospectus, submitted to St. Martin's Press at the invitation of Thomas Broadbent and Barry Rosinoff, expanding on the ideas of the earlier essay on American constitutional sources. Over the next several years the people at St. Martin's continued to support me in this endeavor. I want especially to thank Bertrand W. Lummus for assembling a keen and judicious team of professional reviewers; Ellen Wynn, whose interest served to allay the pressures of manuscript production; and Richard Steins and Rebecca Day, who worked on the final stages of production.

Several of the professional reviewers who commented on the prospectus and the manuscript have improved markedly on the tone and substance of this book. At an early, critical stage Alan Wolfe and Charles Hayes encouraged St. Martin's to proceed with the project on the basis of the prospectus. I am indebted to Gregory Casey, Thomas Cronin, Peter Bachrach, and William Morrow for their penetrating appraisals. Peter Stillman's advice and support were indispensable; I could not have gotten along without him. He performed admirably and amazingly in the diverse roles of friend, critic, counselor, and arbiter. Diane Hammond, a friend and companion, read the manuscript in galleys and made numerous stylistic improvements and some of real substance. Any errors or shortcomings are solely my own.

Frank M. Coleman

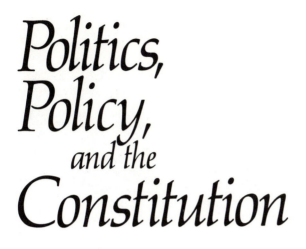

Politics,
Policy,
and the
Constitution

CHAPTER 1

What Is Politics?

To begin the study of American politics, we should ask ourselves what we want to know, a question that turns on the prior question, "What is knowledge?" One answer supposes that we have knowledge only of "facts" existing "out there" in the world independently, as it were, of the person who knows them. Acquiring knowledge, in this view, is a process of acquiring facts, a great many of them, from a variety of sources—such as the daily newspapers, six o'clock news, news magazines, and other journals of opinion. In such a view, knowing the facts is virtually an end in itself. Thus, to know American politics is to know the sum of many facts, much as the addition of many potatoes will yield a five-pound sack of them.

I call this a *tabloid* version of political knowledge because it appears to draw its inspiration from the newspapers. Because a tabloid version of knowledge—which will be avoided in this book—is common in this culture, it is worthwhile to illustrate it, to suggest what may be wrong with it and to provide an alternative view. One detective drama, in particular, illustrates this idea of knowledge with staggering simplicity. Even though the example is a bit dated—"Dragnet" and its star, Sergeant Friday, were popular during the 1950s—it represents an outlook that continues to have a firm hold on the popular imagination.

Friday was so named because the cases to which he was assigned always came in on Friday afternoon at 4:30 P.M., quitting time for most people in the workaday world. Friday (played by Jack Webb) always began his investigation that very afternoon, in the course of which the following series of questions, or something very near to it, would invariably occur. For background, Friday would ask, "What do you do for a living?" "Do you have relatives in Los Angeles?" "Have you lived at this address for very long?" Then the questions would turn in an alarmingly specific direction. "Where were you at 10:00 P.M. last Tuesday?"

As Friday bore in on the specific questions the suspect, incapable of concealing his anxiety any further, would stammer out the question, "What, Sergeant Friday, do you want to know?" Hat pushed back on his head, weary but hiding his exasperation, Friday's response was always the same: "Just the facts, sir [ma'am], nothing but the facts."

Quite a few texts on American politics set for themselves the task of supplying the same sort of information. These texts are written from an approach best described as *descriptivist,* or using the example here, a "Sergeant Friday" perspective. An example of this outlook, based on a fact-minded approach to knowledge, is the following:

> Everything in this book describes what *is,* not what ought to be. There are no articles urging citizens to vote more intelligently or Presidents to dedicate themselves to history rather than to politics. These selections *describe;* they do not cheer or deplore.[1]

This concept of knowledge is not wrong; rather it is incomplete and misleading. Of course we want the facts about the American political system. We want a rather large amount of uncomplicated information about bureaucracy, the presidential primaries, leading decisions of the Supreme Court, interest group activity, and so on. No one will get very far in analyzing American politics without basic information of this sort, and let me quickly add that this book attempts to supply it in abundance. But there is something slipshod and dissatisfying about this concept of knowledge. One might ask, "Where do you stop?" Is it important to know the guest list at the inaugural balls? What about a biography of each member of the cabinet? Should we know the street address of the Pentagon? What rule do we use to tell us which facts we can safely ignore?

Another problem not faced squarely by the Sergeant Friday approach is that the facts do not speak for themselves. They do not say the same things to all people. Although Sergeant Friday puts his questions to the quavering suspect in the flat tones of the professional, as though he were inquiring about samples of rock brought from the ocean floor, it is evident that he employs a mixture of personal and professional standards of judgment, hidden from view, about the "relevant" facts. Friday uses these hidden criteria, which he calls "hunches," to tell him when a witness is lying or knows more than he is telling. A hunch is an interpretation of the facts, or slightly differently, a theory about the facts. That is, a hunch is an arrangement of the facts supporting one interpretation of events and not another. But hunches are not the basis on which cases are brought to trial. And theories will not gain wide acceptance unless they contain criteria which enable us to test their version of the truth. At some point, Friday will have to make explicit the criteria which support his interpretation of the facts.

Sergeant Friday's concept of knowledge is incomplete, therefore, on several counts. It hides the need to set forth significant criteria to determine the important facts; it does not provide a scheme for classifying the facts; and finally, it does not provide a means for testing an interpretation of the facts.

We are going to much trouble to belabor poor Sergeant Friday who, after all, is only trying to do his job, dutifully collecting the facts. The reason is that all texts on American politics, even the descriptivist ones which claim not to be, are theory infected. They present an interpretation of the facts of American political experience, *theirs.* This text is no exception, but there is a difference. By denying that their version of events is interpretive, descriptivists hope to escape defending the criteria which support their outlook. Like Friday they keep their hunches about things secret. This text does not do that.

The approach to political knowledge in this book is *contextual.* To distinguish it from the descriptivist approach, it focuses on the theories which constitute the world of factual experience. More narrowly, the focus is on the theories which constitute the world of American political experience. These theories are the leading interpretations of the constitutional system, linking the fundamental ideas of American political association with the nature of our institutions, patterns of political activity, and characteristic policies. In the following chapter all the leading interpretations of American constitutionalism will be discussed in detail. Great stress is laid on the constitutional system because it most nearly satisfies a quest for knowledge which goes beyond facts to the underlying forces of American political life.

There is another point to be made from the example of Sergeant Friday, after which he will be permitted a deserved rest. We should visualize ourselves, like Friday, as investigators of events. American politics confronts us, after all, as a series of events about which we would like to have an explanation because many of these events affect our lives in dramatic and important ways. We would like to hold persons, or maybe principles, responsible for these events because they shape our lives. Unlike Friday, we should be somewhat more careful about the manner in which we conduct our investigation. To be good investigators, we shall have to improve on a merely factual account of American politics. The presence of controversy about the major facts of our political experience requires attention to theory and interpretation, especially constitutional theory. Additionally, we need to be sure of what we are investigating. What is politics? What is a political event?

SNAPSHOTS OF POLITICAL EVENTS

Our intention is to investigate political events, but the events we are going to investigate are by no means clearly demarcated. That is, there is a great deal of discussion about which events are "political."[2] For the moment, I will sidestep this discussion by pointing to examples which I think illustrate the "political" in life.

The principal figures in these events are perhaps obscure, though well known in their own communities. One is a seamstress, born on an Alabama farm, who never attended college, never spoke in a strident voice, never sought public office, and never had a political following. The other party is an Iowa farm couple. They describe themselves as "average" and "good solid citizens." They farm a 125-acre tract in La Porte City, Iowa, which had belonged to the family since 1852. The values of hard work, discipline, education, and earned respect by which they lived blended perfectly with the La Porte City community.

These people, moreover, did not possess any of the resources sometimes regarded as essential to political activity. They did not have money, a printing press, advance men, speech writers, weapons, organized backing, public office, or pollsters. They were not bereft of the resources needed to become "political," but such resources were in short supply. Finally, the events at which we shall be looking are set into ordinary life. They lack the staging we have become accustomed to: a cast of thousands, klieg lights, balloons, a band, a platform, prestigious figures, campaign buttons, oratory.

SNAPSHOT 1. On December 1, 1955, in the late afternoon, a black seamstress, Rosa Parks, boarded the Cleveland bus in downtown Montgomery, Alabama. She was weary from working long hours on her feet as a salesclerk in Montgomery Fair, a leading department store in the community. Gratefully, she noticed that seats were available on the bus and sat down in the first seat behind the section reserved for whites. As the bus moved through traffic picking up passengers, the remaining seats quickly vanished. To accommodate an influx of white passengers, the bus driver ordered Rosa Parks, along with three other black passengers, to move to the rear. The other three black passengers immediately surrendered their seats, finding a place in the aisle to stand. If Rosa Parks had followed the driver's command, she, too, would have had to stand. A white male passenger, who had just boarded the bus, would take her seat. Rosa Parks, in contrast with the ingrained deferential habits of a century of racial servitude, quietly refused to obey the bus driver's command.[3]

SNAPSHOT 2. The Mullens' half-page advertisement appeared in the *Des Moines Register* on April 12, 1970.[4] Many families at their Sunday breakfast tables were startled into conversation by the half-inch banner headline:

A SILENT MESSAGE TO THE FATHERS AND MOTHERS OF IOWA

Below the headline in smaller type, were these words:

> We have been dying for nine, long miserable years in an undeclared war . . . how many more lives do you wish to sacrifice because of your silence?

To the right of the last word was a small black cross, and beneath it, words as terse as an epitaph: "Sgt. Michael E. Mullen—killed by friendly fire."[5]

The crosses used in this advertisement impose themselves on the viewer's attention. There are fourteen rows of forty-nine crosses each and a fifteenth row of twenty-seven with space left open for one more. A journalist said that the ranks of crosses "so starkly aligned and black against the bleak white page, suggested a photographic negative of some well kept battlefield cemetery viewed from afar."[6] The explanation for the row upon row of crosses appears at the bottom of the advertisement.

> These 714 crosses represent the 714 Iowans who have died in Vietnam.

Near the bottom in the left-hand corner is printed,

> In memory of the Vietnam War Dead whom our son joined on February 18, 1970 . . . and to those awaiting the acceptable sacrifice in 1970 . . .

Across from these words appears the credit:

> Sponsored by Mr. and Mrs. Eugene Mullen, La Porte City, Iowa.

POLITICS AS CONFLICT OVER RULES

What is politics? Based on these examples, politics is conflict over the rules and resources which shape human action in ordered communities. By the community we may mean the nation, social classes, the workplace, the city, the neighborhood, the classroom, the ethnic or racial group. Here I shall mean primarily the national community, and the two examples emphasize political conflict about the rules of human action.

Two decades ago, the simple action of Rosa Parks challenged the premises which ordered human relationships between the races in Southern cities. In the colloquial language of the South, the unwritten rule which her action called into question was that "niggers sit in the back of the bus" and that "niggers give up their seats on the bus to white folks." It is unlikely that Rosa Parks or the bus driver foresaw all the consequences of her refusal, yet each might have known that there was a great deal at stake.

One immediate consequence was that Rosa Parks was arrested, taken to the police station, fingerprinted, and required to pay a ten dollar fine. Another immediate consequence was that a young Baptist minister, Martin Luther King, Jr., was sufficiently aroused by her example to lead a boycott of the Montgomery bus system lasting nearly one year. Desegregation of the buses finally occurred in November 1956, with a federal court injunction prohibiting discriminatory bus seating.

Rosa Parks's action was duplicated in many settings in the South in the late 1950s and well into the 1960s. The issue was first joined in settings where the black people stood on firm constitutional grounds, that is, public facilities such as schools, parks, bus lines, drinking fountains, public bathrooms, hospitals. Later in the 1960s, the issue was extended to whether the police powers of the state could be used to enforce segregation in private facilities "affected with a public interest." Examples are restaurants, movie houses, dime-store lunch counters, motels and hotels. At these facilities black patronage was invited but only in segregated areas.[7] Rosa Parks's simple action culminated in the Civil Rights Act of 1964, which prohibited segregation in "public accommodations that affect interstate commerce."

Following her example, blacks refused to sit in the back of the bus or in the "crow's nest" (second balcony) of the movie house, or to refrain from using the white bathroom, or to accept any one of a hundred indignities and insults in everyday life which arise from segregated facilities. If Rosa Parks's action required blacks to stop regarding themselves as "second-class citizens," or more brutally, "niggers," it also forced on an unwilling white community a reassessment of who they were and what they were doing.

An important characteristic of a conflict about the rules is that it requires a radical reassessment from all parties of what, up to that time, is considered to be a responsible course of action. Such reassessments never occur without the discharge of tremendous social and emotional tension. Martin Luther King, Jr., was well aware of this. Although a practitioner of "nonviolent resistance," he defended the "creative tension" which the actions of the boycotters forced on the reluctant whites.

In the famous "Letter from Birmingham City Jail," King replied to white clergy who looked on the activities of the civil rights movement as "unwise and untimely": "I have earnestly worked and preached against violent tension, but there is a constructive non-violent tension that is necessary for growth."[8]

Like Rosa Parks, the Mullens had had enough. They had voted for Lyndon Johnson in 1964 in hopes that consistent with his public position he would bring an end to the Vietnam War. They were dismayed when in February 1965 Johnson ordered Operation Rolling Thunder, the sustained air bombardment of North Vietnam. In July 1965 the President ordered an increase of U.S. forces from 75,000 to 125,000.[9] The Mullens felt deceived by official statements about the war, and they were disturbed by the absence of a declaration of war by Congress. Their hope, like many other parents, was that the war would be over before their son, Michael, reached draft age in 1968.

In this hope, too, they were disappointed. Michael Mullen was drafted into the army in 1968. In little more than a year he was killed near the city of Tam Ky when a test round of artillery fire fell short of its intended target and detonated near his position. He died, as the army said, from "friendly fire," gunned down by our own artillery.[10] Confusing official explanations of the cause of their son's death were now added to official contradictions about the course of U.S. involvement in Vietnam. These confusions fed each other, linking the senseless death of Michael with the senselessness of the war.

They spoke out through their ad, to sever themselves from further complicity in a war they thought was utterly inhuman. In their view it was the silence of the "silent majority," the apolitical majority, which made the prosecution of the war possible. Their own custom, like that of the community in which they lived, was to bear up, stoically and uncomplainingly, to such adversities as patriotism seemed to require. Silence and sacrifice were the virtues by which they lived. Then Michael was killed. "Our advertisement was our way of telling the world what we thought about the draft, the war, and the loss of life in Vietnam," Peg Mullen said.[11] She urged the people of La Porte City to take a new look at the policy of silence and of answering the draft.

At the end of this analysis, we come to several important conclusions. First, politics takes place in a variety of settings. Events that reflect on national and international policy, such as the action of Rosa Parks and the Mullens, may take place under our very noses. It is misleading to suppose that politics is something appropriated from ordinary people by bureaucrats, elected officials, and statesmen and that only their actions are invested with political significance. Politics has a way of cropping up in ordinary experience.

Second, politics is social in its origin and aims. The Mullens and Rosa Parks sought mutuality with the members of their community by bringing a rankling grievance into the open. Action and speech is the vehicle through which they urged a change of mind. The methods they used to place the issues of racism and the war on the political agenda of the community were open, respectful of the rights of other parties to the controversy, and in keeping with public standards of taste and decency. Yet, at the minimum, reciprocal awareness of the importance of these issues was necessary to maintain the community as a political one. Although the immediate consequence of their actions was to release a frightful amount of tension into the community, the object behind their actions was to reach accord on the rules governing it. Politics involves observable conflict about the rules of human action. But the object inspiring the conflict is to encourage mutuality at a deeper level.

Third, the Constitution, the constituent principles of American political association, exerts an independent influence on the outcome of struggles arising in the political arena. The American political community has traditionally, indeed for centuries, placed great emphasis on free speech, the conscience of the individual, individual dignity, and the like. The departure of their immediate community from these norms in daily practice (the racist South and the stoically silent farm belt) did not lessen the determination of Rosa Parks and the Mullens to act on them. As the conflict about rules escalated in the example of Rosa Parks and the bus driver, we can see that the Constitution tipped the outcome of the struggle in favor of the black seamstress. Similarly, the Constitution afforded protection to the unpopular course of action taken by the Mullens in protesting the Vietnam War. The notion that the Constitution is an independent variable influencing the outcome of political conflicts is extremely important. It is a theme we shall return to many times.

POLITICS AS CONFLICT OVER RESOURCES

Politics is also a conflict over the distribution of resources in human communities. American culture emphasizes material acquisitions—electrical appliances, split-level houses, weapons, accessories, cars, and on and on—so this concept of politics may seem more self-evident than the previous one and is reflected in leading definitions of the "political" in the American scene.

For example, one widely accepted definition is that politics is "who gets what, when, how."[12] Some win, others lose, and in words made famous by Kurt Vonnegut, "so it goes." Closely allied to this view is the one that politics is "influence," a "relation among actors in which one actor induces other actors to act in some way they would not otherwise act."[13] We learn that the things most influential in the lives of individuals and groups are promises of rewards or threats of sanctions. This view is saying, then, that politics is, universally, a relation between a particular A and a particular B, wherein A induces B to do something B would not otherwise do, and probably would prefer not to do, through a promise of rewards or a threat of sanctions.

This view assumes that political actors will seek to organize resources so that they will have maximum influence in particular situations. Thus B will try to develop sufficient resources to exert countervailing power against attempts by A to influence B's conduct. A, on the other hand, will deploy, withhold, or withdraw resources to minimize the costs of influencing B's actions. For the relationship between A and B to hold true, B must always have some resources to employ in resisting A, and A must desist from employing force to coerce B. The moment that force is used the bargaining relationship between A and B breaks down: Outright coercion produces a result which neither wishes. Nevertheless, the logic of the political relationship between A and B strongly implies that A will pyramid resources to present B with a *fait accompli*—an offer that cannot be refused.

This analysis reveals that mutuality is only a peripheral concern for those who use this idea of politics. A seeks to pyramid resources to influence the conduct of B, not to convince B of the merits of a particular course of action. Whether B thinks well or ill of the action desired by A is a matter of secondary interest. Resources may change hands, but neither A nor B seeks to change the other party's thinking.

Another feature of this concept is that it is drearily mechanical. The notion of influentials, the ones who have candy bars, jobs, money, and bombs, pushing around noninfluentials (those without these resources) does too little credit to either party. Certainly there are some styles of political action obviously inspired by this conception. Congressmen are bribed, citizens are intimidated, and liberating efforts are too often crushed. People do change their minds about things sometimes, however, and this concept of politics has difficulty accounting for this factor. It can only account for people who are pushed about.

A final objection is that this conception cannot explain the role of rules in structuring outcomes in the political process. If influence were all that mattered, it would be impossible to account for the final victory of Rosa Parks in the struggle over bus accommodations. Since she had little influence other than her own convictions, she could not have an observable impact on the behavior of others, and hence, could not be political. Constitutional rules existing independently of the parties to the struggle tipped the outcome of the conflict, as it progressed, in her direction.

POLITICS AS CONFLICT OVER RULES AND RESOURCES

In the real world political conflicts center on both rules and resources. The rules, whether law, custom, or the Constitution, are not neutral. They structure conflict, tipping the outcome of political struggle in a particular direction. At the same time, the distribution of resources is a critical factor in determining the capacity of a political actor to mount a contest over the rules. To illustrate these views, we shall first look at the manner in which the leading ideas of the constitutional system influence the allocation of resources. Then we shall consider the handicap presented by modest resources in fighting the rules.

Liberalism is the central organizing idea of American constitutionalism. The liberal ideology holds that the state is created and sustained by the intersection of interests of a whole society of radical individualists. Each of them is disposed by temperament, intelligence, and the history of personal possessions to perceive the good for themselves in radically different ways and ruthlessly to pursue it. The state should be confined to a minimal function in this vision, maintaining the external conditions of public order so that the primary forces in human affairs, private conscience and capital accumulation,[14] can have their way. One preferred way to imagine these political arrangements, virtually a national daydream, is as a society of "cowboys" ("cowgirls" do not have a prominent place in this fantasy) each living on his isolated spread. In this setting, the only government is a sheriff; he intervenes on an occasional and infrequent basis, somewhat after the fashion of Matt Dillon in Dodge City, when it is necessary to prevent bloodshed.

The liberal vision of political arrangements is *traditional* in America, tolerating an internal variety of discourse while remaining the same in terms of its controlling principles; and it is *bipartisan,* transcending party lines. It is something more, therefore, than the platform statements of the political parties or the sayings of great men; it is an imperial political ideology shaping the consciousness of a whole people through their national inheritance. As a tradition of ideas, liberalism lauds the "free enterprise" system and individual rights and subjects the state to repeated and virulent attack. Thus, Henry Thoreau, an exemplar of the liberal persuasion, could say in an antistate mood that the maxim, "That government governs best which governs least," could be replaced with a better one: "That government governs best which governs not at all."[15] Defending the rights of private conscience, Thoreau added, "Any man more right than his neighbors constitutes a majority of one already."[16] William Graham Sumner, a Social Darwinist writing in the late nineteenth century, showed that liberalism sustained a favored position for the capitalist system. Jefferson's phrase about the "pursuit of happiness," he warned, did not mean that the state had a responsibility to assure the happiness of its members. The state was simply there to preserve certain "conditions," such as "liberty for labor and security for earnings," under which the pursuit of happiness could be carried on.[17]

Liberal political views are often asserted with jolting force by major figures in our own day. "Ask not what your country can do for you but what you can do for yourself,"[18] President Nixon advised the audience in his second inaugural address. A few years later, Gerald Ford, as a candidate for presidential office, was reminding audiences across the nation, "A government big enough to give you everything you want is big enough to take from you everything you have."[19] A new wave of liberal revivalism has swept the country with the election of President Ronald Reagan. He repeatedly endorses the liberal vision of political arrangements, including Thoreau's extreme position that the best government "governs not at all." His closing remarks in the final presidential debate evoke the image of a stockade from which, the branding done, the cattle are to be loosed onto the open range. "I would like to have a crusade today. And it would be to take government off the backs of the great people of this country and turn you loose again to do those things that I know you can do so well, because you did them and made this country great."[20]

The first Reagan budget, involving a major reduction in the role of the state in supplying social services, is an excellent illustration of the point that ideas influence the allocation of social resources. The liberal vision is not congenial to the notion that the state should have positive functions such as education, transportation, support of the arts, medical care, housing, environmental safety, or employment. Consequently, many of the programs in support of these functions were cut. The proposed budget, much of which was enacted, provided for reductions amounting to $41.4 billion in 83 major social service programs over the next five years.[21] The specific cuts were food stamps, $11.7 billion; medicaid, $15 billion; student assistance, $9.2 billion; child nutrition, $9 billion; elementary and secondary education, $7.2 billion; health and social service programs, $16 billion.[22] CETA, which provides money for subsidized employment for the poor, will be abolished at a savings of

$3.6 billion. Public service corporations such as AMTRAK and CON-RAIL will have their operating subsidies cut in half or eliminated.[23] It is estimated that $60 billion in resources will be transferred from the public to the private sector through these budget cuts and through a phased reduction in corporate and personal income taxes.[24] Offsetting the reduction in government spending on social services is a proposed increase of $38 billion over the next two years in defense allocations.[25]

To President Reagan and others this description of liberalism may seem far from the mark. Reagan has said that he was formerly a "hemo-philic liberal,"[26] meaning that he "hemorrhaged" support for social service programs, but that he now dissociates himself from these views. Others may point out that "liberalism" is often associated with the social service programs that Reagan is cutting from the budget. Never-theless, historically, there is good reason for persisting in the notion that Reagan is a spokesman for the liberal tradition, perhaps its apotheosis, and that *neo-liberal* should be the term applied to those who approve of the concept of social obligation embedded in the programs scheduled for the budget axe.

Neo-liberalism begins with the observation that human rights were narrowly restricted by spokesmen for the liberal faith to freedom of speech, press, worship, procedural, conscience, capital accumulation, and wage contracts. They argued that the scope of rights to which the liberal state afforded protection should be expanded to include medical assistance, adequate housing, education, social insurance, cultivation of the arts, and a livelihood. The object of this new definition of human entitlements, the neo-liberals said, was to "make the community more of a community," and less a pitched battle between each human and every other, and to confer on the state positive functions to make it more deserving of support.[27] Like liberalism, neo-liberalism embodied both a theory of the state and an economic program. Arising in the late nineteenth century in England and America, it influenced the formula-tion of social policy in President Franklin Roosevelt's New Deal, con-tributed vastly to the Great Society programs of President Johnson,[28] and is currently inspiring opposition to President Reagan's effort to restrict the scope of human entitlements through budget reductions.

Thus the leading ideas of American political tradition shape the distribution of social resources, and the ability of parties to fight the rules is affected by the distribution of resources. Inequities here hinder the capacity of actors to do battle, even when it appears that social gain would follow from modest revision. For example, the city of Philadel-phia has over 30,000 vacant houses. Most of these have fallen into possession of the city or the Department of Housing and Urban Devel-opment (HUD) because of delinquent taxes or mortgage arrears. Neither

HUD nor the city has expeditiously disposed of these properties despite a shortage of desirable housing in the city among low-income groups.[29]

Many of these vacant houses are concentrated in north central Philadelphia, a neighborhood mostly inhabited by low-income blacks. To many of the local residents, stuffed into crime-infested public housing projects, the vacant homes afford an unexpected opportunity— something after the order of found money. The city has two programs for placing vacant homes with new owners. One is an urban homesteading program in which houses are sold for one dollar plus the cost of rehabilitating them. Rehabilitation costs often run as high as $12,000 to $14,000 as determined by bid, well beyond the reach of a really poor family. The other, a "gift property" program, involves the sale of the house to a recipient at a nominal fee ($13.50) on condition that it be brought up to the requirements of city building codes within a year.[30]

The gift property program seems custom-made for north central Philadelphia. The existing rules limit its application in two ways, however. So far the program has been restricted to West Kensington, a low- and middle-income white neighborhood where 1,000 persons have benefitted from its provisions. Additionally, the benefits of the program have been haltingly administered, and there is now a waiting list of 10,000 applicants.[31] The problem for the residents of north central Philadelphia may be defined with precision. How does a politically powerless, low-income black neighborhood expand the provisions of the relevant program to include the north central area and to expedite delivery of services? More generally, how does a group with slender resources fight the rules?

One answer is protest, a political resource used as a last resort by a politically powerless group.[32] In north central Philadelphia protest has taken the form of breaking and entering and occupying homes abandoned by their former owners. Milton Street, a black activist and president of the North Philadelphia Black Development Association, has successfully installed families in abandoned, boarded up, deteriorating homes in his neighborhood. For thirty-seven homeowners the legality of Street's seizures has been sustained after the fact by HUD and the city. City officials did not enforce breaking and entering laws, and HUD sought, fruitlessly as it turned out, a way to make future seizures legal.[33]

The success of Street's method may be credited to his own boldness and to the role of the media in creating a climate of opinion favorable to protest action among "reference publics," that is, constituencies to which responsible officials at the federal and city level may be sensitive. In 1977, Street was one of the few local political figures in the city or the state to appear on the front page of *The New York Times*. [34] A detailed article (June 1977) on his seizure of abandoned homes, the inaction of

HUD and the city, and an inventory of vacant homes in Philadelphia were placed before an influential sector of public opinion. Six months later the *Philadelphia Inquirer,* the city's metropolitan daily, did a follow-up study of Street's protest activities.[35] His fame, measured in news copy, gave him an independent bargaining position with responsible officials at the city and federal level. He used this influence to legitimize the seizures he had already made and to press for an expansion of the gift property program.

It is false to conclude from this example that the strategy of protest is always successful or that newspapers really run the government. In a few select cases, of which this happens to be one, protest may be used as a political resource by a powerless group seeking to win marginal change in the rules. The fruits of Street's activity are these: thirty-seven families in abandoned homes; a bargaining relationship with city and federal officials administering the housing program; and expansion of the gift property program to north central Philadelphia. These results are modest in relation to the achievements of blacks in civil rights. Time will tell whether protest concerning resources will have a like degree of success.

SUMMARY

This chapter stresses the meaning of politics. Before going on to other things, it makes sense to review the conclusion reached and to point to future directions. First, politics is the sphere in which ordinary human beings often express themselves. Newspapers, television, popular journals, and many texts convey the impression that politics occurs on stage, as it were, in Washington or a state capitol. But if our preliminary understanding of the political is correct, politics is as much the property of ordinary citizens as it is the doings of officialdom.

Second, a variant of the point made above, vast resources are not required to engage in political activity. As important as balloons, oratory, and klieg lights are social imagination and a certain amount of boldness. Human qualities are required because politics is sensitive to the rules which organize the community. Politics seeks to encourage reciprocal states of awareness about the need to make adjustments in the rules. Initiating rule change is a delicate matter, requiring the courage and insight of a Rosa Parks or a Peg Mullen no less than organizational clout, campaign funding, the attention of the media, and so on.

Third, there is a tendency for political conflict to escalate. Inescapably, politics is radical, impinging on the rules which bind the community and orient it for action in the world. Whereas the final aim of political action may be to encourage mutuality at a deeper level, as was certainly the case for the Mullenses and Rosa Parks, the immediate result is to release a frightful amount of tension. This tension will spread in widening circles according to the importance of the issue that has been uncovered.

A fourth point is that the Constitution, that is, the organizing rules of American politics, is not neutral among the contestants in the political arena. The Constitution is a hidden actor, working and controlling the process by which political outcomes are decided. The constitutional system, at the least, affords protection to those who are forced back on protest as a means of bringing suppressed conflicts to the attention of the community. Protest was a political resource used as a last resort by the Mullenses and by Milton Street. Unlike Milton Street, Rosa Parks did not seek a political confrontation; but when confrontation presented itself, she did not turn aside. Given her slender resources, it seems fair to say that the constitutional rules were indispensable to her eventual triumph. At the same time, the organizing idea of the constitutional system, liberalism, appears insensitive to the plight of disadvantaged groups. The neo-liberals are correct in arguing that the charter of rights to which traditional liberalism affords protection is excessively narrow.

This discussion sets the stage for the main focus of inquiry in this book, the role played by the constitutional system in shaping the political process. We will show how the Constitution shapes the outcomes of political conflict in relation to the formal institutions of government (the courts, executive, bureaucracy, legislature, and federal system) and informal features of the political process (political parties, interest groups, and corporate power). Different interpretations of the manner in which the constitutional system works will be the main topic of the next chapter.

NOTES

1. Raymond E. Wolfinger, ed., *Readings in Political Behavior* (Englewood Cliffs, N.J.: Prentice-Hall, 1966), p. viii (emphasis mine).
2. For a discussion of competing definitions of the "political," see William E. Connolly, *The Terms of Political Discourse* (Lexington, Mass.: Heath, 1974), chap. 1.
3. See Martin Luther King, Jr., "The Montgomery Bus Boycott," in *America Personified: Portraits from History*, eds. Robert D. Marcus and David Burner (New York: St. Martin's Press, 1974), pp. 387–89.
4. C. D. B. Bryan, *Friendly Fire* (New York: Bantam, 1977), p. 139.
5. *Ibid.*, p. 437.
6. *Ibid.*, p. 139.

7. Harell D. Rodgers and Charles S. Bullock, *Law and Social Change: Civil Rights and Their Consequences* (New York: McGraw-Hill, 1972).

8. King, "Letter from Birmingham City Jail," *America Personified*, p. 393.

9. Bryan, *Friendly Fire*, p. 32.

10. *Ibid.*, pp. 410–30.

11. *Ibid.*, p. 141.

12. Harold Lasswell, *Politics: Who Gets What, When, How* (New York: Meridian Books, 1950).

13. Robert A. Dahl, *Modern Political Analysis*, 2nd ed. (Englewood Cliffs, N.J.: Prentice-Hall, 1970), chap. 2.

14. See Louis Hartz, *The Liberal Tradition in America* (New York: Harcourt, Brace & World, 1955); Karl Polanyi, *The Great Transformation* (Boston: Beacon Press, 1944); H. Mark Roelofs, *Ideology and Myth in American Politics* (Boston: Little, Brown, 1976); and Frank M. Coleman, *Hobbes and America* (Toronto: University of Toronto Press, 1977).

15. Henry D. Thoreau, *Walden and Civil Disobedience* (New York: Signet, 1960), p. 222.

16. *Ibid.*, p. 230.

17. William Graham Sumner, *What Social Classes Owe to Each Other* (Caldwell, Id.: Caxton Printers, 1952), p. 31.

18. Richard Nixon, "Second Inaugural Address," January 20, 1973.

19. *The New York Times*, August 20, 1976, A10.

20. *The New York Times*, October 30, 1980, B19.

21. *The New York Times*, February 20, 1981, A1, 11–13.

22. *Ibid.*

23. *Ibid.*

24. *Washington Post*, February 19, 1981, A17.

25. *The New York Times*, March 4, 1981, A1.

26. *The Official Ronald Wilson Reagan Quote Book* (St. Louis Park, Minn.: Chaim-Pinkham Books, 1980), p. 43.

27. John R. Rodman, ed., *The Political Theory of T. H. Green* (New York: Appleton-Century-Crofts, 1964), p. 52; John Dewey, *Liberalism and Social Action* (New York: Capricorn Books, 1963).

28. Graham Wallas, *The Great Society* (New York: Macmillan, 1914).

29. Mary Walton, "Unrepentant House Snatcher," *Philadelphia Inquirer, Today—The Inquirer Magazine*, January 29, 1978, pp. 12–15, 26–29.

30. *Ibid.*

31. *Ibid.*

32. See Michael Lipsky, "Protest as a Political Resource," *American Political Science Review*, December 1968, pp. 1144–58.

33. Walton, "Unrepentant House Snatcher."

34. *The New York Times*, June 12, 1977, pp. 1, 22.

35. Walton, "Unrepentant House Snatcher."

CHAPTER 2

Conflicting Interpretations of American Politics

Several ideas, of critical importance in defining the outlook of this book and central to everything that follows, will be outlined now. Each of these ideas will be further developed later in the chapter, and as the book unfolds, they will be referred to again and again.

MULTIPLE FORM OF THE CONSTITUTION. The American Constitution is more than the written memorandum of association struck off by the Philadelphia delegates in the summer of 1787. Although we are accustomed to think of it as solely a written document, with seven articles and twenty-six amendments, the Constitution is also a tradition of political ideas and a set of practical political arrangements. To distinguish this idea from the conventional view, I shall call it the *multiple form* idea of the Constitution, or simply the *constitutional system.* The basic idea is one constitution existing in several forms rather than one constitution existing in only a written form.

MADISON: THE FATHER OF AMERICAN CONSTITUTIONALISM. James Madison has the best qualifications for being considered the father of the Constitution. Not only did he have an important role in the debates about the drafting of the written Constitution but also in *Federalist* No. 10 and No. 51, he offers the best theoretical defense of the practical political arrangements underlying the constitutional system. Madison's active political life and writings, therefore, illustrate the concept of a constitution existing in multiple form. No other political figure makes such a substantial and lasting contribution to American constitutionalism.

THE CONSTITUTION AND CONFLICTING INTERPRETATIONS. This chapter deals with the problem of conflicting interpretations of American politics, which are, in essence, conflicting views about the role the constitutional system plays in structuring outcomes in the political process. These views are models of political activity, each offering a different picture of the decisive, underlying forces in political life. Each model establishes a link among the Constitution, the political process, and public policy. The interpretations we are referring to variously assert that the constitutional system favors popular majorities, a judicial elite, a plurality of social groups, an economic class, and a power elite.

Understanding the constitutional system, as we have defined it above, is the key to deciding which among these conflicting interpretations of American politics is correct. The constitutional system offers a useful approach because, as a written memorandum, tradition of ideas, and set of practical political arrangements, it has a decisive impact on the political life of the nation. This chapter will review each of these conflicting interpretations and offer a provisional judgment about their validity, using the notion of the constitutional system as a framework of analysis. The final chapter of this book will return to this topic, seeking to render a final judgment based on all the evidence.

THE CONSTITUTION AS PAST AND PROLOGUE. The American constitutional system is deeply influenced by seventeenth-century English constitutional conflicts and the rise of the commercial Protestant middle class, whose leading ideas were brilliantly summarized in the writings of seventeenth-century liberal-democratic philosophers such as Hobbes and Locke (see Chapter 3). In the course of the eighteenth century these ideas are transmuted into social dogma so that they become the natural basis of political discourse among constitution makers.

Additionally, the elements of the constitutional system pieced together in Philadelphia have an important effect on America's political future. The main features of the political parties, the pattern and purpose of political activity, and the daily practice of American politics are markedly affected by its eighteenth-century constitutional system. This view will be brought out in the later discussions of the party system, the federalist political arrangements, the presidency, power on Capitol Hill, and the judiciary. An issue which these later chapters will raise is whether America's eighteenth-century constitutional system provides an adequate restraining influence on the impact of twentieth-century corporate capital on the political process.

The plan of this chapter is, first, to focus on conflicting interpretations of American politics, judicial supremacy, popular sovereignty, class domination, and power elites. Then, the multiple-form idea of the

Constitution, one constitution in several forms, will be presented in greater detail, and it will be shown that Madison's political writings illustrate this theme. Finally, the chapter will offer some provisional judgments about which among several conflicting interpretations is correct, using our revised understanding of the Constitution as a guide.

CONFLICTING INTEPRETATIONS

POPULAR SOVEREIGNTY

One widely accepted interpretation of American politics, that the people are sovereign,[1] I shall call the popular sovereignty interpretation. *Sovereign* literally means "no higher ruler than," and in this view of American politics there is no higher ruler than the people. The core of this view is that the people are an independently acting ruling authority alive in the course of native history. Periodically, this view asserts, the people vest their power of rule in a presidential leader and/or a political party. President and party seek to capture the public imagination with a compelling statement of current social thinking and to carry these ideas forward through a variety of policy measures.

Since party and presidential leader are indispensable instruments of popular action, there is some confusion among the members of this persuasion about who the "people" are who are sovereign. Popular sovereignty takes the form of sovereignty of the electorate, sovereignty of the political party, sovereignty of public opinion, sovereignty of the titular leader of the party, and sometimes sovereignty of certain "right-thinking" people within the political party.[2] More often than not the hopes and expectations of this interpretation are focused on the titular party leader, especially when he is the president-elect.[3]

JUDICIAL SUPREMACY

Another widely accepted interpretation of American politics is that the people have vested final sovereignty in a pattern of law, the law of the written Constitution.[4] The supremacy of the Constitution is based on the premise that it embodies unchanging principles of right and justice. These principles are interpreted and applied for our own and future generations through the activity of judicial review. It is maintained that the Supreme Court conforms the life of the nation to an ideal pattern of law through case-by-case interpretations of the meaning of the Constitution.

This outlook tends to vest final authority in the members of the

Supreme Court, just as the popular sovereignty interpretation tends to repose ultimate confidence and power in a heroic presidential leader. Constitutional supremacy means in practice judicial supremacy. Upholding this view, one Supreme Court justice stated, "the Constitution is what the Judges say it is."[5] This striking assertion of judicial authority is buttressed by the fact that, ordinarily, members of the Supreme Court speak last on contested issues of public policy.

PLURALISM

A third major interpretation of American politics affirms that neither of the groups just discussed, the electoral majority or the Supreme Court minority, dominates the political process. Instead, it says that a plurality of social and economic groups determine the framework within which popular majorities make their decisions (thus upsetting the popular sovereignty thesis) and that the members of the Supreme Court accommodate themselves to this plurality of groups in the course of making judicial decisions (thus denying the judicial supremacy view).[6]

Elaborating their stand, and contrasting squarely with the popular sovereignty view, the pluralists assert that electoral majorities basically ratify decisions made in advance by active and influential groups. The groups exercising controlling influence vary with the issue under consideration and the political arena in which it arises (national, state, local, or executive, judicial, legislative). In contrast to the judicial supremacy outlook, pluralists believe that the Supreme Court is embedded in the patterns of group compromise. Although the court does speak last on contested public policies, still it must reach an accommodation with any coalition of groups that has captured the White House and one or both houses of Congress. Such an accommodation must be reached because, first, the Senate shares with the President powers of appointment and confirmation of justices. Second, Congress, as a whole, has law-making power over the court's right to hear cases on appeal from lower courts.[7]

The pluralist outlook is more elusive than the popular sovereignty or judicial supremacy interpretations. Generally, it asserts that a plurality of actors *both* in the government and in society is charged with the management of public affairs and that this assortment of groups is loosely controlled by the people exercising their right of choice through elections.

CLASS DOMINATION

A fourth major interpretation of American politics is that of class domination. This view, unlike all the previous interpretations, asserts that power is organized mainly outside the formal institutions of government and is in the hands of the class that manipulates accumulated capital. In contrast to the pluralist view, it holds that a determinate group, whom we shall loosely call "capitalists," decisively influences results on all matters of major social importance.[8] Unlike the popular sovereignty and judicial supremacy views, it believes that this group, outside the structure of governmental institutions, is not accountable to popular instruments of political control. The class domination view goes much further than pluralism in placing institutions in their economic setting and in emphasizing a maldistribution of political and economic resources.

This outlook believes that the maldistribution of political resources arises out of the organization of a capitalist economy. Those who own the instruments of production, who manage them, or who possess the resources to buy them exercise an important influence over the security and livelihood of those whom they employ. The inequalities which originate in private ownership of the means of production spill over into the political arena, where they have a baneful influence on many areas of public policy. In its early phase the class domination theory emphasized the exploitation of the laboring class. The later view extends this point by asserting that the state is used by dominant economic interests as an auxiliary source of capital supply. Thus all groups in society, even, say, the white-collar worker, bureaucrat, or farmer, are disadvantaged by the group that manipulates accumulated capital.

POWER ELITE

Related to the class domination outlook but differing from it in important ways is the power elite interpretation of American politics. This view also finds that multiple inequalities flow from the properties of the American political system. But the explanation of these inequalities is said to lie in the "mobilization of bias" of the American political community rather than in the domination of an economic class.[9]

The mobilization of bias is a cluster of beliefs, ideas, and conventions which guide the operation of political institutions and processes. It involves a tacit agreement among elites, situated at the apex of different power bases—military, political, and economic—to exclude from consideration many matters of major social importance. Efforts to place controversial items on the political agenda and to increase popular participation in decision making are frustrated by covert and sometimes overt action of these elites. This interpretation asserts that elites are able to act in concert, even while deriving power from different institutional bases, because they deal with each other on a relational basis while manipulating all other political actors.

Like the class domination outlook, the power elite theory concludes that existing political arrangements tip outcomes in the political process toward privileged groups. Yet this theory emphasizes the relative autonomy of the political sphere. It tends to explain political inequality as a function of prevailing beliefs, practices, and biases of the constitutional system rather than the resources at the disposal of an economic group. Both interpretations are strikingly different from pluralism, which states that the political system represents a stable balance of social forces, and from judicial supremacy and popular sovereignty, which assert that political institutions are socially progressive.

WHAT THE CONSTITUTION IS AND DOES

We have just seen that the facts of American political experience do not speak to all men alike. Intelligent, well-trained students of American politics look at the system and see very different things. In the midst of this controversy over the basic facts it is unacceptable to adopt a descriptivist approach to the study of politics. A contextual approach, interpreting political events from a broad perspective, is needed to sift the evidence and evaluate conflicting claims to reality.

I suggest that the Constitution offers a useful avenue for approaching the study of American politics, but we must know what the Constitution is and what it does. This sounds like a very straightforward task; however, it is a bit more difficult than it might seem for two reasons. First, we are speaking of an abstraction. Constitutions do not walk the streets and we cannot engage a constitution in conversation. Second, this abstraction, the Constitution, is poorly represented in the literature of American politics. Thus, I shall spend a fair amount of time in this chapter trying to present a clear idea of what the Constitution is and what it does.

The idea of the Constitution embodied in much of the literature and pageantry of American politics is extremely narrow and literal. This idea of the Constitution, which I shall call *literal,* is delivered with uncritical force and naïveté, in a famous passage from an opinion by Justice Roberts, a former judge on the Supreme Court:

> When an act of Congress is appropriately challenged in the courts as not conforming to the constitutional mandate, the judicial branch of Government has only one duty, to lay the article of the Constitution which is invoked beside the statute which is challenged and to decide whether the latter squares with the former. All the court does, or can do, is to announce its considered Judgment upon the question.[10]

It is necessary to say with all the energy one can, at the very start, that an interpretation of American politics based on this understanding of the Constitution is not a particularly interesting or rewarding experience. Further, it is misleading.

Roberts's opinion implies that the Constitution exists solely as a *written memorandum of association* (the Constitution of 1787), and this is the form in which we are most accustomed to thinking about it. Propaganda, show business, and habit collaborate to keep this idea of the Constitution uppermost in mind. The written Constitution is preserved, almost superstitiously, under glass in a fireproof, bombproof vault in the National Archives Building, Washington, D.C. Why? If Washington were bombed and the written document preserved, would we be better off? In other words, patterns of thought appear to be entirely fixed on the written document. To change this habit of thinking may be a difficult task.

The American Constitution does exist in other forms than the written articles of political association, and they have a more immediate impact on the everyday political life of the nation than the lifeless abstraction that Roberts talks about. I shall call this other view the *multiple form* idea of the American Constitution, one constitution in several forms.

Another form in which the Constitution exists is as the *historical commitment of a people to a particular tradition of ideas,* [11] which is the ideology of liberal democracy. The liberal tradition, an overpowering consensus in American politics that underlies both political parties and shapes our major institutions, has remained much the same in terms of its controlling principles for many centuries. This tradition of ideas does not have the legal force of the written Constitution. Yet well-known expressions of it, for example, the *Federalist Papers,* the Declaration of Independence, and John Locke's *Second Treatise of Government,* are sometimes referred to by the Supreme Court in interpreting the written document.

An expression of this historical enthusiasm for liberal democracy is Lincoln's Gettysburg Address. The address is a reminder to the American people that they are created as a community in memory and anticipation by the ancient commitment of the founding "fathers" to liberalism. "Fourscore and seven years ago," Lincoln says, "our fathers brought forth on this continent a new nation, conceived in liberty, and dedicated to the proposition that all men are created equal." The historic commitment to the ideas of liberty and equality needs to be examined in relation to acts in the present, Lincoln points out. *"Now* [emphasis mine]," he says, "we are engaged in a great civil war, testing whether that nation, or any nation so conceived and so dedicated, can long endure." Further, Lincoln avows, this tradition of ideas not only shapes the present but also orients conduct toward the future. "It is for us, the living . . . to be dedicated here to the unfinished work which they who fought here have thus far so nobly advanced." The Gettysburg Address is easily the most eloquent expression of the American commitment to liberalism, the nature of which, Lincoln reminds us, is always in need of reinterpretation in relation to the politics of the current day.

Another form in which the Constitution exists is as *a set of working arrangements.* These arrangements, which enable those engaged in politics in our society to act, may be called the *operative realities* of American politics.[12] To put it bluntly, these operative realities describe the way things really work, for the ideas passed on from generation to generation, the ideas of the fathers, do not exist in remote splendor from the squalid world of political practice. Instead, they exist immanently and actually in the ways in which the political process goes on. The descriptivist literature, discussed in the first chapter, is a good source of information on these working arrangements; the patterns of American politics are set forward in exhaustive and often repetitious detail.

In discussing these working arrangements we shall have to distinguish them from social practices that conflict with constitutional trends. As we saw from the examples of Chapter 1, major ideas of the Constitution may stimulate political action in conflict with the custom of the community. Fortunately, Americans tend to practice politics in a distinctive manner, which makes this critical differentiation possible.

To say that the American Constitution exists in several forms—a written memorandum, a set of political practices, a tradition of ideas—is not to say that America has several constitutions. America has only one Constitution. But it is to say that, contrary to Justice Roberts's belief, our one Constitution finds expression in a variety of forms and affects the quality of our daily lives. In a sentence, the Constitution is the total range of constraints—institutional, ideological, and practical—under which Americans have chosen to live. As such, it shapes the conduct of American politics, affects the design of our institutions, and influences social customs and habits in visible and important ways.

Changing the idea of what the Constitution is changes our idea of what the Constitution does. The concept of its functions is poorly conveyed by the opinion of Justice Roberts, who sees the Constitution as a barrier, apart from the politics of the nation, which important public policy must find some way of surmounting. The task of hurdling this roadblock, left behind through a fit of absent-mindedness or malice, must be attempted for reasons like that given by mountain climbers, "because it's there." In other words, the notion of the Constitution as solely a written document leads to the view that its function is external to political life.

Actually, the Constitution exerts a strong enabling and constraining function on the political life of the nation. It performs an enabling function insofar as it helps our society organize itself politically for action in the world. The Constitution sets out the institutional design, shapes the patterns of behavior, and furnishes the ideas through which the political process occurs. Without the creative functions that the Constitution performs, politics in America would not be possible. By the same token, the Constitution exerts a powerful constraining force on the politics and policies of the nation. Policy options possible in other nations become impractical, even unthinkable, in America.

MADISON: FATHER OF THE CONSTITUTION

James Madison is often presented as the true father of the American Constitution, ahead of such likely candidates as George Washington, Benjamin Franklin, Thomas Jefferson, or John Adams. Madison was the fourth president of the United States (1809–1817), a member of the U.S. House of Representatives (1789–1797), and secretary of state (1801–1809). His notes on the proceedings of the constitutional convention are the main record of issues and spokesmen who mattered in framing the written Constitution.

Belief that Madison is the father of the Constitution does not turn on his part in the proceedings of the Philadelphia convention or on his numerous and successive public offices. Instead, it is based on the fact that Madison co-authored (with John Jay and Alexander Hamilton) the *Federalist Papers,* the best theoretical defense of the Constitution of 1787 and the institutions which it created. The ideas in this defense reach backward in history at the same time that they are carried forward in the practical arrangements of American politics. They are interwoven with American political institutions and processes, establishing a link between theory and practice.

Madison's ideas look backward to seventeenth-century English constitutional conflicts and to the doctrine, established by the first liberal-democratic thinkers, Thomas Hobbes (1588–1679) and John Locke (1632–1704), that the individual is the sole source of right in modern society. Madison shares with these English thinkers the important idea that man is an "independently situated political actor" who both creates and becomes the subject of governmental institutions.[13] That is, each individual is differently constituted in terms of intelligence, temperament, skills, and the history of personal possessions to perceive the good for him- or herself in radically different ways and ruthlessly to pursue it. Political institutions are created and sustained insofar as they afford protection to the personal spheres of property, religion, and opinion marked out by each individual in his or her separate quest for the good things of life.

Speaking of this idea of political man and of its relation to government, Madison says that each man has a "property," by which he means an absolute and exclusive claim to a range of personal goods set apart through the exercise of his talents and faculties. Among the things in which a man has a sense of property, Madison says, are the following: (1) "A man's land, or merchandize or money is called his property." (2) "A man has property in his opinions and the free communication of them." (3) A man "has a property of peculiar value in his religious opinions and in the profession and practice dictated by them." (4) A man "has a property very dear to him in the safety and liberty of his person." (5) A man "has an equal property in the free exercise of his faculties and free choice of objects on which to employ them." "Government," Madison asserts, "is instituted to protect property of every sort";[14] that is, government is instituted to safeguard independently situated actors in the possession of their material goods, opinions, faculties, and all else that expresses their sense of personal liberty.

The same ideas that link Madison to the past also tie him to the present. Rosa Parks's refusal to surrender her seat on the bus, as an example, is logically derived from the ideas of Madison and his English forefathers. Since the authority of political institutions is based on the consent of a society of independently situated actors, government must provide all, rich and poor, smart and stupid, black and white or otherwise, equal treatment before the law and equal access to public facilities. In his own day, Madison avoided the conclusion to which his own political ideas pointed. The black was not provided equal protection under the laws of the states then in force or under specific provisions of the Constitution (see especially Chapter 6). But other generations differently positioned in terms of social circumstance looked upon the same tradition of ideas from a different perspective. Rosa Parks drew conclusions, which Madison chose not to recognize, from the tradition of ideas for which he was a major spokesman.

Similarly, the Mullens' public resistance to military intervention in Vietnam issued from a confident belief that the government would afford protection to each man's "property in his opinions and the free communication of them." Even though the Mullens' advertisement encouraged resistance to government policy, it enjoyed the protection which our institutions are obliged to provide in all spheres for the expression of personal liberty.

If Madison is a pivotal figure, joining the past to the present, he is of equal importance as a link between ideas and political practice. In Madison's *Federalist* essays, ideas emerge as the interior reality of political institutions. His most important contribution is the connection he makes between the idea of the independently situated political actor and institutions based on "countervailing power." Madison argued that the "property" spheres of individuals were best protected by institutions organized on the basis of countervailing power. This concept originally denotes governmental checks on the exercise of power by rival powers; later the idea is broadened to include nongovernmental checks.

Countervailing power has two main forms in Madison's writing: federalism and separation of powers (executive, legislative, and judicial). Together with republicanism (to be discussed at greater length along with federalism and separation of powers), these institutional forms are meant to preserve the liberties of the individual. The main point at this stage is to see that ideas do not exist merely as an abstraction. For Madison they exist in the political process, working themselves out in the patterns of behavior of all participants.

In *Federalist* No. 10 Madison expresses fear that sharp conflicts will arise out of the choices pursued by independently situated actors in the political arena. "Liberty" tends to be expressed in the material choices pursued by individuals in a highly commercialized society, and conflict arises because individuals invest their whole personality in their choice (particularly of material possessions), have differing capacities for realizing their choices, and seek to make their choices prevail over competing interests. Differences in capacity divide society into the rich and the poor, creditors and debtors. Differences in the kind of choices people make, coupled with a determination to make their choices prevail, produce conflict between a "landed interest, a manufacturing interest, a mercantile interest, [and] a moneyed interest, with many lesser interests."[15] The consequence of this intense competition among social interests is general social conflict. In this state men can be relied upon to "vex and oppress each other" rather than to "cooperate for the common good." At the bottom of Madison's account of social conflict is a theory of conflict between discrete and hostile, acquisitive individuals. He makes it the first duty of government to manage this conflict, at once preserving the "diversity in the faculties of [individual] men,"[16] and the stability of political institutions.

Madison's chief technique for dealing with social conflict is an elaborate governmental system of "countervailing power." He sought to check power with power at every level, and thus to withhold opportunities for political domination from any one individual or interest group or combination of groups.[17] His basic vision is that government must be neutral in the clash of economic interests; its role is not that of a positive agent but of a manager of the conflicts that threaten social stability, assuring through the nature of institutional design that opportunities for government domination are withheld from any group. As stated in *Federalist* No. 51, the system of arrangements should array "ambition . . . to counteract ambition." It should establish, in the absence of any norm of public rectitude, "the private interest of every individual" as a "sentinel over public rights." Much of the substance of these remarks is contained in Madison's corrosive parable on government.

> If men were angels, no government would be necessary. If angels were to govern men, neither external nor internal controls on government would be necessary. In framing a government which is to be administered by men over men, the great difficulty lies in this: you must first enable the government to control the governed; and in the next place oblige it to control itself.[18]

Madison puts forward federalism and republicanism as institutions that promote the goal of managing conflict. The principle of federalism operated like numerous watertight compartments on a great ship. As the ship is kept afloat by sealing off the invading water in isolated containers, so the great ship of state would be preserved by compartmentalized power. Federalism separates the use of power by parties acting in the national sphere from those in the state and local sphere of government. Consequently, those who come into conflict in either the national or local sphere can make use of the federal principle to seal off threats to their own power. Madison assured the upper classes that federalism would afford them safe refuge from the democratizing forces at work in the state and local government and thus promote the goal of conflict-management.

> The influence of factious leaders may kindle a flame within their particular States, but will be unable to spread a conflagration through the other States. . . . A rage for paper money, for an abolition of debts, for an equal division of property, or for any other wicked or improper project, will be less apt to pervade the whole body of the Union than a particular member of it.[19]

The attraction of republicanism was that it incorporated more interests distributed over a larger sphere than democracy. To Madison, democracy meant the whole people meeting and deliberating together in a common assembly, a concept that restricted the territorial sphere over which governmental power could be exercised. Republicanism involved the principle of the representation of the people and this allowed an outward extension of the government, thus embracing more interests. More interests distributed over a larger sphere, the key principle, makes it difficult for any one group or combination of groups to "discover their own strength and act in unison with each other" or to "concert and carry into effect schemes of oppression."[20]

Madison's plan for managing social conflict is engagingly simple. First, multiply the parties to the social conflict and fling them into space (republicanism). Afterward, seal them off in separate and isolated compartments of power (federalism).

A related technique used by Madison for dealing with social conflict is the dispersion of the executive, legislative, and judicial powers among separate departments of government. In point of fact Madison did not, as convention has it, provide for a "separation of powers" among the departments; rather he argued the utility of "separate institutions sharing power."[21] Each one of the departments was to share extensively in the exercise of power by the coordinate branches. Thus the legislature shares in judicial power through appointments, determination of powers of appellate review, and creation of federal courts. The executive shares in the legislative power through the veto, state of the union message, assemblage of special legislative sessions, and legislative initiative. The judiciary speaks last on contested constitutional issues involving executive and legislative policy. Each department partially shares in the exercise of power by the others; each department, therefore, must obtain the concurrence of the others in order to get anything done.

Madison's basic vision of the political process is that separate institutions sharing power will force independently situated actors to negotiate their differences rather than fight them out. A political process characterized by negotiations among diverse centers of power offers in Madison's view the best prospect of reconciling the conflicting claims of liberty and stability. His theory, to sum up, looks forward and backward, unifying ideas and political practice; it affords a comprehensive vision of the Constitution existing in a multiple form —as written memorandum, cluster of ideas, and set of practical political arrangements. Most importantly, Madison's theory of politics links the individual to institutions organized on the basis of countervailing power.

CONFLICTING INTERPRETATIONS REVISITED

I started by saying that a correct understanding of the Constitution was the key to evaluating conflicting versions of American politics, an investigative method for discovering whether political arrangements are tipped toward a power elite, a plurality of social and economic groups, popular majorities, a judicial elite, or monopoly capital.

Any judgments offered at this point must be provisional. We have yet to study the historical foundations of American constitutionalism (Chapter 3) and trace the manner in which American politics is shaped by the working out in history of inherited ideas and political arrangements (Chapters 4 through 9). Deciding which among several interpretations is correct is a tricky matter in any event, but I can offer some preliminary judgments about the main patterns of American politics, saving a final summing up for the concluding chapter.

POPULAR SOVEREIGNTY REVISITED

Popular sovereignty is squarely in conflict with Madison's idea that the main purpose of American politics is to preserve the liberties of independently situated actors through a system of republicanism and countervailing power. Madison emphasizes that his system is designed to withhold power from *any* group, "whether a majority or a minority of the whole."[22] He states that republican institutions provide for the representation of the people, but he stresses that countervailing power is meant to assure that the people, considered as a popular majority, "will be broken into so many parts, interests, and classes of citizens, that the rights of individuals . . . will be in little danger from interested combinations of the majority."[23]

It seems inescapable that Madison did not intend the practical arrangements of the Constitution to serve as an instrument for majority democracy through presidential leadership. Further evidence to support this conclusion is provided by the features of the written Constitution. The electoral college was designed to withhold the critical election of the president from the people and to vest it in a college of electors chosen by the state legislatures. The right to vote is not protected by the written Constitution. Unable to agree on the criteria of voting eligibility, the delegates to the Philadelphia convention left the matter to the states, all of whom imposed tax and property restrictions on the voting franchise. A series of amendments is needed in the course of national history, the Fifteenth, Nineteenth, Twenty-third, Twenty-fourth, and Twenty-sixth, to roll back restrictions placed by the state legislatures on the right to vote.

The case for popular sovereignty is not overthrown by these observations. We shall later see that the franchise has been broadened and the electoral college greatly changed. But it is worth noting that democratic participation is an uphill battle in American history. The Constitution, considered as written memo, cluster of ideas, and set of practical arrangements, is meant to frustrate and impede popular majorities.

JUDICIAL SUPREMACY REVISITED

Another interpretation that does not fare well is judicial supremacy. The notion of imposing an ideal pattern of law through judicial interpretation is in conflict with Madison's notion of balancing power among rival institutions. Again, Madison sought to withhold power from any group whether "a majority of the whole," or a minority. He is no more favorable to vesting final authority in a judicial elite than in popular majorities. Group conciliation and compromise are more in keeping with the pattern of Madisonian politics than rule by a judicial aristocracy.

Hamilton, who joined with Madison in writing the *Federalist,* stressed that the judiciary is the weakest branch and, therefore, the department most likely to seek compromise and accommodation with the coordinate branches. He said that the judiciary lacked both the "sword" of the chief executive and the "purse" of the legislature.[24] In the absence of these political resources, Hamilton expressed confidence that the judiciary was destined to become the "weakest of the three departments of power."[25] Shifting attention to the present day, we find that consistently with Madison's basic design and Hamilton's prophecy, the Supreme Court adapts itself to the patterns of group conciliation in performing its rule-making and rule-adjudicating functions (see Chapter 10).

Not only do the practical arrangements of the Constitution weigh against the judicial supremacy view, so do its written provisions. The Philadelphia delegates withheld the power of judicial review from the members of the Supreme Court, surely a curious omission if they wished to make the judiciary the preeminent place of power. When the power of judicial review over the actions of the coordinate branches was asserted by Chief Justice Marshall in the landmark case of *Marbury* v. *Madison* (1803), it came as a great surprise. The evidence indicates that judicial review is a political creation of Justice Marshall in answer to a logical need for a final interpreter of the written Constitution and is not an express and intended function conferred on the Supreme Court by the document itself. It is worth remarking that the significance of Marshall's opinion was overlooked in the heat of the immediate controversy. Not until a full half century later, in the case of *Dred Scott* v. *Sanford* (1857), is the power of judicial review reaffirmed.

To further assess the validity of the judicial supremacy view, we shall have to explore the important limitations that the Supreme Court itself has placed on the judicial function. Only after further study will it become clear whether, as one view has it, the Supreme Court is a "power group" and a "vehicle of revealed truth" whose judgments commonly prevail in the political struggle.[26] At this point, my provisional judgment is that judicial supremacy was not intended by the Philadelphia delegates and does not fit with the practical arrangements of the constitutional system.

PLURALISM REVISITED

Madison's vision of the political process appears to lie closest to the pluralist interpretation. Modern pluralism emphasizes, as Madison did, that politics is a matter of conflict management among a plurality of social and economic groups. However, pluralism shifts the emphasis of Madison from *governmental* conflict and balance to conflict and balance among a diverse composition of *social and economic forces.*[27] Pluralists state that power is distributed noncumulatively among social, political, and economic groups, thus producing the stability desired by Madison rather than the institutional design upon which he had placed stress.

This shift in emphasis is not significant, because it is clear that Madison believed in relative equality among political actors, placing major stress on governmental institutions which would maintain that equality. Pluralism goes beyond this assumption in its assertion that the historical evolution of American society has produced an increasingly even distribution of status, skill, and material goods.[28] The inference to be drawn is that the goals of Madisonian politics, a rough measure of distributive justice flowing from the self-interested activity of individuals and groups, will be more fully realized in our own era than in Madison's. The distribution of resources and balances of the governmental system will prevent any one group from assembling sufficient power to get all of what it wants. But each group will get enough of what it wants to form a vested interest in sustaining the constitutional system.

Although the independently situated actor stressed by Madison is apparently swallowed up by the pluralist emphasis on "group" activity, the goal and conduct of politics remain highly privatized, so much so that pluralism retains its conformity with Madisonian perspectives. A contemporary pluralist, for example, states that each individual in the political arena, whether cabinet officials, administrative staff, committee chairmen, party whips, mayors, even the chief executive himself, is isolated by unique constellations of interests which variably affect *his* "frame of reference," *his* tenure in office, and the pursuit of *his* immediate aims.[29] Political leadership consists in finding the opportunities for direction in the needs of a particular group, becoming its authorized spokesman, and then proceeding to exploit needs elsewhere in the system, through negotiations between independently situated actors, in order to service one's own particular political clientele.

Applying this theory of politics to the office of the president, a modern pluralist advises,

> When we inaugurate a President of the United States, we give a man the powers of our highest political office. From the moment he is sworn the man confronts a personal problem: how to make those powers work for *him.* [Emphasis mine][30]

The practical lesson this manual dispenses, one which can also be gleaned from the *Federalist,* is that the president should "deal in the coin of self-interest" with individuals with whom he shares power.[31]

Pluralists repeatedly emphasize that the political process, consistently with Madison's aim, operates through negotiations among many diverse centers of power. We are told, for example, that in American politics "constant negotiations among different centers of power is necessary in order to make decisions."[32] The constitutional system, another overview states, "assumes a highly individualistic politics with scores of separate officeholders, each backed up by some kind of constituency, engaged in an endless series of negotiations."[33] Congress is deeply immersed in the pattern of negotiations among many individuals, according to another source. He declares that "the very essence of the legislative process is the willingness to accept trading as a means."[34] Another analyst says that the same is true of the president. "The political life of the president is one of constant bargaining—to get the votes to get nominated, to get the votes to get elected, to get the votes to get bills through Congress, to get the votes to get renominated, etc. etc."[35]

Although the evidence is provisional, suggesting that a final conclusion be postponed, neither the popular sovereignty nor the judicial supremacy view appears to correspond to the constitutional arrangements set forward by Madison. Pluralism, on the other hand, at this point in the analysis, appears to conform with Madison's basic intentions.

POWER ELITE AND CLASS DOMINATION REVISITED

Theories of power elite and class domination assert, in contrast to Madison and the pluralists, that political resources are distributed unequally, tending toward a concentration of power in the hands of a determinate group. Further, they assert that the parties to the social conflict are the elite on one side and the masses on the other, not independently situated actors or social groups, and that a gulf divides these two classes concerning their capacity to influence political outcomes. Pluralism and Madisonian theory assume that the parties to the social conflict are relatively equal in status, skill, and political resources; thus, the groups have an equal opportunity to influence the political process. The class domination view stresses that the political process is deflected by powerful groups outside the system of constitutional arrangements. Power elite theory emphasizes that constitutional arrangements tip outcomes toward privileged groups. In contrast, pluralism sees the political process as relatively equitable and conforming to the patterns of the constitutional system.

At the heart of the power elite theory is the view that a bias which favors influential groups and discriminates against noninfluential groups is built into the very structure of American political institutions. Practical political arrangements are nonneutral, it is alleged; instead, they embody as a matter of routine a "mobilization of bias" against noninfluential participants in the political process. Does Madison's vision of constitutional arrangements provide any support for this charge?

It is true that Madison speaks of political institutions suited to managing conflict among independently situated actors, each of whom has relatively equal chances to influence political outcomes. At the same time, he affirms that political arrangements will protect the "permanent and aggregate interests of the community," by which he certainly meant the prominent economic interests of his day, the "landed interest . . . manufacturing interest . . . mercantile interest . . . moneyed interest."[36] Madison says that the regulation of *"these* various and interfering interests forms the principal task of modern legislation" (emphasis mine).

Countervailing power protects the "diversity in the faculties of [individual] men,"[37] but most of all it protects the successful men, those who have outdistanced the others in the competitive scramble for material goods. Countervailing power is intended to secure the possessions and liberties of these men, let us call them the *influentials*, both from attack by popular majorities *and* (paranoiac as it may seem) from attack by other competitive, influential groups. As Madison reveals in talking about federalism, countervailing power is meant to assure the victory of the upper classes against local majorities. "The influence of factious leaders may kindle a flame within their particular States, but will be unable to spread a conflagration through the other States. . . . A rage for paper money, for an abolition of debts, [etc.] . . . will be less apt to pervade the whole body of the Union than a particular member of it."[38] At the same time that Madison gave influentials the reassurance of antimajoritarian constitutional features, he hastened to show them that the system was foolproof; it would protect them from each other as well. To insure that "the private interest of every individual may be a sentinel over the public rights," he arrayed the "ambition" of every man "to counteract [the] ambition" of every other man through a system of countervailing power.[39]

This system is a marvel of ingenuity born of an overmastering fear of leveling, popular majorities, and competitive economic interests. It is also, plainly, a system built around the concerns of the latter group. Madison assumed, without stating all the elements of his case in a clear fashion, that the system of arrangements would force influentials to deal with one another on a relational basis. Those who did not have sufficient resources to push their way into the political process would be dealt with manipulatively. The condition of influentials dealing *relationally* with other influentials and *manipulatively* with all others is assumed by Madison in this statement: "the regulation of *these* various and interfering interests forms the principal task of modern legislation." He does not mention the fate of noninfluential groups, and indeed, in his theory one hears nothing about them. Their very existence is assumed away. Thus, there appears to be some truth to the charge that political arrangements are designed to tip outcomes in the political process toward privileged groups.

By placing *Federalist* No. 10 in its historical setting, scholars have derived a class interpretation of American politics. Charles Beard's *An Economic Interpretation of the Constitution of the United States* (1913) made an enormous stir in intellectual circles when it was first published. Proving that interpretations of politics are themselves a part of politics, Beard's classic essay was used by the Progressive party as a basis for the recall of judicial decisions, popular election of United States senators, workmen's compensation, and other social legislation. Beard quoted liberally from Madison's famous essay in making the case that the "property" Madison wished to protect through government was "personalty" or mobile capital (capital invested in securities, commerce, manufacturing, loans, and land speculation).

Beard pointed out that the majority of delegates to the Constitutional Convention held substantial amounts of property in personalty, especially stocks and bonds floated by the Continental Congress in the course of financing the American Revolution. Forty out of fifty-five delegates to the convention held property in this form in amounts varying from a few dollars up to more than one hundred thousand dollars. The value of this stock had plummeted to less than one-tenth of its face value in the postwar years as it became apparent that the faltering government lacked the powers to make good on its debts. Beard established a strong presumption that the class holding this stock engineered the Philadelphia convention as a means of securing its capital investments. They wanted a strong central government which would have powers of taxation over the states, provide a national bank to fund the national debt, and establish uniform commercial regulations among the states.[40]

Beard's conception of the class that triumphed at the convention has been challenged but not overthrown.[41] An important amendment to his thesis has been offered by Staughton Lynd, *Class Conflict, Slavery and the United States Constitution* (1967). Lynd argues that finance capital, mainly concentrated in the towns and cities along the Atlantic seaboard, required the assistance of landed wealth, located chiefly in Virginia and the Southern states, to produce a victory at the Philadelphia convention. Basically, Lynd asserts, a bargain was struck between personalty and realty (capital invested in agricultural production). Influential capitalist interests dealt relationally with each other, exchanging protection of the slave trade for commercial regulation and the funding of the debt, and manipulatively with noninfluential groups, the blacks, small farmers, tradesmen, and artisans, who constituted the debtor class.[42] To be more specific concerning these transactions, the South had these provisions written into the constitution:

1. No ban on the importation of slaves until 1808 (Art. 1, sec. 9).
2. An obligation to return runaway slaves, that is, "persons held to service or labor" (Art. IV, sec. 2).
3. The slave counting as three-fifths of a person for the purpose of representation (Art. 1, sec. 2).

The class holding mobile capital was particularly benefitted by the following provisions:

1. Uniform rules regulating interstate commerce (Art. 1, sec. 8).
2. Uniform standards of currency, weights, and measures (Art. 1, sec. 8).

3. All debts contracted by the Continental government held valid against the United States under the Constitution (Art. VI, (sec. 1).
4. A federal court system to avoid the need for pursuing debtors through the state courts (Art. III, sec. 1).
5. Full faith and credit provided by each state to judgments enacted against its citizens by the courts of another state (Art. IV, sec. 1).

The class interpretation of American politics as expressed by Beard narrowed the conception of property in *Federalist* No. 10 to mobile capital and asserted that Madison and the framers wished to afford protection to the members of a particular class. Far from wishing to protect the liberties of a society of similarly positioned, economically motivated individuals, Beard implies, Madison wished to advance the goals of a determinate group—finance capital. Beard asserts that the small farmers, artisans, tradesmen, and workers, perceiving what was in store for them under the arrangements provided by the Constitution, sought to oppose its ratification by the legislatures of the states. In this effort they were unsuccessful.

SUMMARY

This chapter asserts that an understanding of the Constitution as written memorandum, tradition of ideas, and set of practical arrangements is useful for analyzing conflicting interpretations of American politics. Analysis of the Constitution in its multiple form through an exploration of the writings of James Madison, "father" of the Constitution, has not yielded a definitive interpretation of American politics because Madison, himself, is subject to more than one interpretation.

The chapter has established, however, that Madison was opposed to popular majorities and that the judicial supremacy interpretation is not easily reconciled with constitutional arrangements. From these considerations I have come to the preliminary judgment that the focus of debate lies between the pluralist interpretation of American politics, on the one hand, and power elite and class domination interpretations, on the other.

Basically, modern pluralism wishes to affirm that the constitutional system operates to this very day in the manner prescribed by Madison. An elaborate system of countervailing power affords protection to the spheres of liberty and property marked out by independently situated actors and social groups. According to this perspective, political arrangements do not inhibit the entry of topical and controversial issues onto the political agenda. Individuals and groups are afforded relatively equal opportunity to place issues on the agenda of public consideration and to decide policy outcomes. Thus, pluralism affirms that the balances of an eighteenth-century constitutional system are preserved to this very day by practical political arrangements.

The power elite interpretation seeks to explain and interpret ambiguities in the constitutional system which Madison and the framers established. The antimajoritarian features of Madisonian politics, along with the underlying assumption that political arrangements should serve the interest of a cluster of economic groups (the landed, manufacturing, mercantile, and moneyed interests), provide evidence for the view that there is a "mobilization of bias" built into the constitutional system. The practical result of influential economic groups dealing relationally with one another and manipulatively with noninfluential groups is to keep important issues from the political agenda. Thus, the power elite view finds a convincing basis in Madison that modern political inequalities are an outgrowth of beliefs, practices, and political arrangements of the constitutional system.

The class domination outlook states that constitutional arrangements are meant to secure the position of an economic class. Certain features of the written Constitution can be explained as the product of agreements between personalty and realty. A *prima facie* case for the influence of economic interests on the political process is provided by the research of Lynd and Beard. Additionally, these were the same groups, "the permanent and aggregate interests of the community," which Madison sought to safeguard from social conflict. Thus, the class domination outlook must be retained, alongside pluralist and power elite perspectives, as a tenable interpretation of American constitutionalism.

NOTES

1. See J. Allen Smith, *The Spirit of American Government* (New York: Macmillan, 1907); Woodrow Wilson, *Congressional Government* (New York: Meridian, 1965); William H. Riker, *Democracy in the United States,* 2nd ed. (New York: Macmillan, 1965); E. E. Schattschneider, *Party Government* (New York: Farrar, Straus & Giroux, 1942); Committee on Political Parties of the APSA, *Towards a More Responsible Two-Party System* (New York: Holt, Rinehart, 1950); James MacGregor Burns, *Deadlock of Democracy* (Englewood Cliffs, N.J.: Spectrum, 1963).
2. Ernest Barker, *Principles of Social and Political Theory* (London: Oxford University Press, 1961), p. 61.
3. James MacGregor Burns, *Uncommon Sense* (New York: Harper & Row, 1972).
4. See Arthur N. Holcombe, *The Constitutional System* (Glenview, Ill.: Scott, Fores-

man, 1964); E. S. Corwin, *The "Higher Law" Background of American Constitutional Law* (Ithaca N.Y.: Cornell University Press, 1955); Charles Howard McIlwain, *Constitutionalism: Ancient and Modern,* rev. ed. (Ithaca N.Y.: Cornell University Press, 1947); Andrew C. McLaughlin, *The Foundations of American Constitutionalism* (Greenwich, Conn.: Fawcett, 1961).

5. Quoted in Alpheus Thomas Mason and William M. Beaney, *The Supreme Court in a Free Society* (New York: W. W. Norton, 1968), p. 1.

6. Robert A. Dahl, *Preface to Democratic Theory* (Chicago: Phoenix Books, 1963); *Democracy in the United States,* 2nd ed. (Skokie, Ill.: Rand McNally, 1973); *Who Governs?* (New Haven, Conn.: Yale University Press, 1961); Nelson Polsby, *Community Power and Political Theory* (New Haven, Conn.: Yale University Press, 1963).

7. Robert A. Dahl, "Decision-Making in a Democracy," *Journal of Public Law,* vol. 6 (1958), 279–95.

8. See James O'Connor, *The Fiscal Crisis of the State* (New York: St. Martin's Press, 1973); Douglas F. Dowd, *The Twisted Dream* (Cambridge, Mass.: Winthrop, 1974); Ralph Milliband, *The State in Capitalist Society* (New York: Basic Books, 1969); Ira Katznelson and Mark Kesselman, *The Politics of Power* (New York: Harcourt Brace Jovanovich, 1975).

9. See Peter Bachrach, *The Theory of Democratic Elitism* (Boston: Little, Brown, 1967); Peter Bachrach and Morton S. Baratz, "Two Faces of Power," *American Political Science Review,* vol. 56 (December 1962), 947–52; "Decisions and Non-Decisions: An Analytical Framework," *American Political Science Review,* vol. 57 (September 1963), 632–42; *Power and Poverty* (New York: Oxford University Press, 1970).

10. *United States* v. *Butler,* 297 U.S. 1.

11. The most striking expression of America's historical commitment to liberalism is found in H. Mark Roelofs, *The Language of Modern Politics* (Homewood, Ill.: Dorsey Press, 1967), chap. 2; *Ideology and Myth in American Politics* (Boston: Little, Brown, 1976); and Louis Hartz, *The Liberal Tradition in America* (New York: Harcourt, Brace & World, 1955).

12. The view that ideas are necessarily dependent on forms of social activity for their operation and existence is set forward in Peter Winch, *The Idea of a Social Science and Its Relation to Philosophy* (London: Routledge & Kegan Paul, 1958), and Michael Oakeshott, *Rationalism in Politics* (New York: Basic Books, 1952).

13. The term *independently situated political actor* is coined by H. Mark Roelofs in *The Language of Modern Politics* (Homewood, Ill.: Dorsey Press, 1967), chap. 2. The notion that Hobbes originates and is the master of the liberal tradition in political thought is held by Leo Strauss, *The Political Philosophy of Hobbes,* trans. E. Sinclair (Chicago: University of Chicago Press, Phoenix Books, 1952); Michael Oakeshott in his introduction to *Leviathan* (London: Basil Blackwell, 1957), pp. lii, and liii; Alexander Passerin D'Entreves, *Natural Law* (New York: Harper & Row, 1951); and C. B. Macpherson, *Possessive Individualism* (London: Oxford University Press, 1962).

14. James Madison, "National Gazette," (1792), quoted in Saul K. Padover, *The Forging of American Federalism: Selected Writings of James Madison* (New York: Harper Torchbooks, 1965), pp. 267–68.

15. *Federalist* No. 10.

16. *Ibid.*
17. See the discussion by George D. Beam, *Usual Politics* (New York: Holt, Rinehart & Winston, 1970), p. 28.
18. *Federalist* No. 51.
19. *Federalist* No. 10.
20. *Ibid.*
21. See the discussion by Richard A. Neustadt, *Presidential Power* (New York: John Wiley, 1960), chap. 3; and Michael D. Reagan, *The New Federalism* (New York: Oxford University Press, 1972), chap. 1.
22. *Federalist* No. 10.
23. *Federalist* No. 51.
24. *Federalist* No. 78.
25. *Ibid.*
26. Alpheus T. Mason, *The Supreme Court: Instrument of Power or of Revealed Truth* (Boston: Boston University Press, 1953).
27. Dahl, *Preface to Democratic Theory,* chaps. 4 and 5.
28. *Ibid.,* p. 137.
29. See David Truman, *The Governmental Process* (New York: Knopf, 1951), chap. 13.
30. Neustadt, *Presidential Power,* preface.
31. *Ibid.,* p. 46.
32. Dahl, *Preface to Democratic Theory,* p. 24.
33. Burns, *Deadlock of Democracy,* p. 87.
34. Truman, *Governmental Process,* p. 368.
35. William H. Riker, *Federalism Origin, Operation, Significance* (Boston: Little, Brown, 1964), p. 93.
36. *Federalist* No. 10.
37. *Ibid.*
38. *Ibid.*
39. *Federalist* No. 51.
40. Charles Beard, *An Economic Interpretation of the Constitution of the United States* (New York: Free Press, 1965), pp. 15–16, 149–50, 169–178.
41. Forrest McDonald, *We The People, The Economic Origins of the Constitution* (Chicago: Phoenix Books, 1963).
42. Staughton Lynd, *Class Conflict, Slavery and the United States Constitution* (Indianapolis: Bobbs-Merrill, 1967).

CHAPTER 3

The Foundations
of American
Constitutionalism

THE PHILADELPHIA STORY

There is a story about the creation of the American Constitution which I am sure that you have heard before. It is not false but conveys much less than the whole truth. Allowing for some variation in the storytellers, it goes something like this.

Delegates from the legislatures of the several states arrived in Philadelphia in the spring of 1787 to consider changes in the Articles of Confederation. Following the Declaration of Independence in 1776, the Articles had been drafted to establish an alliance of the states against Britain in the Revolutionary War. In the course of the discussions which ensued over the spring and summer of 1787, changes were proposed that went far beyond the instructions of the delegates. The constitution submitted for ratification to the states embodied controversial and far-reaching proposals for a new and more centralized form of government.

The delegates to the Philadelphia convention were acting on the charge of the Annapolis convention to develop a form of government "adequate to the exigencies of the Union." This was a convention of commercial states—New York, Pennsylvania, Delaware, Virginia, and New Jersey—which met to consider commerce and navigation in 1786. Implied in this charge was the view, widely held among the commercial and financial class, that the Articles of Confederation were not adequate to the tasks facing the government in the postwar era because the powers to regulate commerce, establish a uniform currency, and levy tariffs and taxes had been withheld from the Continental Congress.

The inability to levy taxes meant that Congress was unable to meet its financial obligations to the investors who had underwritten the costs of the Revolutionary War. Commercial wars arose among the states because of the absence of uniform regulations and tariff structures. Commercial affairs were further disrupted by the inflation of state currencies. Debtors fled to Rhode Island, where their debts could be paid for a trifle in valueless currency. Finally, Congress lacked executive and judicial power over the citizens of the states, a necessary corollary. It only had weak powers of requisition over the states, and the states were in disarray.

We are well into the story at this point. The delegates succeeded in their task through bold experimentation tempered by a spirit of compromise, several of which illustrate the practical gifts of the founding fathers. One of these, always placed in capitals as the Great Compromise, involves the reconciliation between the large and small states over the composition of the national legislature. The essence of the compromise was the creation of a bicameral legislature. The large states agreed to equal representation in the Senate (to their disadvantage), and the small states agreed to a representation on the basis of population in the House of Representatives (to their disadvantage).

Other compromises related to the status of slaves, taxation, and the qualifications for voting and holding office. Economic differences between the North and the South were revealed in the discussion over the slaves. Nonslaveholders wished to ban the importation of slaves and to count them in the apportionment of taxes but not in representation. Slave-holding states held the reverse. The result was the three-fifths compromise, which counted the black people as a fraction for the purposes of taxation and representation and banned the importation of slaves after 1808. Another split which occurred along the same lines involved the power of Congress to tax exports. Southerners feared that imposition of these taxes might injure an export trade in indigo, rice, tobacco, and cotton. Northern merchants preferred an extensive regulation of interstate and foreign commerce to include taxing power over imports and exports. In the compromise, Congress would retain power to tax imports and to regulate interstate and foreign commerce, but it was denied power to impose an export tax on articles shipped abroad by any state.

Many delegates wished to impose property qualifications for voting and holding office. The proposal was defeated, but ironically, not because the members of the convention held any enthusiasm for democracy. It was defeated because the wealthy classes who dominated the convention could not agree on a definition of "property" that was applicable without disenfranchising each other. Some held property in land and slaves; others, in the expanding assets of their business; others, in stocks and bonds. They compromised by leaving it for the states to decide whether these qualifications should be imposed.

Some versions of this story stress the "fight" over ratification. Opponents of the Constitution focused on the absence of a Bill of Rights and the fact that the delegates had exceeded their instructions. In any event, the Constitution was ratified within a year by eleven of the thirteen states, two more than necessary under its provisions. By the time North Carolina (1789) and Rhode Island (1790) got around to ratifying, George Washington was already serving as president.

This account has transformed the framers into legendary figures and imparted an air of mystery to the written document. Of course, the callous attitudes toward the blacks and the propertyless cannot be glossed over. Yet most would agree with William Gladstone, the English prime minister, who said that the Constitution "is the most wonderful work ever struck off at a given time by the brain and purpose of man." This mystique is perfectly captured in the setting in which the Constitution is presently displayed. It sits beneath a gold eagle in the great domed Exhibition Hall of the National Archives in Washington, D.C. Along with the Bill of Rights and the Declaration of Independence, it is put on view in a protective glass case during the day. At night the documents are lowered by elevator into a vault of steel and reinforced concrete twenty feet below the floor. The framers are viewed as demigods who produced an original and lasting method for governing the American people.

The trouble with this story lies in the difficulty of separating truth from fiction. For to begin with, it rests on such a large fiction that whatever truths it manages to convey are insubstantial. A people does not just sit down and strike off in a few months the rules by which it intends to be governed for all future time. To suppose that this is true is to transform the work of the framers into something magical, like a conjuror plucking rabbits from a hat. The illusion nearly succeeds because the account focuses exclusively on the events in Philadelphia. However, if what is wanted is an adequate explanation of a significant human event, the framing of the Constitution, we shall have to fit the actions and thoughts of the framers into the surrounding political culture.

Another problem, which is really just a variation of the first, is that the Philadelphia story does not give much insight into the basic intentions of the framers. The Constitution is often presumed to reflect the interests of the propertied classes in American society.[1] But if one reads the *Federalist Papers* with any care, as well as the debates on the Constitution, one cannot escape the impression that the wealthy classes feared each other as much as they did the propertyless elements in society. Madison, as we have seen, emphasized the necessity of checking the ambition of each man with the ambition of every other man. In this manner the "private interest of every individual may be a sentinel over the public rights."[2] The whole system of countervailing power among the federal and state and local organs of government, and among the executive, legislative, and judicial organs, is tied to a highly pessimistic view of human nature, not to mention a very crabbed notion of the functions of politics. Such a view is not tied in any obvious way to the possession of property. We shall have to look elsewhere for an explanation of this outlook.

A PREFORMATION OF NATIONAL CONSCIOUSNESS

To understand the sources of the written Constitution, we must investigate it as the historical commitment of the American people to a tradition of ideas. Much of what is incorporated into the written Constitution already existed in patterns of thought and political processes worked out before. American political institutions were created by blind enthusiasm for the ideas of liberal democracy as much as by the wit and skill of the assembled delegates. The latter were simply the agents through which these enthusiasms were put into effect. If this is to diminish the importance of the events in Philadelphia, most especially of the compromises—not excluding the Great Compromise—it will be a gain in political insight. American political institutions are the product of an overwhelming consensus on the fundamentals of political association. The areas in which the delegates were compelled to compromise pale into insignificance next to the matters on which they were in agreement.

The notion that there is a preformation of the national political consciousness turns on the observation, which one can confirm for oneself at any moment, that the mind is not a *tabula rasa*. We are born into a sociocultural world, which is a preconstituted and preorganized world, and whose particular structures are the result of a historical process.[3] We acquire a facility for action in this world as we begin to grasp the rules that govern its internal life. Since the rules are uncritically acquired, we tend to associate them with an ineluctable order of nature. It is difficult to imagine, in many cases, how social and political arrangements could possibly be any different than they are. But this is a fallacy. The world in which we live is "natural" only because we have internalized the rules by which it is governed.

If it is true in our own lives that we are uncritically dependent on a host of assumptions and axioms, it is true also of any place and time. It is true of the framers of the Constitution as well as of ourselves. This is the theory of a preformation of the national political consciousness which we shall now explore.

SEVENTEENTH-CENTURY CONSTITUTIONAL CONFLICTS

The most important form in which the American Constitution exists is as an imperial political ideology shaping the consciousness of the American people through their ideological inheritance. The tradition of ideas that has shaped the dominant institutions of our society, liberal democracy, has its origins in seventeenth-century English constitutional conflicts. Therefore, to grasp the seminal ideas of American life we must shift the stage from Philadelphia to seventeenth-century England and the rise of the commercial Protestant middle class.

This is the class through which the claims of modern individualism are advanced with unrivaled force in human affairs. These claims were originally advanced in two main areas of social action, the economic and the religious, but they eventually took form in political demands as well. Insofar as they were advanced in the religious sphere, they took shape in the doctrine of "the sanctity of the inner life."[4] This means that there is no higher authority in human affairs than the conscience of the individual. Public authority, to keep peace in a society of such individuals, must confine itself merely to laying down a rule of action, never meddling in internal affairs of conscience and private belief. At the least, this doctrine requires a separation of church and state, but beyond that it implies safeguards for freedom of expression, of worship, and of assembly. In the economic sphere the claims of modern individualism took shape in the doctrine of "possessive individualism,"[5] the notion that the individual is the sole proprietor of one's talents and energies, owing nothing for them to society. Whatever people set apart through their labor, in whatever amount, is theirs to dispose of as they like. Again, this concept of individualism confines the role of public authority to a minimum. It is the function of a stable order to enforce contracts and provide the minimal regulations necessary to release the energies of acquisitive persons.

Both these doctrines were revolutionary in seventeenth-century English society. The notion that conscience and property were not the business of the state was unacceptable to any self-respecting bishop or king in the Tudor era. But events conspired against the bishops, kings, and nobles. The unusual circumstances that surround the breakthrough of the Protestant middle class into history united the class that was rising to power behind both claims.

The two great themes of sixteenth- and seventeenth-century English constitutional history are the strengthening of the power of the state and the assertion of individual freedom. The former increased as a consequence of the Henrician Reformation (1531). Parliament made Henry VIII supreme head of the Church of England and vested in him powers of appointment to ecclesiastical office and the property of the Church. He sold great parts of the confiscated land to peers, courtiers, and merchants, who resold much of it to smaller dealers. The middle-men of the commercial class bought the land for speculation.[6]

Over time the middle class derived greater benefit from the Henrician Reformation than did the monarchy. Throughout the sixteenth and seventeenth centuries this class sought to augment its political and economic power and to promote reformation of the Anglican Church in accordance with Protestant forms of worship. In the mind of the Protestant middle class, property and religion, secular order and personal freedom, are inextricably associated. The energy and enterprise of this new class was concentrated in the House of Commons, and along this avenue its controversial objectives were sought with ultimate success. The Tudor monarchs, seeking a counterpoise to the landed nobility, cunningly supported the claims of the commercial class and the country gentry. The latter enriched themselves by the practice of enclosure (of land from the common) and the resale of Church lands, whereas the commercial class profited from the growth of economic opportunities in the New World.

Civil war (1642–1646) and revolution broke out in England when the Stuart monarchs tried to change the formulas that had worked under the Tudors. Revolution was produced by the cumulative effect of the policies pursued by Charles I, who discouraged enclosure, restored high church forms of religious worship, effected a marital alliance with the Catholic throne of France, and asserted a right of taxation without Parliamentary approval. Charles I dissolved Parliament on numerous occasions following disputes over ecclesiastical and financial policy. The king seemed insensible to the fact that the whole basis of English society had been surreptitiously revolutionized in the course of the sixteenth and seventeenth centuries. The commercial Protestant class held sufficient power to overthrow any authority inconsistent with the claims of modern individualism. Failing to see this, although he could not have seen it and be king, Charles I lost his head.

The overthrow of papal rule by Henry VIII looks forward, therefore, to the rise of a new class in English society, the civil wars, and the execution of Charles I in 1649. The crucial point is that following the execution of the king, public order must agree with the perspectives of the triumphant middle class. Soon we shall consider two authors, Thomas Hobbes (1588–1679) and John Locke (1632–1704), who put this conclusion on a coherent intellectual basis. These men developed a theory of liberal democratic constitutionalism founded on the revolutionary outlook of the modern individual and the genius of protestantism. They set forward rules of political association which govern American social and political order to this very day; for American political thinkers, themselves British Protestants, selected from the larger world of values those theories for which they had an affinity. There is this difference. The ideas of liberal democracy were unopposed in the American setting, thus transforming them into a total ideology, which is difficult to challenge or even to question. In England, the views of the Tory squire, who stood by monarchy, the Church, and the feudal order, live on in the policies of the Conservative party and, some say, the Labour party.

There is a surprising conclusion to this narrative. Against the backdrop of sixteenth- and seventeenth-century English constitutional conflicts, the framers of the Constitution and the leaders of the American Revolution are conservative figures. The reason is that the American Revolution was built on the successes of the civil wars (1642–1646) and the Glorious Revolution (1688). If we distinguish between revolution, the use of violence to change the principles on which authority in society is constituted, from rebellion, the use of violence to extract short-term gains from presently constituted authority, the events of the American "revolution" belong more to the latter category than to the former.

In the American setting, the colonists employed the same historical props and rhetoric as the Puritan commercial class in its contests with the Stuart monarchs. The Declaration of Independence contrived "to conjure . . . a vision of the virtuous and long suffering colonists standing like martyrs to receive on their defenseless heads the ceaseless blows of the tyrant's hand."[7] It made George III unrecognizable as an "agent of Cruelty and Perfidy, scarcely parallelled in the most barbarous ages, and totally unworthy of the Head of a civilized nation." But many of the issues the document raises, for example, the erection of a "multitude of new offices," seem like nitpicking. The main issues, free trade and no taxation without representation, were long since settled on both sides of the Atlantic as "the rights of Englishmen." As some historians now grant, these issues could have been worked out within a commonwealth of nations framework.[8] But such arrangements were not in existence, and the colonists no longer found it convenient to be governed by the Colonial Office at Whitehall. They wanted a government located on these shores and more friendly to personal and commercial liberty. In the context of affairs we have been looking at, this demand can hardly be described as revolutionary.

A brief look at the events of 1688 and 1776 will show that the main formulas of the sixteenth and seventeenth centuries were still at work. The middle class will rebel against any authority that infringes on the expanding rights of property and conscience. A secular order, indifferent to the affairs of conscience and protective of the rights of property, represents the thrust of the times. In the progress of events, 1642 through 1646, 1688, and 1776, the middle class, as it goes about the business of consolidating its revolutionary gains, becomes increasingly conservative in its attitudes toward property. For this reason it is doubtful that 1688 and 1776 qualify as social revolutions, as we have defined it and as the events show.

The year 1688 anticipates 1776. In 1688 the leaders of the Tory and Whig parties, believing that a Catholic monarch threatened the vested interest in the Protestant Reformation, joined in an alliance to overthrow the ruling monarch, James II, and to invite William, Prince of Orange, a Protestant, to take on the powers of king. The revolution was a palace revolution in which the king, by vacating the throne, assisted in his own overthrow. The revolution did not involve nor seek to conciliate popular demands for a redistribution of property.[9]

"Revolution" is a misnomer in relation to the events that actually occurred. First, 1688 was not a social revolution because Whig liberalism, both in the late seventeenth century and subsequently, was fully as much a defense against radical democracy as an attack on traditionalism. Although the Whigs might appear to be socially progressive in relation to the squirearchy and the clergy of the Tory party, they do not appear in this light in relation to the freeholders and tradesmen who composed the Leveller and Digger parties.[10] The Whig party occupied a position on the social questions of the day roughly intermediate between the Tories and the radical democrats. Of this more later. Second, the revolution was not political because it merely proposed a change in the heads of government. The only principles it clearly upheld were parliamentary supremacy and a Protestant succession, principles far from revolutionary.

Current interpretations of the American Revolution stress that it fails to qualify as a social revolution because, first of all, no social change occurred. America bypassed the feudal stage of history and hence had no feudal social and economic inheritance to surmount. Revisionist historians have replaced the notion of class conflict with Toqueville's famous observation on American equality: "The great advantage of the Americans is that they have arrived at a state of democracy without having to endure a democratic revolution, and that they are born equal instead of becoming so."[11] A comparative study of revolutions points out that the absence of a "social and class movement" culminating in a "victory of the extremists" distinguishes the American revolution from the English (1642–1646), the French (1789), and the Russian (1917).[12]

Second, the revolution was not a political one because it proposed a change merely in the heads of government, not in the principles on which government was constituted. The Declaration of Independence does not set forward novel rights or principles of government. Instead, it seeks to defend existing rights against an unpopular monarch. In many ways the Declaration is a succinct restatement of the Whig rebellion of 1688. One suggestion, having little regard for American pride and pageantry, is that the term "revolution" be dropped and for it substituted the more historically accurate "a conservative colonial rebellion."[13]

The liberal tradition, therefore, is a cluster of ideas which has its sources in English constitutional conflicts of the sixteenth and seventeenth centuries. This tradition was transmitted to these shores where it decisively shaped the fundamental documents of our national existence. To the minds of the framers these ideas were irresistibly attractive and in perfect conformity with "the laws of Nature and of Nature's God." The liberal tradition must be understood to have been in existence, working and controlling all the time, and shaping the characteristics of our national political life. Unquestionably, America is the most vigorous and single-minded representative of this set of ideas in the world today. The major strengths and weaknesses of the republic derive from this fact.

LIBERAL DEMOCRATIC CONSTITUTIONALISM

THOMAS HOBBES (1588–1679)

If Hobbes is placed in the setting of the constitutional crisis we have been talking about, he may be seen as the first competent advocate of the claims of the rising Protestant middle class. It was Hobbes's view that the authority of feudal institutions had been liquidated by the period of the civil wars (1642–1646) and that authority in modern society would have to be the free creation of the absolute will of the individual. The principles of liberal democratic constitutionalism—government by consent, inalienable rights, and a right of resistance—are all derived from this single principle that the sole source of right is the absolute will of the individual. Hobbes was also the first to visualize the pattern and goals of politics in a liberal society. For Hobbes, the function of politics is to manage conflict, which is achieved through a transactional pattern in which disputes are negotiated and compromised rather than fought out.

Hobbes fled to the continent during the period of the civil wars. Thus his defense of the Protestant cause was not by force of arms. But for those with a discerning eye, his treatment of the State of Nature in *Leviathan,* his major work, published in 1651, if not an argument for social revolution, is a recognition that social revolution has occurred. The "state of nature" is a literary device which involves imagining away the presence of constituted authority while retaining, in the mind's eye, the dominant characteristics of the political culture. Insofar as this exercise involves the former, it reveals Hobbes's view that the authority of king and bishops had been taken away by the civil wars. Insofar as it involves the latter, it reveals his awareness that English political culture is Protestant bourgeois. It is Hobbes's clear intention to establish the foundations of a new constitutional order on the basis of the triumphant Protestant culture, one consistent with the revolutionary doctrines of possessive individualism and the sanctity of the inner life.

EQUALITY. Hobbes traces the source of legitimate government to the consent of individuals, taken one by one. He believes that men and women are individually entitled to be consulted on the terms by which authority is introduced into society. He calls the process by which government is created *covenant,* which means an original agreement between each person and every other person. No theorist before Hobbes, and one is tempted to say none since, has so emphatically established the will of the individual as the sole source of right.

Hobbes lays the foundation of liberal democracy because he asserts, with an emphasis that was to endure through two centuries at least, that all persons are fundamentally equal and have equal rights in the covenant. Hobbes states that no person has the right to insist on his qualifications for political rule based on his superiority in intellect, virtue, wealth, or any other attribute. All persons, everywhere, Hobbes insists, are pretty much the same.[14]

Even if men are not equal, Hobbes says, they ought to consider themselves so. Thinking and acting otherwise is very apt to produce social conflict. Since public authority is derived in an equal degree from all parties to the covenant, it must provide the members of society equal treatment before the law. In the apportionment of taxes and conscription for military service, the sovereign will take care to distribute burdens equitably.

CONSENT. The covenant that creates public authority is a promise of transfer of right contingent on safety of performance. Since one's right of self-rule cannot really be surrendered, the promise actually involves a disposition not to resist the sovereign's rule. The individual makes a promise not to resist public authority (1) insofar as other parties make a like promise and (2) insofar as public authority provides a secure social order. But the form of the covenant reserves for the individual the right to be self-ruled when the condition of safety is no longer present. Hobbes gives many examples: A man who throws down his arms and flies from the field of battle does not perform an injustice for which he should be punished; a person who refuses to give evidence against himself does not merit punishment unless he is pardoned in advance; rebels and criminals who resist punishment do not, by resisting, perform any new act of injustice.[15]

Although public order is created by the consent of each individual, it is maintained by sanctions or threat of sanctions. In the most remembered passage of Hobbes, he says, "Covenants, without the Sword, are but Words, and of no strength to secure a man at all."[16] But the authority of the sovereign to wield the sword is derived from agreement, and the state will have a monopoly of the means of legitimate coercion. Power reinforces state authority but does not create it.

INALIENABLE RIGHTS AND A RIGHT OF RESISTANCE. Inalienable rights refers to those rights that cannot be given up in the agreements by which public authority is constituted. When infringed on by public authority or other parties, they furnish the individual with a right of resistance. Hobbes speaks of these rights, not propagandistically, but as a precaution a person of ordinary intelligence would take in the agreement process.

Hobbes is generally supposed to have afforded protection in his doctrine of inalienable rights to physical life alone. He says, for example, that the soldier who throws down his arms and flies from battle performs an act of "cowardice" but not "injustice" because the agreement reserves the right to self-rule when the condition of safety is not present.[17] But the seeds of Locke's and Jefferson's inalienable right to property is also present in Hobbes's doctrine. He says that public order must provide not only "the security of a man's person in his life" but additionally "the means of so preserving life as not to be weary of it."[18] Inalienable rights, he says in another place, "includes all things without which a man cannot live, or not live well."[19] Finally, he says public order must guarantee the "safety of the People," not a "bare Preservation alone" but also "all other Contentments of life, which every man by lawfull Industry . . . shall acquire to himselfe."[20] Hobbes, therefore, defends the right of the modern individual to resist any authority that infringes on the inalienable rights of life and property.

THE MERELY POLICING SOVEREIGN. The function of the government is to provide a framework of order within which each person can pursue happiness as he or she separately defines it. The most important affairs in life, the inner life and economic acquisition, lie outside the scope of the state's authority. The state performs its function well if it maintains a secure order and issues such necessary regulations as will keep individuals from injuring themselves in their separate quests for the good life.

> For the use of the Lawes (which are but Rules Authorised) is not to bind the People from all Voluntary Actions; but to direct and keep them in such a motion, as not to hurt themselves by their own impetuous desires . . . as Hedges are set, not to stop Travellers, but to keep them in the way.[21]

A contemporary of Hobbes observed that the state is obeyed "for better but not for worse"[22] in his political society. He intended the remark as a criticism, but Hobbes might have taken it as a compliment. The critic was a bishop who was speaking up for a feudal order where relationships of authority were on a personal basis; where the relationships involved, as in a marriage, the care of souls as well as the tending of things; and where the relationships were indissoluble and absolute. In Hobbes's theory our obligation is not to a person or group of persons but to an office (or pattern of offices). We are obligated to an impersonal official, like the policeman on the beat, who is there solely to maintain the decencies of civil behavior. The law of the state is confined to actions merely; it cannot meddle in internal affairs of conscience or private belief. Furthermore, our obligation to the state is conditional, not absolute. It is consistent with the conditions under which public order is created to prefer private need to public order in cases of conflict. The case of the recalcitrant soldier is such an instance.

THE PATTERN AND GOALS OF POLITICS. Hobbes reads into human nature, as do many of the liberals who come after him, elements of intense competitiveness, isolation, and struggle. He was not aware that many of these elements are a function of the acquired behavior of persons in a market society. This is a society which produces an extraordinary amount of rivalry and insecurity by transforming all things, humanity included, into a commodity.[23] Reflecting this view, Hobbes says that the value of a man is his "Price" and "as in other things, so in men, not the seller, but the buyer determines the Price."[24] For those among us who have nothing but their labor to sell, this cannot be a reassuring social doctrine. But Hobbes regards the problems of rivalry and insecurity as behavioral, not socioeconomic. Through the literary device of the State of Nature, he sought to scare a society of ruthless individualists, such as commercial Protestantism had produced, into the acceptance of civil authority. He darkly implies that such a society, without the presence of constituted authority, will decline into a chaotic conflict of private wills. Then, to put it in a modern image, there will be no Bloomingdale's, no Strawbridge and Clothiers, no Macy's, no Sears, no Neiman-Marcus, and so on, "and the life of man, solitary, poore, nasty, brutish, and short."[25]

With hindsight one can see that the policing official whom Hobbes installed to avert chaos is inadequate to the task, because the policeman can use but cannot rely on his power to sustain civil order. The moment he uses his power, the individuals or groups with whom he is in conflict recover their original right of self-rule. Compromise, or transactional politics, is a way of adjusting the right of public authority to the right of the individual. So we may reason that public authority in a liberal society will seek to manage conflict through a transactional pattern of politics. This pattern benefits powerful individuals and groups who are able to bend the law to their advantage, but corruption of the political process is only one aspect of the problem. The individuals of whom Hobbes speaks are radically in conflict. It would compromise their freedom least if all others took on the obligations of the covenant, except themselves, leaving them free to prey on all others from outside the law. Thus, in the language of American westerns, there will be a strong tendency for ruthless individuals, even within the bounds of civil society, "to take the law back into their own hands." This is the dark, pessimistic side of liberal politics. It links Hobbes with Madison and the American system of countervailing power in which opportunities for domination are withheld from the grasping hands of any one individual or group.

JOHN LOCKE (1632–1704)

Locke is important chiefly as a vehicle through which Hobbes's new constitutional philosophy of conflict management is transmitted to the

American colonies. Locke is essentially a propagandist, not a political theorist, and he fails to give expression in terms as satisfactory as Hobbes to the constitutional ideas of liberal democracy. Nevertheless, he is in agreement with Hobbes concerning the source, nature, and limits of public authority, and he transmits to America Hobbes's new ideas. Like Hobbes, Locke considers the individual to be freed, in modern times, from all restraints formerly imposed on the right to acquire property. Although Locke does appear to impose certain restraints derived from natural law, a careful reading of his work shows that they are all removed by subsequent passages. Like Hobbes, therefore, Locke defends the absolute rights of the individual to life and property, and he comes to the same inescapable conclusion that where these rights are pushed to the utmost extent, public authority must be empowered to settle conflicts of private right, absolutely.

Several respects in which Locke differs from Hobbes do not affect their fundamental agreement on the nature of authority and the theory of conflict management. Locke vests authority in a pattern of offices, a representative and hereditary assembly and monarchy, rather than a single office, monarchy. The reason for this change is that Locke believes that separate institutions sharing power is better suited to managing social conflict. The change, therefore, is a matter of policy and does not affect the substantive authority of the sovereign, which remains absolute. Second, property absorbs virtually the whole content of Locke's idea of natural right. A substantial narrowing of the claims of modern egoism occurs with his monotonous and exaggerated emphasis on the rights of property appropriation. Third, in Locke sovereignty is transmuted into a social no less than an institutional structure. Parental authority, operating in the social sphere, reinforces the position of the institutional sovereign, operating in the political sphere. Another way of putting this is that with Locke, liberal democracy becomes transformed into social dogma, the transmission of which is the work of the fathers. With the development of social coercion, liberalism is less dependent on institutional forms of coercion.

PROPERTY AS AN ABSOLUTE AND INALIENABLE RIGHT. The thrust of Locke's views on property is conveyed in a famous routine of Jack Benny. Benny is held up in a deserted part of the city by a robber.

Robber: Your money or your life.
Benny: (cups his hand in his chin, taps foot, appears deep in thought, says nothing)
Robber: (exasperated) Your money or your life!!
Benny: (also exasperated) I'm thinking about it!!![26]

We have seen that Hobbes regarded the rights of bourgeois men to life and property as absolute and inalienable. Locke appears to impose restraints on the individual's right to appropriate property derived from the ancient tradition of natural law. The first restraint is *usage,* which limits the individual to the amount of property that he and his family are able to consume. It is a standard of consumption applying chiefly to perishable goods. The second limitation is *sufficiency,* requiring that appropriation cease where the general supply of goods is running out. The third, a limitation of *labor,* requires that appropriated property be the product of one's own industry.[27]

All these restraints are removed or assumed away in a critical chapter of the *Second Treatise of Government* (1686). The chapter, "Of Property," supports the right of possessive individualism, the right of the individual to be the sole owner of his talents and energies, owing nothing to society for them. Whatever the amount of property an individual has is his to dispose of as he likes, no matter what the injury to society. The limitation of usage is overstepped by the introduction of money. Money is not a perishable good, and therefore, one can accumulate as much of it as one likes. Since one can accumulate as much money as one likes, one can also accumulate as much as one likes of other forms of wealth that are convertible into money. Hence, we find Locke justifying the unlimited accumulation of land as well. In this case Locke ignores the conflict with the limitation of sufficiency. Elsewhere, he assumes that a payment of a wage gives a master ownership of the goods set apart through the labor of his servant.[28]

The emphasis on property is reflected in Locke's equivocations on the great social questions of his day. He argues that men are equal and have equal rights of ownership, but he seeks to protect the gains of those who had achieved wealth through spoilation of the monasteries, enclosure, and high rents. For Locke, the wealthy are the "Industrious and the Rational" whose property rights need protection against the "Quarrelsom and Contentious," among whom the Levellers and Diggers were foremost.[29] These groups demanded a redistribution of property, a shift in the burden of taxes, and in general, a successful conclusion to the social movement toward liberation initiated by the civil wars. Against these demands Locke argues for both the inherited and the acquired rights of property and states that the acquisition of wealth, having taken place out of the bounds of civil society, is unregulated by social compact.[30] Both doctrines weigh heavily against the goals of the underclasses. The Glorious Revolution of 1688, which is sometimes said to have been stimulated by the publication of the *Second Treatise,* did not do anything for the propertyless. Instead, as Locke intended, it consolidated the propertied elements in the Whig party behind a supreme legislative assembly, which ruled with the assistance of monarchy if possible but without it if necessary.

To Locke the rights of property are not only absolute but also inalienable. He emphatically asserts that the right to property, unlike the right to life, cannot be given up in the covenant. He declares that the sovereign may rightfully require us to give our life in battle but may justly be resisted if, without the consent of the subject, he seeks to take "one penny of his Money."[31] This is the bizarre tendency of commercial Protestantism in its advanced phase. The driving force which had been enlisted in the service of religious ends becomes an obsession with material acquisition. Locke is transparently in sympathy with the new change in attitude.

> We are not born in heaven but in this world, where our being is to be preserved with meat, drink, and clothing, and other necessaries that are not born with us, but must be got and kept with forecast, care, and labor, and, therefore, we cannot be all praises and hallelujahs, and perpetually in the vision of things above.[32]

INSTITUTIONS MANAGING CONFLICTS ABOUT PROPERTY. Locke worries that public authority might invade the rights of men to life and property and thereby produce instability. Stability and the security of property were connected in Locke's mind, as they were for the framers of the Constitution. He therefore proposes the notion of separate institutions sharing in the power of the state as a way of managing conflicts about property. The rationale is that the sovereign will be forced to negotiate with all influential parties affected by his rule, especially propertied interests. The necessity for negotiations will restrain the sovereign from invading the rights of bourgeois men and, in so doing, undermine his own authority. When these rights are invaded, of course, all parties have a right of resistance. Stability can be achieved by designing institutions that are efficient in managing social conflicts centering on property.

Locke's preference for sharing power does not alter the nature of sovereignty but the manner in which sovereign power is to be organized. The power of the state for Locke and Hobbes is absolute and unitary. Locke states that there is "one, Supreams Power, which is the Legislative, to which all the rest are and must be subordinate."[33] Unlike Hobbes, Locke prefers sovereignty to be vested in a pattern of offices, rather than a single office, but the principle of the absolute authority and power of the state is upheld. In accordance with this view, Locke states that the "Legislative" is "placed in the Concurrence of three distinct Persons,"[34] the monarchy and the offices of a representative and hereditary assembly. None of these several institutions is supreme, because each must have the concurrence of the others to act. But when the several offices concur in the exercise of power, the liberty of the subject is as much restricted as under any form of government. In other words, there is in Hobbes and Locke *one* government possessing absolute authority and power; but the use of sovereign power in Locke's theory is divided among several political offices.

The rationale for this distribution of power, Locke says, is that it hinders the monarch from using the "Force, Treasure, and Offices of Society, to corrupt the Representatives, and gain them to his purpose."[35] Also, it makes it difficult for the members of the assemblies, whether hereditary or popular, to "suit the law, both in its making and execution to their own private advantage."[36] To repeat, separate institutions sharing power provides a way to adjust the conflicting rights of sovereign and subject while preserving the final authority of the sovereign.

SUMMARY

What are the rewards of the investigation we have been pursuing? For one, it should put to rest the notion that American political institutions were improvised by a handful of men in a few summer months in 1787. An adequate account of the events surrounding the framing of the Constitution must surely include a historical enthusiasm for liberal democracy arising out of sixteenth- and seventeenth-century English constitutional conflicts. The major principles and political processes of American politics were all worked out before the constitutional convention. All that remained was to give these principles and processes institutional expression. It was this overwhelming consensus on the fundamental principles of political association which made the compromises of the convention possible, not excluding the Great Compromise. Next to this agreement on the fundamentals, the substance of the compromises that occurred is of small importance.

If the status of the framers is reduced by this account, at least we understand them better, not to mention the Constitution itself. Contrary to much of what has been written about the founding fathers, their writings and speeches indicate a timid reluctance to venture beyond the principles expressed by Locke in the *Second Treatise*. It is clear that they wanted political institutions efficient in managing social conflicts centering on property. The obsession with conflict management and the stability of political institutions is derived from Hobbes by way of Locke. Unlike the liberal theorists who preceded them, the framers were not as good at spelling out the principles to which the working arrangements of American politics are tied. Only by investigating the theories of Hobbes and Locke can we see the connection between liberal democratic principles—such as equality, consent, inalienable rights, right of resistance, and sovereignty—and the patterns of American politics—radical individualism, transactional relations, conflict management. It is often ventured that in America "theory" and "practice" are widely different. But if we look at the principles, institutions, and processes of American politics, we see that they are an internally consistent whole.

Some large questions left unresolved by the "Philadelphia story" also begin to clear up. Why, if the constitution was so clearly the product of the privileged classes, was it immediately ratified and made the supreme law of the land? And why did the members of this privileged class have such an intense suspicion of each other, almost outstripping their fear of the propertyless? The notion of a preformation of national political consciousness is useful in answering the first question. Because neither the framers nor the opponents of the Constitution possessed any alternative political ideas, the Constitution of 1787 triumphed by way of default. The tension between the liberal democratic ideas of freedom and equality was manifest even at this time, but no one knew how to resolve this tension within the framework of the liberal consensus. All were ready to adopt the familiar, even though it was clearly to the disadvantage of some.

The pervasiveness and limitations of the liberal consensus may be more clearly revealed in the attitudes of the framers toward each other than in their view of the disadvantaged. Madison built institutions on the basis of suspicions and fears found in the writings of the early liberals. If we call to mind the ruthless individual of Hobbesian politics, we find a satisfactory explanation for Madison's elaborate concern with power. Only by checking the power of each individual with the power of every other individual could the stability of institutions be assured. The constitutional system of countervailing power, which has no equal anywhere in the world, carries out the pessimistic strain in liberal politics to its ultimate conclusion. These institutions may be stable, but can they govern?

A final contribution of this investigation is to reopen the question of who or what is the final authority in America. The answers most often given are (1) the "people," expressing their will in elections, and (2) the written Constitution as it is interpreted and applied for future generations by the Supreme Court. Both these answers are not very satisfactory, as we have seen in the previous chapter. The view now prevails that Americans had so totally conformed to the ideas of liberal democracy by the eighteenth century that only the contractual metaphors developed by Hobbes and Locke serve to explain political experience. After exhaustive analysis of the origins of American political institutions, one historian says, "This image of a social contract formed by isolated and hostile individuals was now the only contractual metaphor that comprehended American social reality."[37] The final authority that arises out of this contract is not a pattern of law and it is not the people. It is the merely policing sovereign of Hobbes's thought.

This concept of the state, as a policeman who maintains the boundaries of permissible actions in a society of near lawless individuals, reemerges in Hamilton's conception of the office of the chief executive and the tendency of the framers toward a more centralized form of government to check the disarray of state and local governments. Hamilton spoke in behalf of an "energetic" executive, a term connoting the coercive power of the state, who would safeguard the existence of government and property "against the enterprises and assaults of ambition, of faction, and of anarchy."[38] He boldly proposed to strengthen the coercive arm of the state in preparation for the expected clash with propertyless elements in society. Siding with Hobbes, he foresaw the need for a unitary executive who would draw the sword, if necessary, to safeguard public order. Institutions managing social conflict, the preferred solution of Locke and Madison, worked only in relation to those who had nothing to lose from revolt.

The concept of the merely policing state is one of the many elements of a preconstituted world inherited from the founding fathers and transmitted into the present day. For evidence, we need look no further than the presidency of Ronald Reagan. Asked as a candidate to elaborate his vision of the presidential office, he replied (with his liberal ancestors, Hobbes, Locke, and Hamilton), "Government exists to protect us from each other."[39] Following his election, President Reagan reminded a convention of the International Association of Chiefs of Police that the fabric of American civilization depended on their efforts. In colorful imagery, evoking Hobbes, he said, "You are the thin blue line which holds back a jungle which threatens to reclaim this clearing we call civilization."[40] Functions sometimes vested in the state, such as education, employment, medical care, guardian of public resources, friend of the indigent, transportation, municipal planning, and support of the arts, are not congenial with the notion of the minimal, merely policing state. Consequently, it should come as no great surprise to find that President Reagan's 1982 budget proposed the elimination or reduction of many programs in support of these functions.

The preconstituted world of American liberalism has the force of public convention behind it, so much so that the likely derivation of the leading ideas of the Reagan administration is secondhand from American folklore rather than firsthand from Locke, Madison, or Hamilton.

One only has to attend to the mythic role of "sheriff" in the Hollywood version of the wild West to grasp the source of inspiration of Reagan's idea of the chief executive. The sheriff, in keeping with the notion of a minimal, merely policing government, loosely presides over a society of trigger-happy cowboys. By applying sanctions and threats of sanctions on necessary occasions, the sheriff seeks to persuade this society of cowboys, one step removed from the violence of the state of nature, not to "take the law back into their own hands." The function of the sheriff is to survive, and he does so by establishing a presumption that violence will be punished. This role is reenacted on television screens and in public theaters countless times in ritual celebration of the organizing ideas of the American political community.

NOTES

1. This is the new orthodoxy even among those of rival persuasion. My own version of events is drawn from some of the following works: Thomas R. Dye and L. Harmon Zeigler, *The Irony of Democracy* (Belmont, Cal.: Wadsworth, 1970); Kenneth M. Dolbeare and Murray J. Edelman, *American Politics,* 2nd ed. (Lexington, Mass.: Heath, 1974); Michael Parenti, *Democracy for the Few* (New York: St. Martin's Press, 1974); Ira Katznelson and Mark Kesselman, *The Politics of Power* (New York: Harcourt Brace Jovanovich, 1975). The general version of events contained in these works is based on the pathbreaking but much criticized work of Charles Beard, *An Economic Interpretation of the Constitution of the United States* (New York: Macmillan, 1913). For a critique of Beard see Forrest McDonald, *We the People* (Chicago: University of Chicago Press, 1963), and Robert E. Brown, *Charles Beard and the Constitution* (Princeton, N.J.: Princeton University Press, 1956). An attempt to make a balanced appraisal is offered by Lee Benson, *Turner and Beard: American Historical Writing Reconsidered* (New York: Free Press, 1960).
2. *Federalist* No. 51.
3. Louis Hartz, *The Liberal Tradition in America* (New York: Harcourt, Brace & World, 1955); Alfred Schutz, *On Phenomenology and Social Relations,* ed. and with an introduction by Helmut R. Wagner (Chicago: University of Chicago Press, 1970); J. Donald Moon, "In What Sense Are the Social Sciences Methodologically Distinctive?" delivered at the 1974 Annual Meeting of the American Political Science Association, Chicago, Ill., August 29–September 2, 1974.
4. C. B. Macpherson, *The Political Theory of Possessive Individualism* (London: Oxford University Press, 1962), chap. 2.
5. Robert Paul Wolff, *The Poverty of Liberalism* (Boston: Beacon Press, 1968), chap. 1.
6. Following are some of the works on which I have relied in discussing the constitutional crisis in England in the sixteenth and seventeenth centuries: Christopher Hill, *The Century of Revolution: 1603–1714* (New York: W. W. Norton, 1961); *Puritanism and Revolution* (New York: Schocken Books, 1958); G. M. Tre-

velyan, *History of England: The Tudors and Stuart Era,* vol. II (New York: Doubleday, Anchor Books, 1952); J. R. Tanner, *English Constitutional Conflicts of the Seventeenth Century* (Cambridge, Eng.: Cambridge University Press, 1962); Eduard Bernstein, *Cromwell and Communism* (New York: Schocken Books, 1963); Roger Lockyer, *Tudor and Stuart Britain: 1471–1714* (London: Longman Group Ltd., 1974).

7. Carl Lotus Becker, *The Declaration of Independence* (New York: Harcourt, Brace, 1922), p. 207.

8. Charles Burton Marshall, "American Foreign Policy as a Dimension of the American Revolution," in *America's Continuing Revolution,* eds. Irving Kristol *et al.* (New York: Anchor Books, 1976), pp. 345–67).

9. Angus McInnes, "The Revolution and the People," in *Britain After the Glorious Revolution,* ed. G. Holmes (New York: St. Martin's Press, 1969), p. 81; Tanner, *English Constitutional Conflicts,* p. 265.

10. C. B. Macpherson, *The Political Theory of Possessive Individualism* (London: Oxford University Press, 1962), chap. 3; and Bernstein, *Cromwell and Communism.*

11. Robert E. Brown, *Reinterpretation of the Formation of the Constitution* (Boston: Boston University Press, 1969); and Hartz, *The Liberal Tradition in America.*

12. Crane Brinton, *The Anatomy of Revolution* (New York: Random House, Vintage Books, 1965), pp. 24, 100, 190.

13. Daniel Boorstein, *The Genius of American Politics* (Chicago: University of Chicago Press, Phoenix Books, 1953), p. 70.

14. Thomas Hobbes, *Leviathan,* ed. and with an introduction by C. B. Macpherson (Baltimore, Md.: Penguin Books, 1968), chap. 13. The opinion that Hobbes originates and is master of the liberal tradition in political thought is put forward by several eminent scholars. See Leo Strauss, *The Political Philosophy of Hobbes,* trans. E. Sinclair (Chicago: University of Chicago Press, Phoenix Books, 1952), pp. 154–61; Ernest Barker, *Greek Political Theory* (New York: Barnes and Noble, 1961), pp. 42–46; Macpherson, *Possessive Individualism,* pp. 72–79.

15. *Ibid.,* p. 270.

16. *Ibid.,* p. 223.

17. *Ibid.,* p. 270.

18. *Ibid.,* p. 192.

19. *Ibid.,* p. 212.

20. *Ibid.,* p. 376.

21. *Ibid.,* p. 388.

22. John Bowle, *Hobbes and His Critics* (New York: Oxford University Press, 1952).

23. Karl Polanyi, *The Great Transformation* (Boston: Beacon Press, 1944), chap. 5; and Macpherson, *Possessive Individualism,* p. 41.

24. Hobbes, *Leviathan,* pp. 151–52.

25. *Ibid.,* p. 186.

26. I am indebted to Mark Roelofs for this insightful application of Jack Benny's comedy routine.

27. John Locke, *Two Treatises of Government,* ed. and with an introduction by Peter Laslett (New York: Mentor Books, 1965), *Second Treatise,* secs. 27, 28, 30, 31, 36.

28. *Ibid.,* secs. 37, 45, 50; and see the discussion by Macpherson, *Possessive Individualism,* pp. 197–220.

29. *Ibid.,* sec. 34.

30. *Ibid.,* secs. 27, 72, 50.

31. *Ibid.,* sec. 139.

32. As quoted in Sheldon Wolin, *Politics and Vision* (Boston: Little, Brown, 1960), p. 298. See R. H. Tawney, *Religion and the Rise of Capitalism* (New York: Mentor Books, 1963), and Max Weber, *The Protestant Ethic and the Spirit of Capitalism,* trans. Talcott Parsons (New York: Scribner's, 1958).

33. Locke, *Second Treatise,* sec. 149.

34. *Ibid.,* sec. 213.

35. *Ibid.,* sec. 222.

36. *Ibid.,* sec. 143.

37. Gordon S. Wood, *The Creation of the American Republic: 1776–1787* (New York: W. W. Norton, 1972), p. 601.

38. *Federalist* No. 70.

39. *The New York Times,* July 16, 1980, A14.

40. Quoted in the *National Journal,* October 3, 1981, p. 1774.

CHAPTER 4

Political Parties, Power Brokers, and Democratic Participation

This chapter will apply the idea of the constitutional system to a discussion of the national party system. One of the major preoccupations of Madison, a concern derived from his liberal ancestors, Hobbes and Locke, is with institutions suited to managing social conflict concerning inequality of property. As we saw before, Madison thought that an "extensive federal republic" would be best suited to this task because it flung the conflicting parties into space and thereafter sealed them off in insulated chambers. Madison explicitly rejects democratic institutions on the basis of his Lockean concerns with stability and the management of social conflict.

The consequence of these political arrangements for the growth of the American national party system is a dependence on decentralized cadres, or parties. The constitutional system encourages the distribution of power among a small group of influentials, which I shall call *power brokers*, situated at different levels of the federal system (national, state, and local). Although the relationships among them are nonhierarchical, collectively they occupy a power "plateau" from which the general electorate, that is, the "people," is excluded. The power brokers deal relationally with each other in a bargaining style of politics and manipulatively with those outside the power system. Power in the political system is sometimes compared to a flat-topped pyramid (a "strata-archy" rather than a conically shaped "hierarchy"), with a number of actors, influentials, and political entrepreneurs occupying the top level.[1]

I shall show that Madison succeeded in his intended object, weakening the capacity of democratic majorities to participate actively in the political process, but that this very success has robbed institutions of a basis of democratic consent and undermined the credibility of the parties as instruments of government. These harsh views are based on the current decline in political partisanship, rampant voter apathy, and the rise of organizations for independent candidates. The political parties have further shown they are unable to employ new methods of political communication, chiefly television and direct mail, to cultivate party support. Some say that if trends of the past decades continue, the study of the two-party system in texts on American politics will be a thing of the past.[2] Although recent times have brought the issue of the survival of the political parties, and indeed of democracy, to a crucial pitch, its sources lie in the past. The present crisis of the two-party system will furnish the background for a discussion of the nature of and prospects for democratic participation at the end of the chapter.

CONSTITUTION AGAINST DEMOCRACY

The Madisonian constitutional system structures political arrangements that favor power brokers, each dealing with one another on an individualistic basis in the coin of self-interest. Madison was not friendly, in fact he was decidedly hostile, as were many of his associates, to political parties, "a majority of the whole,"[3] seeking to transmit popular enthusiasms through the instruments of party government.

Madison always approached politics as though he were a wary cop trying to separate the contestants in a tavern brawl. Like any good cop, Madison sought to reduce the scope of conflict. The contestants were to be cordoned off so that the onlookers, the unruly mob, would not transform the brawl into a riot. Once the contestants were isolated, Madison sought to break them into small groups, dispersing the brawl so that the contagion of conflict would not affect the whole. Then, one by one, the effort would be made to dampen the conflict within the smaller groups.

"Democracies," Madison says, "have ever been the spectacles of turbulence and contention; have ever been found incompatible with personal security or the rights of property; and have in general been as short in their lives as they have been violent in their deaths."[4]

Democracy, in Madison's mind, was biased toward expanding the scope of social conflict.[5] This factor justified the elites of this period in developing techniques for narrowing the scope of conflict, deflecting the course of democracy from majoritarian to brokerage politics. Madison proposed three techniques for reducing the scope of social conflict: (1) reducing the number of contestants, (2) dispersing the contestants, (3) cordoning off the arena of conflict.

To reduce the number of political contestants, Madison argued at the Philadelphia convention for property and tax-paying restrictions on the right to vote. As noted before, however, the delegates could not agree on what types of property were to be the basis for exclusion. Moreover, Madison's proposals in behalf of franchise restrictions were opposed in principle by Benjamin Franklin and George Mason.[6] Mason doubted that property was a mark of good character, as Madison contended, or that the propertyless were any less responsible than the wealthy classes. Benjamin Franklin spoke in behalf of a representative system of government which would include those who had fought in the Revolutionary War. The compromise reached was that voting qualifications would be the same as for the lower house of the state legislature. This outcome was actually a victory for Madison because all the states imposed property or tax-paying restrictions on the voting franchise (Figure 4–1). Madison could take satisfaction in the knowledge that participation was reduced, as he desired, but not so much as to rob the institutions of their reputation of being rooted in democratic consent.

The absence of a constitutional right to vote has created problems for democratic participation which persist into the present day. Restrictions imposed by the states against blacks, women, eighteen-year-olds, and the District of Columbia have been dealt with after the fact and only through the cumbersome process of constitutional amendment (Fifteenth, Nineteenth, Twenty-Third, Twenty-Fourth, and Twenty-Sixth). Until such time as Congress acted, other agencies unsuited to this political struggle, the Supreme Court most notably, reluctantly intervened to protect the rights of disenfranchised groups. Thus, democratic participation in elections is an uphill battle in American political history. Through piecemeal victories against the biases of the constitutional system, excluded groups have gradually won a limited right to participate in the political process.

Another technique of conflict management was cordoning off the arena of conflict. The indirect method of electing members of the Senate and the president insulated the political process from unwholesome popular pressures. Members of the Senate were to be chosen by the legislatures of the states. The indirect election of the president through nonpopular institutions, the state legislatures and the electoral college,

FIGURE 4-1

The Duration of Property and Taxpaying Restrictions in the Franchise, 1776–1860

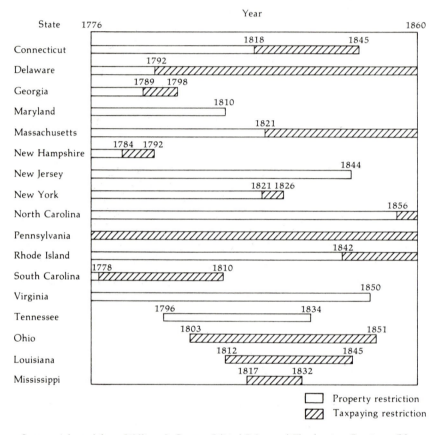

SOURCE: Adapted from William J. Crotty, *Political Reform and The American Experiment* (New York: Thomas Y. Crowell, 1977), p. 12.

was aimed at keeping the people away from so critical a task.[7] The president is now thought to be the instrument of popular majorities, especially when he has a majority of the same party in one or both houses of Congress. However, this conception of the office is far from what Madison and his colleagues intended.

The electoral college system was intended to vest the power of choosing the president in a body of electors themselves selected according to a method preferred by the state legislatures. Whether the electors were to be chosen by legislative appointment, gubernatorial appointment, or by popular election was thought to be a decision best left to the states. Most of the delegates to the convention assumed that the members of the electoral college would be chosen by the state legislature after consultation with the people.[8] Each state was to be allowed a number of electors equal to its total number of senators and representatives.

The electoral college system did not take into account the operation of party caucuses collaborating with particular candidates. In 1804 the Constitution was amended to preclude a tie vote between presidential candidates of the same party. The Twelfth Amendment required the members of the electoral college to cast a separate ballot for president and vice-president, thus avoiding the outcome of the 1800 election when Burr and Jefferson received the same number of electoral votes.

Although parties have drastically changed the manner in which the electoral system operates, the bias against a direct reflection of the wishes of popular majorities is still preserved. As it stands now the electoral college has been democratized in the respect that electors are chosen by a plurality of the popular vote within each state. Each slate of electors is committed in advance to the candidate who has received the party nomination. Discretion in the choice of the president by the state legislature or electoral college is eliminated. However, the electoral college majority (270 votes) is not an accurate reflection of the popular majority because each state receives two additional electoral votes by virtue of its representation in the Senate. This system gives the less populous states a slight edge that would be lost if only the popular vote were counted. Some analysts argue that the present system actually gives the electoral balance to minority groups in populous urban industrial states.[9]

To offer an example, Gerald Ford could have won the 1976 election by a shift of 9,245 votes in the states of Hawaii and Ohio even while losing the popular tally by 1.7 million votes. In 1960, a switch of only 8,891 popular votes from John Kennedy to Richard Nixon in Illinois and Mississippi would have denied either candidate an electoral college majority. In 1888, Benjamin Harrison polled 95,713 fewer votes than Grover Cleveland but received an electoral majority.[10] These instances and others like them have kept alive movements for reform.

Dispersing the parties to the social conflict is the third means employed by Madison to manage political struggle. He dispersed the powers of government so that the contestants in the political struggle would themselves be dispersed beyond the remedy of political combination. A government of dispersed powers will break society "into so many parts, interests, and classes of citizens, that the rights of individuals, or of the minority, will be in little danger from interested combinations of the majority."[11]

A fear of democratic participation so vast as to inform all of one's thinking about politics must have a specific object. If we cast about in the writings of the framers for the particular source of their fears, we find it in a collective dread of the propertyless and the blacks. Madison acknowledges a deep-seated fear of a black population regularly dealt with on a manipulative basis by influential groups in the political process.

> I take no little notice of an unhappy species of population abounding in some of the states who, during the calm of regular government were sunk below the level of men; but who, in the tempestuous seeds of civil violence, may emerge into human character and give a superiority of strength to any party with which they may associate themselves.[12]

Noting the commercial class of Massachusetts had to finance its own army to put down Shays's rebellion, Hamilton points out that the new federal army will save them time, expense, and needless anxiety. Daniel Shays, a veteran of Bunker Hill, assembled an insurgent army of farmers and laborers in Western Massachusetts in the summer of 1786. He led these ragged forces against tax collectors and sheriffs attempting to repossess farms on behalf of creditors. Writing in 1787, Hamilton says,

> The tempestuous situation from which Massachusetts has scarcely emerged evinces that dangers of this kind [domestic revolt] are not merely speculative. Who could determine what might have been the issue of her late convulsions if the malcontents had been headed by Caesar or Cromwell? A strong military force in the hands of the national government is a protection against revolutionary action.[13]

The framers had good reason for fearing democracy. Expansion of the political agenda under a democratic regime would have included the dissatisfactions of the blacks and the propertyless and therefore would have rocked the government. Thus the framers built a bias against democracy into the very structure of government. This was an unusual step, distinguishing the American polity from, say, party government in Great Britain. In the latter country, the checks imposed on the majority party in government by an opposition party and an unwritten constitution are thought to be sufficient. These checks are not only consistent with the spirit of democracy but also essential elements of its operation. The framers went beyond this system by seeking permanent institutional safeguards against democracy. The role of an opposition party was not enough; the government, itself, had to be secure from party rule. A consequence of this antidemocratic bias is that government and political parties, to this day, survive at the expense of democratic participation.

DECENTRALIZED CADRE PARTIES

The two-party system, as we now know it, is decisively affected by the characteristics of the constitutional system. Historically, and to this very day, the American party system consists of decentralized cadre parties. The cadre, or "skeletal" party, is historically associated with the genesis of liberal democratic institutions in England and the need for a suitable organization to represent the outlook of the Protestant middle class. A distinguishing feature of the cadre party, as one analyst notes, is that it is constituted by "a small group of activists, a self-selected party elite that *is* the party." All the major functions of the party are performed by this group of activists who "make its decisions, raise its funds, pick its candidates, shape its issue stands and platforms, and decide its strategies." The commercial Protestants who run the party apply principles of operation carried over from business. They run an "entrepreneurial party, selling their candidates and platforms to cagey political consumers."[14] There is a sharp distinction between the party and the electorate in this vision. The party elite is organized, active, and influential, whereas the electorate is passive, uninformed, and only intermittently engaged in politics.

The methods and goals of the cadre leadership reflect Madison's thinking about politics, fulfilling the role of power brokers. The style of operation is bargaining and negotiation among established influentials. The leadership performs a brokerage function among candidates, officeholders, and spokespersons for interest groups. An individual who possesses money, glamor, skills, following, ambition, or some combination of these elements is co-opted by the leadership and matched up with a collection of interest groups recruited on a similar basis. This improvisation of candidates and interest groups is called a party and sold to the electorate in the most attractively packaged fashion. The payoff for the brokerage function is the capture of office and all that goes with it. With the patronage and other rewards accruing to the acquisition of office, the cadre leadership is able to defray its own expenses in time and money.[15]

The selection of issues and candidates takes place at the level of government for which office is sought. The organization of the leadership of the political parties is imitative of the federal structure of government. Each party has a national party committee, the Democratic National Committee and the Republican National Committee, and party organs at the state, county, ward, and precinct levels of political organization. Although on an organization chart, the national party committee stands at the head, this picture is a distortion. The units of party organization at the state and local level make their own selection of issues and candidates apart from the wishes of the national committee. Additionally, each of the political parties has congressional campaign committees, one for each house, and they make independent decisions regarding campaign spending and issues. For the most part, each of the party units mentioned has independent sources of revenue to run its operations.[16]

The independence of the various levels tends to make the office of national chairman a weak post. In an interview in December 1977 as he stepped down as chairman of the Democratic National Committee, Kenneth Curtis, former governor of Maine and successor as party chairman to Robert Strauss, confessed that he basically didn't like his job. Asked whether the chairmanship was a "lousy job," Curtis replied, "That's one way you could put it." He added, "Did you ever try to meet the payroll every two weeks of a bankrupt organization and try to keep 50 state chairmen happy?"[17]

All efforts to give the national committees a role in selecting candidates and issues have failed. A Democratic Advisory Council was established by the political forces who campaigned for Adlai Stevenson following his election defeat in 1956. The Stevenson forces wished to substantiate a record for the party in Congress and to prepare in advance for the presidential race in 1960. Although the council was composed of illustrious members of the Democratic party, such as Harry Truman, Eleanor Roosevelt, and Walter Reuther, nevertheless, Lyndon Johnson and Sam Rayburn, the Senate majority leader and speaker of the House, rebuffed invitations to attend its executive sessions. A perceptive onlooker commented, "Without the participation of the congressional leaders, the Advisory Council was reduced to little more than a star-studded discussion group operating on the fringes of the party."[18]

A similar attempt was made by the Republicans after Nixon's defeat in 1960. The All Republican Conference (1962) and the Critical Issues Council (1963) also had an illustrious membership as well as Eisenhower's blessing. Notwithstanding, Charles Halleck and Everett Dirksen, the House and Senate minority leaders, refused to attend the conference sessions and persisted in putting on their own "Ev and Charlie" political show.

The weakness of the national committees serves to underline the fact that the political parties are basically federations of cadre leaders loosely held together by an extensive process of bargaining and negotiation. At the national party conventions, this bargaining process is clearly displayed. If the accommodations among the cadre leadership succeed, the federation will be maintained for the purposes of electing the presidential candidate. The front runners for the party nomination will ardently strive to conciliate all factions within the party in hopes of drawing their support in the campaign. However, if these negotiations fail, there is little that the national party or its endorsed candidate can do to impose sanctions. At the local level the cadre leadership may declare the national candidate *persona non grata,* as did the Texas Democratic leadership in discouraging state visits by Hubert Humphrey in the 1968 election. Or an interest group which has traditionally been an element of the party coalition may announce its intention to sit out the election. The "neutrality" of the AFL-CIO toward the McGovern/Nixon contest in 1972 was severely damaging to McGovern's chances of election.

Analysts of the 1972 and 1976 Democratic party conventions report a trend toward tripartite bargaining arrangements among candidate organizations, issue blocs, and the regular party leadership. George McGovern's relatively weak organization forced him to depend on caucuses led by women, youth, and blacks at the expense of his ability to accommodate the regular party leadership. By comparison the strong organization mounted by Jimmy Carter in 1976 and the declining strength of reform groups placed the candidate in a secure bargaining relationship with all groups.[19] In 1976 women constituted 34.3 percent of the delegates, compared with 38 percent of all delegates in 1972; blacks made up 10.6 percent of the delegates, compared with 15 percent in 1972; persons thirty years old or younger constituted 14.8 percent, compared with 21 percent in 1972.[20]

The primary interest of the cadre leadership is in the co-optation of influentials and in winning elections. Between elections the party leadership makes little effort to increase its membership through voting registration drives and education of the public. The lack of interest of the elective leadership in Congress to proposals for national voting registration is typical (see Table 4-1). With the weakening of ties between ethnic groups and the political parties, the cadre leadership has turned to Madison Avenue to provide the emotional hype needed to put their candidate across. Its thin commitment to its electoral constituency elicits from them a weak response. Being affiliated with one of the major political parties means very little. Americans may, most do, identify themselves as Republicans or Democrats. Yet this identification may not involve even such feeble participation as voting for the party candidate, and it certainly does not require higher levels of participation such as

TABLE 4-1

Socioeconomic Characteristics and Nonregistration of Voters, 1972 Presidential Election[a]

Social Characteristic	Percent Not Voting	Percent Not Registered
Age		
18–20 years	51.7	41.9
21–24 years	49.3	40.5
25–29 years	42.2	33.9
30–34 years	38.1	28.8
35–44 years	33.7	25.2
45–54 years	29.1	20.7
55–64 years	29.3	19.8
65–74 years	31.9	21.5
75 years and over	44.4	29.3
Sex		
Male	35.9	26.9
Female	38.0	28.4
Race		
White	35.5	26.6
Black	47.9	34.5
Ethnic origin		
German	29.2	21.0
Italian	28.5	22.5
Irish	33.4	23.3
French	36.8	27.3
Polish	28.0	20.2
Russian	19.5	14.3
English, Scottish, Welsh	28.7	19.9
Spanish	62.5	55.6
(Mexican)	(62.5)	(54.0)
(Puerto Rican)	(55.4)	(47.3)
(Other Spanish)	(64.5)	(63.2)
Years in school		
Elementary:		
0–4	67.0	51.8
5–7	55.7	40.5

TABLE 4-1

Socioeconomic Characteristics and Nonregistration of Voters, 1972 Presidential Election[a] **(continued)**

Social Characteristic	Percent Not Voting	Percent Not Registered
8	44.8	32.0
High school:		
1–3	48.0	37.0
4	34.6	26.0
College:		
1–3	25.1	18.3
4	17.7	12.9
5 or more	14.4	11.2
Employment status		
Employed	34.0	25.7
Unemployed	50.1	41.3
Occupational grouping		
White collar workers	23.6	17.6
Blue collar workers	45.8	35.1
Service workers	41.4	31.8
Farm workers	36.4	24.0
Home ownership[b]		
Own home	16	NA[c]
Rent	44	NA

[a]These U.S. Census figures do not include military personnel or institutionalized populations.
[b]These totals are taken from the Gallup poll as reported in AVM Corporation, *The Tally Sheet* (Fall, 1971), p. 15.
[c]NA—Figures not available.

SOURCE: Adapted from William J. Crotty, *Political Reform and the American Experiment* (New York: Thomas Y. Crowell), pp. 54–55.

joining the party, attending party meetings, contributing to the party coffers, or campaigning for the party candidate.

Style is substance. The overall effect of the parties' methods of operation is to further the antidemocratic biases of the constitutional system. The blacks and the propertyless are not excluded from the franchise as they were in Madison's era. But the methods of operation, dealing relationally with other party leaders, ignoring voter registration, co-opting influentials who may help the ticket, soliciting funds from producer groups, are much the same as they were in Madison's day and they have the same effect.

A contemporary profile of nonvoters (Table 4-1) shows that the basic patterns of exclusion, originating in Madison's time, persist into our own. This profile is drawn in careful detail by a modern student of voting behavior.

> Far fewer blacks than whites register or vote. The majority of Spanish-speaking people, who may face citizenship difficulties as well as language and cultural barriers, do not vote. . . . Forty percent of the unemployed are not registered and 50 percent do not vote (compared with 26 percent and 34 percent, respectively, for those with jobs). A majority of the least educated (four or less years of formal education) are unenrolled and two-thirds do not exercise the franchise. Of those with four years of college, only 13 percent remain unregistered and only 18 percent fail to vote. White collar personnel register and vote on almost a 2 to 1 ratio over blue collar workers and on both counts do substantially better than service and farm workers. . . . Homeowners are far more likely to enroll than those that rent. . . . Forty percent of the under 25 are unenrolled and one-half of this age category does not vote.[21]

Through the operation of America's decentralized cadre parties the main characteristics of an eighteenth-century constitutional system have slipped into the twentieth century. As in Madison's day, a range of noninfluential groups are excluded from effective participation by the working arrangements of politics. Conversely, groups with high socio-economic status participate at a much higher rate. In terms of ideology and methods of operation, the national political parties are more alike than dissimilar because of the constraints imposed by the Constitution (as memorandom, ideology, and practice).

Occasionally, the cadre leadership tips its hand by taking overt action to limit the political agenda and to exclude noninfluential groups from the political process. One example is the bipartisan reaction of the leaders of the Republican and Democratic parties against the community action programs of the Johnson administration. In an unusual step, the government called for the "maximum feasible participation" of the poor in the war against poverty. Through neighborhood organizations, assembled by the Office of Economic Opportunity (OEO) or its local representatives, the poor were to be drawn into the process of identifying major grievances and the programs most suitable for dealing with them. Such an activity would have an obvious and immediate democratizing influence on the political process, and one might reasonably expect that the party leadership would welcome such a development. This was not the case. Both Richard Daley (Democrat), mayor of Chicago, and William F. Walsh (Republican), mayor of Syracuse, loudly protested against the formation of neighborhood organizations independent of the control of city hall and party leadership. Nor were they alone. In time, this bipartisan coalition brought a complete halt to the community participation program.[22]

Such items on the political agenda are startling because they are there so seldom. By and large, the methods of operation of the cadre leadership are enough to limit the agenda of politics without the need for overt action of the sort undertaken by Mayor Daley and Mayor Walsh. It is in the items never placed on the political agenda that the political parties most clearly reveal their commitment to an eighteenth-century Constitution.

One of these items is the socialization of the uses of capital corresponding to the activity of the state as an instrument of capital accumulation. As we shall see in Chapter 5, corporate industry has diverted the resources of the state in selected areas—transportation, energy, housing—to its own purposes. Corporate industry, by its own action, has broken down the divide between the public and private sector and created a rationale for direct government supervision of the economy. In keeping with the logic of the new situation a distinguished economist, John Kenneth Galbraith, asserts, "The Democratic Party must henceforth use the word socialism. It describes what is needed."[23]

The political parties, accustomed as they are to restricting the agenda of politics and limiting the framework of democratic discussion, have not begun to grasp the problem that corporate capital has set for them, let alone sought to educate and organize the public to make a proper response. Party elites conventionally deal on a relational basis with influential producer groups. Similarly, producer groups impartially distribute their largesse to the elites of both political parties. For example, the oil and gas industry made substantial contributions to Sam Rayburn and Lyndon Johnson, speaker of the House and Senate majority leader, throughout the 1950s to assure safe appointments to key committees (House Ways and Means and Senate Finance) on the depletion allowance.[24] In the election campaigns of 1974 and 1976, Republicans and Democrats on the Senate Finance Committee were the recipients of campaign support from the same industry. Oil corporations made contributions to the Nixon reelection campaign in 1972, illegally and legally, in staggering amounts (Table 4–2). Such contributions help to explain why there is no movement afoot by the political parties to socialize the oil and gas industry. Although these contributions are perhaps atypical, the tendency of well-heeled producer and professional groups to work across party lines with strategically placed influentials in Congress and the presidency is long-standing. Given the relationships just described it is unlikely that the political parties are going to mount an offensive against the favored position of corporate capital.

The cost of not dealing with the impact of corporate capital in the political process and related problems of resource allocation and distribution will be increased apathy and indifference from citizens. "Voters are not fools," one analyst has reminded the elite democrats.[25] Thus, we can safely predict that the parties will not attract much more attention and support from the electorate until they are more responsive to the relationships between the public and private sector and the politics of resource allocation. In our era the parties are presented a momentous challenge by the relative sophistication of the voting population and the existence of difficult social and economic issues. Judging from the past the parties will take up such issues when they are compelled to do so by insurgent groups. As the rising levels of participation in the presidential primaries of 1968 show, the parties are most likely to elicit public interest when used as vehicles by insurgent groups for issues lying outside the boundaries of elite consensus.

TABLE 4-2

Oil Corporation Contributions to the Nixon Campaign, 1972

Company	Total Contribution ($)	Secret Contribution ($)
1. Gulf Oil Co.	1,176,500	1,132,000
2. Amerada Hess Corp.	261,956	211,000
3. Getty Oil Co.	179,292	77,500
4. Standard Oil (Calif.)	166,000	102,000
5. Sun Oil Co.	157,798	60,000
6. Pan Ocean Oil Corp.	137,035	—
7. Phillips Petroleum Co.	137,000	100,000
8. Exxon	127,747	100,672
9. The Williams Companies	117,596	—
10. Shaheen Natural Resources	104,000	—
11. Ashland Oil, Inc.	103,500	100,000
TOTALS:	2,668,424	1,883,172

Source: Adapted from William J. Crotty, *Political Reform and the American Experiment* (New York: Thomas Y. Crowell, 1977), p. 147.

INTERESTING TIMES

The Chinese have a proverbial curse: "May you live in interesting times." There is accumulating evidence that the times in which we live are "interesting" in the fateful way intimated.[26] Several trends seen by students of political parties and voting behavior foreshadow the collapse of the present two-party system: falling rates of voter participation, a decline in political partisanship, and a tendency for political incumbents and challengers to form independent organizations. Reform movements in the political parties are desperately trying to stave off collapse by democratizing the existing cadre parties in the direction of increased participation. Playing a pivotal role in this struggle, along with the distribution of power among competing elites, is an eighteenth-century liberal antidemocratic Constitution. In this section, attention will be focused on evidence of atrophy and decline in the major political parties.

DECLINE OF VOTER PARTICIPATION

One of the trends pointed to with alarm is that voting participation in presidential elections has been declining steadily since 1960. In that year 62.8 percent of the electorate turned out to give a razor-thin edge to John F. Kennedy over Richard Nixon. Then there is a period of decline, with 61.9 percent of the eligible population voting in 1964 and 60.9 percent in 1968. In 1972 a significant drop occurs: 55.4 percent of the persons eligible went to the polls. This decline continued into the 1976 presidential elections, when 53.3 percent of the voting population participated.[27] Further, of all Americans over eighteen, 27 percent voted for Carter, 26 percent voted for Ford, and a whopping 47 percent stayed home. Since Carter won only slightly more than one-half of the vote, roughly 25 percent of the electorate chose the president. It might be said that the real winner on election day was "none of the above."

This trend continues unabated into the election of Ronald Reagan. Only 52.4 percent of the nation's 160,491,000 eligible voters took part in the election, the lowest turnout in a presidential election since 1948 when 51.1 percent voted in the contest between Harry Truman and Thomas E. Dewey. Low turnouts have a particularly adverse effect on the Democratic party candidate. Many nonvoters tend to lean Democratic. They are the young (under thirty-five), the minorities (especially blacks and Hispanics), the less educated, and blue-collar workers.[28]

FIGURE 4-2
Turnout of the Eligible Electorate in Presidential Contests,
1824–1980

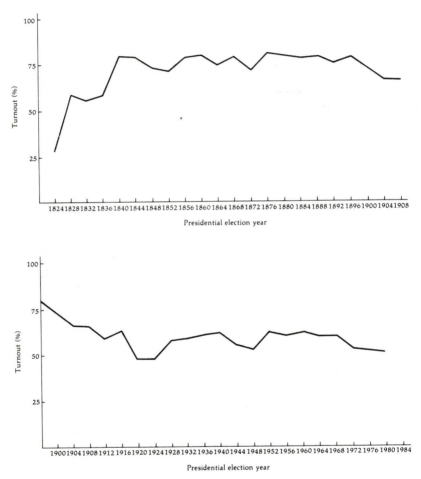

SOURCE: William J. Crotty, *Political Reform and the American Experiment* (New York: Thomas Y. Crowell, 1977), p. 48.

A distressing paradox is that the decline in presidential voting has occurred at a time when many positive steps have been taken to increase voter turnout. The media have provided mass exposure of the electoral process and have entered into the reporting of the presidential primary campaigns in depth and with gusto. The national government and the states have not been inactive. There has been a steady expansion of the number of states providing for presidential primaries coupled with the removal of obstacles to voting, such as literacy tests and poll taxes. The Voting Rights Act (1970) enfranchised millions of black voters. Many states have made voter registration easier; twenty-five now permit post-card registration, and Oregon, Wisconsin, Maine, and Minnesota have established election day registration. North Dakota requires none at all. In 1980, the national government, through the Federal Elections Commission, provided substantial sums to contenders for the presidency in primaries as well as in the general election. It provided $31 million in matching funds for ten Democratic and Republican candidates competing for the party nomination. This sum was followed by an allottment of $63 million for Carter, Reagan, and Anderson (who received $4.1 million) to use in the general election campaign. The major political parties received $8.9 million each to operate their party conventions and $4.7 million to spend on their party candidate.[29] These funds are made available for distribution through the dues checkoff on income tax returns. Their general aim is to make presidential candidates less dependent on contributions from the rich and to reduce the importance of wealth as a criterion of candidacy.

A reason sometimes given for the drop in voting turnout is that a new group, the eighteen-year-olds who were given the right to vote by the Twenty-sixth Amendment (1970), has entered the voting population. This group, consisting of approximately twenty-one million eighteen-year-olds, is unaccustomed to the intricacies and exasperating features of the registration process. Accounts on the optimistic side view the present rate of voting turnout as a transitional phase. They predict that voting participation will stabilize at 55 percent to 60 percent after the new group of eighteen-year-olds is processed for registration.[30] A comparison is often made to the drop in voting turnout when women received the right to vote through the Nineteenth Amendment (1920). During the period required by the new group to overcome the hurdles of registration, the turnout of voters fell to 50 percent (Figure 4-2).

The absolute number of voters who remain indifferent to election results is staggering in a nation claiming to rest on democratic consent (Figure 4-3). The year 1968 offers an interesting standard of comparison because the turnout (60.9 percent of the eligible voters went to the polls) is high in comparison with recent times. Forty million qualified voters stayed home in that year. A popular vote of 500,000 (six-tenths of 1 percent of the total vote) meant the difference between the victorious Republican candidate (Richard Nixon) and the defeated Democratic candidate (Hubert Humphrey). An analyst notes, "The number of non-voters in this election could have reversed the winner's plurality 80 times over."[31] In the election of 1972, to offer a further basis of comparison, sixty million people did not vote. This "nation" of non-voters exceeds the total population of France, West Germany, Italy, Mexico, Canada, and the United Kingdom combined. If placed within specific territorial boundaries, it would constitute the world's eighth largest country.[32] As formerly noted, a substantial portion of this nation of estranged voters is poor, black, blue collar, and young. In 1976 only 42 percent of those eighteen to twenty-four bothered to vote; those twenty-five to thirty-four did better at 55.4 percent.[33]

As we look into the political future, the forecast for voting participation is not encouraging. If we assume with the optimists that the voting turnout will stabilize at 60 percent, and if we suppose that current population projections will hold constant, then the United

FIGURE 4-3
Voting Age Population and the Number of Nonvoters in the United States, 1952–1972

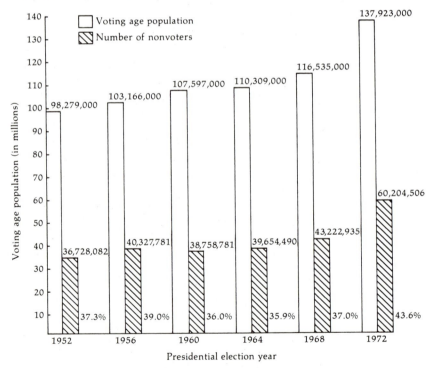

SOURCE: Adapted from William J. Crotty, *Political Reform and the American Experiment* (New York: Thomas Y. Crowell, 1977), p. 50.

States may have 122 million nonvoters by the year 2000. "Even in an age of statistical and every other type of overkill, these figures are striking,"[34] an analyst observes.

To avoid a time when the majority of the electorate is not voting (and possibly to improve his own prospects for reelection), President Carter proposed in his first year in office a new national initiative in which registration and voting on the same day and postcard registration would become the law. These proposals were modest, falling far short of the enrolling procedures used in other Western democracies, which achieve a higher turnout than in the United States. Italy, West Germany, France, Great Britain, and Canada, for example, have created national electoral commissions charged with the task of enrolling eligible voters. By placing the burden of registration on the state rather than on the private citizen, these countries achieve a rate of participation 15 to 30 percent above that in the United States.[35] Carter's registration proposal (along with one for electoral college reform) was opposed by the Republican party and failed to win the enthusiastic backing of the elective leadership of the Democratic party.

DECLINE OF PARTISANSHIP

Another trend that is upsetting traditional expectations about two-party democracy is the increase in independent voters and a related decline in political partisanship. Since 1952 a team of scholars at the Center for Political Studies, University of Michigan, has been asking a representative sample of the voting population a series of questions concerning their voting behavior. The responses are then projected on the voting population at large. The principal question put to the sample population is the following:

> Generally speaking, do you usually think of yourself as a Republican, a Democrat, an Independent, or what?

In the 1950s this research showed that 22 percent of the population classified themselves as Independents. In the late 1960s, an increase in the proportion of Independents became noticeable, and this growth intensified in the early 1970s. By 1973, the Independents comprised 31 percent of the population. The Independent voter is now the second largest group in the voting population after Democrats, 45 percent, and well ahead of Republicans, 22 percent (Figure 4-4). A high percentage of the youngest group of the voting population classify themselves as Independents. By 1968, over one-half of the Independents were drawn from this group (Table 4-3).

FIGURE 4-4
The American Electorate—A Profile

The American Electorate—a Profile

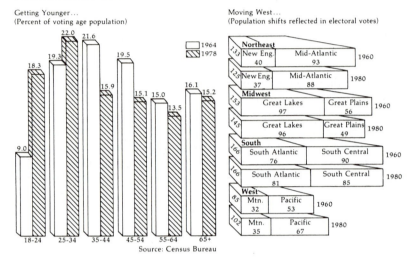

Getting Younger...
(Percent of voting age population)

Moving West...
(Population shifts reflected in electoral votes)

Source: Census Bureau

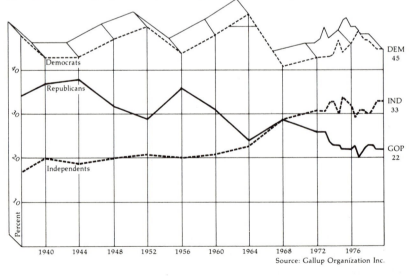

...and Becoming More Independent
(Q: "In politics, as of today, do you consider yourself a Republican, Democrat or independent?")

Source: Gallup Organization Inc.

SOURCE: Adapted from *National Journal*, October 20, 1980, p. 1727.

TABLE 4-3

Proportion Independents by age, 1952–1974

Age	1952	1956	1960	1964	1968	1972[a]	1974[a]
21–25	25	37	39	33	53	51	53
26–30	32	31	26	29	41	50	42
31–40	23	26	27	26	29	40	39
41–50	26	21	25	24	31	30	37
51–65	19	24	21	18	24	26	32
66+	20	13	13	14	15	19	23
Average percent Independent among those over 30	20	22	22	21	26	28	34
Difference between youngest and over 30	3	15	17	12	27	23	19

[a]For 1972 and 1974 the youngest age group is 18 to 25.

Source: Adapted from Norman H. Nie et al., *The Changing American Voter* (Cambridge, Mass.: Harvard University Press, 1976), p. 60.

CANDIDATE ORGANIZATIONS, MEDIA, AND MONEY

If the political parties arouse little except apathy from the electorate, the candidates hope to survive through independent organizations, a trend evident among candidates in all spheres of political activity. This trend both reflects and exacerbates the confusion of the electorate. If the political parties collapse, and some predict that they will before very long, the candidates hope to salvage their own political fortunes from the ruins. An observer neatly summarizes this trend:

> Today, you really don't have slates (of party candidates), with a few exceptions, anywhere in the country. The Senators run their own campaigns, the Congressmen run their own campaigns, the state legislators run their own campaigns, and the sheriff runs his own campaign. Before, it used to be that the party's name was in big letters [on campaign literature] and that the candidate's was small. Now it's just the opposite. I can show you hundreds of brochures where candidates are hiding their affiliation.[36]

A tendency to rely on the media and the demise of ethnically based party machines in the big cities contributes to the disintegrative effects of independent organizations. In Chicago, Pittsburgh, Philadelphia, and New York, ethnic ties to party machines have survived into the present day. These ties are undergoing dissolution, however, as the state takes over the social welfare functions formerly supplied by the party precinct organization. Since the precinct level no longer has the capacity to deliver lopsided votes of the immigrant and working class populations, candidates are turning to independent organizations and to the media. The expensive medium of television has transformed the old party machines into museum pieces, relics of the nineteenth century. The notion of progress is allied with the new medium. A journalist offers the interesting comparison, "What the railroad was to the first half of 20th century politicking, television has become to the second half."[37]

Examples of independent organizations for the presidential office are provided by the election of Richard Nixon and Jimmy Carter. In 1972 the Nixon White House staff set up a Committee to Re-Elect the President (CREEP) which had a separate staff, financing, and locale from the national party headquarters of the Republican party. The CREEP staff was devoted exclusively to the reelection of the president. One of the reasons Republican candidates for Congress had trouble unseating incumbent Democrats in that election is that the staff had dried up the funds needed to wage a successful campaign. CREEP soaked up an estimated sixty million dollars in campaign funds, none of which was diverted to the task of electing congressmen and governors (see discussion, Chapter 9). The staff ran the total presidential campaign, and the national party organization was relegated to an inconsequential role. Before, during, and after the campaign the White House staff was transformed into a way station for the members of CREEP.[38]

Jimmy Carter's election in 1976 is another example of this phenomenon. Following a pattern set by John Kennedy in 1960, Carter built a strong organization in his home state, in this case a good two years before the national party convention. Using this as a base of power, he ran successfully in a number of presidential primaries, collected the support of the regular party leadership (Daley was still important), amassed a delegate total sufficient to win nomination on the first ballot, and appeared in person at the convention. Carter picked up a check from the Federal Election Commission for $21.8 million to defray the expense of his independent organization in the general election after the convention.[39] Carter's organization was maintained in Atlanta, Georgia, physically separate from the Washington site of the national party headquarters. After the election, the candidate's organization metamorphosed into the White House staff.

The trend toward independent organizations is as evident in House and Senate races as in contests for the presidency. Generous staff allowances enable congressional incumbents to form the nucleus of an independent organization with expenses partially defrayed by the government. The percentage of staff assigned to home districts by House members has more than doubled, from 14 percent in 1960 to 34 percent in 1974.[40] To offset the moods of a volatile electorate, representatives seek to combine a powerful district staff operation with the chairmanship of a subcommittee. Incumbency, however, is no longer a sure thing. In 1980, many incumbent Democrats in the House and Senate were swept from office by a tide of presidential voting which was running in the other direction.

The trend toward independent organizations is not a departure from Madisonian notions of politics. Rather it is a new variation on old principles of private entrepreneurship which have inspired politics in America from the beginning. The political parties have never been more than the temporary intersection of interests of independently situated actors, loosely held together in unstable combinations by the cadre leadership. As the ethnic ties which sustained the position of the cadre leadership have been weakened and as the new technologies of political communication—direct mail advertising and television—have been strengthened, it is natural, in accordance with the controlling principles of American liberal tradition, for these old principles to reassert themselves. The weakness of party organization in America is shown in its feeble organizational response to the challenge presented by the new era of television campaigning. The strength of the liberal tradition is shown by the tendency to use the new technologies of communication to buttress independent organizations.

More money than ever before is being spent on political campaigns, and an increasing proportion of it is going toward new media techniques. In 1964, presidential primary and general election expenditures by all candidates was $60 million, and in 1968, $100 million. The total expenditure for the 1980 election, counting both primary and general election expenditures of all candidates, was approximately $250 million. Of this amount, Reagan spent $62 million; Carter, $56.1 million; and Anderson, $12.5 million.[41] Overall expenses have similarly risen in congressional campaigns. In 1972, House campaign funds from all sources were $38.9 million, and in 1978, $92.2 million. In the Senate, $23.3 million was raised for the election in 1972, and $66 million for the campaign in 1968.[42]

Unlike the presidential primaries and general elections, congressional elections are regulated but not financed by the provisions of the Federal Election Campaign Act (1974). This circumstance has forced congressmen into dependence on individual contributions and PACs (fund-raising committees called Political Action Committees). A study of House and Senate campaigns shows that the proportion of contributions provided by individuals and PACs has risen in the period from 1972 to 1978 while the proportion contributed by party organizations has declined. Further, the number of PACs organized by business and professional groups far outstrips the number sympathetic to labor; the total contributions of the business and professional PACs also exceed the labor fund-raising committees.[43]

As previously stated, much of the money now being spent on political campaigns is going to new media techniques. Political rallies and mass gatherings at the public square are a thing of the past. The electorate sits passively, unceremoniously, perhaps sullenly, waiting for political news through the television tube and the mailbox. In 1980, the Carter campaign allotted almost the total amount of its $19.5 million in media expenses to television; the Reagan campaign spent $10.5 million in television advertising.[44] Record amounts were spent on direct mail advertising in the 1980 campaign. This technique involves segmenting the electorate by race, income, religion, sex, voting behavior, and contribution record; storing of this information on computer tapes; and then matching the tapes with an electronically typed form letter aimed at the political outlook of the recipient. To the recipient, the letter appears to be personally typed from a sympathetic ally in an important cause.[45]

Use of this technique by Richard Viguerie, sometimes called the "godfather of the new Right," was credited with unseating many incumbent Democrats in the House and Senate during the 1980 general election.[46] Viguerie's National Conservative Political Action Committee (NCPAC) sent out 100 million pieces of mail at 30 cents per individualized computer typed first class letter. No less than television, the use of the direct mail advertising technique has moved into the era of big business.[47]

COMPETING IDEAS OF DEMOCRATIC PARTICIPATION

If the much vaunted two-party system collapsed tomorrow, why should anyone regret it? By the admission of its principal advocates, it chiefly serves the need of media gurus—the cadre leadership, independently-situated, wealthy, glamorous political incumbents, the spokesmen for the business and professional PACs—in short, the diverse collection of economic interests, dressed up in modern fashion, served by Madison's political arrangements. If the people, organized behind majoritarian political parties, are locked out of the system of government by these arrangements, why should they have any regrets about its passing?

One outlook on the present disarray argues, in essence, that it is not the two-party system that is in need of modification but rather our idea of democratic participation. Despite admitted deficiencies, the present system offers the public a choice of policies and candidates following an open and announced intraparty struggle for power. Democracy is preserved through the choice the electorate makes following the aftermath of elite competition. Proponents of this perspective, the politics of *elite competition,* would like to save, through moderate reform, the two-party system and the constitutional system that undergirds it.

Another outlook, *participatory democracy,* receives the news about voter apathy, independent organizations, and decline in partisanship as a matter of the chickens coming home to roost. The cadre leadership, by its structure and operating methods, has discouraged public participation in the agenda-setting functions of political government. This political elite, so it is charged, restricts the boundaries of political conflict and tacitly excludes disadvantaged groups from the political process. If the political parties are in decline, so the participatory democrats argue, it is because they are not democratic. We should bid them good-bye and wish them on their way. The constitutional system, which preserves an antidemocratic bias, is a hidden participant in this dispute, siding with the elite democrats.

At issue in the contest between elite democrats and participatory democrats is a different idea of the nature of democratic participation. Both sides use the word *democracy,* but they mean by it very different things. To sharpen this conflict and to obtain some grasp of the leading issues, we shall put a few questions to each side. Who, we shall ask, should participate in politics? What are the forms of democratic participation? What are its goals?

ELITE DEMOCRACY

This view holds that the essence of democracy is the choice of policy and candidates made by the electorate following an open contest for power by the leaders of rival party organizations. A two-party system and democratic government are twin, so it is said, because two parties can preserve the options of democratic choice while providing a stable system. The parties provide an equitable match between the available supply of political and economic goods and the demands of diverse groups. They compete to package their programs and leaders in an attractive manner and make an effort, at least at election time, to involve the public in the activities of choice. Two parties, such as America has, are preferable to a multiparty system because the judgment made by the electorate of these packaging efforts is unspoiled by confused results.[48]

The principal participants in this scenario are the elites who compete among themselves (within the party) and between themselves (between the parties) for the votes of the electorate. The people perform a semipassive function of deciding between fixed outcomes. The elites control the action; the people are chiefly spectators.

The form of democratic participation is voting between the options presented by the result of elite competition. The majority "reigns" but the minority "rules," as one analyst says pithily.[49] The minority rules because the framework within which the majority chooses is circumscribed in advance. This idea of democratic participation may benefit from an analogy with the grocery shopper. As long as the grocery shopper like the voter is not restricted to one brand of soap flakes or one party (a monopoly) or as long as the choices are not meaningless (soap flakes and political parties with identical properties), then democracy and free enterprise may be said to be at work.

The goal of participation is primarily, as in Madison, the stability of the political system. Elites tacitly agree to limit the scope of conflict, reducing participation in politics, and to abide by the results of the conflict as determined in election outcomes. Agreement on the boundaries of political conflict enables elites to stabilize outcomes even while engaging in open competition with each other. Primarily, the public is restricted to ratifying the choices determined by the general boundaries of systemic conflict and the distribution of power among competing elites.

From this perspective the low rate of participation in general elections is not particularly worrisome. Low rates of participation, so it is argued, reduce the number of issues and participants entering the political arena. Distraction is reduced, and the elites can proceed with their work unhampered by concerns about public interference. The systemic virtues of citizen apathy are pointed out in this passage by an elite democrat:

> How could a mass democracy work if all the people were deeply involved in politics? Lack of interest by some people is not without its benefits too. . . . Low affect toward the election—not caring much—underlies the resolution of many political problems. . . . Low interest provides maneuvering room for political shifts necessary for a complex society in a period of rapid change. Compromise might be based on a sophisticated awareness of costs and returns—perhaps impossible in a mass society—but it is more often induced by indifference.[50]

At the same time as they celebrate indifference, elite theorists point out that the *reputation* of democratic participation is good for stability. Democratic elitism hints that elites should engage in the rhetoric of democratic participation, while practically consolidating power and narrowing the boundaries of conflict.

> . . . [I]t is important to continue moral admonishment for citizens to become active in politics, not because we want or expect great masses of them to become active, but rather because the admonishment helps keep the system open, and sustains the belief in the right of all to participate, which is an important norm governing the behavior of elites.[51]

PARTICIPATORY DEMOCRACY

In the view of participatory democrats, the people are presumed to have a right not merely to choose among the available options but also to enter into the process of determining the agenda.[52] This right does not rest on the grounds of a special competence of the sort claimed by elite democrats for the politically influential; rather it is based on a view of human nature.

The participatory democrats see politics as a distinctly human activity.[53] As we mature, we make choices about the rules by which we wish our lives to be ordered; and if our choices are to prevail, we shall be required, at least on some occasions, to discuss and defend them. This discussion about the rules which shape human action in the community is politics. Political activity, therefore, is a vital means of personal growth.

This outlook emphasizes discussion rather than voting as the primary form of democratic participation. Voting, although not excluded, is seen as susceptible to manipulation by elites. Forums where there is a reasonable opportunity to debate the issues are thought more appropriate to the political process. Further, the spectrum of the "political" is greatly enlarged. Political discussion takes place about and within a variety of institutions: the corporate boardroom, the school, the family, the workplace; it is not restricted to the voting booth. Discussion of the role of nongovernmental institutions is warranted, so say these critics, because many of the attitudes we bring with us to the discussion process originate in private settings. Studies show that authoritarian structures of life in the family, school, and workplace limit both the desire and the skill to participate in politics.[54]

The goal of participation is to make the "community more of a community," as the neo-liberals put it, by encouraging a sense of political efficacy in all its members. Participatory democrats believe that this goal is more likely to be achieved if the boundaries of political conflict are widened rather than narrowed in advance by elites. Political elites create a "mobilization of bias," so it is asserted, which has the effect of maintaining systemic stability at the expense of issues of intense interest to the political community. Although the community appears to be in equilibrium, in fact it operates under a coerced consensus which limits the items on the political agenda. Submerged conflicts can only receive a hearing after a violent rupture with the existing mobilization of bias.[55] By inviting public participation in the formation of the agenda, violent outbreaks against the system can be reduced and the community can resolve outstanding issues through a more peaceable, orderly process of discussion.

This view dissents from the outlook that democracy requires a passive electorate. It urges the direct involvement of the public in discussion about the rules by which it proposes to be governed. It makes the assumption that politics is a good outlet for human energies and that the benefits of democratic participation should be widely distributed.

EXAMPLES OF TWO VIEWS

The chief ideas of participatory democracy and elite democracy discussed above are abstractly stated. It may be useful to present them in a concrete political setting so that the main themes may be more clearly grasped. To illustrate some of the tensions of democratic participation which have marked our time, I shall focus on two examples of party politics. The pursuit, capture, and use of power by Senator John Kennedy (Democrat, Massachusetts) in 1960 illustrates elite democracy at work. Contrasting with the Kennedy nomination and election is the insurgent political movement led by Senator Eugene McCarthy (Democrat, Minnesota) in the presidential primaries of 1968. McCarthy's efforts to kindle public discussion about United States involvement in the Vietnam War constituted a serious challenge to elite consensus within the Democratic party. He made effective use of the methods of participatory democracy to obtain a hearing for issues and groups excluded from the political process by the cadre leadership of the Democratic party.

KENNEDY, 1960. In 1960, Kennedy negotiated with one set of influentials to capture the Democratic party nomination, and after the election, he negotiated with another set of influentials concerning the terms by which he was going to govern. The first cluster of elites, the regular party leadership of the Democratic party, was instrumental in eliminating rivals for the nomination within the party.[56] These rivals were

Hubert Humphrey, Stuart Symington, and Lyndon Johnson. As the nominee of the Democratic party, Kennedy promised to "get the country moving again." Yet in negotiating with another set of established interests, the structure of power in Congress and the bureaucracy, Kennedy ended up with a set of policies that closely resembled those of the Eisenhower administration.[57] These policies were more accurately reflected in the statements of Richard Nixon, his Republican rival, than in Kennedy's messages about a New Frontier. Although there may be a difference in the rhetoric employed by competing elites, there is little difference in their substantive exercise of power.

Kennedy captured a sufficient number of delegates to win nomination on the first ballot at the Democratic party convention in Los Angeles in July 1960. He ran in early presidential primaries in New Hampshire, Wisconsin, and West Virginia to demonstrate vote-getting power to the party bosses and to eliminate rivals. Winning in West Virginia, a Protestant state, was especially important. Kennedy took the evidence of his popularity to the regular party leadership, no more than 4 to 6 percent of the membership, who controlled over one-half of the votes at the national convention. In state after state he negotiated with such power brokers as Neil Stabler, Walter Reuther, and G. Mennen Williams in Michigan; William Green and David Lawrence in Pennsylvania; Pat Brown in California; Peter Crotty, Ben Wetzler, and Charles Buckley in New York; Richard Daley in Illinois, to name a few, and so was able to assemble a large bloc of votes by talking to a handful of men.[58]

The coalition of political forces improvised by Kennedy in winning the nomination and the election was of no use to him, so he discovered, in running the country. That is to say, after winning the election in 1960, Kennedy found that he did not know the right men. He knew the men who would be useful to him in acquiring power, but he did not know the men who would be helpful to him in holding on to power through the development and implementation of policy. The Kennedy cabinet, "nine strangers and a brother," suggests that he did not take seriously the idea that the electorate had entrusted him with a particular task. What the New Frontier might mean in terms of policy was anybody's guess.

In negotiating with the "Washington establishment"—the committee chairmen, the powerful heads of subcommittees, and entrenched interests in the bureaucracy—concerning the exercise of power, Kennedy abandoned all the rhetorical excesses of the campaign. He had been extremely effective in the campaign in associating himself with the great men of America's past while linking his opponent to the hapless. At a Democratic rally in Virginia at the start of the campaign, Kennedy showed his skill in the rhetoric of elite competition.

The Democratic party's candidates in this century never ran on slogans like "Stand Pat with McKinley," "Return to Normalcy with Harding," "Keep Cool with Coolidge," and "Two Chickens in Every Pot with Hoover." (Laughter) I don't know what Dewey's slogan was because he never worked it out. . . . Our slogans have meaning. Woodrow Wilson's New Freedom, Franklin Roosevelt's New Deal, Harry Truman's Fair Deal, and today, we stand on the threshold of a New Frontier, for all Americans.[59]

But in accommodating himself to established power in Congress, men such as Harry Byrd, Carl Vinson, and Wilbur D. Mills, Kennedy came to resemble no one so much as Nixon and Eisenhower, the men whom he had debunked in his campaign.

By his message of protest in the arrest of Martin Luther King, Jr. (for trespass in Atlanta) Kennedy was able to stir the interest of black voters. His margin of victory in the states of Illinois, Michigan, and South Carolina may well have been provided by an unusually large turnout of the black vote. Yet it was not until 1963, three years after his election to office, that Kennedy introduced civil rights legislation in Congress, and then it was done only because of irresistible pressure mounted by the black political leadership. Throughout the presidential campaign Kennedy stressed the need to "get the country moving again" on the road to social and economic progress. Yet he initiated tax "reform" legislation weighted toward the interest of business and upper-income groups. He abandoned the effort to create a Department of Urban Affairs and failed to obtain passage of medicare legislation and federal aid to education. On economic issues on which he enjoyed consensus, Kennedy achieved success. These were social security benefits, widened minimum wage coverage, programs to stimulate housing, extension of benefits for unemployed workers, and reduction of interest rates for loans of long duration. All these measures had been sponsored at one time or another by Eisenhower. Kennedy simply made marginal changes in the legacy of the Eisenhower administration, just as Nixon would have done had he been elected.[60]

McCARTHY, 1968. The insurgent movement led by Eugene McCarthy in the presidential primaries of 1968 challenged an elite consensus that had developed around United States involvement in the Vietnam War. McCarthy foresaw a situation in which the electorate would not be presented with a choice of policy alternatives on the war in the general election of 1968. The Republican candidate, Richard Nixon, announced that he had a "secret plan" to end the war but stated no opposition, in principle, to its continued progress. President Johnson, although rarely appearing in public settings, showed no sign of abating the policy of bombing and intervention on which he had embarked. Among the potential challengers to the incumbent president within the Democratic party, none appeared ready to wage a campaign on the Vietnam issue.

McCarthy led the effort to make the presidential primaries a referendum on Johnson's policy of intervention in Vietnam. He entered the New Hampshire primary, obtaining a vote count sufficient to induce Johnson to withdraw his name from the party nomination. Attention now turned to the vice-president, Hubert Humphrey, Johnson's presumed choice as successor. Humphrey failed to dissociate himself from the interventionist position, and so McCarthy, now joined by Senator Robert Kennedy (Democrat, New York), continued the battle by entering the primaries in the states of Indiana, Nebraska, Oregon, and California. Robert Kennedy's candidacy was terminated with his tragic assassination shortly after winning the California primary.[61]

Nevertheless, the popular victories of the collection of antiwar forces in the presidential primaries did not lead to a fair hearing and representation for the insurgent groups at the Democratic party convention in Chicago. The cadre leadership of the party, through its control of the committees on delegate credentials and the platform, denied the insurgent groups a number of seats proportionate to their popular vote in the primary states and blocked discussion of the merits of an anti-Vietnam plank embarrassing to the vice-president. The suppression of the legitimate aims and expectations of the antiwar groups set the stage for a pitched battle between police and McCarthy supporters in Grant Park in the vicinity of the convention grounds. Many news photographers and reporters, attempting to record the scene, were themselves bloodied in the unequal contest.

A commission was appointed by the convention, headed by George McGovern (senator from South Dakota), to investigate the sources of dissatisfaction within the party and to recommend reform. The McGovern Commission found that the regular party leadership had indeed suppressed antiwar sentiments through the process of delegate selection, and it made recommendations aimed at opening up the party to the spirit of democratic discussion. The commission found:

> More than one-third of the delegates who attended the Convention in Chicago were selected, in effect, more than two years before, when the issues, to say nothing of the candidates, had not been clarified. In many states, where delegates are actually selected within the calendar year of the Convention, the individuals empowered to appoint them were themselves selected two to four years before. This means, for example, that by the time President Lyndon B. Johnson announced his decision not to seek renomination, many delegates to the 1968 Convention had, in effect, already been chosen.

Youth participation was a dramatic feature of the politics of 1968, yet in eighteen delegations to the Democratic Convention in Chicago, there were no voting delegates under thirty years of age. In thirteen other state delegations, there was only one voting delegate under thirty. The average age of the Delaware delegation was fifty-three years. Women were also substantially underrepresented, comprising only 13 percent of the total delegates. Ten state delegations did not have the four women required to fill the places assigned to them on the four standing committees of the Convention. Only one delegation of the fifty-five had a woman as its chairman.[62]

The enduring legacy of McCarthy and his followers was not that they changed the course of the Vietnam War. In this effort the antiwar movement was a failure; not until four years later was a Republican president, Richard Nixon, to take the first few halting steps to extricate the nation from the war. Rather the impact of the McCarthy movement lay in breaking up the patterns of elite accommodation, so tellingly described by McGovern. In a period of normal politics, such as characterized the nomination of Kennedy in 1960, we see a passive acceptance of the outcomes of elite consensus, and the costs of imposing the consensus are low. In a period of extraordinary politics, such as characterized the McCarthy campaign in 1968, an important element of the elite consensus is publicly challenged. Although elites may be successful in imposing the consensus on the challengers, the costs of maintaining it go up. The necessity of subterfuge and even coercion to stop the challengers undermined the legitimacy of the consensus achieved by the party regulars. It discredited the Democratic party in the public eye and probably cost the Democrats the White House in 1968. Thus, McCarthy forced the Democratic party to undertake reforms to bring the processes of the party into line with the requirements of democratic discussion.[63] Some adjustment to the politics of political efficacy had to be made by the party if it was to survive.

SUMMARY

The times are "interesting," because they present the national parties with a dilemma and an opportunity. Voter dissatisfaction and decline in partisanship indicate an unwillingness to sustain patterns of elite competition and an interest in the goals of participatory democracy. Groups and issues lying outside the boundaries of elite consensus may be afforded an unusual opportunity by progressive institutional decay and weakening leadership in the national parties. There is a range of policies and reforms, presently ignored by the cadre leadership of the parties, which might furnish the basis for an insurgent political movement. Among these issues are an equalization of patterns of political participation; democratic control over new methods of political communication (direct mail advertising and television); public financing of congressional elections; social control over corporate capital; and equitable policies of medical care, energy conservation, housing, and transportation. These issues afford an opportunity for the mobilization of citizen energies in new and promising directions.

Blocking the path of political change is the constitutional system in which America's decentralized cadre parties are embedded. The constitutional system is not a visible actor on the political scene, producing an observable impact on the behavior of any one individual or group or shaping events in a specific manner. Still it imposes a set of practical, ideological, and institutional constraints which limit the opportunities for democratic participation and the infusion of new ideas into the political process. The constitutional crisis, of which the crisis of the party system is a part arises out of limitations on democratic participation imposed by the founding fathers.

NOTES

1. Thomas Dye and L. Harmon Zeigler, *The Irony of Democracy* (Belmont, Cal.: Wadsworth, 1970), chap. 7.
2. David Broder, *The Party's Over* (New York: Harper & Row, 1971).
3. *Federalist* No. 10.
4. *Ibid.*
5. E. E. Schattschneider, *The Semi-Sovereign People* (New York: Holt, Rinehart & Winston, 1960), chap. 1.
6. William Crotty, *Political Reform and the American Experiment* (New York: Thomas Y. Crowell, 1977), p. 10.
7. Joseph E. Kallenbach, *The American Chief Executive* (New York: Harper & Row, 1966), p. 44.
8. *Ibid.*
9. Theodore White, *The Making of the President: 1960* (New York: Bantam, 1960), chap. 14.
10. Examples cited in *National Journal,* October 8, 1977, pp. 1,574–76.
11. *Federalist* No. 51, Also see Richard Hofstadter, *The Idea of a Party System* (Berkeley: University of California Press, 1969).
12. *Federalist* No. 23.
13. *Federalist* No. 21.
14. Maurice Duverger, *Political Parties* (New York: John Wiley, 1963), bk. 1; Frank J. Sorauf, *Political Parties in the American System* (Boston: Little, Brown, 1964), pp. 42–44.
15. Allan P. Sindler, *Political Parties in the United States* (New York: St. Martin's Press, 1966), chap. 4.

16. *Ibid.*
17. *National Journal,* December 17, 1977, p. 1,972.
18. Daniel M. Berman, *In Congress Assembled* (New York: Macmillan, 1966), pp. 242–44.
19. Denis G. Sullivan, Jeffrey L. Pressman, and F. Christopher Arterton, *Explorations in Convention Decision-Making* (San Francisco: W. H. Freeman, 1976), chap. 5.
20. *The New York Times,* July 12, 1976, C5.
21. Crotty, *Political Reform,* pp. 53–55.
22. Erwin Knoll and Jules Witcover, "Fighting Poverty—And City Hall," *The Reporter,* June 3, 1965, pp. 19–22.
23. John Kenneth Galbraith, "Who Needs the Democrats: And What It Takes to Be Needed," *Harper's Magazine,* July 1970, pp. 43–62.
24. Robert Engler, *The Brotherhood of Oil* (Chicago: University of Chicago Press, 1977), p. 63.
25. V. O. Key, Jr., *The Responsible Electorate* (Cambridge, Mass.: Harvard University Press, 1966).
26. Walter Dean Burnham, *Critical Elections and the Mainsprings of American Politics* (New York: W. W. Norton, 1970), p. 193.
27. *Statistical Abstract of the United States* (New York: Grossett & Dunlap, 1977), p. 467; *The New York Times,* November 7, 1976, sec. D.
28. *The New York Times,* November 24, 1980, A26; *Wall Street Journal,* November 4, 1980, pp. 1, 14.
29. *National Journal,* January 10, 1981, p. 50.
30. William H. Flanigan and Nancy Zingale, *Political Behavior and the American Electorate,* 3rd ed. (Boston: Allyn and Bacon, 1972).
31. Crotty, *Political Reform,* p. 49.
32. Crotty, *Political Reform,* p. 51.
33. *Wall Street Journal,* November 4, 1980, pp. 1, 14.
34. Crotty, *Political Reform,* p. 52.
35. *Ibid.* chap. 3.
36. Paul Weyrich, director of the Committee for the Survival of a Free Congress, quoted in the *National Journal,* October 20, 1979, p. 1,732.
37. *Ibid.,* p. 1,746.
38. Nelson Polsby and Aaron Wildavsky, *Presidential Elections,* (New York: Scribner's, 1976) p. 168; Theodore White, *The Making of the President: 1972* (New York: Bantam, 1973).
39. Jules Witcover, *Marathon: The Pursuit of the Presidency* (New York: Viking, 1977), pp. 348–49.
40. Morris P. Fiorina, *Congress: Keystone of the Washington Establishment* (New Haven, Conn.: Yale University Press, 1977), chap. 7.
41. *National Journal,* January 10, 1981, p. 50.
42. *National Journal,* October 20, 1980, p. 1,746.
43. *Ibid.,* pp. 1,736, 1,746.
44. *National Journal,* January 10, 1981, p. 50.
45. *National Journal,* October 20, 1980, p. 1,733.
46. *Ibid.*
47. *Ibid.*
48. Joseph A. Schumpeter, *Capitalism, Socialism and Democracy,* 3rd ed. (New York:

Harper & Row, 1950); Henry Kariel, ed., *Frontiers of Democratic Theory* (New York: Random House, 1970).

49. Robert A. Dahl, *Preface to Democratic Theory* (Chicago: University of Chicago Press, 1965).

50. Bernard R. Berelson, Paul F. Lazarsfeld, and William N. McPhee, *Voting* (Chicago: University of Chicago Press, 1954), chap. 14.

51. Lester Milbraith, *Political Participation* (Chicago: Rand McNally, 1965) p. 152.

52. Peter Bachrach, *Theory of Democratic Elitism* (Boston: Little, Brown, 1967); Kariel, *Frontiers of Democratic Theory;* Roger W. Cobb, *Participation in American Politics* (Baltimore, Md.: Johns Hopkins University Press, 1972); Dennis Thompson, *Political Participation* (Washington, D.C.: American Political Science Association: Division of Educational Affairs, 1977).

53. Carole Pateman, *Participation and Democratic Theory* (Cambridge, Eng.: Cambridge University Press, 1970).

54. Charles Hampden Turner, *Radical Man* (New York: Anchor Books, 1971).

55. Peter Bachrach and Morton S. Baratz, *Power and Poverty: Theory and Practice* (New York: Oxford University Press, 1970).

56. Theodore White, *The Making of the President: 1960* (New York: Bantam, 1960).

57. Bernard Nossiter, *The Mythmakers* (Boston: Beacon Press, 1964), chap. 1.

58. White, *Making of the President: 1960,* chap. 5.

59. James MacGregor Burns, *The Deadlock of Democracy* (Englewood Cliffs, N.J.: Prentice-Hall, 1963), pp. 306–307.

60. Nossiter, *Mythmakers,* chap. 1.

61. Arthur Herzog, *McCarthy for President* (New York: Viking, 1969); Abigail McCarthy, *Private Faces/Public Places* (New York: Doubleday, 1972).

62. George McGovern, "The Lessons of 1968," *Harper's Magazine,* January 1970.

63. The reform proposals of the McGovern Commission were two-pronged: (1) Procedural changes were proposed to respond to the closed nature of the delegate selection process. The commission recommended that the entire process be conducted within the calendar year of the convention. To insure that the process be made more open, the commission urged that state parties take the following steps: Adopt explicit rules governing the process; forbid proxy voting; forbid use of the unit rule (which binds the whole delegation to the choice of the majority); require that in all but rural areas, party meetings be held at uniform dates, at uniform times, and in public places of easy access; require adequate notice of party meetings involving delegate selection.
(2) Guidelines were proposed to increase the representation of blacks, women, and young people at the convention. The commission proposed that state parties take "affirmative steps to encourage representation on the National Convention delegations of minority groups, young people and women in reasonable relationship to their presence in the population of the state." In 1971, Larry O'Brien, the national party chairman, sent out a letter to all state party officials informing them that they suffered the burden of proof for showing that their selection process had sought to comply with the commission's recommendations. As noted earlier in the chapter, the McGovern reforms led to increased representation for blacks, women, and the young in convention proceedings.

CHAPTER 5

The Political Process

FROM MADISON TO MODERN OLIGOPOLY

This chapter sets forward the view that the political agenda is no longer shaped within conventional boundaries (the courts, executive, legislature, and bureaucracy) by negotiations among a plurality of social groups broadly representative of the interests of a commercial Protestant middle class. Instead, a single group, corporate capital, outside the conventional boundaries of the political system, plays a crucial role in shaping political directions. The major consequence is that the Madisonian basis of constitutionalism, which was meant to preserve the spheres of liberty of independently situated actors, has been upset, the conventional basis of interest group politics has been altered, and we are now entering a period marked by crisis over the practical arrangements of American constitutionalism.

The core values of seventeenth-century commercial Protestantism made an important and lasting contribution to American political life. At the heart of these values is the doctrine of the sanctity of the inner life (the notion that the individual is the highest authority on matters relating to conscience and spiritual welfare) and the doctrine of possessive individualism (the notion that the individual is the sole possessor of his or her talents and energies, owing nothing to society for them). In the economic sphere these values lead to the formation of a market society; each individual is disposed to regard his or her skills as a commodity and to negotiate the highest possible price for them. In the religious and social spheres these values generate a pluralist society; through the intersection of individual choices a rich, varied, and complex group life springs into existence. Politically, these doctrines sustain a merely policing authority. Since the most important matters in life now lie in the private sphere, conscience and accumulation, the proper role of public authority is to interfere to the least possible extent with the personal freedoms of society's members.

These doctrines are originally stated and defended by Hobbes and later propagandized in the writings of Locke. By the time of the American Revolution, they are an article of faith and the basis of public authority on both sides of the Atlantic. In America, these doctrines reappear as a part of the rhetoric of the times and as a basis for pragmatic, political concern. Jefferson's famous declaration of "independence" and the "inalienable rights of man" is the best example of persuasive writing dealing with these themes. Madison expresses a pragmatic concern with the design of political institutions which will afford the best protection to the "property" spheres of a society of independently situated actors. We recall from Chapter 2 his assertion that each person has a personal sphere in which a strong sense of "propriety" is expressed; for some it is "opinion" and the free communication of views; for others it is "safety and liberty of person"; others emphasize freedom of worship; and for most of us, Madison implies, it is ownership of material possessions. Madison argues that institutions based on countervailing power (republicanism, federalism, and separation of powers) are best suited to safeguarding the liberty spheres of independently-situated actors. This is because the parcelling out of power would force an observable conflict on the issues and require a resolution of these issues to be negotiated among influential parties rather than imposed by any single group.

For Madison and his colleagues at the time of the Constitutional Convention the first line of defense for personal freedoms was the practical arrangements of the Constitution, that is, the system of countervailing power. No provision was made for a Bill of Rights, and it was only after objections from some of the firebrands of the American Revolution, John Adams and Patrick Henry, for example, and threats to withhold ratification that the substantive and procedural liberties of the Bill of Rights were tacked on, much in the form of an afterthought. These liberties, whether substantive—as in freedom of worship, press, petition, assembly, and speech—or procedural—protection against "unreasonable search and seizure," double jeopardy, the right to confront accusers, and trial by jury—were broadly accepted by the public and thought to be adequately defended by the justices of the state courts. The role of a national Supreme Court superintending the protection of civil liberties was unfamiliar to the times.

Nor did the framers consider that political parties offered protection to personal liberties. Their position was just the reverse. Political parties animated by leveling popular majorities were a threat, and an elaborate system of countervailing power was needed to protect freedom from the excesses of democracy.

These points are worth underlining because the system of countervailing power has not worked out in the manner visualized by Madison's theory, for a number of reasons. One of these is that the system can guard against indirect exercises of interest group power only through the formal institutions of government. If an interest group directly exercises power to limit the range of options of other groups, apart from the formal institutions of government, the system of countervailing power does not operate. In state and local political arenas where the size and resources of major corporations in relation to local institutions are strikingly evident, the direct exercise of interest group power is very important. (Examples of this point will be offered shortly.)

Second, Madison's theory did not (because it could not) account for the presence of modern oligopoly. The operational success of countervailing power depends on the visible confrontation of interests in the political arena. A visible confrontation occurs when A, let us say, President Ronald Reagan, confronts B, let us say Thomas P. ("Tip") O'Neill, House majority leader, concerning an issue, as for example, the 1982 budget appropriations, which exists demonstrably in the political arena. A painful example of such a confrontation, to be discussed later in this chapter, occured between Senator Russell Long, chairman of the Senate Finance Committee, and President Jimmy Carter over the provisions of the National Energy Plan (1977). By diffusing power, Madison forces political actors visibly in conflict to negotiate their differences or reconcile themselves to stalemate. So far so good. A new situation arises, however, if a powerful group, let us say the oil majors, can encircle A and B, persuading both parties of the merits of an identical structure of preferences, or at least considerably narrowing the difference that exists between them. In this case a sufficiently powerful interest can prevail on a latent issue while bypassing an observable conflict in the political arena. Indeed, the entire arena of political decision-making shifts from the formal institutions of government to the informal basis of power rooted in the economy.

In this chapter, I shall argue that corporate capital deploys a considerable array of resources, chiefly superior organizational capacity and technology along with modern advertising, to decide important questions of public policy in advance of an observable conflict on the issues. Further, even when an issue does enter the political arena, corporate capital tends to prevail because it has previously shaped the structure of public preferences, disposing the outcome of controversy in its direction, and because it has superior organizational resources at its disposal. The consequence is that decision-making power over issues is removed from the formal institutions of government, and the political basis of eighteenth-century constitutional arrangements is destroyed.

I conclude that the system of shared power holding does not safeguard its intended object—the spheres of liberty of independently situated actors. The best way of making this point is by noting the energy-intensive life-style on which corporate America (that is, Westinghouse, General Electric, Exxon, Gulf Oil, Firestone, B.F. Goodrich, Ford, General Motors, and so on) has sold the middle class over the past forty years. The American public is exhorted to believe that the "pursuit of happiness" means a split-level house in the suburbs on a half acre of ground, a two-car garage, a backyard swimming pool, a power boat and private plane, an array of home technologies (central air conditioning, double-door refrigerator, electric range, and television), and an expressway to one's place of work. Energy shortages are now making this life-style unaffordable for all. No matter. Perspectives nurtured by the advertising industry become a part of nature. A middle class persuaded by Madison Avenue over some period of time to "live better electrically," "put a tiger in [its] tank," and "tour the U.S.A. in [its] Chevrolet," views this life-style as among the inalienable rights government is meant to defend.

The government does seek to defend it, for in the main, government has been converted to the mission of corporate America. Through an array of subsidies that support this energy-intensive life-style (tax deductions on mortgage interest, regulated gasoline prices, expressway construction) and a deficiency of real alternatives (conservation and alternative energy programs, urban and intercity transportation, urban renewal), it joins with corporate capital in locking the middle class, and other groups, into the existing structure of public preferences. When the members of the middle class are seen invariably to pursue the same things in the same way, when they do so at the urging of Madison Avenue in apparent conflict with their real interests and in the absence of alternatives provided by the government, one begins to suspect that a system of countervailing power no longer exists.

Oligopoly refers to a cluster of corporations that dominates the market in a particular area. For example, the Big Four in automobile production, General Motors, Ford Motor Corporation, Chrysler Corporation, and American Motors Corporation, account for over 99 percent of domestic output; in farm machinery three firms, International Harvester, McCormick, and John Deere, produce over one-half of all domestic output; in the telecommunications industry Bell Telephone and American Telephone and Telegraph dominate; fifteen major corporations, among them Litton, McDonnell Douglas, Rockwell, Northrop, Lockheed, General Dynamics, and Boeing, receive approximately one-half of the $39 billion let in defense contracts in any given year; oil supply, at least up through 1973 (the year of the Arab oil embargo), was almost unilaterally shaped by the oil "majors," Gulf, Exxon, Mobil, Standard Oil of California, and Texaco. In these cases, prices and production plans are the outcome of interaction with a limited number of dominant firms in the industry; economic planning for as much as 60 percent of manufactured goods produced in the United States[1] is made on this basis.

Oligopoly seeks to prevail on issues of critical importance to the stability and growth of their industry in the market. Oligopoly does not seek to prevail across a range of policy issues; it is not advantageous to do so. Rather there is a strong material interest to influence the political process, when that is necessary, in a highly specific way. In this effort oligopoly is assisted by the expertise of the elites who staff its operations, by the technological resources it can deploy in behalf of its goals, and by the blandishments of the advertising industry. As a very rough estimate of the extent to which the modern corporation seeks to influence the structure of public preferences, $60 billion per year was spent by business on advertising and sales promotion in the late 1960s.[2] Mobil Oil Corporation alone spends $23 million on advertising and sales promotion. When placed alongside the fact that all campaign expenditures in 1972, a presidential election year, totalled a half billion dollars, these expenditures represent a substantial effort to create a climate of opinion favorable to the products, services, and public policies of business enterprise.

To the view that modern oligopoly decisively shapes the structure of public preferences, overturns the balances of an eighteenth-century constitutional system, and narrows the choices of individuals, the reply is sometimes made that residual sources of countervailing power remain in the constitutional system. These residual sources, more often identified at the national rather than the state and local level, exist outside the formal structure of government. Public interest lobbies, organized labor, and intergovernmental lobbies (associations of state, county, and municipal government) are often said to be effective in opposing the modern oligopoly in the political arena. To the extent that these groups are politically effective, there is evidence that the main features of the Madisonian constitutional system linger on into the present day. Thus, in the following discussion we shall pay careful attention to the role these groups play in the political process.

INTEREST GROUPS AND POWER

To grasp the changes in the political process which have occurred between Madison's time and our own, we need to know how interest groups exert power in the political arena. Additionally, we need to know how the constitutional rules of the game shape the competition of interests. As noted earlier, the Constitution is not neutral among the participants in the political struggle. We must pay attention to the manner in which the constitutional system tips power in the political arena, favoring one or another of the contestants.

An interest group is distinguished from other, merely social, groups in that it employs organized and sustained means to maintain and enhance its own interest through the exercise of power over other groups. A collection of boys and girls on the street corner or in the drugstore is not an interest group. They do not fit our definition, because other than taking up a small amount of public space, they are not making demands on other groups. A group of vigilantes getting ready to dispense frontier justice to a gang of cattle rustlers is not an interest group; for although they are certainly exercising power over another group, their efforts are mostly improvisational, not organized and sustained. Vigilantes are ad hoc groups, designed for the needs of the moment and no more.

Lurking behind this definition are two basic assumptions: (1) an interest group has some degree of skill and resources it can use to influence the action of others; (2) an interest group has an objective sufficiently concrete to be explained to others; broad enough to require their cooperation, or at least tolerance, in sustaining it; and sufficiently particularized to encounter opposition from at least some groups.

The strategy an interest group uses to exercise power over other groups varies with the skill and resources at its disposal and, sometimes, the kind of interest pursued. Interest groups with considerable resources at their disposal, as for example a modern corporation, may directly exercise power over other groups who have only slender means to oppose them. Or the interest group, even if it is a powerful one, may enlist the aid of a third party, the government, in an effort to prevail over others in the competitive struggle. In this case an interest group exercises power over other groups indirectly through the intervention of the government.

The distinction between indirect and direct exercises of power helps us to see that the lobbying activities of interest groups do not tell the whole story. *Lobbying* is an effort to exercise power over other groups indirectly by enlisting government power for a particular group. There are 1,773 registered lobbyists in Washington whose job is to cajole, reason, trick, or persuade government officials into doing something for their employers. There are also numerous examples of the exercise of power independent of the government. We shall first turn to current examples of the direct exercise of interest group power in the state and local arena. Later, we shall consider the activities of the notorious, deservedly or not, Washington lobbyists.

PRIVATE POWER IN LOCAL ARENAS

The nongovernmental constraints imposed by interest groups in local political arenas need to be distinguished from the governmental ones arising from activity chiefly at the national level. Only a part of the influence exerted by interest groups on public policy occurs through the impact they make on government decision making. In local political arenas, power over other groups is exercised by corporate industry by withholding skills and resources and by deploying resources strategically. The single-minded pursuit of profits often underlies the manner in which corporate industry allocates its resources, several examples of which follow.

MASS TRANSIT

There is a charming passage in *Ragtime,* a novel set in the early 1900s, which tells of how an immigrant worker, Tateh, and his daughter, travel from New York City to the outskirts of Boston simply by making transfers from one trolley to the next. They board the No. 12 streetcar on the lower east side, ride up Broadway to the Bronx, and then go through a series of Connecticut towns. Two days later, traveling in the electrified cars through a countryside whose sights and smells are unobscured by pollution, they arrive in Springfield, Massachusetts, just outside of Boston. The fare for each ride was about a nickel for Tateh and two cents for his daughter—a total of three dollars and forty cents for both from New York to Boston.

Some experts believe that America had a better mass transit system at the turn of the century than it has now. In its era of ascendancy, the trolley system was cheap to operate, was nonpolluting, and had an excellent network of rail linkages. By making transfers, after the fashion of Tateh and his daughter, people could travel long distances very inexpensively. More money was spent on maintaining this mass transit system than is now spent on public transportation. In 1909, thirty-three cents out of every dollar was spent on some form of public transportation, whereas in 1963 only four cents out of the dollar was allocated for this purpose.[3]

Despite the many desirable characteristics of the street railway and rapid transit systems of the past, the trolley is now used in only six American cities. Virtually the entire trolley system was liquidated during the 1930s and 1940s by the emergence of "transit-holding companies," and of these, the one formed by General Motors, Firestone, and Standard Oil of California was the most powerful and notorious. By convincing the town fathers that progress was allied with conversion to diesel buses, and by arranging a financial package that made this conversion feasible, this collection of motor interests was able to determine the direction of transportation policy in American cities for decades to come, and quite likely for all time. The formation of the transit holding companies provides an important lesson in the exercise of power, unopposed by competing groups, in local political arenas over a significant area of public policy.

The triumvirate, General Motors (GM), Firestone, and Standard Oil of California, operated in the following manner. They formed a holding company, National City Lines, which was bound to purchase vehicles and supplies only from the companies that furnished the investment capital for its activities. The agreement between National City Lines and the triumvirate was to "further the sale and create an additional market for the products of suppliers . . . to the exclusion of products competitive therewith."[4] National City Lines, in turn, sought and obtained franchises from the town to operate the public transit system. The franchise was used by National City Lines to replace street car trolleys with GM diesel buses, running on Firestone tires, and powered by Standard of California diesel oil. National City Lines acquired control over forty-six transit systems in forty-five American cities in a ten-year period (1938–1947). A telling feature of such arrangements is that transportation policy was a secondary interest of companies seeking a larger market for their products. Many cities lost their street railway networks during this crucial period, only to be unable to afford the costs of reconversion at a later date.

Los Angeles is the horrible result, in terms of health, aesthetics and conservation, of the policies pursued by the transit holding companies. At one time, the city was served by three thousand vehicles on lines that radiated seventy-five miles from the city's center. In the words of one transportation specialist, the trolleys were "the nucleus of a highly efficient rapid transit system, which would have contributed greatly to lessening the tremendous traffic and smog problems that developed from population growth."[5] The dismantling of the trolley system contributed to the absolute dominance of the automobile in the region and the generation of the smog. The effects, awful as they may seem, appear to be irreversible. On June 8, 1976, by a 59 to 41 margin, Los Angeles voters rejected a one-cent sales tax increase to pay for the cost of a 232-mile rail system built on freeway medians and other publicly owned rights of way.

It is ironic, after all this, that GM, who engineered the creation of the transit holding companies, should be regarded as having little influence on public policy, and at the same time, that the federal government should be blamed for the deterioration of the nation's mass transit system. Both views misunderstand the way in which interest groups exert power in American politics. It is possible for a group to exert nongovernmental power in local arenas and for the effects to be misinterpreted, thereafter, as the consequences of a negligent public policy. After GM's minor reverses on the issues of installing safety and pollution equipment on their cars, a Michigan congressman said,

> GM probably has the worst lobby on Capitol Hill. It ranks at the bottom in terms of effectiveness. Its Washington operation is the most inept and ineffectual I've seen here. . . . Management has this disdain for relations in Washington.
> GM is constantly getting hit in the back of the head because they don't pay enough attention to Washington. They get more bad surprises than any other firm in the nation, and it doesn't have to be that way.[6]

This view seriously underestimates the success of GM in pursuing its goals without lobbying on Capitol Hill. At the same time, the federal government is blamed for the worst effects of policies which GM, Firestone, and Standard Oil pursued years ago. Cities attempting to reinstitute the abandoned rail and trolley systems of yesteryear blame the federal government for insensitivity to the transportation needs of urban communities. Denver spent $4 million in local funds and $2 million in federal funds merely to study the feasibility of a surface rail system for the city. When the request for federal funds for this expensive undertaking were denied, a local official charged government indifference:

> All the federal rhetoric about local choice, preservation of the quality of life in our urban areas, cleaning up the polluted air, saving our scarce petroleum and using federal funds to assist those cities willing and able to shoulder their own share of the burden are only empty words.[7]

POLLUTION

The previous case represents an instance of an interest group deploying its skills and resources to dominate a significant area of public policy. But interest groups may also significantly affect other groups and the local community simply by withholding resources. By concerning itself exclusively with higher profits and withholding resources for any other purpose, a powerful interest may set in motion an adverse condition which the local community is unable to surmount. In this instance power over other groups is exerted by, in essence, not doing anything.

For example, the U.S. Steel Company was brought to Gary, Indiana, by local lobbyists and political elites seeking employment for the work force. As a by-product of its efforts to produce steel at a low price, the company created serious air and water pollution in the area. In the vicinity of the steel mill, there was a steep increase in health problems accompanied by poor air and visibility. Those who could afford to escape these conditions, chiefly the affluent middle class, moved to new suburban neighborhoods. The adverse effects of this development were soon apparent. The tax base of the city suffered from this departure, and the city could no longer supply its former range of services. Recreational programs were curtailed, school budgets reduced, and garbage and transportation cut back.

The adverse consequences of this exercise of power fell unequally on the members of the Gary community. Those with the lowest incomes, living in the areas of highest pollution, were the most seriously affected by urban decline. They could afford neither an escape to the suburbs nor the respite of a vacation during the summer months when pollution was the most severe. Further, the decline of city services affected their lives more than it did the families of the managerial staff whose needs were met by self-sufficient suburban communities.[8]

Attempts by local groups to make an issue over pollution in the Gary community were unsuccessful. Local elites supported tax exemptions for the corporation, deemphasized local laws regulating its operation, and deflected issues embarrassing to it. The policy pursued by U.S. Steel concerning the conflicts that swirled around it was to do nothing. It exerted significant power over the lives and fortunes of the members of the Gary community by sitting on its corporate hands. A local activist reported his frustration in attempting to arouse company executives. They would just nod sympathetically "and agree that the air pollution was terrible, and pat you on the head. But they never *did* anything one way or the other. If only there had been a fight, then something might have been accomplished."[9]

REDLINING

Redlining is a practice whereby local banks and savings and loan associations withhold conventional mortgage loans from a community, not on the basis of the credit worthiness of the applicant or the soundness of the particular house, but on the very subjective judgment on the part of the lender that the neighborhood in which the property is located is declining. The immediate effect of this policy is to accentuate whatever regressive tendencies might have been present in the community. Those who live there are deprived of an opportunity to improve their homes, and those who wish to move in are deprived of mortgage funds.

The decision to grant loans may be thought to be wholly within the discretion of the lender. However, when the expectation is created that funds will be available for qualified applicants, when the bank is effectively depriving the community of the use of its own savings as capital, when the basis of the judgment to withhold money is a subjective opinion, and when banks and savings and loan associations are sustained in important ways by other public institutions, then the assertion that loan policy is a private banking decision seems unpersuasive. The banks are, in fact, making public policy concerning the residential patterns of whole neighborhoods. In effect, they exert power over all other groups in the redlined community through a self-initiated policy of withholding resources. So far, public institutions have not found a way to impose guidelines on the discretionary power of the banks. A weak policy has been developed to require them to report by zip code number on the distribution of mortgage loans within communities.

The practice of redlining often prematurely decides the fate of once viable inner-city communities. The practice is directed against a stated policy of the federal government to attract the middle class, put off by insipid life-styles in suburbia and mindful of high transportation costs, back into the inner city. The return of the middle class may never occur if the banks continue to redline. A mayor whose community succumbed to redlining testified,

> Buyers and homeowners unable to obtain financing for mortgages and home improvement loans are virtually forced to buy elsewhere, some encouraged to do so by the lenders. Given the lack of money to make necessary repairs, the neighborhood rapidly takes on the appearance of a slum. . . . Owner/occupants representing good, stable families move out; absentee landlords and speculators move in. The prophecy fulfills itself.[10]

PRIVATE POWER IN THE NATIONAL ARENA

Unlike local arenas, the exercise of power in the national political arena is more likely to produce an observable conflict of issues. The public interest lobbies are concerned with bringing topical and controversial issues into public view, and the powers of the national government induce a proliferation of groups to monitor the greater number of governmental services.

Despite the existence of observable conflict on a great number of issues, powerful interests, in general, and oligopoly, in particular, is likely to prevail in any contest to which its resources are committed. There are two major reasons for this: the structural biases of Madisonian politics and the superior organizational capacity of oligopoly.

STRUCTURAL BIASES

Madison's requirement that the government be neutral in social conflict, in fact, operates to the advantage of influential interests. For Madison, politics was a matter of influential group leaders dealing relationally, on a one-to-one basis, with other influential group leaders. The basis of group influence is wealth, cohesiveness, education, organization, and access to public power.[11] The landed, manufacturing, mercantile, and moneyed interests which Madison speaks of possess these resources in greater abundance than other groups in society. In Madisonian politics, groups who do not possess these resources, say they have only numbers and need, will be dealt with *manipulatively,* not relationally, by other group interests.

The result is progressive social and economic inequality. If influentials deal relationally only with other influentials, and manipulatively with all the rest, one can project that differentials in wealth and political efficacy will be widened over time. Madisonian politics embodies a structural bias toward inequality. The only manner in which to correct this tendency is for the state to intervene in behalf of those parties in the social conflict possessing slender resources of influence. This is a line of thought and action prohibited by the structural bias of Madison's politics.

If we focus attention on the modern political arena, we see that these projections are fully realized. Without exception studies show that noninfluential groups, such as blacks, women, Puerto Ricans, the elderly, criminals, the retarded, slum dwellers, mental patients, and migrants, are dealt with in a manipulative and cavalier fashion in the political process.[12] Having little resources other than urgent need, they are singularly ineffective in making an impact on public policy. Although the structural bias of politics imposes similar constraints on all participants in the political process (don't the poor think they are to blame for their condition?), the effect of these constraints falls the heaviest on noninfluential groups. They are the ones who suffer the most from the operational features of the political system.

Producer groups, for example, are regularly dealt with on a relational basis in the political process, whereas consumer groups are dealt with manipulatively. Lynn Stalbaum, lobbyist for three milk cooperatives (Associated Milk Producers Inc., Dairymen Inc., and Mid America Dairymen Inc.), with the help of Secretary of Treasury John Connally, was able to reverse a ruling made by Secretary of Agriculture Clifford Hardin on March 12, 1971, stabilizing milk price supports at 80 percent of parity. Connally was the channel through which the dairy lobbyists conveyed a promise of a $2 million contribution to President Nixon's reelection campaign in exchange for milk price supports at 90 percent of parity. Nixon agreed to increase the price supports to the level desired by the milk producers following a forceful presentation in which Connally pointed out the influence the milk lobby had in Congress and the generosity of the campaign pledge. As it turned out, the dairy lobby contributed only about one-quarter of the funds promised. Yet the $322,500 investment paid off handsomely; the price increase ordered by the administration transferred hundreds of millions of dollars from consumer to producer groups. With the help of the nation's top decision makers, they realized an estimated $1,400 for every dollar invested in the Nixon campaign.[13]

ORGANIZATIONAL CAPACITY

Apart from the structural biases of Madison's politics, another good reason for the success of oligopoly in the political arena is organizational capacity. Giant corporate industry, often compared to a ministate or to a quasigovernmental unit,[14] has introduced a new element into the equation of power not accounted for in Madison's theory. The problem of size is illustrated by the following observations:

> After the Department of Defense with its more than 1 million civilian employees, the largest organizations in the United States are not other branches of government but American Telephone and Telegraph and General Motors, each approaching a million employees, more than the industrial labor force of many nations. The Ford Motor Company, with only half that many employees, is nevertheless larger than any government department except Defense and the Postal Service. By amount of revenue, all of these, as well as Exxon and General Electric, are larger than the governments of California, New York State, and New York City, which are giants among state and city governments. If industrial corporations are compared by output with state and municipal government, sixteen of the largest twenty organizations are corporations. General Motors' sales alone are larger than the gross national product of most nations.[15]

Organizational capacity, combined with a high material incentive to influence the political process and the availability of generous resources, provides oligopoly with strong advantages.[16] In contrast, public interest lobbies lack all the attributes just mentioned. They must improvise an organization and adequate supply of resources out of an assortment of civic activists. There is little material reward for the function they perform, only the satisfaction of having represented the public on some vital topic. It is no accident that the clash of interests in the national political arena often seems a very one-sided affair, especially in cases where a powerful oligopoly commits the forces at its disposal. There are no better illustrations of this fact of modern political life than the effects of oligopolistic organizations on public policies regarding energy, transportation, and housing.

ENERGY. Events of the 1970s confirm that U.S. energy policy is decisively shaped by the domestic oil majors, a "private planning system operating on a global scale," as one source describes it. Elaborating on this point of view, he points out that oil producers are among the largest industries in America. Ranked by assets, they occupy five of the first eight and eight of the first fifteen positions. The estimated value of the seven worldwide oil giants (five American: Exxon, Texaco, Gulf, Standard Oil of California, and Mobil; and two international: Royal Dutch Shell and British Petroleum) is $132 billion. Further, "As of 1970 the first twenty oil companies accounted for 94 percent of domestic reserves, 70 percent of domestic crude production, 86 percent of domestic refinery capacity, and 79 percent of domestic gasoline sales. . . . The majors own or have interest in 70 percent of interstate pipelines. They own or lease half of the world's oil tanker tonnage."[17]

The ordinary operations of the members of the oil industry daily bind them together in a community of interests which has broad implications for energy policy. Among the practices and arrangements that foster this community are "patents, banking ties, common capital underwriters and accounting services, interlocking directorships through a third firm, bidding understandings in relation to public lands, recognized territorial prerogatives, crude oil and product exchange arrangements and price fixing." To this it should be added that, "expensive continental shelf drillings are undertaken jointly," and that "the vital interstate pipelines are jointly owned."[18] The 800-mile trans-Alaska pipeline is owned by a consortium of Atlantic Richfield, British Petroleum, Exxon, Phillips, Mobil, Union, and Amerada Hess. Abroad the interrelationships that bind the companies together are closer than at home. ARAMCO, the multinational oil corporation based in Saudi Arabia from which as much as 24.2 percent of imported crude oil is received, is jointly owned by Exxon, Standard Oil of California, Gulf, Texaco, and Mobil.[19]

The oil industries have superb lobbying facilities in Washington, far excelling the public interest lobbies who periodically oppose them. The

American Petroleum Institute, the chief center of lobbying activities for the oil majors, has an annual budget of $25 million. Organized along the same lines as the internal departments within the companies—production, refining, transportation, and marketing—it has been in operation for over fifty years, concerting the policy of its subscribing members.[20] Besides the American Petroleum Institute, there are over twenty other trade associations and more than fifty corporations in Washington with offices devoted to lobbying for the petroleum industry. Standard Oil of Indiana, for example, maintains a separate lobbying office in Washington, with expenditures of $2 million per year.[21]

To offer a standard of comparison, the Energy Action Committee headed by James Flug, the principal public interest lobby supporting the main elements of Carter's proposed energy legislation (in 1977), operated on an annual budget of $240,000. These funds were supplied on an ad hoc basis by movie actor Paul Newman and a few of his wealthy acquaintances.[22]

The oil industry influences energy policy through the standard means of campaign contributions, lobbying, retainers (fees), occasional payoffs, and the like. In the past, these contributions had been targeted to political leaders who were strategically placed to shape energy policy. In 1972, President Nixon renewed his campaign pledges to maintain a favorable climate for oil. The campaign committee to reelect the president, CREEP, which operated independently of the Republican National Committee, vigorously solicited funds from the oil majors and independent producers. CREEP received at least $5 million from the oil industry, including illegal cash contributions of $100,000 each from Gulf Oil, Phillips, and Ashland.[23] The oil industry has funneled money into the campaign chests of members of the Senate Finance Committee over a sustained period of time. Three members of this committee— Russell Long, Robert Dole, and Mike Gravel, all from oil-producing states—received a reported $210,000 for their 1974 election campaign. A fourth member, Lloyd Bentsen (Democrat, Texas), who campaigned unsuccessfully for the presidency in 1974, received a reported $135,-000.[24] In the 1976 election, the oil companies contributed over $500,000 to the reelection of nine members of the Senate Finance Committee according to figures released by Congress Watch[25] (an investigative and research unit sponsored by Ralph Nader).

Another way the oil industry has successfully shaped policy, more important than the preceding methods, is by influencing the structure of public preferences. Through advertising, the oil industry (with a great deal of help from the automobile, vacation, appliances, and utilities industries), has created a well-developed set of preferences in behalf of energy-intensive styles of living. Also, it has cultivated the belief that energy resources are inexhaustible and that with the right production incentives, the oil industry will make this living standard, the highest of any nation in the world, affordable to all Americans. Conflicting evidence, that low-income groups must pay as much as 30 percent of disposable income to meet basic energy consumption needs in a period of rising prices, tends to be overshadowed by the dominant motif of increased production.[26]

The preference structure sold to the public during a period of cheap oil and gas has domestic and international consequences. Looking at the international situation, the United States is an energy "junkie," requiring 35 percent of the world's oil supply to satisfy the needs of 6 percent of the world's population.[27] In transportation and household living, the United States sustains an energy-intensive standard of living that outstrips every other nation.[28] The energy needs of the United States force it into competition with friendly industrial allies such as West Germany and Japan. Additionally, the United States bids up the price of oil, placing it beyond the reach of newly developing third world nations seeking to build an industrial capacity. A second point is that the preference structure impedes the ability of our political leadership to convince the public that energy shortages are real and that alternative energy sources and conservation require serious consideration. It is not accidental that two presidents faced with energy crises, Richard Nixon and Gerald Ford, themselves resorted to manipulating public attitudes. President Carter brought a new insistence on the harsh realities of the situation but had to struggle against poor comprehension of the sacrifices that were needed.

Two events in the early 1970s offer convincing evidence that the energy-intensive style to which the nation is accustomed cannot last in its present form. One of these is the Arab Oil embargo (1973). Six Persian Gulf states, as a protest against U.S. aid to Israel, cut off the supply of oil to the United States (and to the Netherlands, France, and Japan). The boycott cut across a range of U.S. policies and institutions. It affected the liquidity supply of the banks and reduced the luxury car inventory of Detroit producers; it closed down schools for lack of heat and delayed motorists who had to wait hours in line for a few gallons of gasoline; it slowed down the progress of controls on environmental pollution, and city dwellers suffered from blackouts because of failed electrical supply. The boycott served notice that the famed U.S. standard of living is not written in stone but dependent, at least in part, on the pleasure of a cartel of oil-producing nations in the Persian Gulf. Reminders of the fragility of this living standard have occurred from time to time since that occasion, most recently in the cutoff of oil imports from Iran in mid-1978. For the most part, OPEC (Organization of Petroleum Exporting Countries, the title of the Arab oil cartel) has shown a canny ability to allay Western anxieties about oil supply while raising the price of its exports.

A second, less heralded event is that domestic production of crude oil peaked in 1970 at 9.2 MMBD (million barrels of oil per day) and, since then, has steadily declined. In 1978, despite production incentives for newly discovered oil, increased domestic exploration for new reserves, addition of new oil from Alaska, and a succession of OPEC price increases, U.S. production fell to 8.7 MMBD. The reverse side of this decline is a sharp rise in the amount of oil that must be imported. In 1973, the United States imported 35 percent of its oil; by 1977, it was importing 48 percent. In 1971, the United States paid $4 billion for imported oil; and in 1973, $8 billion. By 1978, the United States was paying $45 billion for oil imports and was destined to exceed the $50 billion mark in the 1980s.[29] The decline in production of oil has been accompanied by a similar decrease in the production of natural gas, the nation's second most utilized energy resource. The decline in oil and gas production throws doubt on the claim, often made by oil and gas producers, that increased prices will lead to exploration and higher production yields. Producer groups have been unable to increase domestic production despite ample incentives for over a decade.

Not until 1977, President Carter's first year in office, was an effort made to stem the nation's ruinous dependence on foreign oil and to forge an equitable policy of energy conservation. In the preceding years, Presidents Nixon and Ford had dealt with the energy crisis chiefly through public relations, that is to say, not at all. President Nixon announced Project Independence at Disney World, a pledge that by 1980 the United States would be able to meet its energy needs from domestic resources. No responsible person in the president's own administration believed this prediction to be true.[30] President Ford contracted with Benton and Bowles, a New York advertising agency, to come up with a slogan for a volunteer campaign keyed to the nation's economic and energy woes. Benton and Bowles responded with the WIN campaign, an acronym for "Whip Inflation Now," and the president distributed WIN buttons.[31] Like Project Independence, the WIN campaign conveyed the pleasing impression that the energy dilemma could be resolved through public uplift.

President Carter declared the "moral equivalent of war" on patterns of domestic energy consumption by appearing before a joint session of Congress to present the main outlines of a national energy plan (NEP I) in April 1977. The centerpiece of the plan was a tax on proven reserves of domestic crude oil called COETS (crude oil equalization tax) to bring the price of domestic oil into line with world energy prices. The tax would compel Americans to pay the same price for oil as European nations and Japan, thereby encouraging conservation. Yet the burdens of the tax would be equalized by a system of rebates to the public. By diverting to federal coffers and then to the public the differential between the regulated price of domestic crude oil and the price of oil on the international market (roughly a difference of $4 per barrel at the time), the tax would prevent the oil industry from reaping windfall profits on the greatly increased value of a scarce commodity.[32] Other features of the plan included the allocation of reserve supplies of oil in the event of a future crisis; a tax to encourage major fuel-burning installations (chiefly utilities) to convert from oil and gas to coal within a decade; a tax on "gas guzzling" cars with rebates to fuel-efficient cars; tax incentives for homeowners to install solar devices and conservation improvements; measures to expedite the siting and licensing of nuclear power plants. There was to be a moderate adjustment upward in the price of natural gas, and full deregulation was scheduled for 1985.[33]

The portion of NEP I most stoutly opposed by the oil industry was the crude oil equalization tax. The industry's basic strategy when NEP I came before Congress was to defeat the tax outright or, barring that, to hold the tax proposals hostage to the demand for plow-backs, from the revenues of the tax, for increased exploration. The industry was ably assisted by its access to Senator Russell Long (Democrat, Louisiana), chairman of the Senate Finance Committee and an oil millionaire in his own right, along with eight other members of the committee who were formerly recipients of campaign contributions from the oil majors. The Carter administration's protest that plow-backs could not yield higher domestic oil production based on the known limits of U.S. reserves fell on deaf ears. COETS went down to defeat in the Senate Finance Committee, killing the administration's plan for an equitable pattern of energy conservation.[34]

A new strategy for achieving the same objectives as COETS was devised by the Carter administration in late 1979. The president exercised his authority under the Emergency Petroleum Allocation Act (1973) to deregulate the price of "upper tier" crude oil (generally speaking, crude oil brought into production after 1973) while insisting that the deregulation was tied to the enactment of a "windfall profits" tax (actually an excise tax on domestic oil) to sever the profits of the increased prices from the oil companies. The White House estimated the gross receipts of the tax in the decade 1980 to 1990 at $140 billion. The version enacted by Congress brought substantially more into the federal treasury.[35] The deregulation of upper tier crude oil will make domestic energy much more expensive. However, the tax contains several advantages: (1) it will encourage conservation through raising prices; (2) it will provide the government with funds to stimulate energy diversification, offset the burdens of increased prices on low-income groups, and develop conservation programs; and (3) it will prevent industry from realizing huge gains at the expense of the public.

Industry profits remain high despite the enactment of the windfall profits tax and are projected to remain so for the forseeable future. In proposing the windfall profits tax, President Carter said, "On the battlefield of energy we can win for the nation a new confidence, and we can seize control again of our common destiny." At the same time as this stirring call was being issued, the oil majors were announcing record earnings for the third quarter of 1979. The rise in net income for some oil majors between 1978 and 1979 was as follows: Exxon, 118 percent; Gulf, 97 percent; Amoco, 49 percent; Arco, 45 percent; and Conoco 134 percent. To protect their high earnings position, oil companies were buying into related areas of energy resources and into minerals. A partial listing of takeovers since 1977 includes the following: Atlantic Richfield bought Anaconda, a metals and mineral company; Gulf Oil bought Pittsburgh and Midway Coal; Occidental Petroleum bought Island Creek Coal; Standard Oil (Ind.) bought Old Ben Coal and has offered $1.77 billion for Kennecott, a metals and mineral company.[36] A new trend among oil companies is toward "conglomerate mergers," that is, the purchase of a business in a field unrelated to the takeover company. For example, Mobil Oil Corporation recently announced the purchase of Marcor Inc. (with assets of $2.8 billion), which is the parent company of the Montgomery Ward retail chain. Conglomerate mergers have the merit of securing profits while warding off antitrust actions.[37]

The Carter administration's National Energy Plan made the politics of energy allocation more visible, so there is a clear gain in public enlightenment over the waffling and obscurantism of previous years. But in bringing to the surface the politics of energy, Carter also brought to light the structural biases of American politics and the superior organizational capacity of oligopoly. These features of the modern political process rank alongside the problem of energy imports as one of the most profound and unsettling issues of the 1980s. The structural biases enable powerful interests to shape the political process, covertly, by shaping the criteria of interest (the famed American standard of living) and, overtly, by deploying a range of resources (money, experts, organizational skills, and access). In combination, these forms of private power greatly constrain the efforts of public officials to fashion an energy policy.

The election of Ronald Reagan to presidential office signals the end of the conservationist outlook reflected in the national energy plans of the Carter administration. Many of the preferences of the oil majors and nuclear power advocates are destined to be elevated into public policy by an administration which asserts that the nation is "energy rich," that the solution to problems of supply is to "produce, produce, produce," and which holds that conservation is useless, simply making the public "hotter in the summer and colder in the winter."[38] In keeping with this outlook, President Reagan during his first months in office restored funding for the controversial Clinch River breeder reactor; terminated a range of programs directed to domestic and industrial energy conservation (such as energy performance standards for buildings, performance standards for consumer appliances, loan guarantees for municipal waste reprocessing centers, standby energy conservation plans, residential energy conservation service); deregulated the price on all types of oil (lower tier as well as upper tier); expanded the public lands available for oil leasing and exploration; and explored the possibility of decontrolling the price of natural gas in advance of the expiration of controls in 1985.[39] Although President Reagan temporarily retreated from his plan to abolish the Department of Energy, he destroyed programs directed to conservation and diversification which gave the department its primary reason for existence. Having weakened political support for the department, the President is once more calling for its abolition. The general thrust of these policies is to assure that the nation will resume the energy-intensive consumption habits favored by the oil majors, that the gap between the energy life-styles of lower- and upper-income groups will progressively widen, and that the United States will preempt many of the supplies of oil and gas available to an energy-scarce world.

TRANSPORTATION. One of the areas in which the influence of oligopoly is most apparent is transportation policy. A complicating feature is that the liberal ideology, which is tenaciously held by spokesmen for *both* the major political parties and with particular vigor by President Ronald Reagan, screens the existence of this new situation from view. Whereas we are assured that a minimalist, merely policing state is presiding neutrally over a society of independently situated actors, all of whom are nearly equal in the competition of interests, the state may be observed offering subsidies and tax writeoffs, underwriting capital expenses, and otherwise providing major assistance to modern oligopoly in its effort to dominate a particular sector of economic activity. Curiously, we are given daily assertions that matters are entirely different from what we can observe them to be, and the suspicion is irresistible that without the veil drawn over experience by the rhetoric of liberalism, things as they are could not endure.

The nation's difficulty in forging a transportation policy affords an illustration of this troublesome theme. A public transportation policy was missing from the Carter administration's first national energy plan, which we have just discussed. The enormous revenues generated by the crude oil equalization tax were to be rebated to the public. None were to be spent on public transportation to reduce the extent of energy consumption. The omission seems very curious in view of the circumstance that the private automobile alone consumes 30 percent of the total petroleum used by the nation on any day (about 5.2 MMBD) and that mass transit accounts for only 5 to 6 percent of urban passenger travel.[40] If mass transit ridership increased it would attract passengers from low occupancy automobiles and contribute a major element to the nation's conservation strategy. The gap in the administration's thinking was pointed to by Senator Long, no friend of mass transit, when he objected, "If all [the American people] are going to pay for is a two way ticket for their money to Washington and back, with Washington's expenses deducted on one end, they are going to think we are a bunch of idiots to pass it, and vote us out of office for imposing it on them, and they would be wise to do so."[41]

The reluctance of the Carter administration to advance a public transportation policy can be explained, however, by the merely policing, minimalist role to which the liberal ideology confines the activities of the state. In the area of transportation, the state would be confined to enforcing the customary rules of the road, which ensure that motorists will not harm each other in their separate quests for business, pleasure, and diversion. In line with this minimalist policy, Secretary of Transportation Brock Adams announced at a news conference (June 18, 1979) that he did not expect the automobile's role in filling America's transportation needs to be affected by gas scarcity.[42] Consequently, he planned to proceed with budget cutbacks aimed at reducing the AM-TRAK system and mass transit for the city. The announcement seemed poorly timed, coming a week before OPEC announced another round of price increases, as motorists' tempers flared in cities having spot shortages of gasoline, and as the Carter administration's second national energy plan (NEP II) made an urgent appeal for a public transportation policy. In Dallas a motorist shot another over a place in a gasoline line; attendants were threatened; service station managers required police protection to close the pumps; 750,000 customers were turned away from AMTRAK services.[43] A symbol full of portent for the 1980s is the Los Angeles gas station attendant who strapped a holster to his waist while operating his business. The Carter administration reversed the diverse positions of the Transportation and Energy departments in late 1979 when it tied the revenues from the proposed windfall profits tax to funding of mass transit.[44]

An emphasis on a minimal transportation policy is even more pronounced in the Reagan administration. The Republican party convention urged repeal of the 55 mph speed limit, aimed at saving energy and lives, as an infringement of the personal liberties of motorists. Operating subsidies for urban mass transit systems will be phased out by 1985, and grants to construct new urban rail systems will be sharply curtailed under the budget cuts proposed by the Reagan administration in its FY 1982 budget. Funding for AMTRAK, the intercity rail passenger line, will be cut back by the same budget proposals.[45] Additionally, the Reagan administration has proposed easing or eliminating thirty-five air quality and safety regulations that apply to the automobile industry as unnecessary and excessively burdensome.[46] The president's hostility to public transit is so well known that one Washington wag attributed to him the line, "The only thing wrong with public transit in the cities of this great nation of ours which we all love is that there is no place to hitch your horse."[47]

The minimalist transportation policy defended by Secretary Adams and stressed by the Reagan administration is in keeping with the role customarily assigned the state in a liberal democracy. A nation of independently situated political actors, now housed in private automobiles, should be interfered with as little as possible by a merely policing state. At the most the state, acting in the manner visualized by Hobbes and Locke, should lock up the motorist who shot another over a place in the gasoline line and maintain the customary rules of traffic. These two functions describe the full extent of the role of public authority.

At the same time that we are presented a bipartisan, merely policing public transportation policy by important public spokesmen, we can observe the state underwriting, through direct and indirect subsidies, a private transportation policy whose logic originates in Detroit. The automobile industry has directly affected transportation policy in local arenas of political action in the manner described earlier in this chapter. Beyond these direct effects, the Big Four have combined to obtain vast outlays from the federal government, increasing the power they indirectly exercise over other groups in the political process. In the 1970s the number of cars and trucks in the nation rose by over 4.4 million a year—five times as fast as the population. In the 1950s the consumption of automotive vehicles was 2.2 million annually, and in the 1960s, 3.7 million.[48] Not only are more cars on the road but the rate of growth is rising as well. Without roads on which to travel this expansion of the volume and rate of automobile production would be starkly imbecilic. The federal government, prompted by the autombile industry, has provided the necessary roads.

The Federal Aid Highway Act (1957) provided for the creation of an interstate highway system. It projected that an interstate system of roads 42,500 miles in extent could be constructed for a cost of about $20 billion by 1972. The costs were to be absorbed almost entirely by the federal government from revenues collected from excise taxes on gasoline and automobile-related purchases. Ninety percent of federal funds were available to states participating in interstate construction.[49] Backing the project was a coalition of interests composed of the automobile, oil, rubber, construction, limestone, and asphalt industries; car dealers and renters; bus lines; trucking concerns; and motel owners. A whole new constellation of interests has been spawned by the elements of the interstate system that have been completed thus far. Many of these are grouped close to suburbia, and among them are gas stations, shopping centers, homeowners, and land developers.

At the present time, the cost of the interstate highway system is $87.5 billion. Completion of the interstate system is estimated at well above $100 billion, more than five times the cost initially projected.[50] The Bureau of Public Roads, which has strong lateral ties with congressional appropriations committees and the automobile-oil-construction combine, has presided over the project from the beginning. Located under the Federal Highway Administration in the Department of Transportation, the bureau disburses $6 billion annually in funds for interstate construction.

The indirect subsidy given to the automobile industry by the federal government has contributed to the decline of surface rail transportation and delayed federal monies for urban mass transit. Not until 1974 was federal money supplied for mass transit in substantial amounts; this is several decades after the largesse encouraging automobile usage. Even then the amount available for mass transit is tiny in comparison with that available for federal highways. The National Mass Transportation Act (1974) provided $7 billion in operating subsidies to mass transit through 1980 (about $1 billion annually). The Urban Mass Transportation Administration (also located in the Department of Transportation) allowed $2.2 billion for urban mass transit in its fiscal 1978 budget. Recently, the federal government has allowed major cities to cancel "nonessential" links of the interstate highway system and to shift revenues to mass transit. Critics welcome the change but note that interstate highway construction is still favored by the government. The Highway Trust Fund, which distributes $6 billion annually for the interstate system, remains intact; interstate projects receive 90 percent federal financing in comparison with a lesser rate for mass transit facilities.[51]

Some circumstantial evidence is very strong, as Henry Thoreau said, "a trout in the milk." The evidence points to the conclusion that consumers are so deluged by messages from the Big Four that they tend not to notice the Pinto hobbled by long gasoline lines, the Matador laid in the dust by traffic congestion, or a fortune cast away on an El Dorado. Additionally, the Big Four have encircled the structure of preferences of actors in the political arena—which is why a public transportation policy that would save energy consumption was missing from the National Energy Plan, why $6 billion is annually poured into the interstate highway system, why the price of gasoline sold at the pump for many years was substantially below world prices, why there is a starvation policy toward public transit facilities, why the government does not help the consumer make a more discriminating choice of transportation modes, why each member of the Big Four annually spends $15 million on promotional advertising, why the government now provides $1.5 billion in loan guarantees to the ailing Chrysler Corporation, why a quota on the imports of foreign cars is under consideration by the Reagan administration.[52]

The Big Four, singly or in combination, have exercised power directly over other groups in local arenas of political action and indirectly over other groups in the national political arena. Moreover, they have exercised power, overtly, in relation to other groups on an observable conflict of issues; and they have prevailed over other groups, covertly, by shaping the structure of preferences. We are all familiar with the jingle about "touring the U.S.A. in your Chevrolet." By the same token we are probably all ignorant that gasoline consumption per driver in transit-poor cities like Tucson and Los Angeles is about twice that of transit-oriented cities such as New York or Chicago, or that the exhaust from automobiles contributes about 95 percent of the particulate matter in urban areas.[53] The car manufacturers will try to maintain this balance of knowledge and ignorance, and in this endeavor they are assisted by the biases of the constitutional system, the limitations of American liberal ideology, and the distribution of power in the political arena.

HOUSING. National housing policy is made not by governmental institutions but by a cluster of groups who use it as a means of creating and protecting market advantages. The housing coalition is composed of bankers, builders, realtors, and savings and loan associations. This cluster of interests operates through a variety of interest groups, among them the Mortgage Bankers Association, the American Bankers Association, the U.S. Savings and Loan Association, the National Association of Home Builders, the National Association of Real Estate Boards, and the Chamber of Commerce.

Two basic principles, both of them related to the creation of market advantage, guide the efforts of the housing coalition. One is to stigmatize public housing as an assistance program for the poor. The other is to prevail on the government to provide mortgage insurance chiefly to members of the middle class moving to new homes in the suburbs. Both principles were adopted by the government in the mid-1930s as the foundation of its housing policy. In this fashion the coalition prevented public housing from offering competitive facilities to the middle class. At the same time, the government was drawn into the role of creating an attractive market for banks, realtors, and investors in the suburbs.[54]

Over time, the housing industry coalition has shown remarkable single-mindedness. Its basic policies, originating in the 1930s, are virtually unchanged to the present day. As a key study points out, it continues to operate as a "clientele group," supporting the mortgage finance programs of the Federal Housing Authority (FHA), and as a "veto group," opposing public housing for all except the poor.[55] This coalition got its start by organizing fierce opposition to the public housing program proposed by the 1937 Wagner Act. Sponsors of the legislation were forced to limit eligibility for public housing to the poor as the necessary price for passage of the act.

The "stigmatizing" of public housing as a form of relief flows from not only the desire of the housing coalition to maintain its market advantages but also a bias of the liberal tradition against government provision of social services. It is an interesting and important feature of American politics that an interest group can invoke the prevailing "mobilization of bias" against government programs that threaten its financial interest in a particular area..

But a perceptive international comparison points out that "public housing does not in all societies conjure up grim images of concrete warehouses containing exposed pipes, peeling wall paint, narrow dark stairways, and elevators that stop only on every third floor." In Great Britain and Sweden, a means test is not imposed on applicants and housing is looked on as a service which the government takes pride and satisfaction in making generally available to the public. Conversely, U.S. housing policies lead to problems of "property repair and maintenance, rent arrears, poor housing management, low staff morale, and high staff turnover."[56] Only the elderly, the poor, and problem families inhabit the penitentiaries thrown up in the years following the passage of the Wagner Act. President Nixon observed that "all across America, the federal government has become the biggest slumlord in history."

The fate of the Pruitt-Igoe complex in St. Louis is indicative of the basic flaws in the concept of public housing solely for the poor. Built in 1955 at a cost of $36 million, it was initially hailed as a model of low-income housing. In 1975, after a lengthy history involving all the problems referred to above, the complex was leveled to the ground.

The FHA mortgage insurance program started in the New Deal era along with the public housing program. The former, enacted in 1935, insures mortgages extended by lending institutions. It sets regulations determining the interest charge, the amount of down payment required, and the maximum time period for the mortgages. The chief consumer beneficiaries of the FHA program have been suburban middle-income home buyers rather than working class or poor families residing in the central cities. By insuring well over 90 percent of the appraised value of new homes, the FHA program has enabled millions of Americans to become homeowners in suburbia.[57]

The FHA, until recently, has generally been unwilling to insure mortgages to poor and working class members (particularly blacks) because they have been regarded as bad credit risks. Related to this decision by the FHA has been its reluctance to insure homes in the central city.[58] Not only was the FHA never intended as a program to aid the poor, but also its effect has been to increase the disparities between the haves and the have-nots.

The continuing influence of the housing coalition on federal policy is evident in the details surrounding the passage of the National Housing Act in 1968. On the blue-ribbon committee appointed by President Johnson the members of the housing coalition were heavily represented. The total membership of the Kaiser Committee was eighteen, nine of whom represented the construction industry and three represented financial institutions. It should surprise no one that the committee drafted a proposal to solve the housing shortage by having private developers produce twenty-six million new houses over the next decade. The Kaiser Committee reveals "why federal housing policy promotes home ownership rather than viable public housing,"[59] one study concludes.

COUNTERVAILING POWER REVISITED

The analysis so far projects the view of a political process dominated by powerful oligopolies and influential interests on select policy issues. These groups have upset the relative equality among political actors visualized in the constitutional system. The governmental defenses which Madison set up to guard against the capture of political power have been overrun. Now powerful interests are installed within the very fortifications Madison created, using the government as an ally in their efforts to extend power over other groups. In response to this set of conditions the question arises, "What sources of countervailing power remain to restore equality in the political struggle and the balances of the Madisonian system?"

Answers to this question tend to focus on the activity of social and economic groups rather than the governmental institutions on which Madison placed primary stress. The principal elements of countervailing power are the political parties, public interest lobbies, organized labor, and intergovernmental lobbies.

The basic aim of the public interest lobbies is to make actors and key decisions in the political process visible. By seeking to ensure fair play among the parties to the political struggle, public interest lobbies claim to be partisans of the public interest rather than motivated by private advantage. They are well aware that the system affords many opportunities to exert pressure quietly, at critical points of the policy-making process. They are aware that professional lobbyists such as Lyn Stalbaum, whom we mentioned earlier, prefer to operate as inconspicuously as possible. The professional lobbyist avoids displays of power; he arranges matters so that his clients and the congressman or bureaucrat whom they wish to influence can reach an accommodation out of the public view. Many of the reforms pushed by the public interest lobbies seek to make such arrangements more difficult and more public.

Common Cause is a leading example of a public interest lobby devoted to reform of the political process. It was launched in 1970 by John Gardner, former secretary of Health, Education, and Welfare, as a lobbying organization. It presently has a membership of approximately 265,000, drawn mainly from upper-middle-class professionals. It has an annual budget of $5.5 million; 95 percent of which is derived from dues of $15 per year and contributions of under $100.[60] Common Cause led the fight in the Ninety-fifth Congress for a new lobby registration act. Although it was unsuccessful, its justification was sound. The Federal Lobbying Act (1946) has many loopholes that allow underreporting of spending and registration by professional lobbyists. It is estimated that one-tenth of 1 percent of the total amount spent on lobbying is reported.[61]

Common Cause has sponsored legislation requiring financial disclosure for senior members of the executive branch and Congress, public financing of congressional elections, sunshine laws requiring open meetings, civil service reform, and tighter controls over the intelligence agencies. All these measures are tied to ending the reign of secrecy by which groups manipulate outcomes from behind the scenes. Gardner states that procedural reform is the unifying theme that has enabled Common Cause to find and maintain its constituency.[62]

The focus of Public Citizen, the creation of Ralph Nader, appears to be more diverse than that of Common Cause. This public interest lobby, often Nader personally, appears determined to flush out all hidden interests (nursing home operators, citrus producers, and GM are among them) and to bring them to account. Public Citizen is an umbrella group which employs more than eighty persons in various operating groups. Among these are Congress Watch, Tax Reform Research Group, Health Service Group, Litigation Group, and the Public Citizen Visitor's Center in Washington.[63]

Nader's chief means for bringing influentials to account is exposure. He is a sensational investigative reporter and publicist whose exposés always make good news material. He corners his quarry before the congressional investigative committee (as in the confrontation with GM over automotive safety), pursues them through litigation in the judicial arena (as when the bar associations were held subject to antitrust laws), and harrasses them through disclosures to the regulatory commissions (as in the report on watered orange juice to the Federal Trade Commission). Nader seems to be everywhere, as he must be if he is going to ferret out the exercise of unobserved power in American politics.

His far-flung investigative empire has its comic and serious aspects. Nader is not too far distant from Clark Kent, but a superman who brings wrongdoers to justice through the media rather than through muscle power. Nader, however, does not regard himself as entertainment. On college campuses he challenges the nation's youth to "seize power through citizenship."

> You have numbers, brains, and now the vote. We need your sensitivity. Special interest groups have fielded their team. We must field our team.[64]

The AFL-CIO, organized labor's chief spokesman, represents a working force of over nineteen million union members. It is active and influential on a wide range of issues, which include tax reform, medical insurance, school aid, racial inequality in employment, consumer issues, and many other proposals that affect the distribution of wealth between the working class and management. The AFL-CIO works through its political action arm, COPE, to support candidates, usually from the Democratic party, of whom it approves. After sitting out the 1972 presidential election campaign, the AFL-CIO rejoined the Democratic party in support of Jimmy Carter in 1976 and 1980.

Despite its undoubted clout in national politics, the AFL-CIO both historically and in recent times has been unwilling to use its influence to upset the basic patterns of American politics. On the issues of housing and transportation, labor's commitment to homeownership, jobs, and the family car has been sufficient reason for supporting present subsidies. On issues such as wage and price controls, defense spending, and environmental controls, it has often sided with the business community. Labor has not spoken out on energy, failing to perceive that its interests are directly engaged. It is a leading example of the tendency of out-groups to accept the structural biases of the political process once dealt with on a relational basis by powerful political coalitions.

Like the public interest lobbyists, intergovernmental lobbies are a relatively new generic group in the political arena. Basically intermediaries between the state and local governments and the national organs of government, they include the National Governors Conference, the Council of State Governments, the United States Conference of Mayors, the National League of Cities, the National Association of Counties, and the International City Management Association. These lobbies are on hand in Washington in an effort to convince officials at the national level to provide more federal money with fewer restrictions on the purposes for which it is spent. The constituencies served by the intergovernmental lobbies overlap in many respects with those of the public interest lobbies and organized labor. Together they may be seen as a coalition exercising power against the impact of oligopolistic interests in the political process.

SUMMARY

Public interest groups, organized labor, and intergovernmental lobbies are relatively new political groups trying to deal with a novel political situation. Oligopoly has slipped past the defenses created by Madison against the capture of governmental power by a single group. In important areas of public policy—housing, energy, and transportation—the Madisonian system of countervailing power does not seem to be working, or at any rate, not working very well. In local arenas of political action, countervailing power often does not exist.

The antidemocratic biases that inspire America's decentralized cadre parties make it unlikely that the new position of oligopoly will be challenged by them. The mutual process of co-optation between party influentials and corporate interests makes it more likely that the parties will serve as agents for elevating the preferences of oligopolists into public policy.

An important conclusion of this chapter is that Madison did not provide adequate safeguards to the liberty of independently situated actors through the system of countervailing power. If the constitutional system is unable to afford adequate protection to its most important value, it no longer rests on a secure basis in the political community.

To some extent, Madisonian politics paves the way for the favored position of corporate capital. Madison devised a system whereby influentials would deal relationally with one another and manipulatively with everyone else. Influential groups would be able to prevail, however, only after an observable conflict about the issues. The oligopoly exercising power directly in local communities and shaping the structure of public preferences, thereby avoiding observable conflict, goes an important step beyond Madison's political arrangements. It shifts the political struggle from the formal institutions of government to the economy. Additionally, it suggests that practical political arrangements in twentieth-century America are in conflict with the seventeenth-century liberal democratic values embedded in our eighteenth-century constitutional system. A constitutional crisis, to put it simply, underlies crises in selected areas of public policy, transportation, energy, and housing.

The liberal tradition in American politics has a pivotal position in the new situation. In the beginning, Louis Hartz has written, history was "out on a lark, out to tease men by imitating their dreams with satiric accuracy."[65] The wilderness provided Hobbes's and Locke's vision of independently situated actors in a primitive political society (the state of nature) with touches of verisimilitude; contractual agreement appeared to be a suitable way to get men into political community; the government could reasonably be confined to minimal functions, maintaining public order and managing social conflicts about property. Now Americans cling to their ancient dreams even though they are denied a convincing basis in reality.

In keeping with liberal ideas about minimal government, the Reagan administration insists that neo-liberal programs which enlarge the role of the state must be cut back or eliminated. This wish has been acceded to by a Congress awed by the popularity of the president's position. At the same time that neo-liberal programs are held in check, an enlargement of the responsibilities of the state in other directions is apparent. Modern oligopoly uses the liberal bias against public services to protect its market advantage, it shapes public preferences in behalf of its preferred policies (giving a new meaning and direction to notions about inalienable rights), and it employs the state as an auxiliary source of capital supply. Thus, the revival of liberal ideas by the Reagan administration appears disingenuous; the rhetoric of liberalism is used to manipulate public perceptions, disguising the new arrangements of power from view.

NOTES

1. Charles E. Lindblom, *Politics and Markets* (New York: Basic Books, 1977), pp. 94, 149.

2. *Ibid.,* p. 195.

3. Arnold J. Heidenheimer, Hugh Heclo, and Carolyn Teich Adams, *Comparative Public Policy* (New York: St. Martin's Press, 1975), pp. 172–73.

4. *Ibid.*

5. Quoted in Barry Commoner, "Energy," *The New Yorker,* (February 16, 1976, p. 73.

6. Quoted in Frank V. Fowlkes, "Washington Pressures," *National Journal,* November 14, 1970, p. 2,504.

7. Quoted in Neal R. Peirce and Jerry Hagstrom, "Mass Transit Funds are Rolling," *National Journal,* August 8, 1976, p. 1110.

8. William E. Connolly, *The Terms of Political Discourse,* (Lexington, Mass.: D.C. Heath, 1974), chap. 3; and Matthew Crenson, *The Unpolitics of Air Pollution* (Baltimore, Md.: Johns Hopkins Press, 1971).

9. Cranson, *Unpolitics,* pp. 76–77.

10. Committee on Banking, Currency and Housing, Report No. 94–561, *Depository Institutions Amendments of 1975,* October 10, 1975.

11. David Truman, *The Governmental Process* (New York: Knopf, 1951).

12. Duane Lockard, *The Perverted Priorities of American Politics* (New York: Macmillan, 1971); Michael Parenti, *Democracy for the Few* (New York: St. Martin's Press, 1977); Peter Bachrach, *Theory of Democratic Elitism* (Boston: Little, Brown, 1967).

13. William J. Crotty, *Political Reform and the American Experiment* (New York: Thomas Y. Crowell, 1977), pp. 140–44.

14. Lindblom, *Politics and Markets,* p. 149.

15. *Ibid.,* p. 94.

16. Mancur Olson, *The Logic of Collective Action* (Cambridge, Mass.: Harvard University Press, 1975), chap. 5.

17. Robert Engler, *The Brotherhood of Oil* (Chicago: University of Chicago Press, 1977), pp. 19–21.

18. *Ibid.,* pp. 22–24.

19. *National Journal,* March 4, 1978, pp. 336–40.

20. Engler, *Brotherhood of Oil,* pp. 62–63, 153–54, 184–85.

21. James M. Naughton, "Petropolitics at Work on Capitol Hill," *New York Times* April 3, 1977, Fl, 5.

22. *Ibid.*

23. Engler, *Brotherhood of Oil,* p. 62; Crotty, *Political Reform,* p. 147.

24. Engler, *Brotherhood of Oil,* p. 64.

25. *Washington Post,* November 23, 1977, A4.

26. John Palmer *et al.,* "The Distributional Impact of Energy Prices: How Should the Government Respond?" (Washington, D.C.: Brookings Reprint No. 331, January 1978).

27. David Howard Davis, *Energy Politics* (New York: St. Martin's Press, 1978), p. 1.

28. Joel Darmstadter *et al., How Industrial Societies Use Energy* (Baltimore, Md.: Johns Hopkins Press, 1977), chaps. 4 and 5; also see Dorothy Newman and Dawn Day, *The American Energy Consumer* (Cambridge, Mass.: Ballinger, 1975).

29. U.S. Department of Energy, *National Energy Plan II* (Washington, D.C.: Government Printing Office, 1979), pp. 18, 89.

30. *National Journal,* July 12, 1976, pp. 806–11.

31. Richard Reeves, *A Ford, Not a Lincoln* (New York: Harcourt, Brace, 1975), pp. 159–60.

32. *Wall Street Journal,* October 31, 1977, pp. 1, 23; *Wall Street Journal,* November 15, 1977.

33. U.S. Department of Energy, *National Energy Plan I* (Washington, D.C.: U.S. Government Printing Office, 1977).

34. *National Journal,* September 9, 1979, pp. 1,443–44.

35. *National Journal,* February 23, 1980, pp. 314–16.

36. *The New York Times,* March 16, 1981, D1.

37. *National Journal,* March 14, 1979, pp. 480–83.

38. *The New York Times,* October 30, 1980, B18; *The New York Times,* November 26, 1980, D6; *The New York Times,* March 10, 1981, C1.

39. *The New York Times,* November 26, 1980, D6; *The New York Times,* February 20, 1981, A12; *The New York Times,* February 23, 1981, D3.

40. *National Energy Plan II,* pp. 63–64.

41. *National Journal,* November 5, 1977, pp. 1,716–19.

42. *The New York Times,* June 18, 1979, A1, B8.

43. *The New York Times,* June 26, 1979, A1, B6.

44. *National Journal,* September 22, 1979, pp. 1,556–60.

45. *The New York Times,* February 20, 1981, A12.

46. *The New York Times,* April 7, 1981, A1.

47. Mark Russell at the Shoreham, Washington, D.C.

48. *Washington Post,* November 30, 1977.

49. *National Journal,* November 19, 1977, pp. 1812–15.

50. *The New York Times,* March 1, 1977, p. 14.

51. *National Journal,* March 26, 1977, pp. 464–68.

52. *The New York Times,* February 9, 1981, A1; Emma Rothschild, *Paradise Lost* (New York: Vintage Books, 1974).

53. *Wall Street Journal,* December 30, 1977; Report of the Environmental Protection Agency, Senate Document 92–6, March 16, 1971, p. 3–2.

54. Stephen M. David and Paul Peterson, eds., *Urban Politics and Public Policy* (New York: Praeger, 1973), pp. 3–91.

55. Heidenheimer *et al., Comparative Public Policy,* pp. 74–79.

56. *Ibid.,* p. 74.

57. David and Peterson, eds., *Urban Politics,* pp. 93–103.

58. *Ibid.*

59. Heidenheimer *et al., Comparative Public Policy,* pp. 78–79.

60. Andrew McFarland, "The Complexity of Democratic Practice Within Common Cause," Prepared for Delivery at the 1976 Annual Meeting of the American Political Science Association, Chicago, Illinois, September 2–5, 1976.

61. Senate Government Operations Committee Report on S. 2477, the Lobby Disclosure Act of 1976.

62. McFarland, "Complexity of Democratic Practice."

63. Al Gordon, "Public Interest Lobbies," *Congressional Quarterly*, May 15, 1976, pp. 1,197–1,205.
64. Charles McGarry, *Citizen Nader* (New York: Signet, 1973), p. 252.
65. Louis Hartz, *The Liberal Tradition in America* (New York: Harcourt, Brace & World, 1960), p. 60.

CHAPTER 6

Class, Culture, and the Constitution

In this chapter I will enlarge on the view that a seventeenth-century commercial Protestant culture has trapped America inside an eighteenth-century constitutional system. Therefore, corporate capital is able to dominate political institutions in select areas of public policy—defense, transportation, and energy to name a few outstanding examples —not only, or even chiefly, because of the financial and organizational resources at its disposal, but most importantly because a dominant cultural view obscures at the same time that it shapes social and political reality and the characteristics of the constitutional system. Some of the elements of this view have already been developed in the preceding chapters, enabling us in this chapter to build on what has gone before.

This dominant cultural liberalism is the main agent behind the shaping of the constitutional system. Attention is directed to a preconstituted world of social relations which the delegates uncritically absorbed from the past and blindly transmitted to future generations. This preconstituted world is the dominant culture. It is the "whole way of life, material, intellectual, and spiritual of a society,"[1] and it is embodied in social relations and the circulation of ideas among a people.

The most important teaching of the dominant culture is that we are each radically dissociated egos, independently situated actors to use the customary expression of these pages, each with differing material capacities, talents, and skills, which we may rightfully deploy in the service of our personal freedom. Government in a society of this sort should confine itself to a minimal, merely policing role, so that it might interfere least with the separate quests of each one of us for the good things of life. The most important function of government is to manage social conflict, insuring through the diffusion of power that the state, itself,

131

will not be used to the disadvantage of any one of the participants in this conflict. Thus, the dominant culture exists in a symbiotic and supportive relationship to the political arrangements of the constitutional system, a reflection that strikes one with particular force in the writings of James Madison. In *Federalist* No. 10, as we have had occasion to note many times, the role and functions of the government are set by the dominant enthusiasm of a commercial Protestant culture, that is, managing conflict among the members of a society of radically dissociated egos.

Symbiosis involves the interdependent, mutually supportive relations of dissimilar organisms. In this case, the interrelationship between the dominant culture and the Constitution, both of which are mutually sustaining, yet discrete, entities. This relationship has important political consequences. To the extent that seventeenth-century cultural enthusiasms still dominate American society, and I shall try to show that they do, to that extent Madison's eighteenth-century constitutional arrangements are relevant and useful to the management of social conflict. But seventeenth-century cultural enthusiasms mislead as to the real nature of the conflicts which beset us. Corporate capital has slipped past the defenses Madison and his peers created against the capture of power by a determinate group. In select cases such as energy, transportation, and housing, it prevails where there is an observable conflict on the issues, and beyond this, to a pronounced degree, it shapes the structure of preferences within which debate is carried on by the major participants (Chapter 5).

The new configuration of power introduced by the position of corporate capital imperils the utility of Madisonian constitutional arrangements, and possibly makes them utterly irrelevant. To put it simply, we may need less protection from each other, as Madison and the founding fathers visualized it, than we need protection from corporate giants which dominate important areas of public policy. Yet if we are presently in the midst of a constitutional crisis, a crisis in the principles on which authority in a liberal democratic society has traditionally been constituted, the public has been slow to realize it. One may infer from declining rates of participation in presidential elections a diminishing confidence in the efficacy of institutions and conventional forms of political participation (Chapter 4). Yet so far there appears to be little concern about the stability of political institutions and the survival of the constitutional system. It seems paradoxical that institutions should remain stable and the Constitution held in high esteem when they little serve the purposes of their design.

The view offered in this chapter is that the dominant culture shapes public perceptions of the terms of social conflict, focusing attention on conflicts of private right between social groups (racial, ethnic, and religious), individuals, and geographic groups (urban, suburban, rural, and regional), and away from conflict along the lines of social class or the nexus between corporate capital and the state. The dominant culture plays a dual role, for at the same time that it shapes social and political reality, engendering a host of voluntary associations as we shall soon see, it also screens the reality of class conflict from view. Similarly, at the same time that the dominant culture accentuates conflict along interpersonal, racial, and ethnic lines, it dampens down conflict arising from class divisions. Thus, the dominant culture has an important, hidden function, enabling the political system to bypass systemic disagreements over policy and class conflict, and undergirding the stability of institutions and the constitutional framework.

OBSERVATIONS ON AMERICAN CULTURE AND SOCIAL CLASS

You are leafing through a popular magazine, riding along the highway, or watching television. This time take a second look at the ads, commercials, or billboards. Let's focus on a billboard, possibly an unavoidable thing to do in any event. Billboards tend to dominate the highway scene so that even if you are rushing along at maximum speed in bumper-to-bumper traffic, it is difficult to ignore the fixed stare of the larger-than-life figures who look down on you. For our purposes, the dominance these figures so easily establish is well suited to developing some ideas about political culture in America.

As you approach in the inside lane, a casually dressed, good-looking, bearded fellow casts his eyes on you. He does not look like a stranger. He looks comfortable and familiar, like an old shoe. At the same time, he exudes a certain glamor. He might be a celebrity; occasionally (when there is time for explanation), he is someone on his way up. In any event, he is someone accessible, and he confides to you, as though he were standing in your living room, *"I* [emphasis mine] know my taste." He is referring to a pack of Winstons, which oddly enough, is silhouetted on a blue background just behind his right ear. He is the Winston man who in 1979 made a strong bid to replace the Marlboro man of yesteryear in the popular fancy. The Marlboro man, you remember, is the fellow who knows where the flavor is, in Marlboro country, of course, a place of wild stallions, large spaces, rugged men, snow drifts, and packs and packs of Marlboros.

We have encountered men like this (and women) many times before in identical or similar settings. Possibly, we have met them so often we no longer really look at them. After all, they peer out at us from the pages of every popular magazine and take up a considerable amount of television time, a greater share it seems as the hour grows later. Who are these men and women?

I suggest that they are an archetype, that is, a model or type, of the "choice-making individual,"[2] a permanent structure of the American mind from the beginning and the bedrock of the American constitutional system. The figure on the billboard, in the glamour magazines, on the television screen, wherever he or she appears, is a modern variant of the dissociated, property-possessing, idiosyncratic individual, talked about by Hobbes and Locke, stepped forward from the pages of history and political theory, and enthroned in the midst of a public thoroughfare, a type of marketplace. Here his or her constitutive role in relation to social and political reality may be clearly grasped.

The figure on the billboard is stripped of all the accidents of time and place and family. We know nothing about him in terms of personal biography; our only clue to his nature is that his preferred mode of action in the world is choice making. In Hobbes's and Locke's day, the right of the choice-making individual was primarily expressed in the terms on which authority was to be established in modern society. Their writings were mainly concerned with the type of political institutions that would most nearly reflect the enthusiasms of a whole society of liberated, choice-making, dissociated egos. In modern times, now that the matter of the authority of liberal democratic institutions is settled, attention has turned to the expression of personal choice in material things. Undivided attention can be invested in scotch, cars, trips abroad, appliances, hair sprays, shaving cream, casual clothes, stereos, and so on, because the stability of political institutions seems assured. Although personal choice is now primarily expressed in patterns of consumption, nevertheless, the same idea, a constitutional idea, underlies political arrangements.

As an idea, the choice-making individual is more or less self-consciously used to create and manipulate social reality. I shall deal with the creative side first and then suggest some ways in which Americans are manipulated by their beliefs. The principle of the choice-making, idiosyncratic individual can be used to explain the extraordinary variety of voluntary associations on the social scene. In 1968, there were 10,933 national associations in the United States devoted to everything from sports to education to religion to astrology to popular science. Sixty-two percent of all American adults belong to at least one association (not necessarily a nationwide one), and 40 percent of all Americans say they are active in at least one organization.[3] This bewildering array of organizations has been spawned by the initiative of the choice-making individual, creating and (less often) dissolving groups, as the occasion or the purpose presents itself. A readiness to join, to organize, to improvise a group or association is more common in the United States than in any other nation.

The principle of the choice-making individual is the underpinning of the advertising industry. This gigantic industry with accounts running into the billions of dollars has enormous influence over the public mind. Individuals need some guidance in making their choices, a function the advertising industry has agreeably volunteered to perform. Although the advertising industry did not invent the principle of the choice-making individual—clearly it is a social creation—it has exploited the principle to its ever-lasting good fortune. The industry plays on the emulative side of the choice maker. The idea behind the figure on the billboard—comfortable, casually dressed, successful himself—is that we, too, can become these things, if only we can come up with the money to buy a pack of Winstons. Of course, with emulation comes competitiveness, acquisition, and conflict, matters not dealt with in the picture but certainly implicit in what it tells us.

The notion of the choice-making individual plays a vital role in the two-party system. The essence of democratic choice in America is said to lie in the alternatives set before the electorate by the elites of the major political parties.[4] Even though, as formerly noted, Americans tend to stay away from elections in droves, an enormous amount of attention is paid to elections by the media, not to mention the political science profession. Another trend noted earlier is that a progressively greater portion of the electorate is registering as independent rather than as affiliated with the major parties. In recent years this percentage of the electorate has exceeded the registration of the Republican party. Thus, independents are the second largest political group in America. A large portion of the electorate is either uncertain about a suitable expression of political choice or apathetic about the political choices placed before them or both. The emphasis on free elections in the American political context is explained by reference to the choice-making individual. Yet electoral democracy in America appears to be in trouble.

A flaming romance with the notion of the dissociated individual inspires the movie industry and television. Selecting their figures from all time but aiming their drama at the prejudices of the American audience, filmmakers put forth an unending succession of antisocial antiheroes: international spies, bounty hunters, questionable cops, still more questionable private eyes, confidence men, gamblers, men on the make, men hitting the beach, gangland czars, bounders, gunslingers. It is getting harder to tell the heroes from the villains, because having dissolved society, there is no point of reference. A critic has suggested that Clint Eastwood, the number one or number two box-office attraction at movie theaters for several years, a figure whose movies have grossed over $50 million, is a central metaphor for our time as Nature was for the Social Darwinists.[5] Clint Eastwood may look radical, exuding as he does, a remote alienated, tough attitude, but actually, in the terms we are considering, he is as American as cherry pie, and to mix metaphors a bit, a regular pillar of the community. Eastwood teaches us to regard human existence in terms congenial to the liberal consensus. Life is, we assume after an Eastwood movie, a matter of isolate, lonely, bitter struggle between individuals. What could be more obvious? Further, seeing his .44 magnum tucked under his armpit, the most powerful handgun in the world, we discover what must be done in the ultimate contests over survival. In many ways, Eastwood is a throwback to the American frontier and a more primitive time in the life of the nation.

Billboards, political parties, the movie industry, social groups, television, all tend to give the impression that in America the individual is an unrivaled force in human affairs. To give additional weight to this perspective, Americans enjoy precisely what Hobbes, Locke, and Madison said that political institutions should make possible and insure, freedom of choice. How true is this statement?

To begin we may note that free choice is consistent with a set of severely imposed constraints. A fast-food chain in my town announces, "At Marlow's you have freedom of choice," and markets the alternatives of very old, carcinogenic chicken and questionable hamburger, rumored to be kangaroo meat. In this instance free choice may be a mere matter of naming your poison. To offer another example from the consumer world, consider the case of Levitt Bros. Realty Corp. and the typical Levittowner. Levittowns, which are a totally planned community down to the fire hydrants, offer their clients a choice from among three housing styles, the "Cape Cod," the "Rancher," and the "Colonial," each with the same floor plan, selling for a near identical price. Although it is clear that "choice" is an illusion existing in the buyer's imagination, the illusion is carefully preserved. Do political choice makers, like the consumer who lives in Levittown and lunches at Marlow's, also choose within a narrow framework of alternatives?

The figures on the billboard do not invite attention to differences in material capacity to realize personal choices. To put this another way, important class distinctions are obscured by the notion that we are a society of similarly situated choice-making individuals. Sample surveys reveal that over 80 percent of Americans consider themselves members of the middle class and, therefore, the beneficiaries of a comfortable material existence.[6] It may be that this widespread conception is in part a tribute to the images projected by popular culture. Analyses of the actual distribution of income and wealth in society present a different picture.

Using the index of either income or wealth, there are substantial social and economic, or class, inequalities evident in American society. An economist distinguishes between *income* and *wealth* in the following manner:

> Income is a flow of money and purchasing power over time; wealth a stock of things owned that have market value. Money income includes wages and salaries, social security benefits, dividends, interest and rents received, welfare payments, pensions, alimony received, net income from self-employment (for instance from farming, or by doctors), and other periodic income. Wealth includes automobiles and homes as well as trucks and mines and corporate stock.[7]

The key distinction is that wealth is an income-producing asset; income is used to help meet the necessities of daily living. The wealth of the very rich is convertible into income; yet conversion would expose this wealth to taxation, reducing the portion of aggregate wealth which produces income. Hence the rich tend to obtain an income, like the rest of us, to defray the expenses of daily life, and then to shield wealth from taxation by placing it in tax-exempt municipal bonds.

One fifth of the population owns 77 percent of personal wealth. Much of this is in the form of state and municipal bonds and corporate stock. In 1953, according to one source, 1 percent of the population owned 100 percent of state and local bonds, 77.5 percent of other bonds, 76 percent of corporate stock, and 31.8 percent of U.S. government bonds. A few of the rich are extremely wealthy, the top 1 percent own 30 percent of all wealth; as contrasted with those who are "well off" by virtue of having a high income, the top 1 percent of personal income recipients receive something under 10 percent of income.

The average income of the 10.4 million families in the bottom fifth of the population was $3,054 in 1970, no more than 6 percent of total income received. The average income of the families in the top fifth of the population was $23,100 that year, over 40 percent of the total income received. This distribution of income has remained constant for the past twenty-five years. The tax laws accentuate rather than retard the inequalities produced by wealth and income. The estimated tax rate applying to the poorest segment of the population—those with incomes under $2,000 per year—is 44 percent, a higher rate than any other income bracket.[8]

The dominant culture masks social and economic disparities, enabling elites to direct frustration and resentment downward and away from themselves, and at the same time, narrowing the boundaries of political conflict. The principal evidence in support of this perspective is the American labor movement, which in contrast to European labor parties, has never sought political direction of the state; has never fomented, or wished to foment, social revolution; has concentrated its main energies in negotiating for stable local organization, improved working conditions, and better pay within a stable capitalist framework; and has expressed periodic resentment against welfare "chiselers" and other members of the underclass who are the beneficiaries of state welfare.[9] Victor Gotbaum, the chief spokesman for the civil service unions in New York City, encapsulated the history and objectives of the labor movement in these words: "The labor union movement in this country was built by the hope, the courage, and the strength and the ideals of the outs who wanted in."[10] In short, as Gotbaum suggests, labor has sought an accommodation with the groups in society who manipulate accumulated capital, all within the boundaries of a stable consensus.

Perceptions of class conflict are narrowed from above in America as well as from below. Businessmen commonly report mistrust of the state, as a possible engine of social reform, far beyond the evidence that supports a propensity to act in this direction. It is commonly believed that a new page was written in the history of American capitalism with the New Deal era, that laissez-faire was brought to an end and that the independence formerly enjoyed by business enterprise was taken away by a powerful state bureaucracy. This is not the case, and it would be very, very surprising if it were. The hegemony of Lockian liberal ideas, the arrangements of the Constitution, and the powerful institutional position built up by business in the nineteenth century (see Chapter 13) assured that the New Deal would be a conservative political effort—and indeed it was.[11] American capitalism was saved from its own excesses by a liberal state which agreeably assumed many of its administrative burdens and social expenses. The state provided work relief and unemployment compensation to those injured by the deficiencies of a market economy. It provided social security in the absence of pension benefits administered by the private sector. Compensatory countercyclical fiscal and monetary policy was begun in the New Deal to counteract inflation and recession. Regulatory agencies such as the Securities and Exchange Commission (1934) and the Federal Communications Commission (1934) sought to provide a stable framework for the competition of business interests. In none of these activities did the liberal state intrude on the sacred principle that investment decisions were the sole authority of the private sector. To this day, business rhetoric to the contrary, the American state has the weakest control over corporate investment decisions of any nation in the world.[12] The principal beneficiary of the New Deal reforms is not, as commonly believed, the underclasses, but wealthier groups which successfully focus working class resentment downward at the same time that they use the state as an auxiliary source of capital supply.[13]

Conflict along the lines of social and geographic groups has tended to displace conflict between labor and capital and among socioeconomic classes under the shaping influence of the liberal consensus. The most apparent cases of these forms of conflict are visible in urban settings in the perennial battles over federal housing, urban renewal, and antipoverty grants. Participation in each one of these has consistently set off conflicts among groups in the cities, arrayed along urban or suburban, racial, and ethnic lines, over the use and purpose of federal money. Struggles over the placement of low-income and public housing (which have seen the mobilization of white homeowners, especially), the use of public antipoverty money for the political mobilization of the black and Puerto Rican poor, and the allocation of urban renewal funds to the renovation of central business districts at the expense of housing needs illustrate the sort of conflict touched off by the receipt of federal funds.[14] The general aim of these conflicts resembles the goals sought by the principal figures of the labor movement: to win for excluded groups a position of relative equality within the dominant liberal consensus.

This climate of opinion—the dampening down of class conflict, the tendency to restrict the terms in which political conflict is seen—helps to explain the neutralization of issues and political groups which might reasonably be expected to have an important place on the political agenda. Commonly, we suppose that exclusion of an item from the political agenda is explained by its defeat after an observable conflict. But the hegemony of seventeenth-century Lockean liberal ideas may operate to remove an issue from the political agenda in advance of an observable conflict. The frequent beneficiary of this outcome is twentieth-century corporate capitalism.

As an example, we noted earlier (Chapter 5) that the removal of a proposal for mass transit facilities from the national energy package was a tribute to the law of anticipated reactions. President Carter did not wish to confront two sets of oligopolistic interests, the oil producers and the automobile-highway complex, at one and the same time. It may be added that neither did he wish to assail the well-known preferential structure of the American public. Locke's and Jefferson's verbiage about the "pursuit of happiness" has been transmuted into ownership of two cars, a home on a half-acre of ground, and to be transported by an expressway to one's place of work. The metal cocoons in which Americans enshroud their bodies during their most private hours, the passage to and from the workplace, are the current version of the rights Locke and Jefferson meant for governments to defend. It seems fair to say that the hegemony of seventeenth-century ideas, further interpreted and elaborated on by twentieth-century automobile advertising, cooperated to defeat mass transit as a significant policy option before there was an observable conflict on the issues.

Another inalienable right the president's national energy plan was careful to skirt was the gigantic assets of the oil producers. When the president's plan had been stalled in Congress for six months, causing a famous outburst against the oil producers on which we shall later comment (Chapter 8), a reporter asked the president if divestiture of the oil companies was not a logical and necessary preliminary to the successful passage of his energy policies. Divestiture of the oil producers either vertically according to function (production, refining, distribution, and marketing) or horizontally according to resource base (uranium, coal, oil and gas, solar) is not, itself, a radical proposal for the social redistribution of wealth. Chiefly, it proposes to break up consolidated power over energy resources to give the state leverage in managing supply, price, and public consumption. The exchange between the president and the reporter about divestiture is illuminating. It affords the view that the state is a tacit and silent partner of twentieth-century oligopoly in undermining the seventeenth-century liberal consensus on which its own authority rests.

> Q. Mr. President, if you're serious about the oil industry and the oil lobby working contrary to what you perceive the public interest to be, you've got a club in the closet and that's divestiture. Why don't you move to break them up?
>
> A. Well, there's a matter of raising too many issues at once. And I'm not trying to threaten anybody or use a club. It's obvious that the influence of the oil companies both in the legislative process and the executive branch of government, as well as in the economic structure of the country, is enormous. Part of that is inevitable and part of it is not to be deplored. It's appropriate.
>
> There is a concern to me, for instance, in the uranium industry, which is another major and future alternative for large portions of our energy supplies. The oil companies own about 50% of the uranium deposits. They have substantial holdings in coal. But whether or not divestiture is needed is a matter on which I've not decided, and I don't think that now is the time to go into that detailed study or analysis.[15]

THE DOMINANT CULTURE

The idea of a preconstituted world of social relations which concurrently creates and obscures American political life is in need of further explanation and elaboration. Historical treatment of the dominant commercial Protestant culture, its success in conforming ethnic and racial groups to its main enthusiasms, and the challenge mounted by elements of the counterculture may help carry forward this task. Above all, the burden of this discussion is that cultural hegemony has important political consequences, restricting the boundaries of political conflict and neutralizing controversy over important matters of public policy. The concept of cultural hegemony, central to this discussion, is defined by the theorist most closely identified with it as follows:

> [Hegemony is] an order in which a certain way of life and thought is dominant, in which one concept of reality is diffused throughout society in all its institutional and private manifestations, informing with its spirit all taste, morality, customs, religious, and political principles, and all social relations, particularly in their intellectual and moral connotations.[16]

From the beginning, the dominant culture in America is British commercial Protestant. This culture transmits the notion of the choice-making, independently situated, individual, a Protestant outlook, along with the other intellectual baggage of seventeenth-century liberalism, into the American community. The dominant culture triumphs by way of default, for it has never been stoutly opposed by a competing set of beliefs. This fact places the dominant culture in an unusual position. Its claims about free choice, free elections, government by consent, and the rights of the individual may be asserted without scrutiny or fear of contradiction. Americans have been told that they are free on so many occasions that they believe it as an article of faith. It is characteristic of an overpowering belief that it blocks out contradictory evidence even where it exists in fair abundance. Here, we shall try to adopt a more critical and detached attitude toward the enthusiasms of the dominant culture and pay attention to the constraining features as well.

The idea of a dominant Protestant culture may be contradicted by pointing to the presence of ethnics and blacks on the ballots in electoral campaigns and the lesser importance of WASP credentials in reaching high office in the business and political world these days. Today, we have Spiro Agnew (Greek), Frank Rizzo (Italian), Andrew Young and Kenneth Gibson (black), Tip O'Neill (Irish) to remind us that the WASPs, to some extent, have been shouldered aside and their place taken by aggressive and able spokesmen from diverse ethnic groups. What we are speaking of here, however, is the persistence of a basic set of attitudes, ideas, and practices, received from the past and injected into the culture by a dominant group. It makes little difference that the WASPs have retired from the playing field if the team that replaces them continues to play by the rules which they established. The idea of a dissociated, choice-making individual, which underlies the consumer world, political parties, and social life, is one example among others of the persistence of a powerful idea transmitted by the dominant culture. Insofar as ethnics and blacks are shaped by this idea, and they are, they have not so much altered the culture but changed its outward manifestations.

To say that the members of the dominant culture have lost position and influence is not the same as saying that they are out of the picture. WASPs still continue to exercise a direct influence on the political life of the nation in disproportion to their numbers. A heavily WASP-oriented Republican convention renominated Richard Nixon in 1972. A careful student of American culture, dubbing the convention style "fashionable Protestantism," provides a revealing profile:

> The group was laughably WASP—2% Negro (vs. 11% of the population), 2% Jew (vs. 3% of the population), 15% Catholic (vs. 23% of the population). Not only was the group 82% Protestant (vs. 35% of the population); the leading denomination was Episcopalian (16% vs. 2% of the population), and the lowest was Baptist (7% vs. 13% of the population). . . . The pattern of privilege showed up even in terms of military service. Most of the men were veterans (81%)—Korea and World War II, of course, not Vietnam; and the branch best represented was the Air Force (35% vs. 31% from the Army). These were people in the summer of their middle age (49 years old) and 85% of them had been to college. Almost half belonged to the local Chamber of Commerce, almost a third to the American legion, a fourth to the Masons.[17]

The median income of the delegates, he notes, was twenty thousand dollars a year.

Let us turn from the dominant culture in late maturity to the time of its genesis. The colonists who participated in the American Revolution and ratified the results of the Philadelphia convention were overwhelmingly British Protestant. They constituted at least 75 percent of the three million whites who made up the new nation. Their composition was chiefly English and Scottish leavened by a considerable number of Dutch, Swedish, German, and Irish settlers. Their arrival on these shores took place roughly in the period between the founding of Jamestown (1607) and the outbreak of the American Revolution (1776). In addition to the dominant white population, there were about three-quarters of a million blacks.[18]

The priority of the dominant commercial Protestant element gave them a decisive edge over the successive waves of immigrants who came to America in the nineteenth and early twentieth centuries. The dominant culture is established in the key positions in the professions, public office, trade, and universities. Their influence is exerted through a process of acculturation, not assimilation. By acculturation I mean that the language, political and social values, forms of dress and entertainment, and patterns of work of the dominant culture are adopted. But to a considerable extent, the new ethnic groups sought their intimate friends and marriage partners and live among the members of their own groups. Assimilation of the over thirty-five million new arrivals did not occur.

Although America was spared billboards in the 1830s, the "choice-making individual" was there. To repeat and underline, this is the same figure we have encountered before in the social theories of Hobbes and Locke, and who improvised a whole new set of social, political, and economic arrangements suited to the temper of commercial Protestantism in seventeenth-century England. Commenting on the social characteristics of Americans, Toqueville, a commentator on whom we have relied several times, says,

> The first thing that strikes the observation is an inumerable multitude of men, all equal and alike, incessantly endeavoring to secure the petty and paltry pleasures with which they glut their lives. Each of them, living apart, is a stranger to all the rest; his children and his private friends constitute to him the whole of mankind . . . he exists only in himself and for himself alone; and if his kindred still remain to him, he may be said at any rate to have lost mankind.[19]

The function of the dominant culture, in the beginning and now, is to transmit the values of commercial Protestantism—now we call it derisively the WASP culture—and in so doing, to sustain government in its liberal democratic heritage. Commercial Protestant culture is the womb from which issues all the major ideas of liberalism. Matters we treat as an article of faith—government by consent, sanctity of private conscience and private property, free choice, the merely policing minimal state—became so because of the WASP culture. It shapes the whole structure of our thoughts and aspirations. Already in the eighteenth century Jefferson associates the ideas of liberalism with the "lawes of nature and nature's God," as if to say things could never be any different. The dominant culture is a continuum, without clear beginning or end; it encourages some lines of thought and action and subtly, without our noticing, removes other possibilities from consideration.

One reason the liberal consensus triumphs in America is that natural (physical and social) conditions assist the work of the dominant culture and of political institutions. To a great extent, America *was* the dramatic setting visualized by Hobbes and Locke as the state of nature. The early liberal theorists use this idea, as we said before, as a fiction conveniently symbolizing the conditions of radical equality favored by the Protestants and as a scare tactic to get men to accept the institution of government. Hobbes is especially good in picturing the horrors that would follow if one took away the coercive power of the state. But Hobbes and Locke knew that the prediction of social chaos and the assertion of radical equality were untrue. Feudal institutions and the class structure of England possessed residual strength even after the period of the civil wars and the Glorious Revolution had run their course. Hence, the state of nature was denied a convincing basis in reality.

In America, the situation changes dramatically. The physical and social circumstances of America, in the beginning, collaborated with the liberal theory of the origins of the state. The frontier and the equality of men provided theory with a convincing basis in reality. It is worth repeating the words of a historian who writes that in America "history was out on a lark, out to tease men by imitating their dreams with satiric accuracy."[20]

One of the important features of the new landscape, providing a basis in substance for the liberal vision, was the availability of land. It is no exaggeration, an economist writes, to say that, "land was the single most important fact distinguishing the New World from the Old."[21] The nation could afford to give away land, he notes, and for the better part of the nineteenth century it did so. Two-thirds of the land that is now the forty-eight continental states was transferred from public to private ownership. The Homestead Act of 1862 and the Reclamation Act of 1902 were rooted in Locke's, Jefferson's, and Jackson's visions of a nation of small resident farmers.

In the circumstances of the American frontier, Locke's *Second Treatise* became the manual for social, political, and economic organization. It showed the "Industrious and the Rational" how to go about acquiring riches (through grabbing and holding on), instituting government (through compacts between individuals), and treating neighbors (with respect tinged with diffidence). Not until later was it realized that the laissez-faire policy which guided frontier settlement benefited influential interests—coal, mining, timber, and railroad companies—more than the small resident farmers for whom it was said to be aimed.

As we look out across the American landscape today, we can see that the enthusiasms of the frontier have not changed. They have only taken a new direction. Most male Americans believe, as an article of faith, that the pursuit of happiness entitles them to a free-standing home on a half acre of ground in suburbia. Included in the vision is a two-car garage, an expressway to the place of work, a microwave oven in the kitchen, a color television in the living room, and a wife to manage the details of existence. The West was won in the standard Lockian fashion of grabbing and holding on to land, unlimitedly, as it opened up for settlement. Now the country has opened up a new frontier of shopping malls, freeway oases, Dairy Queens, suburban developments, car lots, X-rated drive-in theaters, filling stations, and other kinds of commercial dross. So driven is the nation by the restless, acquisitive, enterprising spirit of liberalism, that it seems more like a movement than a vessel. America has flung cities into space and covered the country with a lattice of steel and concrete highways (at a cost of $62 billion and up).[22] Thus the country now carries the imprint of the spirit of the American people.

The conditions of equality were also more perfectly realized in America than in England. The inequalities of condition present in America were not a function, as they often were in England, of social rank and station. The titles and privileges of social class were prohibited by the Constitution and they had no basis in the sentiments of the people. Americans, as Toqueville put it, were "born equal" in the sense that they were never required, as a people, to throw off the class structures of feudal society.[23] They were a democratic people from the start. Madison said that the United States was a new experiment in the creation of an "unmixed and extensive" republic. By "unmixed" he meant representative institutions which had their foundation in the people, viewed as a collection of individuals, not a layering of social classes.[24]

Of course, there were inequalities in condition, but they were a function of wealth, sex, and the color of one's skin, not hereditary class. The view among those who counted, the British Protestant commercial class, was that inequalities of condition would be remedied in time by the equality of men in their rights. The deserving among men would take advantage of their equal rights to improve their social and economic position. A social philosophy of "pulling yourself up by the bootstraps" was present in America as early as the eighteenth century. For this reason, liberals can be extraordinarily complacent about racial, sexual, and economic inequality. As long as there is no inequality of birth, "all men are created equal," then men *are* equal. A shrewd observer in the eighteenth century forecast that radical equality would lead in time to radical inequality.

> They [the Americans] all feel that nature has made them equal in respect to their rights; or rather that nature has given them a common and equal right to liberty, to property, and to safety; to justice, government, laws, religion and freedom. They all see that nature has made them unequal in respect to their original powers, capacities, and talents. They become united in claiming and preserving the equality which nature has assigned them; and in availing oneself of the benefits . . . derived from the inequality which nature has also established.[25]

Nineteenth-century WASP culture sought, after the manner of Hobbes and Locke, to free choice-making individuals from government and social responsibilities which might interfere with their right to go their own way. The main vehicles of the Protestant culture at this time were Social Darwinism and Transcendentalism. These schools appeared to encourage rival concerns, the former exhorting individuals to accumulate wealth, and the latter to confront the self in isolation. But they agreed that the most important goods in life were in the private sphere, not in the public, and consequently, they both waged holy war against the state and society in a common crusade to elevate the claims of the individual. They sought to restrict the function of the state, as had Hobbes and Locke before them, to providing a framework of order within which people can pursue private satisfaction free from public interference.

Thoreau, a spokesman for the transcendentalist view, says that government is "an expedient by which men would fain succeed in letting each other alone." To this he adds, "When it is most expedient, the governed are most let alone by it."[26] He says that the maxim that the "government is best which governs least" can be improved on. "That government is best which governs not at all."[27] The transcendentalist attack on the state links up with the Social Darwinist views of William Graham Sumner. Like Thoreau, Sumner was an advocate of the merely policing minimal state. Government should leave the individual alone except to afford protection to persons and possessions from violence. "Liberty for labor and security for earnings are the ends for which civil institutions exist,"[28] and none other. Some thought it was the function of the state to educate, to redistribute wealth, or at least to alleviate misery. Sumner wrote a book in reply called *What Social Classes Owe Each Other*. His answer was succinct, "Nothing." Since social classes owe nothing to each other, the state should not be used as an instrument of social reform. "It cannot be the function of the state to make men happy. They must make themselves happy in their own way, and at their own risk."[29]

The bias of the WASP culture against the state is well known. It transcends political parties, professional occupations, and even markedly different life-styles. For example, in 1976 both Jimmy Carter, the Democratic nominee for president, and Gerald Ford, his Republican opponent, took a strong antigovernment position in their campaigns. A favorite, sure-fire way to capture office in America is to run against the government one wants to take charge of. In 1974, two years before the presidential race, Carter gave Gerald Rafshoon, his media man, a list of words and slogans to use in the campaign. At the top of the list was "not from Washington." The Carter team based its campaign headquarters in Atlanta, instead of the customary Washington site, to dramatize the distance, both geographical and ideological, from the national government. In his primary campaign talks, Carter often reminded the voters, "I haven't been part of the Washington scene."[30]

Ford was another echo of the dominant culture. His favorite line, first used in the acceptance speech and on many occasions thereafter, was "A government big enough to give you everything you want is big enough to take from you everything you have." In 1976, Ford narrowly won the Republican nomination from Ronald Reagan, who brings to the WASP antistate bias movie-star quality. A typical Reagan utterance during the primary campaign was as follows: "It is time to give back to the people of this country the right to run their own country and determine their own destiny—and that has been taken away from us by the central government in Washington, D.C."[31] In his second inaugural address, Richard Nixon expressed the antistate view in language reminiscent of Thoreau and Sumner: "Ask not what your country can do for you," he said; "ask what you can do for yourself."

The joining together of a dominant class interest behind a cultural view of diminishing relevance, backed by the coercive power of the state, suggests that the actual substance of the constitutional system is being eroded although preserved in external forms. Coercion is prescribed for the lower classes and capitalism for competitive capital; concurrently, WASP rhetoric diverts the public from the use of the state as a source of capital accumulation by corporate industry. This schizophrenia is strikingly evident in the policies and public statements of the Reagan administration. Rhetorically, the president assures us that we live in a seventeenth-century world of possessive individualism, thus providing competitive capital and the lower classes with a rationale for budget cutbacks and reduced public services. Operationally, however, the president supports a range of measures—loan guarantees, an adjusted tax structure, an improved regulatory climate, import restrictions, and subsidies—whose chief beneficiary is twentieth-century corporate capital. The president appears not to be aware that he is living in two worlds at once, nor of the profound differences separating them.

Were the dominant culture wholly to succeed in its work of acculturation, we would regard the liberal consensus as identical with pure nature. This reflection prompts a review of features of ethnic culture and the counterculture. These cultural patterns tend to look at the nature and possibilities of human relationships in a different manner, and this difference has produced tension with established political institutions. Ethnic culture, by and large, has accommodated itself to the patterns of the dominant culture; acculturation but not assimilation has occurred. On the other hand, the counterculture is a self-conscious political and social movement which has broken sharply with the stereotypes of the dominant culture. Whereas ethnic groups have periodically clashed with each other and dominant WASP groups, their goals, like those of the labor movement, have been directed to obtaining a place of relative equality and acceptance within the political system. The counterculture, however, has used violence for differing ends: to challenge the liberal consensus and possibly to establish a new basis for social and political authority.

ETHNIC CULTURE

I was standing in front of a church in the west of Ireland, camera in hand, attempting to record the church which I thought just possibly was the place of my grandfather's baptism. The parish priest, who was out cutting his hedges despite the rain, approached me, noted that I was a new man around here, and introduced himself. I must say I was a bit surprised when on hearing my name, he remarked, "Ah, yes, you'd be the sociologist fellow from Chicago." Then he added, "Would you be wantin' your grandfather's baptismal record now?"

I admitted the idea hadn't occurred to me. He shook his head in discouragement. "Ah," he said, "fine sociologist you are."

"Do a lot of people come seeking such records?" I asked.

He nodded gravely. "Indeed they do," he said, "indeed they do. These poor people, you know, they've been in the States for three generations and they come seeking roots; they want to know who they are; they want to know all about their past and ancestors. The poor people, I feel so sorry for them. That's why I had all the baptismal records put on microfilm. It makes it a lot easier for people to find their roots."[32]

This story marks the end of a saga in the lives of many American families. Their ancestors severed roots from their homeland to migrate to America; now they grope among the countrysides of Europe for some part of their lost heritage. Over forty-five million men and women, roughly, immigrated to this country between 1820 and 1970, the major waves completed by the outbreak of World War I. The new immigrant groups were preceded, as we have discussed, by a commercial Protestant population of three million whites, whose immigration was complete by the onset of the American Revolution. Although the new arrivals are more diverse, linguistically and ethnically, from the original settlers, and although they soon outnumbered them, nevertheless, the WASP element exerts an imprint on the political culture far greater than its numbers would suggest.

The first large wave of immigration began in the 1840s and extended to the beginning of the Civil War. In the 1840s some 200,000 immigrants were arriving annually from Britain, Ireland, and Germany. In 1857, a peak year, the Irish famine drove 400,000 people to these shores.

The second wave of immigration, starting in the years following the Civil War and extending to the beginning of the twentieth century, brought millions more. This wave was marked by the inclusion of Scandinavians and many people from eastern Europe as well as the more conventional stock of British, Irish, and Germans. The rate of immigration increased during this period. "In fifteen of the thirty-five years from 1865 to 1900 the annual influx went beyond 400,000 with some 800,000 entering in 1882 alone."[33]

The final population wave, stretching over fifteen years from the turn of the century to World War I, outstripped all previous levels of immigration. A million or more people were now coming to America annually. New groups, the Italians, Polish, Austrians, Russians, and Greeks, were added to immigrant stocks. A halt was called to the successive tides of immigration from European countries at the conclusion of World War I. Restrictive legislation, chiefly directed at non-European populations, made it much more difficult to immigrate to America after this period.[34]

By virtue of immigration, the nation has grown from a population of 3.9 million at the time of the first census in 1790 to 203 million in the 1970 census. The most significant cause of population growth, much greater than births, is immigration. Everyone in this country with the exception of the Indians, the only truly native population, can trace his or her ancestry to the arrival of immigrants from Europe, Africa, Latin America, or the Far East. Immigration from European countries has now slowed to a trickle. In 1973, for the first time in history, more Asian than European immigrants entered the United States. Almost 100,000 from the Far East immigrate to the United States each year.

At this time the major ethnic components of the population are 30 million from Great Britain, 25 million from Germany, 22 million from

Africa, 17 million from Ireland, 10 million of Spanish heritage of whom at least 5 million are Mexican, 9 or 10 million from Italy.

The notion that ethnic groups would "melt" into the dominant British Protestant culture has been discarded. Ethnic groups have shown a remarkable resistance toward assimilation. One explanation for this resistance is that the ethnic group provides an avenue for the acquisition of social, economic, and political power, a sort of "interest" group.[35] It comes into existence because of common origin and cultural background and remains in existence because it furnishes a useful basis for advancement. Ethnic group identity among the Irish, Italians, and Jews tends to bear out this analysis. The political machines of the late Mayor Richard Daley of Chicago, an Irishman, and Mayor Frank Rizzo of Philadelphia, an Italian, demonstrate that clannishness has its uses. The Liberal party in New York City was built on the Jewish vote concentrated in the garment industry.

Another explanation for the survival of ethnic groups is suggested in the quotation that opened this discussion. It can be summarized in a single word, *roots.* This is a value that the dominant culture cannot confer. For this reason, some contemporary spokesmen for ethnic groups reject the goals of acculturation and assimilation. In 1976, a nationwide television audience of sixty million people saw a drama of the African origins of an American family. Entitled "Roots," it dealt with several generations of a black American family, from the moment of captivity in Africa to their eventual release from slavery in the American setting. By implication, the drama encouraged blacks to seek their identity within their African heritage, not within the dominant culture.[36]

The cultural discontent expressed by "Roots" is fed by the poverty, chronic unemployment, malnutrition, and depressed neighborhoods suffered by the members of the black community. Statistics help to tell a part of the story. About one-third of the black population—7.4 million people—lives below the poverty line. The unemployment rate for blacks is about 12 percent, twice that for whites. Among young blacks in urban settings, the unemployment rate may exceed 40 percent. Almost a quarter of all black families receives some form of public assistance compared to one white family in twenty. Black per capita income is about 60 percent of white median income; in 1973, for example, blacks had a median income of $7,596 compared to $12,595 for whites.

Similarly, "persons of Spanish heritage," a category that includes 5.25 million persons of Mexican descent, living mostly in the Southwest and California, and about 1.5 million Puerto Ricans, most of whom live in New York City, are victims of extreme hardship. Twenty-five percent of the nine million Americans claiming Spanish heritage live below the poverty line. Their median family income is slightly better than the figure for blacks but well below the income level of white families. As in the black community, there is a tendency toward insularity, a cultivation of ethnic pride, and an aloof attitude toward assimilation.

Where the lines of ethnic division coincide with significant deprivation, political discontent is greatly accentuated and class warfare may result. As an example of such feeling, one black intellectual, a former Detroit automobile assembly line worker, asserts that the black factory hand is the most exploited of all social groups. They are, he says, "the last hired and the first fired"; they suffer not only from the practices of management but also from the prejudices of their associates in the labor unions. He argues that "inside each American, from top to bottom, in various degrees, has been accumulated all the corruption of a class society, which has achieved its magnificent technological progress first and always by exploiting the Negro race and then by exploiting the immigrants of all races."[37] A similar attitude is expressed by César Chavez, president of the United Farm Workers, in behalf of Mexican-American immigrant workers exploited during the picking season. White workers and professionals sometimes respond by asserting that "reverse discrimination" has overcompensated submerged groups for their previous hardships. We shall consider an example of this outlook later in the Bakke case (Chapter 11).

The course events will take is unknown. Some say that an acculturated black bourgeosie will smother militant demands. Others view black disaffection with the dominant culture, coupled with the aggressiveness of Mexican-American immigrant farm workers, as an ominous sign, especially when these attitudes are linked to the counterculture.

THE COUNTERCULTURE

The theme we have pursued is that Americans, both the wealthy and the underclasses, are mesmerized by the liberal vision of the terms of political conflict. To this day, when the 500 largest industrial corporations in the United States employ over 14 million people and deploy a combined net worth of over 600 billion dollars, when it is clear that the "technostructure" (corporate personnel with requisite managerial skills and technical expertise) of these enterprises have a major influence in political affairs, when surveys reveal that the technostructure is to an increasing degree internally self-perpetuating,[38] social and political groups still visualize the terms of conflict as a battle among lonely and isolated figures, like Clint Eastwood cornering his adversary in a deserted farm house. To put it another way, Americans tend to regard themselves as the choice-making individuals on the highway billboard, without noticing that different social and economic groups are much differently situated in terms of their capacity to realize their choices. By training attention on the narrow band of the conflict in which the public is engaged, the dominant culture helps underwrite the efficacy of an eighteenth-century constitutional system.

Because of the overwhelming triumph of the liberal consensus, one may argue that cultural reappraisal is a necessary preliminary to the consideration of proposals for political change. Labor groups that have directly challenged established "capitalist" groups in the American arena, for example, the International Workers of the World in the 1920s, have been the victims of lynchings and mob reprisals as well as the objects of official oppression. In a setting where all laborers regard themselves as members of the middle class and "expectant capitalists," how could it be otherwise? Cultural reappraisal is the main line of approach taken by members of the counterculture in response to the unique situation of radicalism in America. Aware that radical criticism of institutions is more likely to be misunderstood than subjected to official oppression, they have sought to force members of the dominant culture to reexamine cultural stereotypes and hidden presumptions, and at the minimum, to come to terms with their basic position.

The counterculture refers to a state of mind among a loose collection of intellectuals, blacks, students, women's consciousness groups, labor spokesmen, and environmentalists. As is the case with any new cultural movement, its membership and direction of change is not clearly spelled out. Some of the observable features of the movement are a disregard for the canons of material success and respectability, a rejection of a deodorized and sanitized version of nature ("the plastic setup"), an affinity for communal styles of living, an aversion for the stereotypes of masculine and feminine behavior, and a concern over the progressive obliteration of nature as the "other" (wilderness).[39] The most arresting feature of the counterculture, in relation to the themes developed so far, is that human nature is, in essence, social. The counterculture views a human as an "ensemble of social relations,"[40] that is, a creature who creates, at the same time that he or she is created by, social relationships, rather than the "independently situated actor," a radically nonsocial being whose principal endeavor is extending and amplifying the range of personal choice. This view of human nature pits the counterculture against the dominant culture and links it to a wide cross-section of attitudes among various groups.

The touchstone of this social outlook is that all persons are creative social wills, and as such, they knowingly fulfill themselves in the context of their social needs and resources. Each person is essentially active, a producer confronting nature, but also potentially an artist. All persons, to the extent of their capabilities and opportunities, knowingly embody themselves in their work, whether it is medicine, electronics, farming, hard rock, theater, or welding. In short, people are what they do, but social arrangements should not preclude their doing what they might become. When usefully directed, the productive activity of a man or woman provides the material basis through which others might achieve a release of their creative energies. Social and political arrangements, in this view, should seek to reconcile the aesthetic, productive, and social needs of a person's nature.[41] As a case in point, men should share in the household routine, and managers in the stupefying tasks of assembly-line production. For labor is the specific agency that shapes the world, humanizes it, and helps us to overcome separation from it, ourselves, and our friends.

The attitudes of the counterculture are sometimes found on the fringes of the labor force, not among the union bosses but among some of the workers. Mike Lefevre, a steelworker who lives in Cicero, Illinois, gives concrete expression to these views, as yet unrepresented by official labor spokesmen. Lefevre, who is thirty-seven years old, married, and lives in a two-apartment dwelling with his wife and two children, spends most of his day "pulling steel," that is, loading and unloading bars of steel weighing from 3 to 4 pounds to 400 pounds. Levevre's life, as he is intensely aware, is one-dimensional, for he divides his time between *work,* a period in which mental activity is suspended for the mulish requirements of the job, and *play* (watching television and idling about), a release from work but very like it in requiring minimal thought. *Leisure,* creative time, is missing, and though Lefevre does not have it, he is unusually sensitive to its loss.

Lefevre is a complex man striking out in many directions at once. He is aware that he has been robbed of his leisure and dreams of opening a tavern cum bookstore where laborers and college kids, the ultimate symbol of the leisure class, can get together and talk over ideas.

> I'd like to run a combination bookstore and tavern. (Laughs.) I would like to have a place where college kids came and a steelworker could sit down and talk. Where a workingman could not be ashamed of Walt Whitman and where a college professor could not be ashamed that he painted his house over the weekend.[42]

He knows there cannot be enough compensation for meaningless work and fantasizes about the existence of a building "with all the names" of those who took part in building it.

> I would like to see a building, say, the Empire State, I would like to
> see on one side of it a foot wide strip from top to bottom with the name
> of every bricklayer, the name of every electrician, with all the names. So
> when a guy walked by, he could take his son and say, "See that's me over
> on the forty-fifth floor. I put the steel I-beam in. . . ." Everyone should have
> something to point to.[43]

Lefevre is conscious of the difficulties and ambiguities of holding particular individuals responsible for the failures of an entire system.

> Who you gonna sock? You can't sock General Motors, you can't sock
> anybody in Washington, you can't sock a system.[44]

When Lefevre is not fantasizing or dreaming or smoldering with rage,
he focuses steadfastly, not on social change, in which he has little
confidence, but on the "continuum." Lefevre sees no hope for himself
but believes that he will live on through his children.

> This is gonna sound square but my kid is my imprint. He's my free-
> dom. There's a line in one of Hemingway's books. I think it's from *For Whom*
> *the Bell Tolls.* They're behind the enemy lines, somewhere in Spain, and she's
> pregnant. She wants to stay with him. He tells her no. He says, "if you die,
> I die," knowing he's gonna die. But if you go, I go. Know what I mean? The
> mystics call it the brass bowl. Continuum. . . . This is why I work.[45]

"How do you sock a system?" Good question. Another question:
"What is the system that Lefevre wishes to sock?" He is close to the
charge of Marx that the relationships of production in a capitalist society produce an intolerable blockage of life's possibilities. People work
not for themselves but for a wage, or profits, and at tasks that bear only
a minimal relation to their artistic potential. Men and women struggle
dumbly in a world of flattened perspectives, moving from home to
factory, work to play, anger to infantile fantasy, because capitalist relations of production set them against others and themselves and deprive
them of satisfaction in the fruits of their labor. By the references to
"Washington" and "General Motors," Lefevre may be using a short-
hand to refer to twentieth-century corporate capitalism and the cluster
of institutions set in motion by eighteenth-century constitutionalism.
Possibly Lefevre believes with Marx that these institutions prevent
movement toward a reconciliation of the diverse aspects of human
nature and a more humane society. Whatever his disclaimers about the
futility of "socking a system" or the satisfactions of the continuum, it
is sufficiently clear that men such as Lefevre offer potential grounds for

class conflict and political upheaval. When linked to the views of some among the spokesmen for ethnic groups, they reveal a "system" resting on insecure foundations.

SUMMARY

The figure on the billboard better reminds us of our constraints—that is the main point of this exploration—than our liberties.

The figure symbolizes the constraints of private affluence in the midst of public squalor. Plainly, he has the cash to realize personal choices in consumer trivia. But if we observe carefully, we may notice that the billboard figure is often parked atop a dirty collection of buildings, maybe some of them abandoned, in one of the less select areas of the inner city. His view is impeded by wire and adjacent buildings, and he must stare into the face of a competitor, pushing a different brand, from across the street. His ears are assailed by noise from the traffic below, trash swirls beneath his feet, and it is likely that his eyes smart from the exhaust fumes which hang suspended in the air. The underclasses suffer most from an inequitable distribution of goods and services, but all, including the presumed beneficiaries of the system, suffer from an improper mix of public and private spending.

Additionally, the billboard figure is a cultural stereotype, a product of conventional minds, and he seems not to notice that the "pursuit of happiness" requires that we all go on pursuing the same things in the same way. The range of personal choice is confined to the consumer products of corporate enterprise. We are better informed about the rival claims of cornflakes or cigarettes than about the capacities of public persons and of public institutions. We are taught to exercise fine powers of discrimination in choosing beer, toothpaste, soap, and sundries but seem untroubled by the uneven quality of our urban life. One cultural critic writes that the survival of political institutions in America depends on ignoring politics and worrying instead "about the means of defeating underarm odor, scaly scalp, hairy legs, dull complexion, unruly hair, borderline anemia, athlete's foot, and sluggish bowels, not to mention ferro-nutritional deficiency of the blood, wash-day blues, saggy breasts, receding gums, shiny pants, greying hair, and excess weight."[46] In other words, stability is preserved by endlessly diverting the public with trivia.

The dominant culture is under attack from the counterculture and some elements of ethnic groups. Presently, the chief standard bearer of the dominant culture is an elderly movie actor whose main ideas on social policy are derived from a fascination with the days of the wild

West. Ronald Reagan, whose qualifications chiefly lie in the art of inducing a willing suspension of disbelief, lends an air of credibility to the dominant culture through his formidable acting skills. It is some indication of the mental state of this culture that it is now dependent on fantasy for its survival. But a culture dependent on fantasy is a dead culture. Thus, a cultural interregnum exists in America: one world is dead and the other is struggling to be born.

NOTES

1. Raymond Williams, "Culture," *The Encyclopedia of Philosophy* (New York: Macmillan, The Free Press, 1967).
2. This phrase was suggested to me by H. Mark Roelofs; it happily combines luminous meaning and simplicity.
3. Sidney Verba and Norman H. Nie, *Participation in America* (New York: Harper & Row, 1972), p. 176.
4. Frank J. Sorauf, *Party Politics in America,* 2nd ed. (Boston: Little, Brown, 1972); V. O. Key, *Politics, Parties and Pressure Groups,* 4th ed. (New York: Thomas Y. Crowell, 1958).
5. Kennath Turan, "Clint Eastwood: Mixed Metaphor for Our Time," *Washington Post,* December 23, 1976, C1.
6. Douglas F. Dowd, *The Twisted Dream* (Cambridge, Mass.: Winthrop Publishers, 1974), p. 130; Godfrey Hodgson, *America in Our Time* (New York: Doubleday, 1976), p. 76.
7. Dowd, *Twisted Dream,* p. 286.
8. *Ibid.,* pp. 121–25.
9. See Richard Rubenstein, *Rebels in Eden* (Boston: Little, Brown, 1970), chap. 4; Dowd, *Twisted Dream,* pp. 130–35; Hodgson, *America in Our Time,* chap. 4; Derek C. Bok and John T. Dunlop, *Labor and the American Community* (New York: Simon & Schuster, 1970), chap. 2.
10. Victor Gotbaum, "The Philosophy of a Unionist," *The New York Times,* June 8, 1971, p. 37.
11. Louis Hartz, *The Liberal Tradition in America* (New York: Harcourt, Brace & World, 1960), chap. 10; Thurman Arnold, *The Folklore of Capitalism* (New Haven, Conn.: Yale University Press, 1937).
12. David Vogel, "Why Businessmen Mistrust Their State: The Political Consciousness of American Corporate Executives," Prepared for Delivery at the American Political Science Association Convention, The Palmer House, Chicago, Illinois, September 2–5, 1976.
13. John Kenneth Galbraith, *The New Industrial State* (New York: Signet, 1967).
14. Rubenstein, *Rebels in Eden;* Peter K. Eisinger, "Understanding Urban Politics: Urban Political Conflict," *Polity,* Fall 1976, pp. 219–39.
15. "Transcript of the President's News Conference," *The New York Times,* October 14, 1977, A16.

16. Quoted in John M. Cammett, *Antonio Gramsci and the Origins of Italian Communism* (Stanford, Cal.: Stanford University Press, 1967), p. 204.

17. Garry Wills, *Nixon Agonistes* (New York: Signet, 1971), pp. 220–21.

18. Will Herberg, *Protestant–Catholic–Jew* (New York: Anchor Books, 1960), chap. 2; and Andrew M. Greeley, *Why Can't They Be Like Us?* (New York: Dutton, 1975), chap. 1.

19. Alexis de Toqueville, *Democracy in America,* ed. Phillips Bradley (New York: Vintage Books, 1956), vol. 2, p. 336.

20. Hartz, *Liberal Tradition,* p. 60.

21. Geoffrey Faux, "Reclaiming America," in *Exploring Contradictions,* eds. Phillip Brenner *et al.* (New York: David McKay, 1974), chap. 10.

22. William K. Stevens, "The Superhighway System in 20 Years Has Tied a Vast Nation Together," *The New York Times,* November 14, 1976, pp. 1, 68.

23. Toqueville, *Democracy in America,* vol. 2, p. 245.

24. *Federalist* No. 14.

25. Joel Barlow, *Advice to the Priviledged Orders in the Several States of Europe,* as quoted in Gordon S. Wood, *The Creation of the American Republic* (New York: W. W. Norton, 1972), p. 607.

26. Henry David Thoreau, *Walden and Civil Disobedience,* ed. Perry Miller (New York: Signet, 1960), pp. 222, 223.

27. *Ibid.*

28. William Graham Sumner, *What Social Classes Owe Each Other* (Caldwell, Id.: Caxton Printers, 1952), p. 31.

29. *Ibid.*

30. Quoted in Elizabeth Drew, "A Reporter in Washington," *The New Yorker,* May 31, 1976, pp. 56, 93.

31. Drew, *The New Yorker,* May 24, 1976, p. 107.

32. Greeley, *Why Can't They Be Like Us?,* pp. 191–92.

33. Herberg, *Protestant-Catholic-Jew,* pp. 6–8.

34. *Ibid.*

35. Nathan Glazer and Daniel P. Moynihan, *Beyond the Melting Pot* (Cambridge, Mass.: MIT Press, 1963).

36. Alex Haley, *Roots: The Saga of an American Family* (New York: Doubleday, 1974).

37. James Boggs, *The American Revolution* (New York: Monthly Review Press, 1963), p. 45.

38. For a discussion of the "technostructure" see John Kenneth Galbraith, *The New Industrial State* (New York: Signet, 1967); the institutional position of the five hundred largest industrial corporations is described in Robert Presthus, *The Organizational Society,* rev. ed. (New York: St. Martin's Press, 1978), pp. 6–7, 179–80.

39. For representative literature on the attitudes of the counterculture, see Marc Feigen Fasteau, *The Male Machine* (New York: Dell Publishing Co., 1975); Eli Zaretsky, *Capitalism, the Family, and Personal Life* (New York: Harper Colophon Books, 1973); Philip Slater, *The Pursuit of Loneliness* (Boston: Beacon Press, 1970); David Riesman, *The Lonely Crowd* (Clinton, Mass.: The Clinton Press, 1964);

Herbert Marcuse, *An Essay on Liberation* (Boston: Beacon Press, 1969); Herbert Marcuse, *Eros and Civilization* (New York: Vintage Books, 1962); Charles A. Reich, *The Greening of America* (New York: Bantam, 1971); Theodore Roszak, *The Making of a Counterculture* (New York: Anchor Books, 1969).

40. See Erich Fromm, *Marx's Concept of Man* (New York: Ungar, 1964), pp. 100–105, 206.

41. See Lloyd D. Easton and Kurt H. Gudat, eds., *Writings of the Young Marx on Philosophy and Society* (New York: Anchor Books, 1967), p. 281.

42. Studs Terkel, ed., *Working* (New York: Avon Books, 1974), p. 9.

43. *Ibid.,* p. 2.

44. *Ibid.,* pp. 2, 3.

45. *Ibid.,* p. 10.

46. Marshall McLuhan, "American Advertising," in *Mass Culture: The Popular Arts in America,* eds. Bernard Rosenberg and David White, (New York: The Free Press, 1957), p. 435.

CHAPTER 7

The Federal System

Federal arrangements have been a frequent occasion of dispute among the national and state and local governments. These disputes tend to be cast in the language of legal rights (state sovereignty, states' rights, reserved powers) remote from the racial, economic, and regional grievances that inspired them.

For example, the Whiskey Rebellion (1791), an uprising of Pennsylvania farmers against federal tax collectors, was not so much about states' rights, as some of the protagonists claimed, as whether the federal government could tax corn liquor, a local medium of currency. The Hartford convention (1812), which raised the issue of secession for the first time, concerned New England fears of being overshadowed in the national legislature by westward expansion and Southern dynasty. In the pre–Civil War period the South claimed a legal right of independence partly as a means of deflecting discussion from the issue of the future status of the slave. A similar tack was taken by segregationists in the 1950s and 1960s who wished to prevent integration of black children in the public schools. "States' rights" is a thin disguise of the Western states involved in the "sagebrush rebellion" to permit them an uninhibited exploitation of mineral resources.

These examples are worth remembering because the issue of states' rights has been raised once more (and probably not for the last time), and as before, the causes which surround the legal issue have not been brought into full public view. In his inaugural address, President Reagan declared that failure to recognize the distinction between "the powers granted to the Federal Government and those reserved to the states or to the people" was one of the principal reasons that government had grown in size "beyond the consent of the governed." A restoration of the proper relationships between the state and local governments and the federal government, Mr. Reagan suggested, was one of the most important tasks facing his administration. Such a restoration would

159

contribute significantly to the problem of reducing the overweening size of the federal administration. His tenure in office, he added, was distinguished from the preceding one by its understanding that in the "present crisis" the "government is not the solution to our problem; government is the problem."

As in other times, the controversy over federal arrangements raised by President Reagan's remarks has its source in profound and unsettling political issues. These issues have come to the surface as Reagan has set about dismantling the federal administration and restoring power to the states. At stake, as I shall further develop in the next chapter, is the neo-liberal categorical grants-in-aid programs promoted during the early years of President Johnson's administration (1964). To refresh memory, the neo-liberals observed that the state as descended from Hobbes and Locke protected a narrow scope of human rights. A state that afforded protection merely to private property, free speech, due process, and freedom of religious worship, they argued, was not far removed from the conditions of the state of nature. For the most part, the life of man in civil society continued to be solitary, nasty, poor, and brutish, to paraphrase Hobbes, but now, thanks to the presence of police authority, it was at least somewhat less hazardous and short. By expanding the scope of human entitlements, the neo-liberals said, human potential would be developed and the community, now less dependent on coercion for its survival, would become more of a community. President Johnson grafted this vision of the state to the categorical grants-in-aid program to fashion the Great Society. Anticipating controversy, he targeted specific areas of need—education, legal services, medical care, and nutrition—and he brought the Office of Economic Opportunity, charged with administering the programs, into the White House staff.

President Reagan's attack on a bloated federal bureaucracy is chiefly directed against the Great Society programs inherited from the Johnson administration. Reagan's restoration of federal arrangements, by the same token, is an attempt to return to the ancient cruel beginnings of liberalism, a condition of *homo homini lupus* (man a wolf to man), as Hobbes expressed it, in which the state has a minimal, merely policing, rule over a society of ruthless individualists. Many of the major budget cuts enacted by the Reagan administration are directed to the neo-liberal programs that made up the Great Society: food stamps, medicaid, legal services, and CETA (a successor to the Job Corps). In all, the Reagan administration has eliminated $23.9 billion in categorical grants-in-aid, a 20 to 25 percent reduction in federal spending.

By proceeding systematically, we can participate in the debate initiated by President Reagan on the role of the state and federal arrangements. We shall analyze in sequence the definition, development, origin, operation, and significance of the federal system.

DEFINITION

Studies of American federalism tend to disagree on just about everything, including the merits, definition, and function of federalism in America. Those who disagree on its functions prefer one or another level of decision making in the political system. We hear a great deal of talk about state-centered federalism, new federalism, creative federalism, cooperative federalism, and so on. Each of these adjectives is an expression of preference for a particular level of decision making. Calls for direction from the top, or for innovation from the state and local communities, embody conflicting ideas about how federalism should function.

There are also varying ideas about the merits of the federal system, which is approved or disapproved from different viewpoints concerning the goals such a system of political arrangements should serve. Studies say that American federalism is good or bad, efficient or inefficient, workable or unworkable. These judgments are advanced from different perspectives. Those who favor uniform and national treatment of topical and controversial social issues—poverty, race, land use, pollution, mass transit—tend to disapprove of the federal system because the diffusion of power prevents a general solution to these problems. Reform of the federal system is urged to make it more "workable." Others say that the federal system encourages useful experimentation on social issues among the states and that it encourages citizen participation in politics.

Another point of controversy is the definition of federalism. Controversies over the merits and functions of federalism affect the distribution of power and resources and are, therefore, a matter of appropriate political concern. But a war, the Civil War, has been fought over conflicting definitions. The issue the war posed was whether state sovereignty was consistent with the existence of a legally unified nation. The answer settled by the outcome of the war was *no.* Yet we still hear plenty of talk today about state sovereignty, the erroneous theory of federalism on which the actions of the Southern secessionists was based. Before we make any judgments about the merits and functions of the federal system, we should try to develop an understanding of what it is.

DUAL FEDERALISM

In the traditional view of federalism that prevailed over much of the first 150 years of national existence, the federal and state governments were seen as essentially separate sovereignties, with clearly demarked and independent spheres of activity. These two governments, federal and state, derived their authority from the Constitution, and the authority of the Constitution was based on the consent of the states, not the people. One of the governments operated in the national sphere over matters that were national in scope. The other government operated in the state and local sphere over matters that were statewide and local in nature. Each of the two governments was supreme within its authorized sphere of action. It was the function of the Supreme Court to define these spheres of action, determining whether a matter was national, state and local, or something over which the national and state governments had concurrent jurisdiction. States' rights enthusiasts argued that the Tenth Amendment to the Constitution acted as a positive limitation on the powers of the national government. Only those powers expressly delegated to the national government could be exercised. This view of federalism is summed up in an opinion of Chief Justice Taney in 1859:

> The powers of the General Government, and of the State, although both exist and are exercised within the same territorial limits, are yet separate and distinct sovereignties, acting separately and independently of each other, within their respective spheres.[1]

CENTRALIZED FEDERALISM

In the decades since the New Deal the idea of dual federalism has been discarded by most thoughtful people. The most serious objection to this idea is that it is illogical. There cannot be two "sovereign," or highest, authorities, exercising final authority over the same territorial sphere. One must be the true sovereign. The idea that has come to replace dual sovereignty is that the people have vested final authority in one government, the government of the United States. This sovereignty is undivided but its powers are distributed among rival institutions—federal, state, and local. Each of these institutions shares extensively in the others' exercise of powers. Therefore, instead of separate governments exercising separate grants of power (dual federalism), we have separate institutions sharing in the power of one government (centralized federalism). This is not to say that the rhetoric of dual federalism is dead. We may still have the spectacle of governors protesting the invasion of "states' rights" by their federal partners, a vivid example being provided in 1963 by Governor Wallace, who stood in the doorway of the University of Alabama to block the admission of Vivian Malone and James Hood, two black students. But this posture, for it is a posture, has become absurd. The notion that states were sovereign never really made sense and was never an accurate reflection of political practice. It is now a relic of history.

For an accurate idea of federalism, we should imagine the U.S. government as a marble cake, with a considerable amount of interpenetration and confusion among its parts.[2] When we visualize the exercise of governmental power, we should visualize the mingling and confusion of the elements in the cake. The image to discard is that federalism is a layer cake, with clear division of power among the federal, state, and local layers of government.

Government regulation of the nuclear power industry provides an illustration of the "marble cake" theory of government at work. The site of a nuclear power plant is jointly decided by state officials in cooperation with county and local governments. In reviewing the merits of a proposed site, these officials will be strongly influenced by the environmental impact statement (assessing the effects on water, air, wildlife, minerals, and economy) drafted under the watchful eye of the Environmental Protection Agency. This is a federal executive agency with offices in ten regions of the country. The interval between site and construction approval and the actual completion of the plant is often as long as twelve years. Once a plant is ready to generate power it must obtain an operating license from the Nuclear Regulatory Commission (NRC), an independent regulatory agency of the federal government. Responsibility for insuring the safe operation of the plant is vested in the NRC once the plant becomes operational. Additionally, the federal government through the Department of Energy is responsible for finding a safe means for disposing of radioactive wastes, a by-product of nuclear fission. In fiscal year 1980 the Department of Energy spent $392 million on problems associated with nuclear waste management.[3] However, the states possess veto power over any federal plan relating to nuclear waste management that affects them. It is also significant that the power to set utility rates for the production of electricity from nuclear plants is vested in state public utility commissions. Last, the nuclear power industry, a highly capital intensive industry associated with substantial risk, could not have been initiated without federal support. It is estimated that the federal government has spent between $17 and $24 billion to date on research support for nuclear plant generation.[4]

The elements of this mingling and confusion of functions were brought into sharp focus by the events surrounding the partial meltdown of a nuclear reactor containment vessel at Three Mile Island, Pennsylvania, on March 2, 1979. A relief valve, intended to drain off excess water from the floor of the reactor pile, stuck open, causing a loss of coolant water and precipitating intense heat, which threatened to burn through the containment vessel. In the glare of publicity that followed the accident, it emerged that officials of Metropolitan Edison, the staff operating and managing the plant, were less than fully candid about the extent of the emergency. State and local officials, on the other hand, lacked the experience and competence to deal with a crisis of this magnitude. Consequently, for a period of almost a week following the LOCA (loss of coolant accident), officials of the NRC performed many of the key functions of plant management and dispensed information to the public. In the aftermath of the accident the vexing problem of the future of the plant at that site (and to a large extent, the nuclear industry as a whole) was divided again among federal, state, and local officials. The state public utility commission would decide whether negligence by the electric company required it to absorb the greatly increased expense of purchasing power from outside sources, or whether this expense would be apportioned among consumers in the immediate area. Reorganization of the NRC was recommended by a blue ribbon commission appointed by President Carter to improve supervision of plant operations of the nuclear industry.[5]

The mixture of responsibilities varies among federal, state, and local governmental units according to the function. In the allocation of responsibilities the federal government takes a lead role in weapons research, defense, atomic energy development, post office, space exploration, and energy security. State and local governments have a greater priority in education, police protection, fire fighting, and sanitation. Yet even in these areas there is a mingling and confusion of functions. The large point is that all areas of American government are all involved in all functions.

The American federal system is best conceived as one government serving one people. When we say the "people," we mean the people, taken one by one, as Hobbes and Locke referred to the people, consenting to government as the product of agreements between individuals. The one government is to exercise the total and unrestrained sovereignty which is each person's in the state of nature. The sovereignty of the government is not divided; it cannot be. Instead, the use of sovereign power is divided by a deliberate and set policy among many rival institutions.

DEVELOPMENT OF FEDERAL POWER

Politics, economics, and constitutional interpretation have collaborated to break down the barriers among the units of the federal system and to promote the idea of centralized federalism.

CONSTITUTIONAL INTERPRETATION

The power of Congress to regulate commerce has given the federal government great clout in matters formerly considered state and local. This power embraces all activities—most importantly the power to regulate production, even when the effects are local in nature—which affect the movement of articles from one state to another.[6] Thus defined, this is the principal legal tool employed by Congress to regulate the productive machinery of America's industrial economy. Among the many activities and properties regulated by Congress are labor and race relations; allocation of refined petroleum; the sale of food and drugs; communications and transportation; residential and industrial energy conservation; minimum wages; the price of wheat, cotton, and milk; the marketing of securities; and anticompetitive marketing activities. In the area of commerce there are virtually no barriers to the assertion of federal power. Not for a generation has the Supreme Court invalidated a law of Congress as an invasion of states' rights.

A second path along which federal power has developed is the power to tax and spend for the general welfare.[7] Congress may levy heavy taxes on articles and activities of which it disapproves (white phosphorous matches and gambling), and it may use its tax power to induce states and individuals to undertake certain kinds of programs (unemployment compensation and medical care). To stimulate the creation of state unemployment compensation, Congress set out basic qualifications, established minimal standards of payment, and provided for funding through a tax on all employers. Employers may escape payment of the tax only if they are making a payment to a state program that meets federal guidelines. The states benefit in terms of administrative control and efficiency, if they establish their own programs. All the states, stimulated by the taxing power of the federal government, have done so. Additionally, Congress may regulate behavior by attaching conditions to the spending of federal funds (race relations, for example). The Civil Rights Act of 1964 provides that "No person in the United States shall, on the grounds of race, color, or national origin, be excluded from participation in, be denied the benefits of, or be subjected to discrimination under any program or activity receiving federal financial assistance."

A third path of federal expansion is the power to wage war. The national government is responsible for "the common defense." Ordinarily, by "defense" we mean protective measures against external aggression. Tied to this concept are such legitimate and related functions as recruitment, training and direction of armies, and purchases of weapons and supplies. But the defense function in the modern day has been broadened to include a much greater scope of activities: construction of highways, dams, and bridges; exploration of space; government funding for selected fields of science and research; development of nuclear power; student education in critical fields; and the often abused field of intelligence gathering and research.[8] In these times it seems that the defense power can mean the power to do almost anything. As a case in point, the government relocated many persons of Japanese extraction from the West Coast to internment centers in the middle of the country during World War II. This was held to be a legitimate exercise of the war power by the Supreme Court despite its obvious conflict with constitutional guarantees.[9]

POLITICS

Also encouraging a centralized federalism is the redefinition by political leadership of the boundaries of the federal system and the role of the state. Since the New Deal, attention has focused on national institutions to offset inequalities fostered by a capitalist economy. Presidents are expected to provide national solutions to economic problems whose main effects are felt at the state and local level. The political response to this expectation has generated support for federal assistance to state and local communities, breaking down the conventional boundaries of the federal system, and for the expanded concept of the state embodied in neo-liberal social policy.

As noted earlier, neo-liberalism enlarges the responsibility of the state toward its citizens beyond the familiar freedoms of the Bill of Rights. Not only must the state refrain from interfering with individual rights of speech, property, worship, and assembly, say the neo-liberals, it must also actively seek to extend freedoms that enhance human potential. In this view, the state has an important function in providing housing, education, and health services; protecting the environment from deadly pollutants; nurturing artistic talent; and restoring attractive, humane urban living centers. The freedoms thus protected are often referred to as "positive" since they expand the scope of human development. The "negative" freedoms enshrined by liberal tradition, protecting the individual from state interference, are not discarded by the neo-liberal outlook, only superseded.

The assumption of many state and local problems by national political institutions accompanies the expanded view of the government's role. Many problems thought to be local in nature have been thrust on the national government since the New Deal,[10] a trend accelerated by the Great Society. The Great Society developed the important innovation of joining the grants-in-aid method of distributing federal revenues to the neo-liberal vision of politics. Under this system the federal government sets aside money for housing, welfare assistance, health, cultivation of the arts, security, education, transportation, and pollution control. The states and local communities match this grant with funds of their own and administer the programs under federal control and guidance. These programs directed from Washington are the principal means through which neo-liberal policies have advanced.

The political leadership exerted by President Johnson in behalf of the Great Society illustrates many of the trends just discussed. First unveiled in 1964, the programs were the most ambitious effort in American history to improve the quality of the human environment and the condition of underprivileged groups. Announcing the goals of "Creative Federalism," Johnson stated that programs made possible by national leadership would be carried out by state and local communities. There is no doubt that the volume of federal assistance to the states would have been greater if the nation had not been involved in the Vietnam War at the same time as its "war against poverty."

ECONOMICS

A third reason for the growth of centralized federalism is the economic relationships among the units of the federal system. The expenditures of governments at all levels have increased dramatically in the last two decades. But the revenue sources of the federal government in relation to its expenditures are far more flexible and connected with economic growth than those of the state and local governments. The latter must depend primarily on sales and property taxes; both of these sources tend to grow less rapidly than the economy as a whole and are regressive in their effects. The sales tax is levied on goods regardless of ability to pay. The property tax, which is near its outer limit in many of the old industrial cities of the Northeast, has adverse effects on central city housing stock, applies to all property owners alike regardless of ability to pay, is not fairly assessed, and discriminates against homeowners. Local officials are unwilling to raise property taxes, the only revenue source available to them, despite spiraling expenditures for public services. It is widely regarded as an unfair, unpopular, and inflexible source of revenue.[11]

In contrast, the federal income tax, collected on personal and corporate income, is a "growth" tax. It directly reflects economic growth, providing the federal government with increased tax receipts in an expanding economy. The income tax is also more elastic, flexible, and progressive than sales and property taxes. The federal government, because of the quality of its revenue sources, collects 60 percent of all revenues in the United States. The state governments collect only 21 percent, and local governments only 19 percent of total revenues. What is most important, Washington collects 88 percent of the income tax—the nation's principal growth tax.[12]

These differing tax capacities put pressure on Washington to offset expenses at the local level. In 1954, state and local governments relied on federal aid for 8.5 percent of their revenues; by 1976 the proportion had more than doubled to 19.9 percent. Meanwhile, the amount of federal aid to state and local communities had soared from $3 billion in 1954 to $58 billion in 1976 and $88 billion in 1980. About 17 percent of federal tax revenues is turned back to the states and local communities.

With increasing federal involvement in "local" affairs, the barriers among the units of the federal system have further broken down. Mayors and local officials come directly to Washington, hat in one hand and the other hand outstretched, asking for federal aid. A former mayor of Cleveland put it simply, "Why run to the federal government? Because that's where the money is." A cluster of state, county, and city lobbies now works full time in Washington trying to give the federal assistance spigot another turn.

Federal assistance to the states and local communities occurs in a variety of forms. Seventy-five percent of federal assistance is distributed in the form of "categorical" grants-in-aid. These are grants distributed according to specially designated needs, such as health, safety, law enforcement, education, and research, and according to the ability of recipients to pay matching funds. The poor states have to put up somewhat less in the way of matching funds than the rich ones. Many of the Great Society programs were administered through federal grants-in-aid. This form gives the federal government the most control in targeting the area of need and the means of governmental response.[13]

Twelve percent of federal assistance to the states and local communities is distributed in the form of revenue sharing. Unlike grants-in-aid, there are fewer federal restrictions on the manner in which the money is spent.[14] One-third goes to the states, which may spend it on any normal state activity. Two-thirds goes to the local governments, which must spend it on capital construction or operating costs in eight broad areas: public safety, environment, health, recreation, libraries, social services, financial administration, transportation.

Block grants, which account for about 13 percent of federal assistance to the state and local communities, are more broadly stated than grants-in-aid but narrower in focus than revenue sharing. They bring together grants-in-aid into broad programs that give state and local units some discretion in their direction and use.

This larger discretionary power has brought forth the charge that revenue sharing and block grants are really a hidden means for dismantling programs directed to politically powerless groups. Whereas state governments are often represented as "closer" to the people than an alien bureaucracy in Washington, and therefore better prepared to make decisions affecting their welfare, it is historically the case that the greatest concern for submerged groups has developed at the national level of politics. The most important piece of evidence supporting this view is seen in the Great Society programs. Many of those who are the most vocal in defense of underrepresented groups argue for the retention of categorical grants-in-aid over block grants or revenue sharing for this reason. Former President Carter put the case for categorical grants in these words.

> Categorical grants have been designed as contracts between the Federal government and the state or local government with a clearly understood, predictable sharing responsibility for meeting needs that were identified to be unmet by state and local programs. . . . When these funds are taken away from the poor and put into general revenue sharing or block grants, even the most enlightened legislature is not going to take those funds and put them back into programs that benefit the poor. They are going to spread them uniformly among all citizens.[15]

ORIGIN

The discussion to this point has defined centralized federalism and shown how politics, economics, and constitutional interpretation have worked to develop it further. This is the time to take up a different line of inquiry. What are the merits and functions of federalism in the United States? What purposes does the federal system serve? What are the forces that sustain the federal system both historically and in the present day? These questions are best approached by looking at the intentions of those who framed the federal system, that is, the goals they intended the federal system of political arrangements to serve.

The most developed view of these purposes is found in the *Federalist*

Papers. Hamilton and Madison make clear in these papers that one of the motivating purposes of the elites who framed the constitution was to develop a strong central government, the better to lay taxes and raise armies to defend them from their enemies, both foreign and domestic. The foreign enemies of the founding fathers at that time were England, Spain, and to a lesser degree, France. All the European powers coveted the landed wealth and resources of the New World. Hamilton and Madison never tire of reminding their audience of the dangers which surround them, of foreign powers masquerading as pirates prowling around native shores, and of the trouble and expense of outfitting a navy and a standing army. A federal union, they point out, will have far greater resources at its disposal and, therefore, a greater capability of dealing with external threats to domestic safety.[16]

Hamilton and Madison are equally emphatic about the utility of a centralized federalism in protecting the elite from their enemies at home. Both were keenly sensitive to the hazards of a slave revolt in the Southern colonies and to the dangers of further insurrection by the debtor class. Shays's Rebellion in northern Massachusetts was a reminder, perfectly timed to coincide with the thrust of their argument, of the risks of being inadequately prepared against attacks on property. They point out that a centralized federalism, with adequate police power, will be able to protect the privileged classes against insurrections which the states, individually, would be unable to handle.

Nevertheless, the propertied elite was not just afraid of the lower class and the English, Spanish, and French. They were afraid of each other. Thus Madison and Hamilton assure elites at the state and local level that the police powers of the centralized federalism will not be used against them. Parties in the national sphere will be held in check by rivals for power in the state and local sphere and vice versa.

> Power being almost always the rival of power, the general government will at all times stand ready to check the usurpations of the state governments, and these will have the same disposition towards the general government. . . . If their rights are invaded by either, they can make use of the other as the instrument of redress.[17]

Thus the second basic purpose of the federal system is to manage social conflict. The parties to the conflict are classes, groups, and individuals, and the conflict is waged over the entire federal political landscape. It is a politicized battle of each person against every other person. Conflict is managed by giving parties in the national sphere and parties in the state and local sphere opportunities to seal off threats to their own power.

A third reason for preferring federal arrangements, Madison said, is that it promotes economic freedom. Social conflict is better, he states, than a sacrifice of economic liberties. The optimal arrangement for freedom is a federal system which releases the acquisitive energies of a society of possessive individualists and then manages the ensuing conflict by affording rival economic factions a way to seal off threats to their own power. Federalism, therefore, is a set of practical arrangements designed to foster the ancient enthusiasm of the liberal tradition for private accumulation. Madison referred to this enthusiasm as the "diversity in the faculties" shown by individual men in acquiring and holding on to private property.

The economic ideology that lies behind federal arrangements is sometimes revealed in the modern setting. For example, federalism has been defended by insurance companies and public utilities hoping to escape federal regulation and rate-setting power. It has been promoted by oil companies hoping to win a favorable deal from state legislatures to develop offshore oil. Segregationists and slaveholders, defeated by majorities at the national level, have invoked federal arrangements to obstruct racial justice at the local level. Major corporations uphold the federal principle to block the controls that would follow a federal chartering of corporations. The "sagebrush rebellion" among Western states seeks to strike off federal controls on private development of mineral and water resources within the state. This stance has been hospitably received by the Reagan administration. The president, himself a self-proclaimed "sagebrush rebel," appointed Secretary of Interior James Watt to expedite the removal of federal controls. A sizable portion of the people of Alaska resisted federal efforts to set aside land for national forests and the National Park Service under government protection.

A striking example of the link between federalism and liberal tradition is apparent in the proposed reform of federal arrangements by the Reagan administration. The object is to dismantle the neo-liberal programs of the Great Society and to restore the state to its ancient liberal function of managing social conflict in a society of possessive individualists. The specific means by which the reform is to be carried out are to consolidate the categorical grants-in-aid into block grants and then to reduce the overall amount of the federal allotment to states and local communities. Of the government's 500 categorical programs to the states, there would be a cut of 25 percent in 85 of the major programs. This cut would be followed by consolidating the major programs into six broad block grants covering health, education, and other social services. Decision makers at the state and local level would have greater authority to decide on the allocation of funds, but the amount of money available would be significantly reduced.[18] Additionally, the Reagan administration seeks to remove federal controls over the development of water, mineral, and timber resources within the states by private interests.

The Reagan reform of federal arrangements is said to promote the cause of freedom. The founding fathers may well have agreed with this interpretation were they present to be consulted. It is worth noting though that the freedom served is the defense of private entrepreneurs against state interference. The liberal state has traditionally, indeed for centuries, been pilloried by rapacious individualists and exploiters as a deadly threat to economic freedom. Not served by the Reagan reforms are the positive freedoms enhancing human potential which the Great Society advanced. Many groups at the state and local level will be seriously handicapped by the curtailment of categorical grants from the federal government, and the reduction of the government's protective environmental role will affect everyone.

OPERATION

Federalism creates separate, self-sustaining centers of power, privilege, and profit. When we speak of the federal system we are speaking, as we said before, of *one* governmental system, but its use of power is broadly diffused. An observer of the federal scene states that the power dispersion occurs "over fifty states, and over 80,000 local governments including in round numbers, 3,000 counties, 18,000 municipalities, 17,000 townships, 21,000 school districts, and 21,000 special districts. Within one city there may be five or more 'governments' (county, city, school district, library district, etc.) levying taxes and exercising authority over the same citizens." Another account estimates that the metropolitan area around New York City contains 1,467 distinct political entities.[19]

Each one of these units in the federal system is a base of power. An astute observer suggests that the power base may be "sought and defended as desirable in itself." Or it may be sought "as a means of leverage upon elements in the political system, above or below." Or it may be sought as "a base from which individuals move to places of greater influence in or out of government."[20] The power base may be used for all these reasons in turn, depending on the political skills and motivations of the actors involved. All this is abstractly stated but the consequences are easy to see. The diffusion of power forces a politics of bargaining and accommodation on all actors in the federal system. Each individual in the system, high or low, has a power base. Each requires the concurrence of all the rest, or just about, in order to get anything done. Therefore, each must negotiate with all the others, each dealing in the coin of self-interest.

The large point is, first, that the politics of negotiation between independently situated political actors is a distinctively American style of politics arising out of the arrangements of the political system, and second, that this pattern is imposed on *all* actors in the American political system, no matter how powerful they may look. To drive this point home, we shall look at the constraints imposed on the president of the United States, supposedly the most powerful actor in our political system.

The diffusion of power in the federal system is reflected in the relationships among politicians, even those who are of the same party. A "national" figure must accommodate him- or herself to those who have a power base at the state and local level, as Franklin Delano Roosevelt learned when he sought to oust a number of Southern and Western Democrats who in his estimation had not been sufficiently loyal to his New Deal programs. The occasion was 1938, an off-year election. Roosevelt had just been elected to a second term, but his programs were encountering opposition from members of his own party and from the Supreme Court. Among his strongest opponents were Senator Walter F. George of Georgia and nine other congressmen, each of whom faced primary battles in their home states. If they won the primary, reelection in the general election was virtually assured. Roosevelt, with some encouragement from his inner circle, decided to turn the primary contest into a referendum on his New Deal. He picked out candidates at the state and local level who, he said, reflected his ideas more closely than the incumbents. The people, he said, should send these men to Washington and not the incumbents.[21]

An opportunity to make known his displeasure with incumbent Democrats was made available to Roosevelt by an invitation from the city of Gainesville, Georgia, to dedicate a square named in his honor. At the ceremonies, Roosevelt shared the platform with Senator George and Governor E. D. Rivers. Roosevelt hoped that Rivers would run against George in the primary, and he lavished attention on him while ignoring George. Later, when Rivers declined to run, Roosevelt recruited another candidate, Lawrence S. Camp, U.S. district attorney in Atlanta. Appearing in another Georgia visit, on this occasion with both George and Camp on the platform, Roosevelt made explicit reference to George's indifference to New Deal programs. The president said that voters should follow a test of party loyalty in casting their primary ballot:

> First, has the record of the candidate shown, while differing perhaps in details, a constant active fighting attitude in favor of the broad objectives

of the party and of the Government as they are constituted today; and, secondly, does the candidate really, in his heart, deep down in his heart, believe in these objectives.[22]

Applying this test to George, the president made clear, would result in his being voted out of office. "I regret," he said, "that in the case of my friend Senator George, I cannot answer either of those questions in the affirmative." The audience reacted to this judgment with mixed applause and boos. Roosevelt shook hands with George who said, "Mr. President, I want you to know that I accept the challenge." "Let's always be friends," Roosevelt answered.[23]

Roosevelt's effort to use his national prestige and personal magnetism in engineering the defeat of party rivals was a total disaster. A power base successfully maintained at the state and local level was more than enough to offset the influence of the party's most powerful figure. Only one of the congressmen against whom Roosevelt campaigned was defeated in the party primary, and this was attributed to the candidate's own shortcomings, not to the intervention of Roosevelt. Senator George was returned to office. The lesson to be learned is that the federal diffusion of power equips each political actor with a point of leverage. A politics of accommodation of interests must be practiced even by figures who look high up in the federal hierarchy.

Not only party figures but also local officials may have an almost impregnable position. These officials, too, must be dealt with on a one-to-one basis by those who are nominally situated above them. Roosevelt's efforts to remove Robert M. Moses, chairman of the Triborough Bridge and Tunnel Authority (TBTA) of New York City, offers a useful illustration of this point. The year is 1934, and Roosevelt has been in office for two years. Through the Secretary of the Interior, Harold Ickes, he issued an executive order stating that no official working on a government project could simultaneously hold local political office. The order was directed against Moses, who was not only head of the TBTA but also a member of the N.Y.C. Planning Commission and construction coordinator, another city post. Moses, as chairman of the TBTA, was using federal funds to construct the Triborough Bridge, a gigantic structure, as all his projects were, spanning the Bronx, Queens, and Manhattan. Roosevelt knew that Moses had too much tied up in his city posts to resign from them. He thought that the executive order would force Moses's resignation from the chairmanship of the TBTA, and thus from a role in the construction of the Triborough Bridge, scheduled for completion by 1936. He secretly communicated to Mayor La Guardia through Ickes that funds for the construction of the bridge would be cut off unless Moses resigned.[24]

The move to force the resignation was purely a matter of spite and rivalry between power barons. The fight was waged across the entire landscape of federal politics for over a decade. It had its sources in the period 1924 to 1928 when Moses was president of the Long Island State Parks Commission and Roosevelt was chairman of the Taconic State Parkway Commission. Both were rivals for New York State money to advance construction on their favored parkway projects. Moses obtained priority for his projects from the State Parks Council, and the fortunes of Franklin D. Roosevelt and the Taconic State Parkway languished. But Roosevelt was the favorite son of Al Smith, governor of New York, to succeed him. This Roosevelt did, becoming governor of the state in 1928, using this as a power base from which he went on to capture the presidency in 1932. When he became president, Roosevelt thought the time was opportune to settle a score with his old rival.

Again, Roosevelt was totally unsuccessful and for much the same reasons. Moses, at the state and local level, was an exceedingly powerful figure in his own right. Quite simply, Moses was the most powerful builder the nation has ever known. He completed capital construction projects in the vicinity of New York City that were estimated at $27 billion, including seven bridges, ten expressways, public housing, parks, swimming pools, and playgrounds. In the course of building these projects Moses had gathered about him a formidable coalition that included mayors, governors, insurance salesmen, members of labor unions, bond underwriters, lawyers, bankers (especially from Chase Manhattan), members of the hierarchy of the Catholic Church, Jews, Irishmen, Tammany machine politicians, realtors, department store magnates, philanthropists, journalists, and on and on.[25] Many of these elements rose up in a furor when Roosevelt's aim was disclosed, and in the end La Guardia found a face-saving gesture for the president and Ickes. The executive order was rescinded and Moses continued as chairman of the TBTA well beyond the days of Roosevelt and the New Deal. He kept the post until he overreached himself in dealing with another power baron, Governor Nelson A. Rockefeller,[26] but that is another story.

Such practical lessons are not lost on those who must make the system work the only way it can—through a politics of accommodation between independently situated actors (power brokers) dealing with each other in the coin of self-interest.

SIGNIFICANCE

There are two kinds of criticism of the federal system, one that social ills follow from its operation; the other, that particular injustices are the result of the great variety and confusion of state legislation. As an example of the latter, one author notes that North Carolina punishes homosexual acts committed in the privacy of the home with life imprisonment. Alabama and Minnesota may jail a person from five to twenty years for the possession of marijuana, and in Texas one may be imprisoned two years to life for this offense.[27] The inconsistent state standards in imposing capital punishment have resulted in a ruling from the Supreme Court that it is a "cruel and unusual punishment" within the meaning of the Eighth Amendment. The court did not say that capital punishment inherently violates the Eighth Amendment. It stated that legislators must provide standards for both judge and jury by which to weigh the penalty in the light of the individual's character and the circumstances of the crime. Many states have reimposed the death penalty after narrowing the standards by which it may be imposed.[28]

Another oddity of the federal system that encourages uneven standards of justice concerns the laws of incorporation. New Jersey and Delaware are favored by the legal staffs of major businesses. These states have been in competition since the late nineteenth century to pass the most relaxed laws concerning corporate offenses—watering stock, collusion on prices, institutional racism, bribery of public officials, monopolistic practices, and pollution. Delaware has won in the competition for lax standards because Woodrow Wilson, former governor of New Jersey (and later president of the United States), instituted reforms dealing with incorporation which brought on a decline in business.[29] Under the constitutional rule requiring "comity," each state must extend "full faith and credit" to the laws of any state under which any business is incorporated. A state cannot bar a corporation from trade or business within its environs because its own laws set a higher standard of practice.

The reason that Delaware is anxious to have businesses incorporate in its state is money. In 1971 the revenues of the State of Delaware from corporation franchise taxes and related corporate income totaled $55.5 million. The total revenues of the state were $246 million; thus corporations contributed 23 percent of the state's income. The present popularity of Delaware as a haven for major corporations is due to the revisions to the Delaware General Corporation Law executed in 1967. An investigative account reports that among other things:

> . . . (1) officers and directors of corporations could be indemnified for all court costs and settlements of criminal and civil cases without court or shareholder approval; (2) management was given the power to merge subsidiary corporations without shareholder vote; (3) only directors, not shareholders, may propose amendments to the corporate charter; (4) plans for loans to officers, stock options, stock bonuses, and incentive compensation were allowed without disclosure to shareholders; (5) the board of directors

cannot be held legally responsible for knowing—or learning—about price-fixing practices in the corporation they supposedly manage.[30]

Of *Fortune* magazine's 1,000 largest industrial corporations, 134 incorporated or reincorporated for the first time in Delaware in the years 1967 to 1974. By late 1974, Delaware was "home" for 448 of the 1,000 largest corporations—including 52 of the largest 100 and 251 of the largest 500.[31]

These vagaries and anomalies of the federal system fall with unequal effect on the members of society. Certain groups—homosexuals, murderers, corporation executives—are singled out for exceptional treatment, whether beneficial or injurious. In another area the federal system is criticized because of the general social ills that follow from its operation. Chief among these is the criticism that federalism obstructs national political initiatives for resolving important problems in society. Today's national political initiative concerning the major problems of race, urban poverty, or energy tends to become a pitched battle tomorrow between elites situated at different levels of the federal system. The system promotes conflict management between elites, not a concerted effort to advance major social needs.

> Those who value the virtues of decentralization, which writ large are virtues of freedom, need not scruple at recognizing the defect of those virtues. The defects are principally the danger that parochial and private interests may not coincide, or give way to, the nation's interest. The necessary cure for these defects is effective national leadership. . . . The centrifugal force of domestic politics needs to be balanced by the centripetal force of strong presidental leadership.[32]

Others say that the president, no less than any other actor, must take part in the decentralized bargaining which is the essence of the federal system. The political life of the president, it is pointed out, is one of constant bargaining with state and local power barons on whom his own political survival is dependent.

> In short, the life of a President, who is the main national official, is one of constant bargaining—to get the votes to get nominated, to get the votes to get elected, to get the votes to get bills through Congress, to get the votes to get renominated, etc. etc.[33]

Thus, in the latter account, federalism does not offer the president a point of political leverage in carrying out major policy initiatives. National political figures, such as the president or a prominent senator or representative, may have important advantages flowing from the tax sources of the central government. The categorical grants-in-aid programs offer them a major advantage over state and local political leaders in setting the direction of public policy. Nevertheless, the decentralization of power affords power barons, situated as Robert Moses or Senator George were atop a local power base, substantial means of opposition and resistance. As a consequence, federal programs run the hazard of becoming a private power battle between elites activated by different constituencies.

There is little doubt that federal arrangements tip the role of the president toward that of a power broker and away from that of a realigning force in the political system, and tip politics toward the liberal conception of the role of the state and away from the neo-liberal view of the state's responsibilities to its citizens. The political system is tilted in the direction of conflict management and away from concerted efforts to develop national solutions for glaring social ills. The genius of the Reagan administration is that it has been able to tap the ancient enthusiasms of liberal tradition which sustain federal arrangements in a new and modern political setting.

NOTES

1. *Ableman* v. *Booth,* 21 How. 506 (1859), cited by James L. Sundquist and David W. Davis, *Making Federalism Work* (Washington, D.C.: Brookings Institution, 1969), p. 6. See the discussion by Kenneth T. Palmer, *State Politics in the United States* (New York: St. Martin's Press, 1972), p. 23; also, Richard H. Leach, *American Federalism* (New York: W. W. Norton, 1970), chap. 1.

2. Martin Grodzins, "Centralization and Decentralization in the American Federal System," in *A Nation of States,* ed. Richard A. Goldwin (Chicago: Rand McNally, 1963), pp. 1–23; and "The Federal System," in *Goals for Americans* (Englewood Cliffs, N.J.: Spectrum Books, 1960), pp. 265–82.

3. U.S. Department of Energy, *National Energy Plan* II (Washington, D.C.: Government Printing Office, 1979), p. 112.

4. *National Journal,* April 28, 1979, p. 677.

5. *Report of the President's Commission on the Accident at Three Mile Island* (October 1979).

6. Carl Brent Swisher, *The Growth of Constitutional Power in the United States* (Chicago: Phoenix Books, 1966), pp. 77–89; Alpheus Thomas Mason and William Beaney, *The Supreme Court in a Free Society* (New York: W. W. Norton, 1968), chap. 7.

7. Swisher, *Growth of Constitutional Power,* pp. 89–97.

8. Adam Yarmolinsky, *The Military Establishment* (New York: Harper & Row, 1971); Seymour Melman, *The War Economy of the United States* (New York: St. Martin's Press, 1971); Swisher, *Growth of Constitutional Power,* pp. 99–102.

9. *Korematsu* v. *United States,* 323 U.S. 214 (1944).

10. Sundquist and Davis, *Making Federalism Work,* p. 11.

11. *General Revenue Sharing,* A-47 (Washington, D.C.: Advisory Commission on Intergovernmental Relations, 1974).

12. Michael D. Reagan, *The New Federalism* (New York: Oxford University Press, 1972), pp. 33–45; Milton C. Cummings and David Wise, *Democracy Under Pressure* (New York: Harcourt, Brace, 1974), p. 86.

13. Rochelle L. Stanfield, "State and Local Governments Struggle to Make Ends Meet," *National Journal,* September 18, 1976, p. 1,321.

14. *Ibid.*

15. *General Revenue Sharing,* A-48, (Washington, D.C.: Advisory Commission on Intergovernmental Relations, 1974), p. 47.

16. *Federalist* Nos. 11, 23. Also see generally William H. Riker, *Federalism: Origin, Operation, Significance* (Boston: Little, Brown, 1964), chap. 2.

17. *Federalist* No. 28.

18. *The New York Times,* June 1, 1981, A1, 13.

19. Harold Seidman, *Politics, Position and Power,* 2nd ed. (New York: Oxford University Press, 1976), p. 164; Robert C. Wood, *1400 Governments* (New York: Anchor Books, 1964).

20. David Truman, "Federalism and the Party System," in *American Federalism in Perspective,* ed. Aaron Wildavsky (Boston: Little, Brown, 1967), pp. 81–109.

21. Louis W. Koenig, *The Chief Executive,* rev. ed. (New York: Harcourt, Brace, 1968), pp. 105–07.

22. *Ibid.,* p. 106.

23. *Ibid.,* p. 107.

24. Robert A. Caro, *The Power Broker* (New York: Vintage Books, 1975), chap. 22.

25. *Ibid.,* chap. 33.

26. *Ibid.,* chap. 46.

27. Theodore J. Lowi, *American Government: Incomplete Conquest* (Hinsdale, Ill.: Dryden Press, 1976), pp. 140–41.

28. Lesley Oelsner, "Now Clearly It Is a Burger Court, Just Right of Center," *The New York Times,* July 11, 1976, E8.

29. Ralph Nader, Mark Green, and Joel Seligman, *Taming the Giant Corporation* (New York: W. W. Norton, 1976), p. 57.

30. *Ibid.,* pp. 58–59.

31. *Ibid.,* p. 57.

32. Grodzins, "American Federal System," p. 282.

33. Riker, *Federalism,* p. 93.

CHAPTER 8

The Congressional Establishment

This chapter stresses the theme that Congress, to a greater extent than its rival institutions, the executive and judiciary, reflects the decentralized bargaining features of the Madisonian constitutional system. Students of congressional politics often comment on the manner in which the distribution of power among the chairmen of standing committees and subcommittees deflects attention from national issues and encourages bargaining among many independently situated actors. These chairmen perform a brokerage function, negotiating with other chairmen and representatives to protect their policy turf, constituency, clientele, and incumbent status. So preoccupied are congressmen with protection of their carefully marked out power base that they often seem to be indifferent to matters of major social importance, the very issues we expect them to be concerned about.

Imagine a trip to the Capitol building, which is a large, sumptuous, sprawling affair, laid out in an era when the conservation of heat and the efficient use of space were not uppermost in men's minds. The impression is fostered by the newspapers, public figures, and much popular literature that important debates take place in these dignified surroundings. The comings and goings, meetings and adjournments, speeches and debates are published in considerable detail by the press, above all by the *Washington Post,* the best daily popular source on congressional activities. However, attendance on the floor of the House or Senate hovers around 15 to 20 percent of the membership in the course of normal proceedings. Of those members who are present, no more than a handful are paying the slightest attention to Senator or Representative *X,* who is giving a speech. Most of those present are huddled in small groups, talking among themselves, or strolling about on the floor looking, so it seems, for something they misplaced.

The conventional notion that Congress is the center of an ongoing debate on public affairs has been checked. Congressional decision making reflects the biases of the constitutional system. Elected officials are not placed in charge of public policy and thereafter held responsible for events that are a product of their decisions. Instead, the framers viewed political parties linked to a broad electorate with suspicion and fear; they successfully organized a bias against political parties and democratic participation into the constitutional system. Instead of vesting power in an elected group or party and seeking to make them publicly accountable, the constitutional system encourages the creation of power barons, and then sets them to guard each other. Congress reflects this pattern. Congressional politics is a matter of power brokers dealing relationally with those with whom power is shared and manipulatively with those outside the power system.

Imagine another trip to the Capitol Building, this time armed with the knowledge that decision-making power in Congress is diffused, that it is more likely to rest with the committee and subcommittee chairmen instead of majorities on the floor of the House or Senate. Will these chairmen provide access to the debate on national issues for which we have been searching? Here is one reporter's experience, a veteran of congressional in-fighting, who sought to find out how President Carter's National Energy Plan (1977) was doing one year after its presentation to Congress. To obtain access to the conference committee charged with resolving differences between House and Senate versions of this legislation, this is what the reporter had to do:

> Go to the third floor of the Capitol on the Senate side, walk through the swinging doors to the Senate Document Room, breeze past the gate where people wait for copies of bills, go straight ahead and up a ramp, turn right into a long, dingy hallway, proceed through the hall and down a short flight of steps, turn right at the first landing and go up two steps, take a quick right and left around a corner and climb three steps into a spacious corridor painted aquamarine, move up to the second panelled door on the right, numbered S-334 and wait, and wait, and wait for somebody to come out and tell you what was going on inside. . . . No matter how you got to the door of S-334, you could not get inside unless you carried the proper credentials.[1]

Even after initiation into the intricacies of congressional politics, it is still far from simple to elicit information on matters at the center of discussion and decision. The instance just mentioned is in many ways atypical. Most standing committees and subcommittees hold public sessions, where conflict over the substance of public policy is observable, and these conflicts may be pushed to a vote within committee and on the floor of the House or Senate. Nevertheless, highly sensitive national issues (the natural gas compromise forged by the conference committee just mentioned will cost the public $70 billion by 1985) occur offstage, as it were, outside the range of public view.[2] The process of congressional politics, transactional relations between committee and subcommittee chairmen, is not neutral but tips power into the hands of a few influential people on many occasions. Most important, major conflicts regarding the substance of policy often are not openly debated and decided.

STRUCTURES OF POWER

Many studies talk about the "structure of power" in Congress. Generally, these studies search for a single group, or groups, which exercise power over the substantive content of legislation, but the interesting finding is that these studies disagree with one another.[3]

One candidate for power-holder is the elective leadership of the Senate and House. For example, Speaker of the House of Representatives Tip O'Neill (Democrat, Massachusetts) and Senate Majority Leader Howard Baker (Republican, Tennessee) are featured in the pages of *Newsweek* and *U.S. News and World Report.* Another candidate is the committee chairmen, or alternatively, the subcommittee chairmen, of Congress. Although these people are less likely to have their pictures disseminated to a mass audience, it is often argued that they exercise far more power than the elective leadership over the actual substance of legislation. Still a third group, really a constellation of groups, is the "subgovernments" of Washington. By this term is meant an alliance of interest groups, bureaucrats, and congressmen organized around a particular piece of policy turf—defense contracts, interest rates, farm supports, decontrol of energy price regulation, highway funds, tax write-offs, public health, and the like. In this case, attention is directed to the institutional setting of power on Capitol Hill (the producer and consumer groups, research institutions, intergovernmental lobbies, labor unions, and trade associations, which surround Congress and activate its power levers) as much as to the formal processes of congressional decision making. The implicit view is that these groups have as much to do with making policy as elected representatives and appointed officials.

There appear to be several power structures in Congress, and analyzing each one will tell us something about power in the national legislature.

ELECTIVE LEADERSHIP

Elective leaders are like the "captains" of the team that has the most votes in Congress. Before the beginning of each congressional session, Republican and Democrat party caucuses—"team huddles,"—are held to vote on leadership, rules, and committee appointments. Usually, these caucuses begin in December for the House of Representatives, the larger institution with the most business to transact, and early January for the Senate. The first vote taken at the beginning of a congressional session ratifies the decisions of the party caucuses. This is the only time that the members of the political parties can be relied on to vote together as a unit.[4] The vote on the organization of power is one which each member of the majority party has an interest in sustaining and each member of the minority party, in opposing. At all other times party unity means very little.

Among the leadership posts, the office of the speaker of the House and Senate majority leader are by far the most significant. Through control of procedure, persons holding these posts acquire influence over the substantive content of legislation. The powers of the speaker for the House, for example, include the following:

> He must recognize any member who wishes to speak on the floor; he rules on the appropriateness of parliamentary procedures; he determines the presence of a quorum . . . he votes in case of a tie; he counts and announces votes; he decides in doubtful cases to which standing committees a bill will be assigned; he appoints special or select committees; he appoints the House members to each conference committee; and he maintains decorum in the chamber.[5]

Another important power acquired by the speaker in recent years is over appointments to the Committee on Rules (subject to approval by the party caucus). Taken together, one expert observes, these powers extend fairly broadly "across the stages through which legislative proposals must pass before they emerge as law." Thus, the "scope of his procedural influence" is more important than any particular power.[6] Altogether, the speaker influences legislation by placing himself at the center of negotiations on the timing of bills brought to the floor of the House, the recognition of members who wish to speak on a bill, the appropriateness of a parliamentary tactic, and so forth. A powerful speaker, such as Sam Rayburn was, manages the business of the House almost invisibly through procedure.

Rather small powers of the speaker may sometimes count for a great deal. One of these, for example, is to appoint the members of ad hoc committees, apparently no great matter. However, the power was used by Tip O'Neill to appoint an ad hoc committee, constituted of the several House committees dealing with energy legislation, to consider President Carter's first national energy plan. The effect of the creation of the ad hoc committee was to deprive the chairmen of the standing committees of their normal share of influence over energy policy. Plainly, the object of O'Neill's ploy was to avoid the jurisdictional warfare of the House and to structure a legislative decision favorable to the president. It should be noted that the ad hoc committee had no legislative power. That remains, as always, with the standing committees and the full House. But it did serve to unify the deliberations of the relevant committees (Ways and Means, Interstate and Foreign Commerce, Science and Technology, Interior and Insular Affairs, Public Works, and Transportation).[7]

Like the speaker of the House, the Senate majority leader gains control over policy through his power over the legislative schedule and the division of labor among the committees. He has slightly more power than the speaker in the timing of legislation and over the chairmen of the standing committees. He picks and chairs the Committee on Committees, which is responsible for making committee assignments in the Senate, and the Policy Committee, which directs the legislative schedule. On the other hand, the speaker of the House only acts in an advisory capacity to the Committee on Committees (which makes committee assignments for House Democrats). An ambitious Senate majority leader, such as Lyndon Johnson was, uses his position at the center of the Senate communications process to inform himself and to shape the preferences of senators on legislation. Acting in the diverse roles of switchboard operator, memory bank, and computer, Johnson found that he could build majority coalitions of senators whose reasons for voting on legislation were fundamentally opposed.[8]

The title of *party whip* is misleading in connoting the functions of the second most important elective office in the House and Senate. The term comes from *whipper-in,* the man assigned in English fox hunts to keep the hounds from straying. Actually, the whips are more likely to use cajolery and tact in attempting to persuade the hurried members of the party to appear for important roll-call votes and to vote with the party. The office of House majority leader was hotly contested in the Ninety-fifth Congress between rival factions of the Democratic party led by

Phillip Burton (California), a reform liberal, and Jim Wright (Texas), a moderate. Wright won the contest by one vote, giving a conservative accent to the leadership of the House and Senate.[9] The post of whip is often a stepping stone to the position of Speaker of the House.

Do the procedural powers of the elective leadership constitute a power structure? Probably not. For one thing, Baker and O'Neill themselves would be the first to repudiate the notion that they exercise power over legislation. Such denials may not be conclusive but they give pause. The elective leadership regards itself and is regarded as "brokers, favor doers, agenda setters, and protectors of established institutional routines," not as "program salesmen or vote mobilizers," as one observer puts it. Both the speaker and majority leader, he adds, counsel members to "vote their constituencies."[10] Former Senate Majority Leader Robert Byrd, for example, used to study the voting records of his colleagues as a basis for advising them on roll-call votes. His neutrality was praised by Abraham Ribicoff (Democrat, Connecticut), a liberal who clashed with Byrd on welfare legislation. "He keeps the machinery of the Senate in fine tuned shape."[11] Another example of neutrality is O'Neill's impartial distribution of $150,000 in personal campaign funds among 182 Democratic challengers or incumbents in the 1976 congressional elections. Liberals or conservatives, newcomers or oldtimers, each got $500 from O'Neill for campaign spending.[12] The career of the elective leadership is not based on party crusades but the personal obligations they accumulate through accommodations, courtesies, and small favors.

The weak position of the elective leadership, extending to procedural controls alone, is a reflection of disunity and conflict within the political parties. The parties are not composed of like-minded people but are a loose coalition of state and local forces animated by widely disparate goals.[13] The unity the party presents in organizing power and establishing rules at the outset of Congress is very superficial. It rapidly evaporates as the party takes up the task of government. The idea of liberating the majority party in Congress to enact a legislative program through its elective leadership, a goal often mentioned by reformers, is seriously weakened by the fact that the parties are composed of factional elements unresponsive to a common program of action. The elective leadership is not the power structure of Congress.

COMMITTEE AND SUBCOMMITTEE CHAIRMEN

Up until recently most students of Congress would have agreed with the thrust of a statement by Woodrow Wilson: "I know not how better to describe our form of government in a single phrase than by calling it a government by the chairmen of the Standing Committees of Congress."[14] Wilson did not make the statement because he wished to celebrate the powers of the committee chairmen. Rather he wished to identify the group that he thought possessed substantive power over legislation and to describe the effects, mostly bad, which followed. The committee chairmen held great power in Congress and generally in the political system.

Today, Wilson's estimate would be significantly revised in at least two ways. The president has taken a far greater role in shaping legislative policy, thanks in part to Wilson's own example in presidential office. Second, it is no longer the case that the committee chairmen exert unrivaled sway over legislation coming before their committee. Changes instituted by the Democratic caucus in the House of Representatives have brought about a devolution of power to subcommittee chairmen.

The work of Congress is performed through standing committees. These committees have come into and remained in existence because they perform a variety of political and administrative functions. They coalesce expert views on controversial issues and problems; they oversee administrative programs; they facilitate a distribution of the congressional work load; they provide a decent burial for inept proposals; they provide a forum for the expression of conflicting views about the merits of legislation. Not least of these functions is that they serve to create independent centers of power for career-minded congressmen. They are "the great baronies of congressional power. Many of them look outward in jealous competition with the President, with their opposite committee in the other house, and with the whole house of which they are a part."[15] The jurisdictional authority of each standing committee is fixed by the rules of the respective chamber; the rules confer authority on the committees to analyze, evaluate, and report on legislation within their area of expertise.

There are twenty-two standing committees in the House and eighteen in the Senate. The committees are sometimes ranked in terms of status and prestige. For example, the top six in the Senate are Appropriations, Foreign Relations, Finance, Armed Services, Judiciary, and Interstate and Foreign Commerce. In the House the six most influential are said to be Rules, Appropriations, Ways and Means, Armed Services, Judiciary, and Interstate and Foreign Commerce.[16] To the individual congressman seeking incumbency, the prestige associated with a particular committee may not be the relevant consideration. He may be far more interested in a less prestigious assignment, say Agriculture or Interior and Insular Affairs, where he can serve the bread and butter interests of his constituency. Posts on the committee on House Administration or Veterans Affairs, although lowly in terms of prestige, are useful because they exert leverage on all other congressmen. Some committees, such as Education and Labor, attract members who are media-conscious, sometimes called the "show horses" of Congress, whereas other committees, like Appropriations and Ways and Means, attract those with an appetite for drudgery, the "work horses" of Congress.[17]

Formerly, the chairmen of the standing committees were selected by party caucus on the basis of seniority, a policy which brought to positions of leadership congressmen from safe districts. Many of these constituencies, located in the South, regularly returned congressmen to office by a 55 percent margin or better. Also, the powers of the committee chairmen were considerable, and tales about them are legendary. Once asked if he would accept the post of defense secretary, Carl Vinson, former chairman of the House Armed Services Committee, said, "I would rather run the Defense Department from down here." In brief the chairmen were empowered to call committee into session, to recognize the membership to speak on a bill, to arrange for witnesses to speak on a bill, to bring proceedings to a vote, and to designate the chairmen of the subcommittees of the standing committee (which gave the chairman considerable influence over the junior members).[18] These powers gave the chairman considerable say over the substance of legislation reported out of committee. Today, chairmen of the standing committees are no longer automatically selected on the basis of seniority. In addition, the powers of the subcommittee chairmen have been increased at the expense of the committee chairmen.

The end of unquestioned seniority rule in Congress came in January 1975. The Democratic party caucus, aided and abetted by seventy-five freshmen Democrats, deposed three of the most senior committee chairmen in the House and forced the resignation of a fourth.[19] Wright Patman, 81 years old and a member since 1929, lost the Banking and Currency Committee chairmanship to Henry S. Reuss of Wisconsin, 62. W. R. Poage of Texas, a member since 1935, was deposed as chairman of the Agriculture Committee in favor of Thomas S. Foley of Washington, 45. F. Edward Hebert of Louisiana, 73, a member since 1941, was deposed as head of the Armed Services Committee; Melvin Price from Illinois was designated as the new chairman. Wilbur Mills, 65, a member since 1939, resigned the chairmanship of Ways and Means for reasons of health, but his removal had been all but certain if he had not stepped down voluntarily. In 1973 the party caucus voted to subject any chairman to a secret ballot vote at the request of 20 percent of the caucus. This rule change gave committee members a way to retaliate against chairmen who used their powers in an arbitrary or discriminatory fashion, and the new powers were quickly put to use in the purge of 1975.

As the powers of the chairmen have waned, those of the subcommittee chairmen have increased. A series of rule changes in caucus (called "reforms") have made the latter powerful figures in their own right. These rules changes and their result are summarized as follows:

> First, in 1971 members were limited to the chairmanship of one subcommittee. Senior members who were hoarding chairmanships were forced to relinquish them to less senior members. Later, in 1973, a subcommittee "bill of rights" further reinforced the devolution of power. No longer could full committee chairmen arbitrarily designate subcommittee chairmen. The full committee or subcommittee seniority (depending on the wishes of the committee Democrats) would henceforth determine subcommittee chairmanships. Subcommittee jurisdictions were fixed; full committee chairmen could no longer assign vague jurisdictions in order to maximize their own flexibility in assigning legislation. Subcommittees were guaranteed adequate budgets and staffing; no longer could a full committee chairman starve a subcommittee or pack its staff with his minions. The full impact of these changes has yet to be determined, but it is clear that the twenty-two full committee chairmen in the House have been weakened and the one hundred forty-two subcommittee chairmen have been strengthened.[20]

Parallel changes have occurred in the Senate so that it, too, practices "government by subcommittee." The congressional establishment has been demoted from barons to baronets.

Observers of Congress now talk about it as an institution in which "a relatively large number of individuals have a piece of the action."[21] The power structure of the committee chairmen has dissolved beneath the repeated attacks of the Democratic party caucus and the subcommittee chairmen. According to the new view, power in Congress, to an extent never equalled before, is situational and mercurial, requiring the consent of many independently situated political actors in order to get anything done. The notion that these changes represent "reforms" should be regarded with suspicion, however. Actually the changes may have been prompted by a desire to carve out independent spheres of policy influence, the better to promote the goals of incumbency and irresponsible private power.[22] This interpretation of the recent changes is in keeping with well-known constitutional enthusiasms for the diffusion of power, the evasion of responsibility, and the politicized battle of each against every other.[23]

SUBGOVERNMENTS

Subgovernments are triadic relationships among congressmen, interest groups, and bureaucrats; once formed, these relationships draw on the powers of each of the parties to form a minigovernment virtually impervious to influence or control by the formal institutions of government. Subgovernments are created and sustained by the intersection of interests of independently situated actors in Congress, in the bureaucracy, and in interest groups, each one of whom perceives a mutual advantage in a permanent and informal alliance. The essence of the arrangement is that each party perceives a different yet mutual advantage in creating and maintaining it. The bureaucrat swells the number of his office staff and increases his budget; the congressman maintains incumbency; and the spokesman for the interest group extends and promotes the goals of his clientele.

Examples of subgovernments in Washington abound. So influential are they in shaping policy that there is much justification for considering them the "true" government, or more cautiously, the coequal of formal governmental institutions. Among them are agribusiness; the automobile-highway-oil combine; the liberal-labor lobby; the military-industrial complex; the financier-developer-contractor alliance; and the rivers-harbors-dams complex.

Among these subgovernments, the military-industrial complex has received the most attention. It is an alliance of the chairmen and subcommittee chairmen of the Senate and House Committees on Armed Services and Appropriations; the various military associations on Capitol Hill (Navy League, Association of the U.S. Army, Aerospace Industries Association, etc.); major industries dependent on defense contracts (Ling-Temco-Vought, General Dynamics Corp., Lockheed Aircraft Corp., etc.), and the Pentagon. From the perspective of Congress, the most arresting feature of the complex is that it was rooted in a Southern quadrumvirate until 1971: Richard Russell of Georgia, John Stennis of Mississippi, Mendel Rivers of South Carolina, and George Mahon of Texas. Each of these men saw "Pentagon capitalism" as a means of economic recovery for a region of the country completely bypassed by the Industrial Revolution and hard hit by the Great Depression (1932).[24] Militarist and patriotic sentiments in the South made this variety of capitalist enterprise more salable than might have been the case elsewhere in the country. From their respective positions as chairmen of the Senate or House Armed Services Committees (Russell and Stennis; Carl Vinson and Rivers) and chairman of the House Subcommittee on Defense Appropriations (Mahon), these Southern congressmen were well situated to ally themselves with entrepreneurs in the defense industries, the military, and the bureaucracy. The consequences of this alliance are swollen defense budgets, incumbency, and congressional districts bulging with air bases, forts, space installations, and defense plants.

So successful have Southern congressmen been in deflecting defense appropriations into their areas that congressmen from the Northeast formed a coalition to protect their fair share of defense appropriations. Having witnessed the marvels of Pentagon capitalism in rescuing the South from economic depression, these congressmen now saw it as a way to rescue failed capitalism in their own region. Michael Harrington (Democrat, Massachusetts), a congressman who was formerly a vociferous opponent of the Vietnam War and defense spending, led the coalition. In 1977, coalition leaders demanded in a letter to President Carter that he declare a "moratorium on all activity by the Department of Defense associated with the closure . . . of military installations . . . in our 16 state area."[25] The letter stated that the security of the United States was threatened just as much by the economic stagnation of the Northeast and Midwest as by potential enemies abroad. The coalition's nine-member task force included four members of the House Armed Services Committee, three members of the Appropriations Committee, and a member of the Ways and Means Committee.

Another complex which pressed Carter hard is that of rivers, harbors, and dams. Carter prepared a "hit list" of eighteen dams, scheduled for construction by the Army Corps of Engineers and Bureau of Reclamation, which he proposed to eliminate from the federal budget. His action followed a campaign pledge "to get the Army Corps of Engineers out of the dam-building business." "I personally believe we have built enough dams in this country and will be extremely reluctant as President to build any more,"[26] the candidate said. But the Army Corps of Engineers has powerful friends in Senate and House committees on public works and the interior and in local constituencies, which is why two year's after the preparation of the list, along with the fever of reelection, the corp's biggest, most questionable project, the Tennessee-Tombigbee Waterway, was rushed along with Carter's support. Also, work is proceeding full speed on the big Richard C. Russell dam in Georgia, a project that Carter once went to great lengths to condemn.[27] In this matter, as in other conflicts with subgovernments, the president and Congress are natural adversaries. Only by doing battle with Congress can the president hope to gain control over the sprawling bureaucracy and the policies it administers.

The analysis of subgovernments tends to break down the boundaries between Congress and surrounding institutions. It shows that Congress shares power over legislative policy with the executive and bureaucracy and with elaborate constellations of private power (interest groups). It is plain that in many cases, the power wielded by actors in the private sphere equals or exceeds the power exerted by parties in the public sphere. To the extent that this is true, legislative policy is not shaped by any determinate group *in* Congress. Rather it is shaped by a confluence of groups, both public and private, who collaborate for ends that are distinct yet related: power, profit, and incumbency.[28]

PROCESS, OBJECTS OF DECISION, AND REPRESSED INTERESTS: A CASE STUDY

The previous section has identified a relationship between the structure of power in Congress and the process of congressional decision making. To the extent that the elective leadership in Congress is a power structure, debate and decision making occur through organized opposition along party lines. The majority party in this scenario can be counted on to support the elective leadership both in committee and on the floor of the House or Senate; the minority party can be counted on to oppose. "Reformers," such as Woodrow Wilson and others, argued that this is the way Congress ought to work. They believe that a strong elective leadership, held accountable to a party caucus, enables the electorate to hold a definite group, the party leadership in Congress, responsible for a coherent legislative program. In fact, the dispersion of power on Capitol Hill, mirroring the political biases of the founding fathers, promotes a political process consisting of bargaining relationships between influentials.

The passage of the National Health Service Corps Act (NHSC) by Congress in 1970 will help to illustrate that the process of congressional decision making is extraordinarily complex and labyrinthine, involving numerous power brokers in an endless series of negotiations over the substance of policy. This account is sympathetic toward the process of congressional politics, increasing its value for illustration. Before taking up this case study, however, it is useful to discuss two criticisms of Congress concerning its decision-making process.

One of these is that matters of major social importance are not an "object of decision" of policy makers in America generally, and members of Congress in particular. By an *object of decision* we mean an event that we have the knowledge and resources to bring to pass.[29] If it is a hot summer's day and you had the foresight to purchase a fan during the December sales, cooling off lies within the range of your objects of decision. If you have been coached on your tennis backhand, are in position soon enough, and are being pressed at the net, a backhand down the line lies within the range of your objects of decision. Without the backhand or the fan, you would have to lob (if you knew how to lob) or drown in a pool of sweat.

What is true for individuals is true for societies. Societies organize themselves, politically, technically, and economically, to place certain events within the range of decision for its members and to withhold others from consideration. Given the arrangements of American society, the purchase of a new car (on credit) is an object of decision for many graduating seniors. Nevertheless, new energy, safety, and environmental standards are beginning to affect the kind of car that is available for purchase. Emission controls, standards of gasoline consumption, and safety specifications all illustrate this trend. We have reasonable expectations that public institutions, the Congress especially, will deliberate about public needs, resources, and knowledge, the better to preserve an optimal framework for making public choices. At the least, we expect that deliberations about the structure of public choices will be made public. The preservation of options in the public sphere, for clean air, good schools, and efficient energy consumption, affects the quality of our lives in ways which are no less critical than the preservation of options in the private sphere, a backhand down the line or a fan. Discussion about the preservation of such options is educational; it is near the essence of what is meant by government by consent.[30]

The charge is made that the process of congressional politics, transactional relations between power brokers, is not educational—it does not serve to inform the public—and that it does not offer an opportunity for systematic review of important policy options. A related criticism is that congressional decision making does not serve "repressed interests,"[31] that is, interests of a segment of the population lacking access, lobbying staff, advertising space, and organization. In this view the process of congressional politics is biased toward the interests of those groups who are in need of least protection. These are important criticisms of congressional government, and it is useful to keep them in mind.

The National Health Service Corps was designed to reallocate medical doctors to areas where inadequate medical services existed. Men and women who served in communities designated as "doctor deficient," such as a slum or a remote farming community, would be paid salaries by the federal government and would be exempted from their normal two-year military obligation. The immediate aim of the act was to serve as a "marriage bureau" between doctors and needy areas; its ultimate intent was to encourage doctors to establish a permanent practice in understaffed communities. The legislation provided that the NHSC be administered by the Public Health Service, an administrative unit of the

Department of Health, Education and Welfare (HEW), now the Department of Health and Human Services (HHS). The act provided funding of $10 million in the first year, $20 million in the second year, and $30 million in the third year.[32]

Passage of the act was the product of joint efforts of numerous parties. An important figure was a Seattle pediatrician, Abraham Bergman, who divided his time between his medical duties at the Seattle Children's Hospital and that of unofficial medical advisor to Senator Warren G. Magnuson (Democrat, Wisconsin). To Bergman goes most of the credit for pushing Senator Magnuson's staff into action. Yet the NHSC would have gone nowhere without the reputation, skill, and influence of Magnuson and the diligence of Eric Redman, a junior staff member fresh from college, assigned to work on the bill as a part of his summer staff responsibilities. Magnuson is the fifth-ranking senator in terms of seniority and chairman of the Senate Subcommittee on Health Appropriations, a critical point of leverage in relation to other Senate committees dealing with health legislation and with HEW. Eric Redman, the author of this case study, plainly took a personal as well as a professional interest in the passage of the legislation, and it is his personal concern with the outcome that provides not only a refreshing account of the legislative process but also the human ingredient that meant the difference between success and failure in obtaining its passage. Finally, we need to mention Paul Rogers (Democrat, Florida), chairman of the House Health Subcommittee, who cosponsored the House version of the NHSC.

The NHSC is one of those objects of decision about which we might reasonably expect congressmen to be interested. Affording medical staff to deficient areas filled a need not provided for by other federal legislation and at modest expense. It was a matter of shifting the knowledge and resources of the medical profession to a clear area of need, while at the same time making it reasonably attractive to doctors to fill the needs that had been identified. Doctors tend not to serve in slum areas and farming communities because of social drawbacks, reduced level of compensation, and personal hazard. This sort of problem is reflected in the fact that New York State in 1970 had three times as as high a physician-population ratio as Mississippi. But Senator Javits reportedly complained that "despite the glut of doctors on Park Avenue [in Manhattan] there were parts of the state with only one doctor for 15,000 people."[33] The problem of maldistribution is accentuated by the trend toward medical specialization; it is the general practitioner who serves in underrepresented areas. Despite these circumstances, the chief obstacles to passage of the act did not arise from the medical profession (Fifteen hundred members of the Student American Medical Association volunteered for service in the National Health Corps the first year, more than HEW could feasibly process) but from ideological opponents of the act ("socialized medicine") and the legislative process itself.

At first the legislative strategy called for Magnuson, as chairman of the Senate Subcommittee on Health Appropriations, to earmark funds from the Public Health Service (PHS). Magnuson's committee handled over $40 billion in health appropriations annually. With the cooperation of the surgeon general, head of the PHS, the funds could be used to establish an experimental health service corps, the model for future legislation along these lines. The strategy was rejected after learning that the PHS lacked proper authority to direct medical care to anyone other than "traditional beneficiaries" (Indians, merchant seamen, and prisoners). A second strategy was to amend the Public Health Service Acts of 1970, then in consideration by the Health Subcommittee of the Senate Committee on Labor and Public Welfare. This strategy probably would have succeeded. However, President Nixon ordered the invasion of Cambodia in the summer of 1970, bringing to a halt all normal operations of the Senate and House except the functions of committee staffs. Congressmen and their personal staffs were totally immersed in a government-induced constitutional crisis which did not subside until June. When Redman returned to the business of the NHSC, the Public Health Service Amendments Act had been reported out of committee to the floor of the Senate. There was still a chance that Magnuson could amend the bill from the floor, but this strategy would be irregular. Substantive policy changes are seldom introduced without first being considered by the responsible committee. Magnuson would be in the position of defending a fairly controversial proposal without backing from the Committee on Labor and Public Welfare or HEW.

This development forced the proponents of the NHSC, Bergman, Redman, and Magnuson, back to their own resources. They would have to write their own bill. Assistance in drafting the legislation was sought from Dr. Egeberg, assistant secretary for Health and Scientific Affairs, a division of HEW. Egeberg, something of a maverick in the Nixon administration, promised staff assistance, which he was unable to deliver. His nominal subordinates in HEW refused to support a program strengthening PHS which the Office of Management and Budget and the president's own White House staff were seeking to dismantle. Twenty-seven cosponsors were found for the bill in the Senate, among them some Republicans. Such support is useful for showing that the bill is safe; there is strength in numbers. The bill was assigned to the Committee on Labor and Public Welfare, chaired by Senator Yarborough (Democrat, Texas), for hearings and a report on its merits.

At this point something happened which was quite small but which is typical of the manner in which Congress conducts its business. It was late in the session, August 25, when Redman received a call from Lee Goldman, a staff member of Senator Yarborough, arranging a luncheon appointment for the following day. At the luncheon Goldman got right down to business. He would expedite Senator Yarborough's schedule, allowing consideration of the NHSC bill by the Committee on Labor and Public Welfare in this congressional session, if Redman would use his influence with Magnuson. "I know there are some specific things Yarborough would really like to see Maggie put in that bill," Goldman said. Lamely, Redman replied that he lacked the sort of influence to play the game. He was a junior staff member on board for a limited period of time, not one of the senior staff with independent standing with the senator. That pretty much concluded the discussion with Goldman until he happened to mention, in the way of small talk, that he planned to become a lobbyist for the Association of American Medical Colleges the following year:

> "Well," I said casually, "if you're going to lobby for the AAMC, I guess you'll be seeing a lot of Senator Magnuson next year."
> For the first time during our luncheon, Goldman's composure seemed to change. We moved on to other topics, but before we parted outside the restaurant, we had more or less agreed that perhaps three days *might* be sufficient to prepare for a hearing.
> Twenty minutes later, back in Magnuson's office, I received a call from Goldman.
> "I just talked with Senator Yarborough," he informed me. "Hearings on S. 4106 [the NHSC bill] will be held this Friday."[34]

Following the successful hearings conducted by Yarborough, a favorable report was still not forthcoming from the committee. Republicans, opposed to the Occupational Health and Safety Act, could not produce enough votes in committee to kill the bill, but they could collaborate to deprive the committee of a sufficient number of senators (a quorum) to transact business. Failing the muster of a quorum, neither the NHSC nor the OSHA could reach the floor of the Senate for a vote. Again, Redman needed to intercede, this time with a top aide of Senator Javits (Republican, New York). He pointed out that Javits had supported the bill in committee and that it seemed unfair to kill the proposal because of opposition to another bill. Javits agreed with this reasoning and enlisted the aid of his fellow Republicans in producing a temporary quorum. The NHSC bill was reported out of committee and passed on the floor of the Senate by an overwhelming vote.

Meanwhile, the bill had come to a complete standstill in the House of Representatives. Magnuson had worked out an agreement with Paul Rogers, chairman of the Health Subcommittee of the House Committee on Interstate and Foreign Commerce, to introduce legislation in behalf of the NHSC at the same time on the floor of the House and Senate. The Washington *Evening Star,* trying to startle a few readers and to sell a few newspapers, had headlined the joint introduction of the legislation, "Bill Seeks Care of Poor by Government Doctors." Tim Lee Carter (Democrat, Kentucky), a member of Rogers's subcommittee, had immediately informed him that he was withdrawing support for the bill, and Rogers received a telegram from a group of Florida doctors expressing opposition. The bill was "socialized medicine." Rogers withdrew as cosponsor of the bill (he was facing a general election in a few months), stating that given its present ideological coloration, it could never get out of subcommittee.

Rogers won reelection to Congress handily. With the glow of electoral victory to inspire him, he subdued his anxieties about the socialist aspects of the national health service corps and introduced the legislation in the House. The bill was immediately referred to his subcommittee on health. After two days of hearings, it was reported out of subcommittee to the full (standing) Committee on Interstate and Foreign Commerce, where it was voted on and cleared for action.

Carter assisted Rogers's efforts to speed the passage of the bill through the Health Subcommittee. The congressmen overcame their initial doubts because the socialism which the bill provided benefited their own heavily rural, medically-understaffed communities. By and large the saying is true that America prescribes capitalism for the poor and socialism for the rich. One exception to this rule is the rare socialist project which benefits the rural and ghetto constituencies, of which the NHSC is an example. If the American Medical Association had entered the fray, it is doubtful that such socialism would have prevailed. As the early ambivalence of Rogers and Carter illustrates, rural legislators are easily scared off by the cant of established wealth and of privilege masked as professionalism.

Each bill introduced in Congress is, as one observer graphically states, "a Pauline in perpetual peril," an "Eliza crossing the ice."[35] Fewer than 3 percent of the bills introduced in Congress become public laws. In the ninety-second Congress (1971–1972), 25,354 bills were introduced but only 607 became public law.[36] The NHSC had eluded premature death in the Senate Labor and Public Welfare Committee because of the timely interventions of Redman in securing hearings and a quorum. Despite the noncooperation of HEW and the initial delay in the House Committee on Health, the bill had reasonably good prospects for passage in the ninety-first Congress. But the difficulties were far from over.

Unlike the Senate, in the House bills reported out of committee do not go directly to the floor for action by the full chamber. Instead, for reasons attributed to the press of legislation, bills face the intermediate step of consideration by the House Rules Committee. This committee is often compared to a traffic cop. It expedites the flow of legislation in the House by stipulating the rules under which a bill shall be debated, how long and by which parties, and whether amendments may be offered from the floor or not. Unlike a traffic cop, however, the committee is not neutral about the matters it advances for consideration. It can and does use its formal powers to handicap or to block legislation of which it disapproves. In 1961, the membership of the Rules Committee was increased from twelve to fifteen, the object being to break up a conservative coalition of Southern Democrats and Republicans that blocked much legislation. This tactic has met with modest success. Today, as before, the Rules Committee can still deprive the House of an opportunity to consider legislation favorably reported out by one of its own standing committees.

The powers of the Rules Committee are at their height in an "adjournment crush," the period at the end of a congressional session when a multitude of bills are awaiting consideration and action on the floor of the House. By deciding which bills will advance and which will be delayed, the Rules Committee can virtually determine what will become law and what not. This is precisely the moment when the NHSC came before the Rules Committee. It was mid-December, quite late in a congressional session, which by law was required to expire on January 2, 1971. Seizing the opportunity which the moment presented, the Republicans on the Rules Committee requested a personal interview with President Nixon. They pointed out to him that of the sixty bills awaiting action in the House, only a small number, no more than twelve, could receive attention on the floor. If he would indicate which twelve he wished to go forward, they would take care of the rest. Surprisingly, and surely to his later regret, Nixon did not take advantage of the opportunity being handed him. The Republicans were giving him a chance to kill in secrecy and stealth bills which he later sought to block, publicly and unsuccessfully, through the pocket veto. The Republicans returned to the Rules Committee without instructions, and thus the NHSC, along with other administration-opposed legislation, escaped a beautifully timed, nicely calculated ambush. Along with a handful of other bills, the NHSC was reported out of committee to the floor of the House. The rule issued by the committee allowed a two-hour debate on the bill, rather a lot of time for the end of a congressional session, and amendments from the floor.[37]

The NHSC legislation passed by a considerable majority in the House. Even so, the bill was still in peril. What happened next underlines the truth of a principle which I have asserted in another place. Ours is not, as we are often told, a constitutional system of separation of powers. It is a constitutional system of separate institutions sharing power.[38] Each one of the institutions of government—executive, legislative, and judicial (and federal, state, and local)—shares extensively in the exercise of powers allocated to one of its corivals in the system. In the present instance, the power in which both legislative and executive institutions shared was the legislative. "I am part of the legislative process," President Dwight Eisenhower said as preface to his veto of a bill passed by Congress. But there are other techniques, more refined and subtle than presidential veto, by which the chief executive can shape legislative outcomes.

There is, for example, the *pocket veto.* The pocket veto may be exercised when there are fewer than ten workdays remaining in a congressional session (Sundays and holiday recesses not counting). In this event, the president may prevent legislation from becoming law simply by failing to sign it. In all other cases, the president must sign the bill (whereupon it immediately becomes law), fail to act on it (whereupon it becomes law within ten congressional workdays), or veto it. If he vetoes the legislation, Congress may override the veto by a two-thirds vote of each house (whereupon the bill becomes law). If Congress fails to override the veto, the bill does not become law. In the waning days of the Ninety-first Congress, Redman and his cohorts extended themselves mightily to remove the possibility of a pocket veto. They calculated that if they could get the NHSC on the president's desk no later than December 19, more than ten congressional workdays (excluding Sundays and holiday recess at Christmas and New Year) would remain in the session scheduled for termination on January 2. Thus the possibility of a pocket veto would be averted. A pocket veto was feared because HEW, at the direction of the White House staff and the OMB, had testified against the legislation in the House subcommittee on health.

In his efforts to avoid a pocket veto Redman lost the battle but won the campaign. The weak point in the plan was the system of separate institutions sharing power. The House version of the NHSC was rushed to the Senate on December 19, where by prearrangement the Senate agreed to the House version of the bill by a simple voice vote. But it was not immediately forwarded to President Nixon for action as Redman planned. Before the bill is sent to the chief executive, it must be signed by the speaker of the House and the president pro tem of the Senate. The latter is the vice-president of the United States, who presides over the Senate as an element of his official duties. Frequently, given the demands on his time, the vice-president will designate an alternate to act in his stead. The engrossing of bills to be forwarded to the president is normally a routine matter. Speaker of the House Carl Albert signed the NHSC on December 19. But Vice-President Spiro T. Agnew put in a call to the Senate clerk on December 19, reserving his personal right to sign the bill rather than having his alternate (who can be any senator) act in his behalf. Thus the bill languished in the well of the Senate until December 22, preserving for Nixon the option of the pocket veto.

Nixon had used the pocket veto to thwart the Family Practice Act, a bill of Yarborough's designed to train more family doctors. This veto was unconstitutional because it was announced by the White House during the Christmas recess while Congress was still officially in session and it stimulated a storm of controversy in Congress and in the press. To avoid further controversy over pocket vetoes dealing with medical legislation, Nixon signed the National Health Service Corps Act into law.

Does the passage of the NHSC support or does it conflict with the view that congressional decision making neglects matters of major social importance and is inattentive to repressed interests? The evidence based on this case is ambiguous. The NHSC was indeed signed into law, but almost inadvertently; that is, it became law by fluke. At several points in the legislative process, the act advanced in defiance of the laws of probability and logic.

Miraculously, Abraham Bergman, a political activist as much as a pediatrician, repeatedly intervened to provide rural and ghetto communities with a spokesman for their medical needs. The organized interests, the American Medical Association and American Hospital Association, which exercise a near monopoly over licensing, the supply of physicians, the distribution and cost of services, and rules governing hospitals, did not feel their powers of control sufficiently threatened to oppose the NHSC. In the absence of this opposition, the interests of a repressed segment of the population were voiced and acted on.

By a coincidence, it so happened that the legislative assistant for Yarborough, Goldman, who was to become a lobbyist for the AAMC the following year, was susceptible to influence by a person from Magnuson's office and agreeable, therefore, to hold hearings on an accelerated schedule. *By chance,* Redman learned about the difficulties of Yarborough in getting a quorum of his committee and so was able to intervene to obtain the cooperation of the Republican members. *Fortunately,* Rogers and Carter changed their minds about the socialist aspects of the NHSC.

In a fit of absent-mindedness, Nixon failed to avail himself of the opportunity presented by the Republican members of the Rules Committee to kill off the bill. *By the greatest good luck,* Nixon created such a row about the pocket veto of other medical legislation that he retreated from the pocket veto of the NHSC. Thus the outcome is not at all reassuring. It suggests that social knowledge and resources are allocated in an aimless, inattentive, and almost haphazard manner. It carries the implication that repressed interests require a zealot to speak for them and that dominant groups must be caught napping for action to occur.

The element of fluke in the passage of the NHSC is borne out in other case studies of the legislative process. The Civil Rights Act of 1960 was brought to the floor of the Senate by the legerdemain of Lyndon Johnson, then the Senate majority leader. Johnson opened the floor to amendments on an unrelated bill, knowing that amendments to Senate bills need not be germane to their substance. The Civil Rights Act of 1960 was an amendment to a bill providing for the leasing of officers' club facilities, and it was only debated and acted on in the Senate because the senators thought they were going to talk about something completely different.[39] The Education Bill of 1960, a bill providing for federal aid to public schools, was struck down by the Rules Committee after being passed by majorities on the floor of the House and Senate. Minor differences between the House and Senate versions required that the bill be sent to a conference committee. Bills going to this committee from the House must first pass through the Rules Committee. Here the bill met an unexpected end as Congressman Delaney, a Catholic, voted against the bill, along with fiscal conservatives and segregationists, because it provided no federal aid for parochial schools.[40] Similarly, the final version of the Full Employment Act of 1945 was opposed on the floor of the House and Senate by its original sponsors. In its initial version the bill was to guarantee work to all who sought it, a commitment keenly felt toward the returning veterans of World War II. In its final version, as Alben Barkley put it, the bill guaranteed "everyone who wanted a job the right to go out and look for one." The bill was so marked up in committee to make it acceptable to its opponents that the original sponsors ended up by opposing it.[41]

As a postscript to this discussion, the National Health Service Corps is among the government programs proposed for elimination by the Reagan administration in its 1982 budget. No new scholarships will be awarded because of the administration's finding that the problem of access to medical care in areas formerly regarded as deficient is now "virtually eliminated."[42] Current scholarship holders will be allowed to finish their studies, but no new scholarship money will be made available. Additionally, Senator Magnuson was among the six Democratic senators defeated in a reelection bid in 1980. The fate of the NHSC is gravely in doubt, given the upper hand conservative liberalism has in the Senate, along with the inroads it has made in the House. This outcome offers further grounds for thinking that America's commitment to the ideas and practical arrangements of liberalism is a misfortune; many worthwhile social experiments, such as the NHSC, are never tried, and when they are, given a premature burial.

PROSPECTS FOR REFORM

Efforts to reform Congress, a recurrent feature of American politics, are often inspired by news of some fresh scandal. Select committees on reform are then invested with the public relations function of smoothing and tempering public opinion. One of the directions of reform is the *internal structure of power* in Congress. From Woodrow Wilson (who inveighed against the evils of the committee system) to Richard Bolling (Democrat, Missouri), a contemporary reform spokesman, there have been many attempts to give the elective leadership of Congress greater powers over the committee and subcommittee chairmen (subject to review and approval by the party caucus), the better to hold them responsible for the content of legislative policy. These efforts are inspired by the belief that majorities in the Senate and House are progressive and that, in any event, major social issues should be discussed and decided on in an open manner.[43]

A second direction of reform has dealt with the *jurisdictional alignments* of the major committees in Congress. The efforts to reorganize the committees and subcommittees in the House that share in the formation of energy policy provides a good example. In 1974, two years after the Arab oil embargo and several years before President Carter presented the nation's first National Energy Plan (1977), Representative Bolling cochaired with David Martin (Republican, Nebraska), a select committee which investigated the merits of reshuffling the functions of the many energy policy-making committees (among several other matters of investigation). The Bolling committee proposed the creation of a new energy and environment supercommittee, which was to be carved out of the warring jurisdictions of the relevant committees. The Bolling committee found that tax incentives for exploration and discovery were concentrated in the Committee on Ways and Means; that the nuclear energy industry was presided over by the Joint Committee on Atomic Energy; that regulation of prices for oil and natural gas fell within the purview of the Interstate and Foreign Commerce Committee; that Naval petroleum reserves were the responsibility of the Armed Services Committee; that mining regulations were set by the Interior and Insular Affairs Committee; that energy power administrations, dealing with hydropower, were under the direction of the Public Works Committee; and that proposed federal energy agencies were reviewed by the Government Operations Committee.[44]

The Bolling committee's recommendation in behalf of an energy supercommittee was defeated by the House. To facilitate House consideration of the proposed National Energy Plan (1977), the speaker appointed members to an Ad Hoc Committee on Energy. This committee did not provide a jurisdictional change in the House committees and subcommittees shaping energy policy; its functions were restricted to coordinating the activities of its members, not to drafting legislation. The Ad Hoc Committee was dissolved, having served its purpose, following the enactment of the National Energy Plan into law in 1978.

Today, with eighty-three House committees and subcommittees asserting jurisdiction over some aspect of energy policy, the situation is even more complicated than in 1974. A major new standing committee in the energy policy field has been created, the Committee on Science and Technology, which exercises responsibility among other things in alternative energy, synthetic fuels, and fusion. The confusion in House deliberations on energy policy is illustrated by the fact that President Carter's proposal to develop synthetic fuels (1979) was reported by the Banking, Finance, and Urban Affairs Committee instead of by one of the three standing committees with leading jurisdiction in energy policy, that is, Interior and Insular Affairs, Science and Technology, and Interstate and Foreign Commerce. House rules give the Banking Committee control over programs to assure the continued supply of materials needed for national defense; the committee prevailed on the speaker to obtain jurisdiction over the bill on this basis. The confused situation has given new impetus to efforts of the select committee to create an energy supercommittee. Legislation to this effect will be introduced in Congress in 1980.[45] By comparison, the complexion of energy policy-making committees in the Senate is more simplified, with two standing committees, the Committee on Finance and the Committee on Energy and Natural Resources, sharing responsibility for reporting energy legislation.

A third significant direction of congressional reform is toward *campaign financing*. Large sums of special interest money, formerly used in the funding of presidential primary campaigns and the general election, are now being deflected into congressional races. The Federal Election Law (1974) authorized public financing for presidential campaigns, which has released the funds now going to congressional candidates. The avenue through which these funds are contributed is political action committees (PACs), which may be corporate, trade and professional, labor, or ideological. The PACs are headquartered in Washington, D.C., with branch offices in state and local communities. Donors to the PACs are limited to $5,000, and PACs may contribute no more than $5,000 to the election of a particular candidate.[46] There is no upper limit on the total contributions a candidate may receive from supporting PACs. Various kinds of PACs furnished House candidates with 25 percent of their campaign funds and Senate candidates with 13 percent in 1978. The number of PACs has more than doubled (to more than 1,000) since 1975.[47]

Along with the tendency toward independent candidate organizations (Chapter 4) and the proliferation of subcommittee chairmen in Congress, the PACs have further enhanced the advantages of incumbency. Congressional incumbents typically hold a two-to-one edge in financing over challengers.[48] A Common Cause report puts the issue sharply: "The money flows to incumbents because it is an incumbent who has the power. . . . The result is that in Congress today we have neither a Democratic nor Republican party. Rather we have an Incumbency party which operates a monopoly."[49] Another trend that PACs intensify is toward increasing sources of congressional campaign support from business, professional, and ideological groups. At the end of 1977, business PACs numbered 550, up from 139 in 1975. The number of trade associations and ideological PACs increased from 318 to 556. During the same period, labor political action committees increased from 201 to 234. The combined receipts of business PACs totalled $11.7 million in 1977, and receipts of labor PACs totalled $7.2 million.[50] The American Medical Association, through its political action committee, AMPAC, is far and away the leading contributor to congressional campaigns. AMPAC contributed more than $1.6 million to candidates for Congress in 1977 and 1978 and expected to contribute at roughly the same level in 1980.[51]

Reformers say that the most direct way of dealing with the flood of money to congressional campaigns is by public financing of House and Senate elections with accompanying spending limits. One proposal sponsored by Common Cause and several key figures in the House is to provide five $10,000 payments to candidates from the federal government. Each payment would have to be matched by $10,000 in private contributions, not exceeding $100 each. A candidate who takes the money would agree not to spend more than $150,000 unless his or her opponent refused public spending. In that case, the ceiling would not apply. The money would come through a $1 checkoff on the federal tax forms, the same source of money that is tapped for presidential campaigns.[52] So far this proposal has not won the support of either political party.

CONCLUSION

The varieties of reform, structural, financial, and jurisdictional, have not fared well in recent sessions of Congress. Why not? The answer should be seen against the structural and constitutional biases described in this and other chapters. Because the political parties are in decline, it does not make a great deal of sense to vest hopes in a structural reform that places greater authority in the hands of the elective leadership. The trend toward diffusion of power among the committees and subcommittees and the formation of subgovernments—military-industrial, petrochemical, rivers-harbors-dams, automobile-oil-highway—both reflects and exacerbates the disintegration of the political parties. Now, virtually every congressman, if he so desires, has an opportunity to head up a subgovernment, a baronetcy instead of a barony if you please, but still an independent piece of political turf from which to accumulate incumbency and power.[53] Redrafting of jurisdictional alignments, as proposed in the reforms of the select committees, would break up some of these policy domains, requiring those who preside over them to seek new conquests. Reform of campaign finances runs up against similar considerations. Put simply, it would interfere with the monopoly control of office enjoyed by the incumbency party.

Above all, the constraints imposed by the constitutional system on political action weigh against the prospects for reform of Congress. The trend toward diffusion of power; the decentralized bargaining relationships among subcommittee and committee chairmen; the formation of subgovernments dominating particular spheres of policy; the declining strength of the political parties and elective leadership; the sprawling, disorderly battle tempered by negotiations—all reflect important features of constitutional arrangements created or set in motion by Madison and the founding fathers. All these features stand in the way of the goals of the reformers. One consequence of the projected failure of political reform is that matters of major social importance, energy policy, health care, and urban politics, will not become the focused object of discussion and decision by members of Congress. The institution of Congress, and congressmen individually, so it appears, are afflicted by a permanent blindness built into the nature of American political institutions and the constitutional ideas used in their design.

NOTES

1. Richard Corrigan, "The Sunshine in Room S-334," *National Journal,* April 4, 1978, p. 681.

2. Richard Corrigan and Richard Kirschten, "The Energy Package," *National*

Journal, November 4, 1978, p. 1,764; *Washington Post,* April 22, 1978, A1, 6.

3. Robert Paul Wolff, *The Poverty of Liberalism* (Boston: Beacon Press, 1968), chap. 3.

4. V. O. Key, *Politics, Parties, and Pressure Groups,* 4th ed. (New York: Thomas Y. Crowell, 1958), chap. 24.

5. Richard F. Fenno, Jr., "The Internal Distribution of Influence: The House," in *The Congress and America's Future,* ed. David B. Truman, (Englewood Cliffs, N.J.: Prentice-Hall, 1965), p. 59.

6. *Ibid.*

7. Richard L. Lyons, "House Energy Unit Relies on Ashley's Harmonizing Talents," *Washington Post,* April 26, 1977, A2.

8. Nelson Polsby, *Congress and the Presidency* (Englewood Cliffs, N.J.: Prentice-Hall, 1965), pp. 43–45.

9. Mary Russell, "House Democrats Elect Wright Leader By One," *Washington Post,* December 7, 1976, A1.

10. David R. Mayhew, *Congress: The Electoral Connection* (New Haven, Conn.: Yale University Press, 1976), p. 100.

11. Martin Tolchin, "Byrd Persuasive as Senate Chief," *The New York Times,* March 27, 1977, pp. 1, 44.

12. Mary O'Neill, "O'Neill: Parlaying Popularity and Power," *Washington Post,* December 31, 1976, A1.

13. Key, *Politics, Parties, and Pressure Groups.*

14. Woodrow Wilson, *Congressional Government* (New York: Meridian Books, 1960), p. 82.

15. Stephen K. Bailey, *Congress in the Seventies* (New York: St. Martin's Press, 1970), pp. 52–53.

16. *Ibid.*

17. Mayhew, *Electoral Connection,* pp. 123–25.

18. Daniel Berman, *In Congress Assembled* (New York: Macmillan, 1966), chaps. 6 and 7.

19. Michael J. Malbin, "House Democrats Oust Senior Members from Power," *National Journal,* January 25, 1975, pp. 129–34; "House Reforms—The Emphasis is on Productivity, Not Power," *National Journal,* December 4, 1976, pp. 1,731–37.

20. Morris P. Fiorina, *Congress: Keystone of the Washington Establishment* (New Haven, Conn.: Yale University Press, 1977), p. 64.

21. Bruce I. Oppenheimer, "Subcommittee Government and Congressional Reform," *DEA News Supplement,* Summer 1976, S-10.

22. Mayhew, *Electoral Connection,* pp. 94–96.

23. See Wilson, *Congressional Government,* p. 77.

24. James Clotfelter, *The Military in American Politics* (New York: Harper & Row, 1973), chap. 7; and Seymour Melman, *Pentagon Capitalism* (New York: McGraw-Hill, 1970).

25. George C. Wilson, "16-State House Coalition to Battle Base Closings," *Washington Post,* April 27, 1977, A1, 6.

26. Walter Pincus, "When a Campaign Vow Crashes into a Pork Barrel," *Washington Post,* April 1, 1977, A1, 6.

27. *Ibid.;* and see Grant McConnell, *Private Power and American Democracy* (New

York: Vintage Books, 1966), chap. 7; and David Truman, *The Governmental Process* (New York: Knopf, 1958), chap. 13.

28. Roger H. Davidson and Walter J. Oleszek, *Congress Against Itself* (Bloomington: Indiana University Press, 1977), p. x.

29. Robert Paul Wolff, *The Poverty of Liberalism* (Boston: Beacon Press, 1968), chap. 3.

30. Ernest Barker, *Essays on Government* (London: Oxford University Press, 1965), pp. 56–85.

31. Robert R. Alford, *Health Care Politics* (Chicago: University of Chicago Press, 1975), p. 14.

32. Eric Redman, *The Dance of Legislation* (New York: Simon & Schuster, 1973), pp. 31, 225.

33. Arnold Heidenheimer, Hugh Heclo, and Carolyn Adams, *Comparative Public Policy: The Politics of Social Choice in Europe and America* (New York: St. Martin's Press, 1975), p. 39.

34. Redman, *Dance of Legislation,* p. 113.

35. See the foreword by Richard Neustadt in Redman, *Dance of Legislation,* p. 12.

36. *Congressional Record,* November 8, 1972, D1,227.

37. Redman, *Dance of Legislation,* pp. 240–42.

38. Richard Neustadt, *Presidential Power* (New York: John Wiley, 1963), chap. 3.

39. Daniel M. Berman, *A Bill Becomes A Law,* 2nd ed. (New York: Macmillan, 1966), pp. 57–59.

40. Robert Bendiner, *Obstacle Course on Capitol Hill* (New York: McGraw-Hill, 1965), pp. 186–89.

41. Stephen Kemp Bailey, *Congress Makes a Law* (New York: Vintage Books, 1964), chap. 8.

42. *The New York Times,* February 20, 1981, A13.

43. Richard Bolling, *House Out of Order* (New York: Dutton, 1966).

44. Davidson and Oleszek, *Congress Against Itself,* p. 61.

45. "Staff Report to the Select Committee on Committees on House Committee Energy Jurisdictions," *National Journal,* October 6, 1979, p. 1,652.

46. *National Journal,* November 24, 1979, pp. 1,982–84.

47. *National Journal,* April 8, 1978, pp. 557–61.

48. William J. Crotty, *Political Reform and the American Experiment* (New York: Thomas Y. Crowell, 1977), p. 114.

49. *National Journal,* August 9, 1980, p. 1,308.

50. *National Journal,* April 8, 1978, pp. 557–61.

51. *National Journal,* December 1, 1979, pp. 2,017–22.

52. *National Journal,* April 8, 1978, pp. 557–61.

53. Fiorina, *Congress,* p. 66.

CHAPTER *9*

Presidential Power: Its Pursuit, Use, and Abuse

I think the Founding Fathers expected the President to be the leader of our country. The President is the only person who can speak with a clear voice to the American people and set a standard of ethics and morality, excellence and greatness. He can call on the American people to make a sacrifice and explain the purpose of the sacrifice, propose and carry out bold programs to protect, to expose and root out injustice and discrimination and divisions among the population. He can provide and describe a defense posture that will make our people feel secure, a foreign policy that will make us proud once again.

> Governor Jimmy Carter, quoted in an interview with the *National Journal* (August 7, 1976)

■

I think my biggest mistake has been in inadvertently building up expectations too high.

> President Jimmy Carter in a December 28, 1977, television interview; quoted in the *National Journal* (January 1, 1978)

■

We will need . . . what the Constitution envisioned: a Chief Executive who is the vital center of action in our whole scheme of government.

> Senator John F. Kennedy, speech to the National Press Club (January 14, 1960)

■

I would say the problems are more difficult than I imagined them to be. The responsibilities placed on the United States are greater than I imagined them to be, and there are greater limitations upon our ability to bring about a favorable result than I had imagined them to be.

> President John F. Kennedy, midterm television conversation on the presidency (December 17, 1962)

OFFICE OF THE PRESIDENCY

Our main concern in this chapter is with the office of the presidency and the limits of presidential power. By the office, I mean an institutional personality created by the Constitution and later developed by history, statute, personal initiative, and custom; by the limits of power, I mean the constraints imposed by the office on the man. I shall argue that the eighteenth-century attributes of presidential office poorly prepare a president to reconcile democracy with the expanding influence of corporate power over public policy in the twentieth century.

To focus attention on presidential office reverses the emphasis to which we are accustomed. Customarily, attention is focused on the personality of the president, for to be elevated to presidential office is to achieve celebrity status. The food preferences, hobbies, motor skills, pastimes, aesthetic tastes of presidents receive intense speculation; barometric readings of national moods and prospects are based on a single presidential press conference. The newspapers both create and feed on a vast and seemingly inexhaustible appetite for details about the president's daily round of activities. A picture of the president on the front page helps to sell newspapers. In this chapter, however, I shall show that the office shapes the man to a greater extent than is commonly supposed.

The Constitution is something more than a written memorandum of association: It exerts both an enabling and constraining influence on practical politics (Chapter 2). The Constitution imposes two major roles on presidential office: One demands that the man in office will be the personification of national sovereignty; the other requires that he will be a power broker.

PERSONIFICATION OF NATIONAL SOVEREIGNTY

The constitutional idea of the president as personification of national sovereignty is derived from the theories of Hobbes and Locke. Both had argued that there must be an authority of the last resort, a sovereign bolstered by the power of the sword, to survive in contests with the ruthless individuals produced by capitalism. Hobbes said that the state must have a right equivalent to that claimed by the near lawless individuals of the state of nature; its authority must be absolute, for that was the extent of the claims of modern individualism. In a similar manner Locke held that the executive possessed an indefinite discretionary power to act "without the prescription of the Law, and sometimes even against it," where the preservation of society and civil order were at stake.[1] In the writings of Hobbes and Locke, especially the latter, the preservation of society through the power of the state is tied to the preservation of the rights of property.

Hamilton read into the office of the American chief executive the doctrines of state sovereignty derived from the theories of Hobbes and Locke. For Hamilton, the president was the visual embodiment of the absolute power of the state. Writing under the pseudonym Pacificus, while serving as Secretary of Treasury in Washington's cabinet, Hamilton argued that Article II of the Constitution was an indefinite grant of power to the chief executive.

The occasion for Pacificus, as the tract came to be known, was the Proclamation of Neutrality issued by George Washington in 1793 concerning the conflict between England and France. The proclamation aroused sharp criticism among the Jeffersonian Republicans; they asserted that America had abandoned her former ally in the revolutionary struggles against England and that the chief executive lacked authority to determine the course of foreign relations. In reply, Hamilton noted that the language of Article II, "The executive power shall be vested in a President of the United States," suggested a sweeping grant of power, not limited by any of the succeeding clauses. Even though the Constitution did not provide specific authorization for the president to conduct foreign relations, neither did it prohibit it. The president could, therefore, take any action not specifically denied by the Constitution or reserved to one of the coordinate branches of government. The only limits on his powers of initiative were those set by rival institutions, Congress and the judiciary, with whom the president shared power.[2]

In *Federalist* No. 70, written a few years before Pacificus, Hamilton makes clear that his interest in the powers of the chief executive is linked to a concern for the rights of property. "Energy in the Executive," a euphemism for the coercive power of the state, "is a leading character in the definition of good government." An "energetic" executive is good because it is "essential to the protection of the community against foreign attacks." It also protects business success from those who have fallen prey to the evils of commercial capitalism. Hamilton says, "[Energy] is not less essential to the steady administration of the laws; to the protection of property against those irregular and high handed combinations which sometimes interrupt the ordinary course of justice; to the security of liberty against the enterprises and assaults of ambition of faction and of anarchy."[3] Hamilton straightforwardly proposed to strengthen the hand of the state, which is identical with the president's hand, in preparation for the inevitable crunch with the propertyless.

Besides the sweeping grant of power vested in the chief executive by the loosely drawn language of Article II, other provisions of the same article are based on a conception of the president as the embodiment of state sovereignty. Article II says that the president shall be a single rather than a multiple head of government. Further it states that the president shall have the power to "receive Ambassadors and other public ministers," the power "to grant reprieves and pardons for Offences against the United States, except in Cases of impeachment," and the responsibility "to see that the laws be faithfully executed." The power to "recognize" other countries and to seek recognition gives the president final judgment on a claim made by a ruling group in another country to control its territory and population. Logically, such a judgment can only be made by one who possesses a similar power in relation to the domestic population of his own nation. The power to grant reprieves, pardons, and amnesties involves the power of life and death over all individuals who may be a threat to the internal order and security of the United States. Finally, the power to "take care that the laws be faithfully executed" confers on the president the responsibility to preserve the public order and safety, and the implicit right to use whatever means are needed to execute this responsibility. Acting under this general blanket of authority, presidents have seen fit to suspend the writ of habeas corpus, to impose martial law, to call out the state militia, to seize property and install wiretaps, and to embark on a range of other, similarly extraordinary actions.

Thus, Hamilton's conception of the president as the embodiment of state sovereignty is not a matter of mere historical curiosity. The idea has been repeatedly invoked in the course of American history and has inspired a vast chronology of presidential initiatives. One scholar complains that "Taken by and large, the history of the presidency is a history of aggrandizement."[4] Yet if the preceding account is correct, aggrandizement is built into the conception of the office. The difficulty of setting bounds to presidential power arises from the circumstance that the Constitution is on the president's side.

Perhaps in no other area has the doctrine of presidential sovereignty been more strikingly asserted than in foreign relations. Public statute, presidential initiative, custom, and the Constitution all combine to give the president virtually unlimited authority to initiate and terminate hostilities. In the months preceding the Civil War, Abraham Lincoln instituted a blockade of Southern ports, suspended the writ of habeas corpus, and called out the state militia for a period of ninety days. Theodore Roosevelt fostered the creation of an insurgent government in Panama (in order to secure U.S. canal rights through the isthmus), then sent in U.S. troops to protect these rights from attack by Columbia. Franklin Roosevelt placed the country on a belligerent footing with Germany before World War II by trading U.S. destroyers for British naval bases in the Indies. Harry Truman committed American naval, land, and air forces in South Korea to repel invading North Korean troops. Truman claimed a U.N. Security Council recommendation as the basis for his action; and Congress promptly passed necessary implementing legislation to support it. Both Presidents John Kennedy and Lyndon Johnson sent troops and supplies to South Vietnam in the early 1960s, intervening in an internal civil war. The consequence of this policy was to place the U.S. government on a belligerent footing with the National Liberation Front and later with the North Vietnamese government. President Richard Nixon ordered an invasion of Cambodia in 1972, a country few Americans had heard of, and used funds allocated to another department in order to finance it.[5]

Provisions of the War Powers Act of 1973 seek to curb the authority of the president to initiate and terminate hostilities with foreign powers. The act states that the president has authority to commit U.S. forces only pursuant to a declaration of war, specific statutory authorization, or national emergency created by an attack on the United States. Yet the act recognizes ambiguous situations when the president may act without specific authorization from Congress. For example, the act urges the president "in every possible instance" to consult with Congress before committing U.S. forces or placing them where hostilities may be imminent. Tacitly, the act recognizes the right of the president to intervene militarily even while appearing to disclaim it.

The record of judicial review of the assertions of presidential power is uneven. In *U.S.* v. *Curtiss Wright Export Corporation* (1936) the Supreme Court stated that the president was "sole organ in external relations" and that his powers in this field did not flow from "affirmative grants of the [written] constitution." In *Korematsu* v. *U.S.* (1944) the Court upheld the right of the chief executive to relocate 112,000 Japanese residents of Western states, two-thirds of whom were natural-born citizens. They were removed from their farms and herded first, into camps, later into so-called relocation centers in the deserts of California, Arizona, Idaho, Utah, and Colorado. Yet the Court denied that the president's responsibility to "take care that the laws be faithfully executed" justified seizure of the property of the Youngstown Sheet and Tube Co. (1952). President Truman claimed that continued operation of the plant (closed by a strike) was indispensable to the prosecution of the war in Korea. Additionally, the Court denied an injunction against publication of top-level studies of the process of government involvement in Vietnam in *The New York Times* and *Washington Post*. "National security," the Court held in *New York Times* v. *U.S.* (1971), better known as the case of the Pentagon Papers, did not justify prior censorship. In *United States* v. *Nixon* (1974) the Court denied that the president could withhold tapes of conversations between himself and members of his staff on the grounds of "executive privilege." The right to withhold information, the Court said, can only be maintained to "protect military, diplomatic, and sensitive national security secrets."

POWER BROKER

The role of power broker is not spelled out in the written Constitution but is implicit in its practical arrangements and the tradition of ideas that inform it. In Chapter 2, I stressed that the constitutional system is based on the notion of independently situated actors, people who differ radically from each other in temperament, biography, intelligence, and personal possessions and ruthlessly deploy power in the service of their discrete interests. Madison designed institutions that would induce these rapacious parties to negotiate with each other rather than fight out their differences. The key to his plan is the creation of many, independent, self-sustaining centers of power, thereby giving each interest in society the means of resisting transfers of power and forcing parties to the social conflict to negotiate with each other. This plan is summed up in two phrases: "ambition must be made to counter-act ambition" and "the design of institutions must remedy the defect of better motives."[6]

The manner in which the practical arrangements of the constitution impose a brokerage role on political actors, the president included, has been alluded to in earlier chapters. Thus it is not surprising to encounter these opening words from a modern manual on the presidency: "When we inaugurate a President of the United States we give a man the powers of our highest public office. From the moment he is sworn the man confronts a personal problem: how to make those powers work for *him.*"[7] The perception of politics as the acquisition, enlargement, and collision of personal power is typical of liberalism. It is the sort of problem that Madison posed at the foundation of the republic and resolved through the practical political arrangements we have been describing.

The essence of the solution is that the president should "deal in the coin of self-interest"[8] with those with whom he shares power. The president, whoever he may be and whatever his political backing, must bargain extensively with, among others, the major economic pressure groups (corporations, producers, civil service workers, labor unions, military complex), ethnic groups, entrenched interests in the bureaucracy, and influential people at the state and local level. The power brokers with whom the president must deal are, more often than not, quite powerful figures in their own right. The "power" of the presidency, therefore, is not the power of "command"; rather it is the power to "persuade" independently situated brokers that what the president wants is within their interest and capacity to perform.[9]

PRESIDENTIAL POWER

Whereas the constitutional system confers vast, coercive power on the president as the personification of national sovereignty, it limits the political power available to him in his role as power broker.

However, the notion that the presidency is a powerful political office is cherished by the popular sovereignty theory of American constitutionalism. This view holds that the people are an independently acting, ruling authority, alive in the course of native history, and that periodically, this ruling power is vested in a party and/or heroic political leader. The president should prevail over actors in the political process, according to this view, since he is the instrument of the popular will. This view is often united with the belief that the president is the champion of the underdog and the socially oppressed; he makes democracy work by exerting influence in behalf of underrepresented interests in the political process.

Presidents, themselves, frequently lend support to this view of presidential power (see the quotations from Carter and Kennedy at the beginning of the chapter). Theodore Roosevelt, another example, asserted that the presidency afforded a "bully pulpit," a commanding position from which to shape and lead public opinion. Woodrow Wilson provides the most forceful case for presidential leadership. He said that the president is, at once, the choice of the party and of the nation and that if he chooses to exert political leadership, "no other single force can withstand him, no combination of forces will easily overpower him."[10] An exaggerated view of the political power of the presidency —virtually a myth of presidential leadership—has arisen from such statements.

The founding fathers visualized the presidency as the visible symbol of state power, while ensuring through indirect election and a limited term of office that its occupant would be politically weak. According to Hamilton, executive energy was to be used in keeping off foreign marauders and preserving the relationships of commercial capitalism. This conception of the office has little to do with political leadership, winning and keeping a public following through the skillful presentation of new and persuasive ideas. It has much more to do with the negative characteristics of the merely policing sovereign in the theories of Hobbes and Locke. The president, as Hobbes's sovereign, was merely to preserve the exigencies of public order by waving the sword over his head on necessary occasions.

It may be considered that with the passage of time, and with the rise of political parties, nominating conventions, enlargement of the franchise, media age, public funding of presidential races, and so on, the narrow conception of presidential office held by the founding fathers has been undone. On the other side is the apparent lack of public interest in presidential elections and the failure of the principal candidates and of the cadre leadership of the political parties to arouse the public from apathy. To reiterate, slightly more than one-half of the eligible voters participated in the 1981 election. Since Ronald Reagan won 50 percent of the popular vote, about 25 percent of the eligible voters determined the election of the president. This is not a comforting margin of victory and may not accurately speak for public opinion. The negative conception of the merely policing sovereign lives on in President Reagan's statement that the chief function of government is to "protect us from each other."[11]

The strengths of the constitutional system are most apparent when there is a need to check abuses of executive power, for example, the events surrounding Watergate. The system in this instance worked effectively to bring down a president, Richard Nixon, who committed serious and successive abuses of state power. On the other hand, the weaknesses of the constitutional system are glaringly evident when there is an apparent need to mobilize public support behind a pressing national issue. The Carter administration attempted to exert political leadership for the need to fashion a coherent national energy policy. The structure of preferences shaped by the oil industry, along with its superior organizational capacity, defeated this effort. With the election of Ronald Reagan to presidential office, many of the preferences of the oil industry have been elevated into public policy.

Before evaluating the strengths and weaknesses of presidential office, it is first necessary to familiarize ourselves with the manner in which presidential power is captured and put to use.

PURSUIT OF PRESIDENTIAL OFFICE

The life of the president, one observer notes, is one of "constant bargaining—to get the votes to get nominated, to get the votes to get elected, to get the votes to get bills through Congress, to get the votes to get re-nominated"[12] and so on *ad infinitum*. The life of the president as power broker begins on the road to the White House; if he is to pursue his quest for office with success, he must exert considerable skills in face-to-face negotiations with state and local party leaders, campaign contributors, union officials, and public groups whose support he will need. A study of Jimmy Carter's quest for the party nomination and presidential office is entitled *Marathon,* [13] an apt metaphor in a number of ways. A marathon is a race conducted over a great distance (Carter began his quest for the presidency five years before the party convention); it is a solitary endeavor to reach a distant goal (Fritz Mondale bowed out of the race, saying that he could not bear the prospect of a "whole year sleeping in Holiday Inns"); and eventual success goes to the runner who endures longer than his rivals (among Carter's most admired attributes was "staying power," or sustained drive).

We suspect that it has never been true that "Any American boy can grow up to be president," but the particular ways in which the statement needs to be qualified are not self-evident. First, there are legal criteria which must be satisfied. The Constitution states that a president must be thirty-five years of age, a natural-born citizen, and a resident of the country for fourteen years before becoming president. Second, there are conventional criteria which in many ways are more interesting; they acquire greater force by virtue of being unofficial and assure that the man selected as president will be the independently situated, commercial Protestant whom we have been talking about from the beginning. Among these unwritten rules are that the candidate must be male; have a successful record in business, law, or high public office; be an inveterate joiner of organizations; and have a stable family life. No Jew has ever been a serious presidential candidate, nor have any women or blacks, and only one Catholic (John F. Kennedy) has ever been elected to the office.

Beyond these written and unwritten criteria, a candidate must have certain political assets. He must have a "power base," an office serving an important constituency of interest which can be used to garner additional support and public visibility. Of course, the best place to run for presidential office is from the office itself, and the second best place, from the vice-presidency (vice-presidents placed in nomination by the president to succeed him are invariably nominated by the convention). After these posts, a Senate or gubernatorial position from a large populous, urban-industrial state, contains many advantages. One can be certain of running against a much larger field of rivals as an out-party candidate rather than as an incumbent president or vice-president. The odds of defeating an incumbent president seeking renomination are extremely discouraging, whereas the chances of obtaining the nomination improve against a field of roughly equal competitors.

Since the late 1920s a proven strategy for capturing the party nomination is to advance to an early lead in the presidential primary states while, concurrently, establishing a solid organizational base in the party convention states. Seven candidates who won the nomination for the first time—Herbert Hoover, Al Smith, Dwight Eisenhower, John Kennedy, Barry Goldwater, Jimmy Carter and Ronald Reagan—have used this strategy with success. All of these won nomination on the first ballot; Roosevelt, who employed an identical strategy to capture the nomination was denied first-ballot success by the two-thirds rule not repealed until 1936.[14] An illustrative case, mentioned earlier, is Kennedy's plan for winning the nomination in 1960. Kennedy ran well in the primary states (New Hampshire, Wisconsin, and West Virginia), eliminating weak rivals and demonstrating that his Catholocism was not a serious liability. He took the evidence of his popularity to the convention states and persuaded the party bosses to throw delegate support to his cause. The support of the party regulars who controlled over 60 percent of the delegate votes at the national convention was decisive in giving Kennedy a first-ballot victory.[15] The strategy crosses party lines. Goldwater closely imitated Kennedy's plan in winning the Republican nomination in 1964.

Reforms set in motion by the excesses of Watergate and rioting at the Democratic National Convention in 1968 (see Chapter 4) are intended to democratize the nomination process. The general direction of reform is two-fold: first, to provide public funding for candidates, thus reducing the influence of money; second, to enlarge the number of states selecting delegates by a primary ballot, thus reducing the influence of party bosses.

The Federal Election Campaign Act Amendments of 1974 are an attempt to reform the campaign abuses of the 1972 presidential election when CREEP collected an estimated $45 million in unreported campaign contributions. A substantial portion of these funds were illicitly acquired from corporate donors. The act establishes a $1,000 per person limit on contributions to any one candidate's primary, runoff, and general election campaigns, together with an overall limit of $25,000 on contributions by a single individual to all federal candidates in any one year. Organizations of all kinds are limited to $5,000 per candidate per contest. There is no limit on how many donor groups an organization may create; it is possible that state or regional affiliates of consumer, producer, or labor groups could each contribute a maximum amount of $250,000.[16]

Additionally, the federal treasury will pay qualified candidates seeking their party's presidential nomination an amount equal to the contributions received by the candidates beginning with the first day of the presidential election year. The matching funds will be for all contributions of $250 or less. Although contenders are not prohibited from seeking larger donations, these cannot be included in the sum that the government will equal. To be eligible for matching funds, a potential nominee must raise contributions (of $250 or less) in excess of $5,000 in each of twenty states, the object being to show that the candidate has wide support among a diverse number of party contributors. Each candidate is eligible for a total of $5 million in matching grants, providing that no candidate receives more than 25 percent and no party more than 45 percent of the available money.

An increased number of states is using the primary system of delegate selection. This reform was set in motion by the McGovern Commission, which recommended the selection of delegates through presidential primaries in the same year as the convention and the participation of excluded groups (blacks, women, minorities) in the convention process. Reforms recommended by the commission were acted on in many states, much to everyone's surprise, bringing about a change in the proportion of delegates selected by conventions as opposed to primaries. When Kennedy ran for the nomination in 1960, over 60 percent of the delegates to the national party convention were selected by local party conventions. In 1976, 75 percent of the delegates attending the national convention were selected by presidential primaries.[17]

New presidential candidates come forward every four years; yet the system which elects them, barring the reforms and changes noted, is old. The system is intended to reflect the prejudices of the Whig gentry who founded the nation and drafted its rules of political association. It is not surprising, therefore, to discover a certain degree of homogeneity among presidential candidates, even those of rival party affiliation. Ronald Reagan and his opponent, Jimmy Carter, resemble each other in many nonsuperficial ways. As out-party candidates, Carter in 1976 and Reagan in 1980, there are important similarities in political background, as well as in the tactics and substance of their political campaigns. The differences between the two men were exaggerated by the presidential race in 1980, after Carter belatedly was compelled to defend the neoliberal record of the Democratic party and government regulation of the private sector.

To begin with, both Carter and Reagan meet and exceed the unwritten criteria of presidential candidacy. The physical circumstances of their private lives—Carter as manager of a peanut farm in Georgia grossing over $1 million per year—and Reagan as owner of a lavish ranch in California—provide the Whig version of the "independently situated political actor" with a basis in economic reality. As political candidates with the usual WASP and family attributes, Carter and Reagan may be seen as defending a particular life style rather than

promoting a novel stand on political issues. Both employed their prominence to become governors of developing Sunbelt states. Jimmy Carter
was a one-term governor of Georgia (1970–1974), and Reagan presided
over California as governor for two terms (1966–1974). Both men used
their office to gain access to party notables at the state and local levels
while remaining aloof from the "mess" in Washington.

Tactically, there are many similarities between the political campaigns each waged as out-party candidates. Both men established independent organizations in their home states well in advance of the party
convention whose nomination they hoped to capture. Carter, along
with some of his close associates, decided to contest the Democratic
nomination five years before the party convention (1976). Reagan used
a cluster of advisors, sometimes as a consulting group and sometimes
as a candidate's organization, over a seven-year period. An incumbent
president, Gerald Ford, defeated his effort to obtain the nomination in
1976; but Reagan triumphed in 1980 against a field of candidates (Howard Baker, George Bush, John Connally), all of whom had national
political experience. Before announcing their candidacy, both men trav-
eled extensively on the "mashed potatoes" circuit, talking to state and
local party leaders whose services might be useful to them in the general
campaign. The preconvention strategies of Carter and Reagan focused
intensively on the early primary states (New Hampshire, Wisconsin,
Florida, and North Carolina) in March and April and on an early convention state which a packed field of candidates might overlook (Iowa).
Both won nomination on the first ballot and relied heavily on the media,
rather than party organization, to mount their general campaign.

Carter in 1976 and Reagan in 1980 ran substantively insurgent
political campaigns, emphasizing their position as outsiders, decrying
the mess in Washington, and fully exploiting the liberal anti-state bias.
Reagan's desire to remove "government from the backs of [the] people,"
and to "turn [the people] loose again" to resume the hostilities of the
prepolitical state is too well known at this point to be given further
emphasis. The similar outlook adopted by Jimmy Carter in 1976 is
shadowed by his years in presidential office. As an insurgent candidate
in 1976, Carter could sound very much like the Republican Reagan in
1980. He emphasized the need to decentralize power, to cut down on
federal spending, to provide incentives to the private sector, to emphasize work rather than welfare, to streamline and cut back on the sprawling federal bureaucracy, to reduce taxes, and so on.[18] Carter, like Reagan, cast Washington in the role of a distant, oppressive, colonial power
and signaled that his election would restore certain ancient liberties
which the Republican administration had somehow wrested away.

The point is not to insist that there is no difference between presidential candidates. Of course, there is. The point is not to be fooled. The similarities between presidential candidates are at least as important as their differences. They are late representatives of the Whig elites who have ruled the country from the beginning, and their public stance often typifies this attitude. As candidates and officeholders, they enhance this privileged position at the same time as they provide public service. By running for office, they afford the public the opportunity to participate vicariously in the life of the Whig gentry and to help sustain it.

USE OF PRESIDENTIAL OFFICE

The newspapers are often full of talk about the difficulties of a president with "the lower end of Pennsylvania Avenue," that is, Congress. Such references are often followed by an exhortation on the editorial page that the president should exhibit "strong leadership." Strong presidents are those who prevail in the tussle with Congress by mere force of personality and by skillfully using the powers of their office to maximum advantage. Weak presidents, on the other hand, are those who shrink from battle with the legislature, preferring to take a narrow view of the powers, perquisites, and responsibilities of the office they occupy. The credits in the history books and newspapers, of course, go to the presidents who show the lower end of Pennsylvania Avenue who is in charge.

This view of presidential office is defective, and taken in the main, mistaken. Oddly, this perspective ignores many interesting and important features of the political geography of Washington. A good look shows that the real source of such difficulties as a president may face lies in northwest Washington, where most of the major consumer, producer, labor, and public interest groups are located, rather than in the southeast where Congress, the Library of Congress, and the Supreme Court are. Within a stone's throw of the White House are the AFL-CIO headquarters, the American Petroleum Institute, the Edison Electric Institute, and the National Rifle Association, all of which have much to do with shaping public policy. To direct attention to Congress as the focus of presidential concerns is to miss the larger context. To pick up on a point made earlier, the president must be "persuasive," not only with the groups with which he shares power on Capitol Hill, but also with the major economic pressure groups (corporations, civil service workers, producers, labor chiefs, military armaments manufacturers), public interest groups, the media, entrenched interests in the bureaucracy, and so on.

Presidential office confers certain powers (think of them as levers) which can be activated in face-to-face negotiations with shared power holders to obtain a desired result. Among the power levers we shall discuss in this section are the veto, publicity, budgetary initiative, appointments, and executive reorganization. Other powers of presidential office will be discussed later because of their frequent abuse: impoundment, reprogramming and transfers (of budget items), executive privilege, patronage, and maintenance of public order. The levers of presidential power are activated by the president in his role as power broker to bargain for the support of groups whose assistance he needs. The setting of this bargaining may be the Rose Garden of the White House, but the mechanics of the political relationship are unchanged.

The levers of presidential power are chiefly useful when there is a visible confrontation of interests in the political arena. When modern oligopoly has shaped the structure of public preferences in advance of an observable conflict on the issues, the range of presidential powers will have a limited effect on political outcomes. An example is seen in the effort of the Carter administration to change the energy-intensive life-style to which the oil industry and utilities has accustomed the public over the last thirty years. Carter made little headway in obtaining congressional and public support for the passage of the National Energy Act because of the accepted structure of preferences. We shall give renewed attention to this example after a discussion of the powers of presidential office.

BUDGETARY INITIATIVE

The president, with the assistance of the Office of Management and Budget, takes the initiative in setting forth the priorities of the federal budget. These priorities are stated in general terms when the president delivers the state of the union address to a joint session of Congress in the first week of January. A detailed breakdown of proposed allocations and projected revenues follows the address within a matter of weeks. The Office of Management and Budget, with consultation from the Council of Economic Advisors and experts in the Treasury, undertakes the process of assembling the $300 billion budget twelve months before its introduction in Congress and twenty-two months before the beginning of the fiscal year in which the funds appropriated by Congress are to be spent. For example, preliminary work on the final budget drafted by the Carter administration began in January 1980; a drastically revised version was submitted by the Reagan administration to Congress on February 19, 1981; the appropriations by Congress based on the administration's request will be used in fiscal year 1982, which begins October 1, 1981, and ends September 30, 1982. Congress has about ten months (January to October) to hold hearings, exercise oversight over the program offices, authorize expenditures, and appropriate money.[19]

Since the budget determines "who gets what, when, how," it is a major instrument of presidential power. The Reagan administration seized on the budget as its chief instrument to roll back the tide of neo-liberal programs spawned by the Great Society and to confine the government to the merely policing role visualized by the founding fathers. Leading the effort to gain acceptance for a proposed slash of $41.4 billion in the Carter budget was Reagan's appointee to the Office of Management and Budget, David Stockman. In hearings before the House Committee on the Budget, Stockman said that "The idea that's been established over the last ten years that almost every service that someone might need in life ought to be provided, financed by the Government as a matter of basic right is wrong."[20] This dictum is directed against the neo-liberal critique of the liberal state. Since one cannot feed, clothe, educate, or improve oneself with free speech, free press, and procedural due process, the neo-liberals argue, the state ought to assume responsibility for providing some of these needs. The neo-liberals also assert that medical care, education, housing, and nutrition are as much a human entitlement as the procedural liberties emphasized by conventional liberal ideology. The debate over the Reagan budget is, in essence, a debate between contrasting visions of the role and responsibilities of the state, liberalism versus neo-liberalism.

VETO

The president may use his veto powers to bargain with the elective leadership, committee chairmen, and subcommittee chairmen concerning the substance of legislation. President Carter used the threat of veto power at least twice to amend legislation under consideration in Congress, once to scale down appropriations for the Department of Health, Education, and Welfare, and on another occasion, to eliminate nine out of eighteen dams on a "hit list" of pork barrel expenditures.

Although the veto may be effective in preventing legislation that the president doesn't want, its utility is doubtful in obtaining passage of legislation that the president does want. The effectiveness of the veto is further reduced when opposed legislation is tied to an appropriations measure needed by the government.

PUBLICITY

An important resource of the president is his universal recognition by the public and the comparable obscurity of the average representative.

Studies suggest that only 49 percent of the electorate can identify their congressman. The president can cheaply satisfy a legislator's need for recognition by inviting him or her to the White House for a bill-signing ceremony or for picture-taking sessions and by awarding various mementos from the presidential office. Additionally, the president has the opportunity to shape public opinion on important and controversial issues through the state of the union address, special presentations to joint sessions of Congress, and televised presentations to a nationwide audience. These resources confirm Theodore Roosevelt's observation that the office is a "bully pulpit." On the other hand, it is important to remember that the structure of preferences shaped by the private sector imposes boundaries on the ability of the president to determine the course of public policy. Producer groups spend over $60 billion annually in shaping public choices for transportation, energy, and housing. All these areas overlap in important ways with public policy. As a specific example, Mobil Oil Corporation spends over $23 million annually on public relations and has announced an interest in buying a major urban daily newspaper. This sum exceeds the amount spent by either of the major party candidates on televised advertising in the 1980 presidential campaign.

APPOINTMENTS

The president appoints approximately 2,500 people to positions in the top levels of his administration, which helps him to exert influence over the administration of policy and programs in the upper reaches of the federal bureaucracy. The most sensitive appointments are to positions on the White House staff; 60 aides are thus appointed, without the advice and consent of the Senate. Second, in order of importance and political affiliation with the president are appointments as secretary, undersecretary, and assistant secretary of the departments, along with the administrators and deputies of the independent agencies; 800 appointments are made to these posts, with the advice and consent of the Senate. A third category consists of appointments from the "excepted service" of the civil service, so named because these persons are exempt from the customary requirement of competitive examination and consideration. About 500 appointments are made in this category, without Senate confirmation, principally from members of the academic and business community.[21] The persons appointed in these posts serve in politically sensitive staff positions to cabinet and subcabinet level officials. Finally, 1,100 appointments are made by the president from supergrade positions in the career civil service, without the advice and consent of the Senate.

EXECUTIVE REORGANIZATION

The president has a limited power to reorganize the executive branch. In all cases where the proposed reorganization is major, such as creating or eliminating an agency or increasing or decreasing the authority of an agency, he must proceed with a legislative proposal to which the Congress assents.[22] The president may reorganize the White House staff at his convenience, but he must obtain approval by joint resolution of Congress for significant changes in the Executive Office of the President. President Reagan's proposed abolition of the Department of Energy, the Department of Education, and the Environmental Protection Agency is a major change in the composition of the executive branch. Thus it would have to be embodied in a legislative proposal and win passage in Congress to take effect.

How useful are the levers of presidential power in exerting leadership over an important area of public policy? To provide an example for study, let us reconsider the effort to win passage of a national energy plan (NEP) in the Carter administration. As the centerpiece of Carter's domestic legislative program, this plan almost totally consumed his early years in presidential office. By calling it "the moral equivalent of war," the president placed the full weight of his political prestige behind the proposed legislation. He appeared before a joint session of the Senate and House to present the main features of the plan in April 1977. Briefly, to recapitulate, these elements were to reduce further dependence on oil and gas as the principal energy source, thereby reducing dependence on the importation of oil from the OPEC states at the same stroke. Concurrently, the plan sought to provide inducements for shifting to coal and nuclear energy among industrial users. A crude oil equalization tax to bring domestic crude oil production into line with world energy prices and a conversion tax to induce industrial users to convert from oil and gas to coal were the chief means employed by the plan to realize these objectives. The NEP sought to create additional strategic petroleum reserves in the event of a future interruption of oil supplies. Additionally, the plan sought to provide inducements for energy conservation and experimentation with renewable energy resources.[23]

The crisis atmosphere which has pervaded the attempt to fashion energy policy is informed by the realization that future OPEC oil embargos of the sort that occurred in 1973 would have crippling effects on the U.S. economy and that even without an interruption of supplies, the United States is progressively dependent on resources that are in dwindling supply both domestically and internationally. Today, the United States relies heavily on its least plentiful resources, oil and gas. These resources supply 76 percent of U.S. energy needs although they make up only 7 percent of the nation's energy supply.[24] In 1970 domestic oil production peaked at 9.6 million barrels a day and began to decline rapidly. As a result, by 1973, when the embargo began, 35 percent of the oil consumed in the United States came from abroad. By 1976, with demand rising once again and domestic production falling to around 8 million barrels a day, Americans were importing 40 percent of the oil they consumed. In 1977 oil imports climbed to a record 8.6 million barrels a day, or 46 percent of U.S. energy needs.[25]

At one time or another, and sometimes in combination, presidential responses to the energy crisis have included deception, threat of invasion (of the OPEC states), moral suasion, and brokerage politics. None of these responses has worked so far, and the weight of the evidence strongly suggests that the United States is incapable of developing a coherent energy policy despite its obvious need for one. One of the initial responses to energy shortages in the Ford administration involved the role of the president as the personification of national sovereignty. In January 1975, first Secretary of State Henry Kissinger, then President Gerald Ford, and next Secretary of Defense James Schlesinger (formerly secretary of energy), all speculated aloud in public forums that military action against the OPEC states was a possibility in the event that the Western world was undergoing "actual strangulation." At the time it was widely acknowledged that by dangling the possibility of intervention before the oil producers, the administration hoped to achieve its objectives (lower prices) short of the actual use of force.[26]

President Carter committed the prestige of his office to a national energy plan. He asserted to a joint session of Congress that public institutions must now take responsibility for the allocation of energy resources. "The first principle [of the NEP] is that the energy problem can be addressed only by a Government that accepts responsibility for dealing with it effectively, and by a public that understands its seriousness and is ready to make necessary sacrifices."[27] This assertion was preceded by the now famous declaration that the energy problem presented the country with "the moral equivalent of war," and moreover, a proper resolution constituted a "test of our basic political strength and ability."[28] The president expressed confidence in the ability of the nation and its institutions to withstand this test. "But we have met challenges before and our nation has been the stronger for it . . . I am confident that together we will succeed,"[29] in getting the NEP enacted and implemented.

The House approved the NEP in a form closely resembling the version proposed by the president. The Senate, by contrast, struck down all the proposals at the heart of the plan—the crude oil equalization tax, price controls over natural gas, and utility rate reform. Producer groups with access to the Senate Finance Committee held hostage elements of the plan dealing with domestic crude oil and natural gas in exchange for plow-backs, rebates, and higher prices under phased decontrol; utility companies withdrew the teeth from proposed reform of utility rate structures by making them advisory only.

The president attempted to free the NEP from the Senate impasse in a nationally televised press conference six months after the introduction of the legislation in Congress (April to October 1977). He began by saying that nothing had changed his mind that the energy crisis was "the moral equivalent of war." The seriousness of the crisis, he emphasized, had grown more acute with the passing months. He then attempted to rally the public, consumer groups, and congressional elements favorable to the NEP by a stinging attack on the oil industry. The president asserted that producer groups were attempting to extract windfall profits from the scarce energy sources of oil and gas. "Our proposal, if adopted, would give the oil companies, the producers themselves, the highest price for oil in all the world. But still they want more." The "moral equivalent of war," the president concluded had been transformed into "the biggest rip-off in history."[30]

Public reaction to the president's remarks split along two main lines. Oil industry spokesmen blamed difficulties on a flawed energy program. Supporters of the program blamed the president for having failed to sell it to the public. Whichever is correct, and perhaps neither, the result of the attempt by the president to demonstrate public leadership on the energy problem was the same—it had failed utterly. In the ensuing months the president and his aides followed the only course of action left open to them. They began to negotiate quietly behind the scenes with the producer and utility groups who had bottled up the legislation. Newspapers reports in March and May 1978 carried accounts of the "sweeteners" being offered to producer interests to support the crude oil equalization tax and price controls on natural gas. Among these were such benefits as higher prices for tertiary oil production (oil produced by using high-cost chemical injection techniques); subsidies for converting oil shale, coal, tar sands, or solid waste into liquid fuels; additional funds for research into synthetic fuel products; and phased decontrol of natural gas through 1985 at higher prices than formerly proposed.[31]

The events surrounding the passage of the National Energy Act (1978) illustrate the limits of presidential power. The levers of presidential power can loom large in relation to shared power holders on Capitol Hill and in the bureaucracy. At the same time, they can be tiny in relation to the array of influences which can be mobilized by modern oligopoly when its vital interests are affected. Carter became "Washing-tonized," as the newspapers put it, the moment he perceived that nei-ther public nor party support for the National Energy Plan would be forthcoming and concluded that he must negotiate with powerful pro-ducer groups who held the plan hostage to favorable terms. The critical moment came slightly after a year in office and is candidly acknowl-edged in the quotation already referred to, "I think my biggest mistake has been in inadvertently building up expectations too high." At the time that Carter made this statement, public ratings of his performance were at their lowest. The president drew the appropriate conclusion that "negotiations dealing in the coin of self-interest" were what his own political survival and the passage of the National Energy Plan required. He abandoned his role as the "crusading populist from Plains, Georgia," and took up the role of power broker dictated by the logic of the constitutional system. In the end, President Carter got the National Energy Act he had requested, but it lacked the features of equity and conservation on which he had formerly insisted.

ABUSE OF PRESIDENTIAL OFFICE

The American presidency went through a troubled period in the 1970s. On June 16, 1977, the *Washington Post* published a special anniversary edition of the fifth year of the break-in of the Watergate apartment complex. The *Post* was not celebrating the event but calling attention to its significance. The "cover-up" of the break-in by high officials of the Nixon administration, including by his own admission the president himself, led to his resignation from office. On August 9, 1974, Richard Nixon, thirty-seventh president of the United States, resigned office rather than face certain impeachment by the House of Representatives and trial by the Senate. In the presidential race of 1976, Carter, against the advice of his staff, refused to make an issue of Gerald Ford's pardon of the former president. Both candidates seemed united in a determina-tion to avoid mention of the impact of Watergate on presidential office.

The importance of Watergate for students of the presidency is that it has generated a new interest and concern with abuse of presidential power, that is, abuse of the influence conferred by office. Presidents, of course, are not the only political actors prone to abuse of the powers and perquisites of office; but there are grounds for believing that some of the powers of the presidency are especially susceptible to such abuse. Be-yond those already mentioned (budgetary initiative, veto, and public-ity), there are a range of others (executive privilege, secrecy and classification; patronage, impoundment, reprogramming and transfers; and maintaining public order) that are an occasional source of damaging and sometimes illicit actions. Following is a brief record of abuse in the last two decades.

PATRONAGE

At the president's disposal are powers of appointment to federal judgeships, ambassadorships, cabinet and subcabinet positions, and positions as federal district attorney. He may use these powers to reward those who have worked hard in the election campaign, to co-opt those in his own party who are in incipient opposition, and to recognize independently powerful figures whose support he needs. Generally, the higher the level at which appointment is made, say cabinet level, the more it is a recognition of the independence and power which the appointee possesses.

One way the president's appointive powers has been abused is through the sale of opportunities in the federal service, especially prestigious ambassadorships. An appointment to one of the highly desirable European posts is a possibility for contributions above a certain size to the party coffers. It is far from coincidental that the most substantial contributions, $100,000 and over, are made by wealthy persons who receive assignment to a West European country. As in other things, the Nixon administration extended the practice of sale of ambassadorial posts to the point of wretched excess. In his administration, about 30 percent of the foreign envoy posts were awarded to noncareer personnel. The total amount of donations came to $1.8 million, and most of it (72 percent) was contributed before a set disclosure date.[32]

The abuse of appointive powers in the Nixon administration led Carter to issue a strong statement in behalf of appointment based on merit while he was campaigning for office. He particularly emphasized that federal judges and district attorneys "should be appointed strictly on the basis of merit without any consideration of political aspects or influence. . . . [B]lue ribbon selection committees should be utilized to provide recommendations to the president when vacancies occur."[33] Carter's statement was a clear signal to district attorneys that they could expect to remain in office as long as they were doing a good job. It was also a recognition of the importance of their work at the state and local level of politics. The most effective, perhaps sole, combatants of political corruption at that level are district attorneys who possess the investigative powers and, by and large, the independence to carry out their tasks without interference from local political figures. In the states of

Illinois, New York, Maryland, and Pennsylvania, district attorneys have played a critical role in prosecuting corruption in high places.

Carter was reminded of his campaign stance when he removed David Marston, a Republican, as district attorney for eastern Pennsylvania, on January 24, 1978. By his own admission, Carter received a phone call from Congressman Joshua Eilberg (Democrat, Pennsylvania) requesting him to expedite Marston's removal. Carter instructed Attorney General Griffin Bell to find a replacement for Marston shortly thereafter. Carter's swift response to Eilberg's call and the subsequent removal of Marston would have been unexceptional except that the president had made meritorious appointment an issue in the campaign, Marston had an outstanding record as a prosecutor of corrupt officials in Philadelphia politics, and Eilberg himself was under investigation for wrongdoing. In the short span of six months Marston, a former aide to Senator Richard Schweiker (Republican, Pennsylvania), had prosecuted several top officials in Pennsylvania politics, including former House Speaker Herbert Fineman and former State Senator Henry J. Cianfrani. Marston's impartiality was underscored by his first conviction, obtained against Theodore S. A. Rubino, one of the most powerful politicians in Republican-dominated Chester county. Marston was investigating the substantial legal fees obtained by Eilberg's law firm (in the amount of $500,000) for services rendered to Hahneman Medical Hospital when he was removed. Following Marston's removal, Eilberg was indicted and convicted of using his influence to secure a loan for hospital construction and of profiting from the transaction.[34]

IMPOUNDMENT, REPROGRAMMING, TRANSFER

The president has a variety of powers at his disposal to reverse—at the administrative level, a congressional budget decision of which he disapproves. He may spend monies for purposes not authorized by Congress (reprogramming and transfers), or he may not spend monies for purposes directed by Congress (impoundment). Impoundment originated as a practice in Franklin Roosevelt's administration when Congress voted lump sums for the war effort. Funds that exceeded the war-making need were impounded at the discretion of the president. Truman, Eisenhower, and Johnson continued the practice of impoundment, largely confining it to military spending. With Richard Nixon came a quantum leap in claims of presidential power to withhold money mandated by Congress. The administration confessed to impounding $12.2 billion in 1972. Some estimates place the amount at $28 billion, including programs of which the administration disapproved, such as food stamps, cancer research, rural environment assistance, low-rent public housing construction, and the VA hospital system. More than $9 billion for water pollution control was impounded.[35]

Under special conditions the president may take money from one project and "transfer" it to a different one. The Defense Department, for example, possesses legal authority to transfer up to $600 million "when it is important to the security of the United States."[36] Acting under this blanket of authority, Nixon transferred $100 million in defense appropriations to support the invasion of Cambodia in 1970. The Cambodian invasion was a self-declared presidential war against a country that had the misfortune of being too weak to repel forces hostile to the United States.[37]

Through "reprogramming," money spent on some project Congress has approved is deferred by the president for some project not approved. In 1971, the navy sought to reprogram the $139 million appropriated for the purchase of a tanker and salvage tugs to begin instead construction on a much coveted nuclear aircraft carrier. Navy requests for appropriations for the aircraft carrier had been denied by Congress on several occasions. When the reprogramming of funds was discovered, the outcry was so great the navy was forced to back down. It is estimated that the Defense Department reprograms $1 billion annually.[38]

EXECUTIVE PRIVILEGE, SECRECY, AND CLASSIFICATION

The president has the power to withhold information from Congress and the press even though it is needed to supervise the operations of government. The reasons given for withholding information—"public interest" and "national security"—may sometimes be valid; yet this power has been used to cover up instances of presidential wrongdoing, mismanagement, or usurpation. "Executive secrecy" was the basis for withholding information from Congress that the United States carried out more than 3,900 bombing missions over Cambodia. America's adversaries in the Far East, the North Vietnamese, Cambodians, Russians, and Chinese, knew of the bombing runs before Congress, the institution with the formal power to declare war.[39] In another instance, to encourage oil exploration in the Mideast, the State Department permitted the oil majors to formulate joint policies without fear of antitrust action. This exemption was not divulged to congressional committees responsible for exercising oversight over the Departments of State and Justice. In another example, executive agreements between the United States and Ethiopia, Spain, and the Philippines were not revealed, even though military support was pledged. To give the agreements force, congressional action was indispensable.[40]

The most dramatic assertions of a right to withhold information in the public interest were made in the Nixon administration. In the Pentagon Papers case, the administration sought to enjoin publication of high-level executive memoranda showing that the Johnson administration had been moving in opposite directions in the national campaign of 1964—away from the Vietnam War in public statements and toward deeper military involvement in private. The government contended that it possessed an "inherent power" to prevent the publication of documents when such exposure would constitute a grave threat to national security.[41] Additionally, the government said that publication of the memoranda would retard efforts to bring an end to the war, precisely what those who sought publication *(Washington Post* and *The New York Times)* said they were trying to do by bringing the documents to light.

President Nixon refused to comply with the subpoena of the House Judiciary Committee inquiring into the grounds for his impeachment. The subpoena requested him to release tapes of conversations between himself and his staff occurring on selected dates during the week after the Watergate break-in. Nixon stated that the tapes were information protected by "executive privilege," that is, information which is the president's right to withhold in the national interest. In the Supreme Court case growing out of this contest, *U.S.* v. *Nixon* (July 1974), the Court upheld the doctrine of executive privilege but not the president's particular application of it. The right to withhold information, the Court said, can only be maintained "to protect military, diplomatic, or sensitive national security secrets." Nixon's compliance with the Court order to release the tapes sealed his fate.

MAINTAINING PUBLIC ORDER

The Constitution places the responsibility on the president to "take care that the laws be faithfully executed." Pursuant to this duty, he has been provided with statutory authority to call into the federal service state militia forces (the National Guard) and to use them, as well as U.S. armed forces, to suppress an insurrection against a state or to quell "unlawful obstructions, or combinations, or assemblages, or rebellion against the authority of the United States." The president acts to restore public order upon the request and in consultation with the state's legislature or governor.[42]

It is one thing for the president to intervene to safeguard life and property in a case of civil disorder and quite another to use his police powers to suppress legitimate dissent. The president may use his policing role to identify dissidents as lawbreakers and to arouse public fears which can only be allayed through presidential action. Such an abuse of the president's power occurred in the summer of 1970 when, as John Mitchell, attorney general and political confidante of President Nixon remarked, it appeared that the president was "running for sheriff."[43] Mitchell was referring to the fact that Nixon was criss-crossing the country in Air Force One, the presidential plane, delivering a set policy speech on the uncertain condition of public order. The occasion was the off-year congressional elections.

With some variations, the same speech was given over and over at commencement exercises, party conventions, professional and labor associations, and town gatherings. It went like this: "Our fundamental values are under bitter and even violent attack. We live in a deeply and profoundly unsettled time. Drugs, crime, campus revolts, racial discord, draft resistance—on every hand we find old standards violated, old values discarded."[44] The specter of domestic civil war was raised by the "forces and threats of force that have racked our cities and now our colleges." Six students had just been killed by the National Guard at Kent State University. The president revealed that his hand was already at the national sword ready to draw it if civil conflict broke into the open. "Force can be contained. We have the power to strike back if need be, and to prevail. . . . It has not been a lack of civil power but the reluctance of a free people to employ it that has so often stayed the hand of authorities faced with confrontation."[45] In short, the president was inviting his audience to regard him as a police officer, a sheriff, as Mitchell observed, alert to protect them from immediate and present dangers.

The record shows that Nixon did not stop at the rhetoric of a police state but also took action to bring such a state into existence. A remarkable, yet unpublicized, event of Nixon's first term of office was the development of the Huston Plan. The plan urged that elements of the existing intelligence agencies, the Defense Intelligence Agency, the National Security Agency, the Federal Bureau of Investigation (FBI), along with the Secret Service and elements of the Departments of Justice, Treasury, and Defense, be consolidated into one unit for surveillance of American citizens engaged in dissent. It called for a new grant of authority to include "surreptitious entry" (burglary), opening mail, and wiretapping.[46] Huston, the author of the plan and a member of the president's White House staff, did not shrink at the creation of a right-wing police state. In one memo he noted that "If the government is free to determine the national conscience, it is free to force adherence to it."[47]

Fearing a loss of power and disliking his rivals in the intelligence community, Hoover, director of the FBI, opposed the plan. Mitchell, the attorney general, boggled over the provisions authorizing burglary. Thus the plan was never implemented in the full-scale version conceived by Huston. Yet the evidence shows that it was implemented piecemeal, with Nixon's knowledge and consent, during 1970 to 1974. All the intelligence agencies increased their surveillance of domestic dissident groups during this period. On occasion, they did not stop at the illicit techniques of gathering information advocated by Huston. For example, CHAOS (in the CIA) compiled 13,000 files including individual folders on 7,200 Americans. The documents in these files and related materials included the names of more than 300,000 persons and organizations.[48] The FBI used its COINTELPRO (counterintelligence program) against a wide variety of groups on both the left and the right. Hoover officially discontinued the program in April 1971, after documents disclosing some aspects of it were stolen from the bureau's office in Media, Pennsylvania. Evidence suggests that the bureau has continued to operate the program on an unofficial basis since then.[49]

A second move toward the creation of a police state was the installation of a "plumbers unit" in the basement of the White House in 1971. There was nothing wrong with the pipes in the White House; the unit was for plugging leaks in the national security system. The most spectacular of these emissions was the release of the Pentagon Papers to *The New York Times* in June 1971. Egil Krogh, head of the plumbers unit, was authorized by the president to use any means—burglary, wiretapping, opening mail—both to plug the leaks and to discredit Daniel Ellsberg, source of the big leak to the *Times*. Acting on this authority, Krogh, along with some of the parties who were later to bring us Watergate—E. Howard Hunt, Gordon Liddy, and Bernard Barker—broke into the offices of Dr. Lewis J. Fielding, Ellsberg's psychiatrist, in hopes of finding damaging evidence against Ellsberg in his files. They found nothing of value, nothing, that is to say, which would be of value in discrediting Ellsberg. There is little to distinguish the Fielding break-in (September 1971) and the Watergate break-in (June 1972), except that the parties were caught in the latter act. In both cases, the president sought to hide actions suppressing dissent under the protection of "national security" and "public order." The Fielding break-in is an instructive case of the lengths to which the president was prepared to go and did go when the opportunity arose. On a national television interview with David Frost, Nixon threw a blanket of approval over these and other high-handed actions of his administration. He told Frost, "when the President does it [or orders something to be done], that means that it is not illegal."[50]

THE PRESIDENCY AND THE SYSTEM

At noon on August 9, 1974, a new president of the United States was sworn in, his predecessor having resigned under threat of imminent impeachment and removal because of abuses of presidential office. Later that day, the minority leader of the United States wrote the following note by hand, as befit the dignity and antiquity of the proposed recipient:

> August 9, 1974
> The Honorable James Madison
> Sir:
>   It worked.
>   Sincerely,
>   Hugh Scott
>   United States Senator

No one watching the crisis of the Nixon presidency in 1973 and 1974 could miss this constant invocation of the framers of the Constitution; it was then, and not in the overpublicized and commercialized bicentennial celebration of two years later, that Americans rediscovered their eighteenth-century origins. A *New Yorker* editorialist, for example, commented at the outset of the crisis that the republic was being saved from presidential tyranny not by any action on the part of the American people but by "the long arm of the Founding Fathers reaching down across two centuries . . . we didn't save the system; the system saved us." And looking back on the crisis in the very last days of the Nixon presidency, a journalist was reminded of James Madison's observation (in *Federalist* No. 51) that only by creating a constitutional system in which "ambition must be made to counteract ambition" and "the interest of the man . . . connected to the constitutional rights of the place" could the government be required to control itself. Ultimately, it was the self-interest of congressmen and federal judges in preserving the rights of their branches of government that brought Nixon down, which was "how the framers of the Constitution understood . . . it would work."[51]

To elaborate these themes a bit, it was precisely for ruthless, possessive individualists such as Nixon, whom Madison anticipated would be coming down the pike, that drastically negative features were built into our institutions. Madison clearly assumed that each actor in the political process would employ the power of the state ruthlessly to further his individual interest and those of supporting political clienteles. Wiretapping was beyond his ken, but burglary, petty corruption, and subverting the political opposition were not. Madison proposed to politicize the war of each against all. Ruthless individuals, now disarmed because of Hobbes and Locke, would be encouraged by the design of institutions to negotiate their differences rather than fight them out.

I would like to make two quick points illustrating the application of these constitutional ideas to the crisis of the Nixon presidency and Watergate. First, in the end, ruthless individuals could not be sovereign as they would dearly have liked. The political system is sovereign, otherwise there would have been a breakdown, a shoot-out on the White House lawn over the possession of the tapes, which no one wants. At one point, Nixon took the position that *he* would review the tapes sought by the House Judiciary Committee on Impeachment to determine what offenses, if any, were committed, a position neither the committee nor the Supreme Court found acceptable. Therefore, the decisions of the Supreme Court interpreting the constitutional rules are accepted as binding by all parties even if with great reluctance (see Chapter 11). Second, conspiracy, a conspiratorial lunge for power, is forbidden by the characteristics of the Madisonian constitutional system. Whatever Nixon's actual intentions were, and we may never know, he committed successive and sufficiently serious abuses of the powers of presidential office so that it became tantamount, at least in the eyes of shared power holders, to a conspiratorial grab for the aggregate of state power. The Madisonian system seeks to defeat conspiracy because, by definition, a conspirator upsets a distribution among relatively equal power brokers. To the extent that America has a valid concept of constitutionalism, this is it. Stability is purchased by managing social conflict and equipping all parties with the institutional means to bring down a would-be conspirator.

"The system" worked in 1973 and 1974, according to the views of thoughtful journalists and politicians close to the centers of power; probably most Americans accepted this view. The "system" that worked is at bottom a constitutional order classically liberal in its fear of power, in its concern with balancing power, and in its reliance on individual self-interest to achieve this goal. If Watergate and the forced resignation of Nixon show the American constitutional system at its dismal best, what of the new challenges the system was required to face in the 1970s, specifically the energy crisis referred to earlier?

Precisely those features which support the view that "it" (the Constitution) works, as Senator Scott asserts, throw doubt on the utility of the system when looked at from a different angle. The system is not well suited to providing a publicly agreed on resolution of major social problems such as those presented by the energy crisis. Solutions like those forthcoming in the National Energy Act (1978) were chiefly the product of bargaining among shared power holders largely outside public view. In these bargaining sessions among the president, or his authorized representatives, and shared power holders on Capitol Hill and the producer groups, much that was of substantial importance to the public was abandoned or amended away.

As proposed, the National Energy Plan sought to shift the national resource base from oil and gas, which are in diminishing supply, to coal and nuclear resources (in the intermediate term) and conservation and renewable resources (in the long term). The plan that was enacted placed even heavier reliance on scarce resources of oil and gas. Carter spokesmen justified this change by noting that the dollars extracted from higher prices would go into the pockets of domestic natural gas producers (rather than into the robes of Arab oil sheiks) and that new and unexpected sources of natural gas had been discovered (concurrently with higher prices). The proposed plan sought to equalize the burdens of higher energy prices and conservation through a system of rebates to the consuming public. All features of the rebate plan were removed from the legislation enacted by Congress. Additionally, as noted earlier, the enacted legislation provided subsidies, tax benefits, investment incentives, and even a depletion allowance (for geo-pressurized methane). In the end, producer groups would be able to retain a major portion of the windfall profits arising from shortages plus pocketing funds to engage in experimental recovery techniques, exploration of new resources, and new extraction methods.

The setback encountered by the president and his aides arises from the same features of the constitutional system celebrated by Senator Scott: its distrust of public power; its presumption against nonprivate (common or public) goods; its reluctance to assign important tasks to the public sphere; its emphasis on a transactional, bargaining style of politics carried on between independently situated power brokers; its vision of politics as solely concerned with the management of social conflict. All these negative features built into the structure of institutions considerably undermine the influence and authority of public figures, most significantly, the president, saddled with the responsibility of facing up to the major issues of the day. When these systemic features are coupled with the impact of the modern corporation on the political process, one is forced to conclusions very different from those of Senator Scott. It (the Constitution) does not work. As I emphasized earlier (Chapter 5), the modern corporation benefits from the practical arrangements of the Constitution because it already has an organizational capacity and a high material incentive to gain access to the political process, and it enjoys a considerable advantage on consumer issues where the public is uninformed and unorganized. The weaknesses of the constitutional system and of presidential power are clearly displayed in the attempt to enact an equitable plan of energy conservation.

NOTES

1. John Locke, *Second Treatise,* sec. 160.
2. See the discussion in E. S. Corwin, *The President: Office and Powers,* 4th rev. ed. (New York: New York University Press, 1974), chap. 1.
3. *Federalist* No. 70.
4. Corwin, *The President,* pp. 29–30.
5. See the discussion in Joseph E. Kallenbach, *The American Chief Executive* (New York: Harper & Row, 1966), chaps. 14–16; and William E. Mullen, *Presidential Power and Politics* (New York: St. Martin's Press, 1976), chap. 2.
6. *Federalist* No. 51.
7. Richard E. Neustadt, *Presidential Power* (New York: John Wiley, 1970), preface.
8. *Ibid.,* p. 46.
9. *Ibid.,* chap. 3.
10. Woodrow Wilson, *Constitutional Government in the United States* (New York: Columbia University Press, 1961), p. 68.
11. *The New York Times,* July 16, 1980, A14.
12. William H. Riker, *Federalism: Origin, Operation, Significance* (Boston: Little, Brown, 1964), p. 93.
13. Jules Witcover, *Marathon* (New York: Signet, 1978).
14. James W. Davis, "The Road to the White House," in *The Presidential Office,* eds. Sidney Wise and Robert Schier (New York: Thomas Y. Crowell, 1968), pp. 81–113.
15. Theodore White, *The Making of the President: 1960* (New York: Signet, 1960), chaps. 5–6.
16. *National Journal,* August 4, 1979, pp. 1,282–86.
17. Witcover, *Marathon,* p. 144.
18. *Ibid.,* p. 582.
19. Richard M. Pious, *The American Presidency* (New York: Basic Books, 1979), p. 268.
20. *The New York Times,* March 29, 1981, sec. 4.
21. Pious, *American Presidency,* pp. 217–18.
22. *Ibid.,* pp. 214–15.
23. Executive Office of the President, *National Energy Plan I* (Washington, D.C.: U.S. Government Printing Office, 1977).
24. Aspen Systems Corporation, *Energy Source Book* (Columbia, Md.: An Aspen Publication, 1977).
25. *Wall Street Journal,* October 31, 1977, pp. 1, 23.
26. *Wall Street Journal,* January 10, 1975, editorial page; *The New York Times,* January 20, 1975.
27. Executive Office of the President, *The National Energy Plan I* (Washington, D.C.: U.S. Government Printing Office, 1977), p. 26.

28. *Washington Post,* April 21, 1977, A1, 21.

29. *Ibid.*

30. *Washington Post,* October 14, 1977, A1, 8.

31. *Washington Post,* March 15, 1978, A1, 7; May 12, 1978, A9; May 15, 1978, A8.

32. William J. Crotty, *Political Reform and the American Experiment* (New York: Thomas Y. Crowell, 1977), pp. 157–64.

33. Carter Platform Committee Presentation, cited in "How They Stand: Presidential Candidates' Positions" (Washington, D.C.: Common Cause, 1976), p. 102.

34. See *Philadelphia Inquirer,* January 26, 1978; *Washington Post* (January 31, 1978) A1, 8, 9.

35. Mullen, *Presidential Power,* p. 67.

36. *Ibid.,* p. 72.

37. *Ibid.,* p. 82.

38. *Ibid.,* p. 71.

39. *Ibid.,* p. 82.

40. *Ibid.*

41. Jonathan Schell, *The Time of Illusion* (New York: Vintage Books, 1975), pp. 151–54.

42. Kallenbach, *American Chief Executive,* p. 463.

43. Anthony Lukas, *Nightmare: The Underside of the Nixon Years* (New York: Viking, 1976), p. 4.

44. Schell, *Time of Illusion,* p. 37.

45. *Ibid.*

46. Lukas, *Nightmare,* p. 31.

47. *Ibid.*

48. *Ibid.,* pp. 36–37.

49. *Ibid.*

50. *The New York Times,* "The Week in Review," May 29, 1977, p. 1.

51. Quoted by William B. Hixson, "Liberal Legacy, Radical Critique," *Commonweal* (October 13, 1978), p. 647.

CHAPTER 10

The Federal Bureaucracy

AMBIVALENT ATTITUDES

One of the several attitudes expressed about the role of bureaucratic government in the United States is forcefully represented by President Ronald Reagan. It is plain that in his view, and those of many others who share this perspective, the federal bureaucracy is a scandal, nuisance, and intrusion. This outlook is born of the liberal antistate bias which restricts the function of the state to a merely policing role. That is, the state best serves the acquisitive energies of a society of commercial entrepreneurs when it abstains from social interference. Reagan asserted while running as a candidate for presidential office that abolition of the Energy Department was the most important contribution he could make as president to the solution of the national energy problem. We should look for a solution to the energy crisis, he said, "to the genius of industry, the imagination of management—not to some sprawling Cabinet office in Washington which never should have been created in the first place."[1] A similar proposal urging the abolition of the Environmental Protection Agency and the Occupational Health and Safety Administration was made by Reagan on the grounds that the agencies unnecessarily interfere with private enterprise.[2]

In contrast, a neo-liberal views the bureaucracy as a force for social improvement. In this vision, the bureaucracy is a necessary social instrument which can supply a range of human entitlements neglected by the liberal vision of politics. It is not enough, the neo-liberals argue, to provide a society of independently situated actors with rights of free speech, freedom of worship and press, procedural liberties, right of assembly, right to bear arms and so forth, because none of these rights assures that society will be able to provide for its collective preservation and betterment. Neo-liberals view bureaucratic government, as expressed in the New Deal and Great Society, as an alternative to the

238

limitations of the liberal state. Through the bureaucracy a broader scope of human entitlements, embracing education, housing, minimum income, medical care, unemployment compensation, and nutrition, can and should be supplied by the state.[3] The sharp contrast between the liberal and neo-liberal visions of the role of bureaucracy is manifest in the budget cuts of the Reagan administration. The main thrust of the cuts is directed against neo-liberal programs, such as food stamps, medicaid, child nutrition, and student assistance, associated with the Great Society.

A third view of the bureaucracy is as a passive, yet unwitting instrument of class rule. It notes that the state and the modern corporation exist in an an interdependent relationship, with most of the advantages weighted toward the corporation. The state, through the chief executive, seeks to provide a regulatory framework and fiscal policy which will encourage business expansion; to a greater or lesser degree, depending on the incumbent president, the state will also seek to apply environmental controls and work regulations which require industry to absorb the social costs of its productive activity. On the other hand, the corporation seeks to use the state as an auxiliary source of capital supply, as a means of offsetting some of the more obnoxious by-products of capitalist production, such as unemployment and pollution, and as a safety net, guarding against the consequences of market failure. The state functions as an instrument of private capital accumulation when it deploys resources, invests in human expertise, directs scientific research, and in some cases, actually supplies the finance capital, thereby directly adding to the wealth of specific productive activities.[4] Despite much talk about the free enterprise system, market forces, and the like, the state often engages in this type of activity, thus erasing the boundary line between the so-called private and public sectors. Airports are constructed, loans are issued, costly research projects are funded, shipbuilding is subsidized, railroads are nationalized (automobile manufacture may be next), sewage plants are located, highways are laid out, and insurance schemes are devised.[5] The state picks up the bill for these activities, funneled through bureaucratic programs, and for many more like them. To the extent that the corporate sector evades the social expense of capitalist production and employs the bureaucratic arm as a way to accumulate physical, human, and financial capital, the bureaucracy may be seen as an instrument of a class, the executive managers in the corporate sector, who deploy accumulated capital.

The center of the conflict, it will be argued in this chapter, is between the neo-liberal and corporate-dominated vision of bureaucratic government. Funds and services diverted to the corporate sector undermine the capacity of the liberal state to transcend its own limitations.

The enhanced productivity and profits flowing from state intervention are privately appropriated rather than directed to neo-liberal social ends. Thus, the state is perpetually thrown back on its ancient, liberal foundations, dependent in the end on a large measure of social and state coercion to sustain itself. In an earlier time, this bias may have been enough to assure the government a legitimate standing in the political community. Now, however, the neo-liberal vision of the scope of human entitlements is shared especially by those social groups who are its beneficiaries. Deprivation of entitlements may lead to a crisis of legitimacy for American political institutions at the same time that the corporate sector may be publicly perceived to use the state as a source of capital supply.

CONTROLLING THE BUREAUCRACY

Just as a variety of perspectives compete to shape the role of the federal bureaucracy, so it is that control over the activities of the bureaucracy is exercised by a variety of institutions. It is pardonable to suppose that the chief executive, who has major appointive powers to high-level administrative posts, is the figure who has the greatest measure of influence over the federal bureaucracy. This impression, although not unsound, needs to be qualified in a number of ways.

First, the federal administration is divided into several layers, White House staff, executive office of the president, cabinet, executive agencies, and independent regulatory agencies, each of which has a different political and legal relationship with the president, which in turn qualifies the power he exercises over them. These differences in legal and political relationships will be described later. The point now is that the president does not exercise uniform control over all the federal administration; on the contrary, his control varies with each component.

Second, the power over the budget and certain appointive powers are shared between the president and Congress. Although the president has enormous powers of initiative to shape the priorities of the administration by drafting the budget and selecting officials for administrative posts, the exercise of these powers requires congressional review and concurrence. Thus Congress shares control over the activities of the federal bureaucracy with the president. Remember the response of Senator Russell (Democrat, Georgia), chairman of the Senate Committee on Armed Services, to President Harry Truman's invitation to assume the post of Secretary of Defense. He is reported to have answered, "Why, I would rather run the Defense Department from down here" (Congress). Congress is an avenue through which clienteles of bureaucratic programs may appeal to reverse a decision lost at the administrative level. So-called "iron triangles" are formed out of triadic relationships among congressmen, clientele, and middle-level bureaucrats, each striving (sometimes for different reasons) to retain a program that has been axed from the presidential budget.

Third, the modern corporation influences the activities of the federal bureaucracy through a variety of means. It shapes the structure of public preferences with a potent blend of advertising, technological innovation, and organizational capacity; its top management is appointed to key administrative posts; its profit margin is considered indispensable to economic stimulus and social welfare. Political leadership observes a deferential role in relation to the requirements of the corporation for a stable regulatory framework, an auxiliary source of capital supply, incentives and safeguards for new investment, and a favorable tax structure. The reverse side of the liberal antistate bias is an exaggerated estimate of the capabilities of the modern corporation for solving a host of social ills and, therefore, a determination to withhold little from its requests. President Reagan's statement that we may expect a solution to the energy crisis from "the genius of industry, the imagination of management," that is, from the petrochemical industry, affords an illustration of this side of the liberal bias.

WHITE HOUSE STAFF AND EXECUTIVE OFFICE

The problems of executive control over the bureaucracy arise from the variety of institutions and perspectives just described. The "ordeal of the executive," as it is sometimes called, is created by the circumstance that the president has limited influence over an administration of which he is the nominal head.[6] This problem is not a new one but is coeval with the constitutional system of separate institutions sharing power and with the rise of the modern corporation. The problem reached an acute stage for the first time in the administration of Franklin Roosevelt. At that time the federal administration tripled in size because of the accumulated responsibilities of World War II and New Deal legislation. A committee of scholars, the Brownlow Commission, studied the problem of executive control and declared that the president needed professional staff assistance to enable him to supervise the far-flung activities of his administration.

Out of the proposals of the Brownlow Commission (1936) has evolved the present-day White House staff and executive office of the president (EXOP). These professional staffs have two primary functions. First, they seek to exercise countervailing power over the partial and vested interests of the administration. By various forms of intervention in its operations, they seek to make the policies of the president prevail. Their second function is to operate for the president at a level that requires the collaboration of two or more departments. For example, the Bureau of the Budget assembles the budget of the federal administration presented to Congress in January of each year. The Treasury Department possesses much of the staff capability for this task but is an interested party in the outcome. The Bureau of the Budget, on the other hand, can be counted on to be responsive to the policy wishes of the president.

The White House staff and EXOP have differing legal and professional relationships with the president. What is more, each of these staffs has a different relationship with the president than all other elements of the federal administration.

The White House staff is the unit of federal administration closest to the president. Its members are appointed by the president without the advice and consent of the Senate, and they are removable by the president at will. Their influence in dealing with other parties in the administration is wholly derived from the president. Their function is to represent the president in the administration, in Congress, to the press, and to the public. Members of the staff are often selected from those employed by the president in winning the nomination and election. Having coached the candidate in a winning strategy for the capture of office, their efforts now turn, as members of the president's White House staff, to the considerable task of keeping him there.

So intimately are members of the president's White House staff connected with the person of the president that they are seldom directly quoted and they are never invited to give testimony in Congress (as are members of the executive departments).[7] This intimacy has its privileges, since there is a particular élan associated with carrying out the high duties of the executive office; but it also has its price. There is a complete turnover of White House staff with each new occupant of the executive mansion. One exception to this rule was Lyndon Johnson's efforts to bridge the gap between the Kennedy wing and the Southern wing of the Democratic party by retaining the slain president's personal staff. But Johnson, even while persuading the Kennedy staff to stay on, brought in his own press secretary and retinue of speech writers.

The size of the White House staff varies between 450 to 600 aides and operates on a budget of approximately $16.5 million per year.[8] All members of the White House staff have a close relationship to the president, but there are still great differences in the professional role they satisfy. The staff may be generally divided between those who are preoccupied with the president's future as a career politician and those who are recruited because of their expertise in some critical area of policy. The former roles are fulfilled primarily by those who serve as the president's chief of staff, press secretary, and chief domestic policy advisor. Special assistants to the president in military affairs, energy policy, science, foreign relations, and health are examples of the latter.

To illustrate, the most sensitive political posts in the Carter administration were held by Hamilton Jordan, assistant to the president and chief of the White House staff; Jody Powell, press secretary, and Stuart Eizenstadt, assistant for domestic affairs and policy. Jordan used the levers of presidential power to cajole and coerce shared power holders—congressional barons and baronets, labor leaders, members of the administration, public interest groups, trade association representatives, and many others—to support the general aims of the Carter regime. The task of presenting the president to the public in a favorable light fell to Jody Powell; this is always a challenging assignment requiring wit, patience, command of the facts, and candor. Stuart Eizenstadt, a lawyer by training, emerged from the comparative obscurity of the Carter campaign to a position as the chief draftsman of presidential policy on urban affairs, executive reorganization, wage and price controls, health, and energy. Each of these men, both as campaign staff and as presidential aides, bent their main efforts to the task of furthering the political career of the president.[9] A triumvirate of James Baker, Edward Meese, and Michael Deaver perform similar functions in the Reagan administration.

Each president has his own distinctive "brain trust" on the White House staff as well as his own entourage of political cronies. Two of the top appointments on the Carter White House staff, James R. Schlesinger, assistant to the president, and Zbigniew Brzezinski, assistant for national security affairs, were made because of their expertise in foreign affairs and energy management, not because of their skills in election campaigns.

Schlesinger, a former defense secretary, CIA director, and atomic energy chairman, was given the task of assembling the first National Energy Plan (NEP I) for presentation to Congress, and staff from the various departments were assigned to him on a temporary basis. He moved from his post on the White House staff to a position as secretary of energy as soon as the cabinet-rank department was created by Congress in 1977. Nevertheless, the acrimonious and sustained battle over NEP I, culminating in the defeat of many of its major provisions, was regarded as a personal defeat for the secretary no less than for the president. Schlesinger's resignation, therefore, was among those the president accepted in a cabinet "shake-up" in July 1979, preparatory to Carter's reelection bid in 1980.

The appointment of Brzezinski to a position on the White House staff and to the National Security Council as assistant for national security affairs was correctly interpreted by analysts as a decision to retain control over foreign policy in the White House rather than delegating the major policy-making role to the State Department. Brzezinski, who has been in and out of the federal administration as a foreign policy analyst since the Kennedy era, upstaged two secretaries of state, Cyrus Vance and Edmund Muskie, to retain primacy of White House control. He arrived at this position through the "community," a small group of experts and university professors who influence foreign policy in indirect ways through established forums of opinion.[10] Among the outlets of the community are professional journals *(Foreign Affairs* and *Foreign Policy)*, the op-ed pages of the *Washington Post* and *The New York Times,* testimony to congressional committees, and conferences with government officials at Brookings Institution (Washington, D.C.) and the Council on Foreign Relations (New York City). Conversely, the appointment of Alexander Haig as secretary of state and Richard Allen as special assistant for national security affairs in the Reagan administration is taken as a sign that major responsibilities in foreign policy are to be delegated to the secretary rather than the White House.

Unlike the White House staff, EXOP is an extension of the administrative functions of the presidential office. It does not seek to reflect the personality of the president, as does the White House staff, but to carry out the supervisory responsibilities of his office. This differing professional relationship with the president is symbolized by the fact that EXOP is, for the most part, housed across the street from the White House in the Blair House and in the new Executive Office Building. The White House staff is entirely quartered in the White House itself. The members of EXOP are appointed by the president by and with the advice and consent of the Senate. However, they are removable by the president at will. Since members are chosen for nonpolitical professional capabilities, some do remain on board in the administration when a president leaves office.

One of the most useful tools of executive control, which has been lodged in EXOP from the beginning, is the Office of Management and Budget (OMB), formerly called the Bureau of the Budget. The OMB seeks to draft a budget that reflects the president's priorities in areas such as defense, housing, social services, transportation, space exploration, health, and education. Conflict between the department heads and the president over these priorities is not infrequent, thus transforming the OMB into a scene of intense struggle over the composition of the federal budget. Additional functions performed by the OMB are clearance and referral. The office refers all requests originating in Congress for information about the administration's position to the appropriate department or agency. When the reply is forthcoming, the OMB checks to see whether it agrees with the president's general position.[11]

The OMB played a key role in the early months of the Reagan administration by revising downward those portions of the 1982 budget allocated to social services and increasing the portion allotted to defense. David Stockman, Reagan's appointee as director and a former representative from Michigan, was thrust into an unusual public role, atypical of the self-effacing practices of former OMB directors in carrying out this budgetary reallocation. He obtained estimates of the Carter budget in the transition period before Reagan's inauguration, acquired Reagan's approval for the budget changes following inaugural ceremonies, informed the incoming Cabinet secretaries of the proposed changes in private sessions at the OMB, and helped the White House staff and Reagan prepare the main outlines of the state of the union message on the budget to a joint session of Congress on February 18, 1981. Since that time, he has appeared before congressional committees and subcommittees as well as in the media on numerous occasions to defend the proposed budget cuts. In some quarters, these cuts in social services are viewed as a radical departure from past political arrangements. Much depends on the time frame in which events are viewed. Certainly, it arrests the neo-liberal momentum generated by the expansion of the Great Society programs of the early 1960s and the latter part of the 1970s. In the time frame of the history of the American republic, however, Stockman and Reagan simply propose to restore the liberal state to the archaic principles on which it was founded. This is not a radical but a conventional position.

The second most important element of EXOP in relation to domestic policy is the Council of Economic Advisors (CEA). The CEA was created by the Full Employment Act of 1946, and its function is to provide advice to the president on fiscal policy. Fiscal policy deals with the broad outlines of taxation and spending used to counter inflation and recession and maintain a given standard of employment (6 percent unemployment is considered "acceptable"). Unlike monetary policy, which deals with money supply and is set by an independent agency (the Federal Reserve Board), fiscal policy lies to some extent within the range of the president's influence. The economic predictions of the CEA, although presumptively a matter of professional opinion, nevertheless are tinged by the political framework. On the eve of the 1976 election the CEA issued public statements about a decline in the Consumer Price Index and in the rate of unemployment. These announcements were timed to coincide with Gerald Ford's message to the electorate, "The nation is on the march toward full economic recovery and a better quality of life for all Americans."[12]

The National Security Council (NSC) is the president's most important source of staff assistance in formulating military and foreign policy. Its emergence within EXOP is closely associated with the cold war posture assumed by the United States in the post-World War II era. No central machinery existed to coordinate advice given the president in containing the perceived threat of U.S.S.R. expansion. The National Security Act (1949) created the council and designated the president, vice-president, secretary of state, and secretary of defense as permanent members. Auxiliary members who almost invariably attend its sessions are the director of the CIA, the president's special assistant on national security affairs, and the chairman of the Joint Chiefs of Staff.

In former administrations, the deliberations of the NSC have been markedly influenced by the president's own special assistants on military and foreign affairs. Kennedy relied extensively on McGeorge Bundy, a White House special assistant, to plan and coordinate policy using NSC staff to assist him. Similarly Johnson relied on Walt Rostow, special assistant on national security, to provide direction to the U.S. intervention in Vietnam. The consequence of vesting these staff functions in the White House is to divest the secretaries of state and defense, to some extent, of their expected role in the formulation of policy.

CABINET

At this point we need to pause and take stock of the much different relationships that exist between the president and his cabinet. Collaterally, we need to look at the relationship between cabinet staff and their clienteles. There is a broad coincidence of goals between the president and staff at the levels of administration we have discussed so far. Although the White House staff and EXOP serve the president in different ways, one staff promoting the presidential office (EXOP) and the other promoting the political ambitions of the occupant (White House staff), the professional career of both staffs is entirely dependent on helping the president realize *his* objectives. This is not true of the cabinet.

Members of the cabinet are appointed by the president by and with the advice and consent of the Senate. Appointments are frequently made on the basis of the "acceptability" of the appointee to his or her clienteles. For example, the president will consult the AFL–CIO about the appointment to labor secretary, business groups about the treasury secretary, the Farm Bureau Federation about the secretary of agriculture, and so on. This practice suggests that presidents stand to gain or lose power through their appointments as much as they expect to confer it. Elevation to a cabinet post is a recognition of the independent standing of the appointee in relation to a particular clientele.

A president may remove a cabinet official at will, although the independent standing of most appointees inhibits presidents from exercising this power. Rather than publicize differences between himself and the constituencies a cabinet officer serves, a president will normally adopt a conciliatory approach. Executive "control," one of the themes we have been pursuing, is hard to achieve when a cabinet officer has superior relationships with congressional committees or subcommittees, interest groups, and the staff of his or her department.

"The members of the Cabinet are a President's natural enemies,"[13] one observer comments. This statement should alert us to the fact that we have entered a different world in describing relationships between a president and his cabinet. The battles between them are not personal and idiosyncratic as the quote suggests. Such differences may arise but that is not what concerns us here. Persistent and enduring conflicts among the rival elements of a capitalist economy are transmitted to the cabinet, where they are fought out in conflicts over policy and for slices of the federal budget. The members of the cabinet and the president often position themselves on different sides of this conflict, presidents aiming to exert a modicum of control over the budget and cabinet staff pushing to serve the demands of their clienteles.[14]

Generally, one may distinguish three types of relationships between cabinet departments and their political clienteles. First, there are departments, such as defense, transportation and energy, which are substantially influenced by oligopolistic interests. These try to control the program and budget of a cabinet department related to the market sector in which their influence is dominant. Second, the Departments of Health and Human Services (HHS) and Housing and Urban Development (HUD) seek to fulfill the neo-liberal vision of the political community. They are responsive to a much different clientele, consisting primarily of the poor, the unemployed, the elderly, the illiterate and undernourished, the underemployed, and the migrant worker. Their ability to serve this constituency is often frustrated by the biases of the liberal ideology and the need to compete with corporate-dominated departments for scarce resources. Third, there is a cluster of departments, agriculture, labor, and interior, for example, which serve the needs of a diverse clientele. Elements of corporate capital, competitive capital, and submerged groups compete to shape the priorities of these departments, leading to their designation as cross-pressured. This classification scheme is further elaborated in the following discussion.

CORPORATE-DOMINATED DEPARTMENTS

The Departments of Defense, Transportation, and Energy principally serve the interests of different sectors of oligopolistic activity. Although a reciprocal relation between the department and its clientele is apparent, the preponderant influence is exercised by the affected business. The oil majors (Exxon, Gulf, Mobil, Shell, Standard of Indiana, Texaco, Atlantic Richfield, Standard of California) dominate the extraction, refining, transportation, and marketing of oil and gas, the nation's principal energy sources; the Big Four in automobile production (Chrysler, Ford, General Motors, and AMC) contribute over 90 percent of American car products; fifteen corporations alone receive approximately one-half of the $39 billion let in defense contracts in any given year. As suggested before, these industries have a big incentive to influence governmental action in highly specific ways and possess ample resources for this purpose. Energy, defense, and transportation are outstanding examples of problems of bureaucratic control arising from the size and influence of corporate industry.

The influence of the petrochemical industry and the automobile manufacturers on public policy has been extensively discussed in Chapter 5. Attention will be confined, therefore, to oligopolistic influence on defense spending.

Important evidence of oligopolistic influence over defense expenditures is that it rises against a backdrop of easing international tensions and tends to be bipartisan. Whether the president is a Republican or a Democrat, the fifteen industries receiving the lion's share of contracts for equipment and research do very well. The top ten industries in rank order of size of contracts obtained in fiscal year 1979 were General Dynamics, McDonnell Douglas, United Technologies, General Electric, Lockheed, Hughes Aircraft, Boeing, Grumman, Raytheon, and Tenneco.[15]

The 1977 budget proposed to Congress by departing president Ford provided for a 9 percent increase in defense spending, a total of $101 billion. The funds allotted to research and testing rose by 16 percent, to $11 billion, signifying that spending on new weapons design would go up in future years. Most significantly, the "obligational authority," money authorized for expenditure in future years, increased by 14 percent, to $113.1 billion, which meant that defense spending would rise at a faster rate in the years after the 1977 budget.[16]

President Carter continued these policies in the 1981 budget submitted to Congress. It provided for a 3.3 percent increase in defense spending, adjusted for inflation, to $142.7 billion. It projected a steadily rising defense budget over the next five years, from 23.7 percent of the national budget to 25.4 percent, reaching a projected total of $225 billion in 1985. Most importantly, the 1981 budget called for a 21 percent increase in defense research, which often supplies the basis for greatly increased defense expenditures in future years.[17]

President Reagan continues this trend, proposing a $38 billion increase in defense spending over the projected Carter figures in the next two years. Overall he has requested a $184 billion increase in defense spending authority over the next five years,[18] surrounding these requests with an escalation in the rhetoric of confrontation with the Soviet Union.

Taking cover in their responsibility to protect national security, presidents often find that it is easiest to succumb to a rising level of defense expenditures. A succession of presidents, Kennedy, Johnson, and Nixon, persuaded Congress to sink over $1 billion into the SST (supersonic transport), a transport plane designed by one of the major defense contractors for commercial carriers. The sonic boom produced by this plane in flight finally discouraged its further production. Nixon persisted for many years in an effort to obtain funds for a $50 billion antiballistic missile shield long after a succession of experts had discredited the idea.[19] He helped the Lockheed Aircraft Corporation obtain $250 million in government loans, putting the taxpayer in the position of absorbing cost overruns on Lockheed's Cheyenne military helicopter and C-5A military transport plane.[20] When Carter cancelled production plans for the $21.4 billion B-1 bomber, the decision was received with near shock by the press. In the past, presidents had shown their willingness to underwrite even the most expensive and crackpot ventures in military technology, and the media's reaction revealed that the decision was unusual, an exception to the rule. Plans for reviving production plans for the B-1 are underway in the Reagan administration.[21]

Not all defense expenditure is for military hardware and research. Roughly one-half of the defense budget in a given year is spent on the salaries and pensions of the 2.1 million men and women in uniform, plus 1 million civilian employees and retirees. Defense industries employ 1.7 million more, and an estimated 2 million people depend on the trickle-down effects of military spending. Estimates reveal that the defense industries employ about one-fifth to one-third of all U.S. scientists and engineers. Thus the Pentagon is responsible for about 7 million jobs out of a total labor force of 96 million.[22]

SOCIAL SERVICE DEPARTMENTS

The Departments of Health and Human Services (HHS) and of Housing and Urban Development (HUD) serve very different political constituencies, ones lacking the financial clout, organized backing, managerial expertise, and technical qualifications of the corporate sector. Additionally, the biases of the liberal ideology are weighted against state intervention to offset the burdens of submerged groups, and the objectives of social services are limited to managing social conflict and stabilizing public order.[23] The more ambitious aims of the neo-liberal political outlook, to use the bureaucratic arm of the welfare state to "make the community more of a community," face an uphill battle in this political setting.

Given public hostility to welfare assistance and the competition for scarce budgetary resources, presidents have often found it advantageous to take a neutral stance toward the activities and programs of HHS (formerly HEW) and HUD. Presidents are keenly aware of the political trade-offs involved in allocations to the corporate sector, especially to defense spending, against the need to appease elements of the neo-liberal persuasion. This stance is illustrated by newspaper comment on Carter's 1981 budget. *The New York Times* observed that the president had "produced a fairly middle of the road election year budget for the fiscal year 1981, tilted toward conservatives with a reduction in the deficit and higher military spending but sparing [neo-]liberals any major cutbacks in social programs.[24] "Occasionally, a president will justify budget cuts by deflecting attention toward those who are the recipients of federal relief and away from the maldistribution of wealth. For example, Nixon prefaced 1973 budget cuts in HEW and HUD with the statement that we (the public) should be "charitable to those who can't work without increasing the tax burden of those who do."[25] The statement was not calculated to produce a fresh outburst of social generosity.

President Reagan seeks to forge a political coalition out of the bias of liberal ideology against welfare assistance and the influence of the corporate sector on defense spending. As noted, the 1982 budget proposes deep cuts in social service programs and a corresponding emphasis on increased defense spending. Whether the president can reduce the scope of human entitlements at the same time as neo-liberals press for their expansion will be a hard-fought question for the next decade.

HHS serves the nation's 26 million poor through a variety of programs, none of which precedes the Great Depression. A capsule description of some of the most important of these programs is provided by the *National Journal.*[26] Among those mentioned, the ones proposed for heavy cuts in the 1982 budget are aid for families with dependent children (AFDC), food stamps, and medicaid.

AID FOR FAMILIES WITH DEPENDENT CHILDREN (AFDC). This program provides $9.7 billion annually to the children of families with no source of income because of death, physical or mental disability, or lack of employment. Twenty-two states withhold relief under AFDC if the male head of the house is unemployed for reasons other than physical or mental disability. The fifty states make their own determinations of the amount of money needed by families with dependent children. The monthly needs for a family of four (three children) range from $187 in Texas and $200 in North Carolina to $497 in Hawaii and $456 in Wisconsin. A common criticism of the program, in addition to these disparities, is that it provides an incentive to the unemployed male head of the house, in the states noted, to leave the household.

SUPPLEMENTAL SECURITY INCOME (SSI). Under this program the federal government directly disburses $6.1 billion annually to the elderly, blind, and disabled. The government guarantees $167.80 per month to individuals and $251.80 to married couples, and if a recipient has other income, his or her SSI payments are reduced below the maximum. Unlike AFDC, the federal government totally administers the program rather than using the states as a conduit of funds, which produces a more uniform distribution.

MEDICAID. This program reimburses the states for medical services, including hospital care, nursing home care, and physician services, for all persons eligible for SSI and AFDC. The states may include persons in the medicaid program and increase the range of services beyond the required basics at their own expense. The expense of this form of aid, $14.7 billion annually, has transformed it into a hot item of controversy in federal and state relationships. All the states with medicaid programs pay for some of the medical services beyond the federal requirements. As with AFDC, the federal government pays from 50 percent to 78 percent of the medicaid costs.

FOOD STAMPS. Whether or not they are on welfare, families qualify for food stamps if their net income (after deduction for taxes, union dues, child care, and other expenses) is less than a fixed amount, in 1981 $533 per month for a family of four. A family of four may purchase $166 worth of food stamps—the minimum the Agriculture Department regards as necessary for an adequate diet—with a share of its net income. Families that make less than $30 a month get their food stamps free; others pay about 20 percent to 25 percent of their income to buy them. The federal contribution is the difference between the $166 and the family's payment for the food stamps. Cost of this program is $4.8 billion annually.

GENERAL ASSISTANCE. This is the one major welfare program that is financed and administered strictly at the state and local level. State or county governments in forty-two states use their own money to pay benefits to a variety of groups not covered by federal programs: the working poor, the long-term unemployed, the temporarily disabled, the migrant worker who does not meet residence requirements, and poor postsecondary students.

Altogether, $36 billion annually is expended through this patchwork of federal, state, and local programs. The federal government's contribution of $22.3 billion is supplemented by $13.6 billion of state and local aid. "Federalizing" the welfare system is often advocated as a means of rectifying spending disparities in those programs that the states administer, such as AFDC and medicaid.

Housing and Urban Development spends $2.5 billion to $3.5 billion annually in housing assistance for low-income groups through programs such as rent supplements, public housing construction, and rehabilitation of existing apartments. The oldest and most controversial part of the federal subsidy program is public housing. Since 1931 one million low-rent units have been constructed in 10,000 projects across the United States, and three million people live in them.[27] Social stigma and underfunding of public housing have played a big part in their failure. The proposed 1982 budget greatly reduces the subsidies allocated to low-income groups by HUD. Programs specified for the heaviest cuts are public housing modernization and subsidized housing.[28]

CROSS-PRESSURED DEPARTMENTS

The departments we have looked at so far are activated by segments of the economy that are uniform in character. Corporate capital is comfortably situated within defense, transportation, and energy; the poor are serviced by HHS and HUD. Cross-pressured departments however, serve not only the elements of corporate capital and the poor but also a third category not yet discussed, competitive capital. The Departments of Labor, Interior, Commerce, and Agriculture serve diverse elements of the economy which pressure each department in conflicting directions.

Competitive capital is distinguished from corporate capital by a number of telling features: (1) The markets served by productive activity are local or regional rather than national or international; (2) the ratio of capital investment to labor productivity is on a much lower scale, because increased productivity is keyed to a growth in employment instead of capital investment; (3) business is unable to insulate itself from the market by control over prices, structure of public preferences, and public institutions; and (4) the labor union movement in competitive industries is weak because of the small scale of production.[29]

One analyst estimates, "Competitive industries employ one-third of the U.S. labor force with the largest proportion in services and distribution."[30] Examples of such industries are restaurants, drug and grocery stores, service stations, garages, appliance repair shops, some elements of the farm industry, small-scale manufacture, beauty salons, and bookstores. In comparison to "organized labor," affiliated with corporate capital, (e.g. the United Auto Workers, International Brotherhood of Teamsters, American Federation of Labor, Congress of Industrial Organizations, and International Association of Machinists), the work force associated with competitive capital is often condemned to material impoverishment. "In 1968 over 10 million workers earned less than $1.60 per hour including 3.5 million paid less than $1.00 per hour," the same analyst notes.[31]

In a heavily cross-pressured department, the secretary cannot be the simple advocate of a homogeneous interest. Instead, in agreement with the general patterns of American politics, he or she must take up a position as the skilled power broker among competing interests. To some extent, the absorption of the departmental secretary in these tasks relieves the president, whose problems of asserting control are extensive, as we have emphasized, of the necessity of taking it on himself. This is not to say that conflicts between the chief executive and cross-pressured departments do not occur. Rather the point is that the position of the departmental secretary is weakened by the diversity of his own or her constituency.

For example, the secretary of commerce is attentive to policy recommendations and suggested appointments made by the Business Advisory Council (BAC), a semipublic group set up during the New Deal to draw businessmen into the tasks of government. This advisory council includes all elements of business in its composition, both corporate capital and competitive capital, though more of the former than of the latter. Thus its policies and suggestions are tinged with the conflicts among competing sectors of the economy. Council membership has always included some elements of small and middle-sized business, but the most influential members in 1955 were "representatives from 2 of the 4 largest rubber manufacturers, 3 of the 5 largest automobile manufacturers, 3 of the 10 largest steel producers, 4 of the 10 largest companies in the chemical field, 2 of the 3 largest manufacturers of electrical equipment, 2 of the 3 largest manufacturers of textiles, 4 of the 16 largest oil companies, and 3 of the largest glass manufacturers."[32] The official position of business on antitrust action is questionable. A secretary of commerce would get conflicting answers, depending on which elements within BAC were consulted.

To take another example, the secretary of labor must service not only the AFL-CIO, which represents the 15 million members of the work force heavily allied with the interests of corporate capital, but also the 10 million or more economically depressed workers who depend on competitive capital. No labor secretary can be everywhere at once and all things to all elements of the labor force, pushing common situs picketing and repeal of Taft-Hartley equally hard with higher minimum wages and expanding professional opportunities for blacks and women. It is possibly for this reason that Carter turned aside the AFL-CIO preferred choice for secretary of labor, John T. Dunlop, appointing instead F. Ray Marshall, better known as a spokesman for, "disorganized" elements of the labor force.[33] Again, "labor" does not speak with a single voice and each secretary designate must face intradepartmental conflicts of some magnitude which absorb much time.

INDEPENDENT REGULATORY COMMISSIONS AND EXECUTIVE AGENCIES

The regulatory commissions and executive agencies have a relationship with the president distinct from any other administrative unit discussed so far. The members of the regulatory commissions are appointed by the president by and with the advice and consent of the Senate. However, they may be removed only for "cause," such as malfeasance of office or neglect of duties, so the Supreme Court determined in the case of *Humphrey's Executor* (Rathbun) v. *United States* (1935). The Court said that the rule-setting and the rule-adjudicating functions of the regulatory commissions distinguished them from the cabinet, which made executive decisions tinged with "politics." The regulatory commissions should be independent of executive control so that they could properly carry out their quasi-judicial and quasi-legislative functions, the Court maintained. In practice, the distinction is hard to maintain. Decisions made by the regulatory commissions, such as who shall be allowed to operate a television station, offer securities on a financial exchange, receive a radio frequency, buy out the business of a competitor, ship natural gas in interstate commerce, or fly an airline route, are all tinged with politics.

The independent executive agencies differ from the regulatory commissions in the respect that each of the former has a single executive administrator who is appointed by the president by and with the advice and consent of the Senate and who, like members of the president's cabinet, are removable at the discretion of the president. The directors of the executive agencies chiefly report to the president rather than a congressional committee, as do the regulatory commissions.

Some of the major regulatory commissions in order of their creation include: (1) the Interstate Commerce Commission (1887) which has rate-setting power over railroads, bus lines, oil pipelines, and trucking companies; (2) the Federal Trade Commission (1914) which has responsibility for assuring fair competition, labeling, packaging, and advertising; (3) the Federal Communications Commission (1934) which regulates all television and radio stations and sets rates for telephone and telegraph companies; (4) the Securities Exchange Commission (1934) which regulates the stock exchanges by scrutinizing the claims of securities offered for sale; (5) the Civil Aeronautics Board (1938) which decides on all routes and fares for domestic and overseas carriers; (6) the Nuclear Regulatory Commission (1974) which licenses the construction and operation of nuclear power plants and enforces safety regulations.[34]

One of the major independent executive agencies is the Environmental Protection Agency (EPA) (1970), which seeks to compel business to assume some of the environmental costs of its productive activity. Customarily, businesses limit expenses to short-term labor and material costs; where production results in environmental degradation, the EPA seeks to impose appropriate costs. Under a variety of environmental statutes, the EPA has regulated the emissions on automobiles, banned the use of DDT, required "stack scrubbers" on coal-fired power plants, imposed controls on the lead content of gasoline, and sought to reduce carcinogens in the water supply. Another agency, the Occupational Safety and Health Administration (OSHA) (1970), seeks to reduce the incidence of employment-related injury, illness, and death among working men and women in the United States. This agency sets standards for exposure to hazardous materials (asbestos, chromium), establishes industry-wide safety procedures, and makes periodic inspections to ensure compliance. In a manner similar to the EPA, OSHA issues regulations requiring business to absorb some of the social costs of its productive activity. A third major independent executive agency, ACTION (1971), administers a variety of programs, many of them a legacy of the Peace Corps, that help the people of other countries meet their needs for trained manpower.[35]

The importance of the work done by the regulatory commissions is illustrated by the accident at Three Mile Island. To reconstruct the incident, a partial meltdown of fuel and casings of the nuclear reactor pile occurred when a malfunction, compounded by operator error, deprived the pile of coolant water. Plans were drafted for a general evacuation to within five miles of the plant because of the threat of radiation but they were never executed. President Carter ordered an inquiry into the causes of the accident and appointed John G. Kemeny, president of Dartmouth College, to be its head.

The Kemeny Commission found that the sources of the accident were both general and specific. A general contributing cause was that the Nuclear Regulatory Commission (NRC) viewed its function as promoting and encouraging the nuclear power industry rather than regulating it. The NRC inspectors relied heavily on the industry's own self-evaluation of its safety measures, did little independent testing of construction work, and made little use of its authority to impose fines for significant violations. A 1978 Government Accounting Office report showed that 500 violations were found in 6,400 inspections but civil penalties were imposed in only 13 cases. A specific problem, highlighted by this incident, was operator preparedness. There were no minimal educational requirements nor psychological fitness tests for operators; an individual could fail the portion of the test dealing with emergency procedures yet still pass the examination and receive a permit to operate.[36]

The Kemeny Commission recommended restructuring the NRC as a way of removing it from an unwholesome relationship with the nuclear power industry and its suppliers. The NRC, the report said, should be established as an independent agency within the executive branch; as such, it would be headed by a single administrator appointed by the president, with the advice and consent of the Senate, to serve a substantial term (longer than the presidential term) but removable at the discretion of the president. The five-member NRC would be abolished. This recommendation draws on the successful experience of the EPA as an independent executive regulatory agency which has achieved relative independence from the industries over which it exercises control.

The Kemeny Commission did not reach the merits of the issue of whether nuclear power should be used as a major source of electric output. In 1978, 13.1 percent of electric output was derived from nuclear energy, and it is projected that 27.3 percent will be derived from this source by 1987.[37] Six of the commissioners, including the chairman, John Kemeny, recommended that no further construction permits for nuclear power plants be issued until a review of the report was made by the president and Congress. A main presumption of the report was that nuclear power could be made safe with proper regulatory control. Also, noteworthy is the commission's view that the agency supervising the nuclear power industry would be less politicized if brought within the executive branch (as an independent executive agency) than if allowed to remain as a regulatory commission. This reasoning runs counter to *Humphrey's Executor* v. *United States.*

Contrasting with the passive regulatory approach of the NRC is the aggressive position taken by the Federal Trade Commission (FTC) in exercising its responsibilities. The FTC is well known for its numerous battles in behalf of the consumer with insurance companies, druggists, funeral directors, used car dealers, and even doctors and dentists. Daringly, it has used its powers to examine the relationships between industry and the government. The FTC pointed out that 2,106 mergers were announced in 1978, a 95 percent increase from 1977 and a 471 percent increase from 1975. The total purchase value of mergers rose from $11.8 billion to $34.2 billion in 1978. The FTC was powerless, it said, to prevent this occurrence because many of the mergers fell into the category of "conglomerate mergers" not prohibited by federal law. Nevertheless, the figures prompted the chairman of the FTC to conclude in testimony before the Senate Judiciary Committee in 1979 that the country was rapidly abandoning the "Jeffersonian [and Madisonian] preference for dispersed power."[38]

The negative attitude of President Reagan toward the work of the independent regulatory commissions and executive agencies is indicated by proposed cuts in the 1982 budget and staff of sixteen major regulatory agencies. The FTC would be required to dismiss 17 percent of its staff and absorb a 10.5 percent budget cut. The EPA is targeted for a 10 percent budget cut and an 11 percent staff cut. Exempt from the cuts is the NRC, which received an 11.5 percent budget increase.[39] The former chairman of the NRC, Joseph Hendrie, who was dismissed by Carter after receipt of the Kemeny Commission report, was restored to his old office. Murray Weidenbaum, the chairman of the Council of Economic Advisors in the Reagan administration, charges that the regulatory agencies have caused a decline in productivity. He states that in 1976, "The total annual cost of federal regulation was shown to be approximately $66 billion, consisting of $3 billion of taxpayer costs to operate the regulatory agencies and $63 billion (or twenty times as much) for business to comply with the regulations."[40] The future role of the regulatory agencies, along with the neo-liberal, social service programs, is one of the core issues of the coming years.

CONCLUSION

Two themes have been pursued in this chapter, executive control of the federal bureaucracy and the competition among perspectives—liberal, neo-liberal, and class interest—to shape the role of the bureaucracy.

The executive office of the president and the White House staff do give the president limited means of exercising power over partial and vested interests within his administration. By acting as extensions of the presidential office (EXOP) and of the personal political ambitions of its occupant (White House staff), both staffs can extend the range of the president's influence over his administration. In the end, however, both staffs depend on his political effectiveness.

The constraints imposed by the constitutional system weaken the capacity of the chief executive to manage the bureaucracy effectively. First, the constitutional system fragments power and provides the means by which most parties can resist transfers of power away from themselves to others. Members of Congress, bureaucrats, and clienteles are potent forces when they cooperate to protect their special preserves from executive management. To put it somewhat differently, there are many official and extraofficial claimants to the time, services, and loyalties of bureaucrats, and many of these parties have some power to push their claims in an aggressive manner. Thus in attempting to control the bureaucracy, the chief executive must bargain and negotiate, a pattern which we have observed repeatedly, with those with whom he shares power.

The fragmentation of power which describes the relationships between the president and his cabinet is accentuated further in his relationships with the independent regulatory commissions. The president is deprived of the means of controlling their activities except by influencing relevant congressional committees. This is not a very promising means of control.

A second bias of the constitutional system thwarting executive control is that the state is given a passive role in managing the private ownership of wealth. The practical arrangements of Madisonian politics, we have seen, retain the upper hand of wealthy groups in the outcome of social conflict. In Hamilton's vision the power of the state is straightforwardly defended to maintain the class basis of social groups. The biases of the constitutional system, therefore, ill prepare the state, and most importantly the chief executive, to reconcile democracy with the expanding role of corporate power in the late nineteenth century, and with accelerated force into the twentieth. Public bureaucracy arises late in America, long after the formation of bureaucracy in the corporate sector, and it is given a limited function. At best, public bureaucracy seeks to alleviate the worst effects of capitalism, and at worst, it falls under the influence of the interests it is supposed to regulate.

The major consequence is that the priorities of modern oligopoly dominate the bureaucracy in important areas. Despite complaints and much rhetoric about the regulatory role of the bureaucracy, the functions it performs chiefly benefit big capital and are indispensable to its survival. Modern oligopoly, especially in energy, transportation, and defense, relies on the bureaucratic machine to provide an auxiliary source of capital supply, to underwrite scientific and technical research, to provide a predictable regulatory environment within which controlled competition may occur, to absorb the administrative overhead of its operations, to serve as the legatee of failed capitalist enterprise, and to absorb the costs of its productive activity in relation to the environment and the work force. The demand for these services from corporate-dominated departments diverts available resources from social service agencies and confines the liberal state to the archaic principles that inspired its creation. A partnership between liberal ideology and corporate capitalism is manifest in the budgetary priorities and programs of the Reagan administration.

NOTES

1. *The New York Times,* February 24, 1980, B4.
2. *Ibid.*
3. Edward S. Greenberg, *Serving the Few* (New York: John Wiley, 1974), pp. 13–17.
4. James O'Connor, *The Fiscal Crisis of the State* (New York: St. Martin's Press, 1973); John Kenneth Galbraith, *The New Industrial State* (New York: Signet, 1967); Michael Best and William Connolly, *The Politicized Economy* (Lexington, Mass.: Heath, 1976).
5. O'Connor, *Fiscal Crisis,* p. 1.
6. David Truman, *The Governmental Process* (New York: Knopf, 1958), p. 395.
7. Patrick Anderson, *The President's Men* (New York: Doubleday, 1968).
8. *National Journal,* February 12, 1977, p. 232.
9. *Ibid.,* pp. 232–36.
10. *The New York Times,* December 19, 1976, E4.
11. Aaron Wildavsky, *The Politics of the Budgetary Process* (Boston: Little, Brown, 1964); Richard Pious, *The American Presidency* (New York: Basic Books, 1979), chap. 8.
12. *The New York Times,* August 20, 1976, A10.
13. Richard Neustadt, *Presidential Power* (New York: John Wiley, 1960), p. 39.
14. O'Connor, *Fiscal Crisis,* chap. 3.
15. *National Journal,* April 7, 1981, pp. 380–81.
16. *The New York Times,* May 3, 1976, C 1–4.
17. *The New York Times,* January 4, 1980, A1, B10.
18. *National Journal,* April 7, 1981, pp. 380–81.
19. Seymour Melman, *Pentagon Capitalism* (New York: McGraw-Hill, 1970), pp. 115–23.

20. *The New York Times,* October 17, 1976, C 1–15.

21. *The New York Times,* September 4, 1979, F1, 10.

22. *The New York Times,* December 19, 1976, E2.

23. Frances Fox Piven and Richard Cloward, *Regulating the Poor* (New York: Vintage Books, 1971).

24. *The New York Times,* January 29, 1980, A1.

25. *The New York Times,* August 25, 1972.

26. *National Journal,* January 8, 1977, pp. 44–45.

27. *National Journal* September 11, 1976, pp. 1,270–78.

28. *The New York Times,* February 20, 1981, A11.

29. O'Connor, *Fiscal Crisis,* pp. 13–15.

30. *Ibid.,* p. 13.

31. *Ibid.,* p. 14.

32. Grant McConnell, *Private Power and American Democracy* (New York: Vintage Books, 1966), p. 278.

33. *National Journal,* January 1, 1977, pp. 16–22.

34. *United States Government Organization Manual* (Washington, D.C.: U.S. Government Printing Office, 1978).

35. *Ibid.* See also *National Journal,* May 12, 1979, p. 773.

36. *Report of the President's Commission on the Accident at Three Mile Island* (Washington, D.C.: U.S. Government Printing Office, 1979), pp. 27–59.

37. *National Journal,* April 28, 1978, p. 678.

38. Quoted in *National Journal,* March 14, 1979, p. 480; see also *National Journal,* October 13, 1979, pp. 1,676–80.

39. *National Journal,* March 21, 1981, pp. 475, 502.

40. Murray Weidenbaum, "Reply," in *Journal of Post Keynesian Economics,* Spring 1980, p. 351.

CHAPTER 11

Justice in America

POLITICS AND THE JUDICIARY

Ordinarily, we do not think of the judiciary as involved in politics. Justices commonly reside in Greek temples. The courtroom is a hushed precinct paneled with rich wood, a setting much too exalted to admit the common concerns of mere politics. Especially it seems that the justices themselves cannot be "political" figures. The design of our courtrooms is such that attention is focused on these judges, who sit above the other participants. No visitor's gallery is allowed to rise above them, and those who work in the courtroom are not allowed to sit or stand at their level. They wear a special costume—a black robe. All must rise when they enter the courtroom and all address them as "Your honor," even though they may be personally despised.

Judges are not thought of as political partly because we have fastened on a narrow and trivial conception of the term. Politics, we think, is conflict over wealth, status, patronage, power. Thus the executive is a political institution because that is where subgovernments contend for mastery over selected areas of policy and power. Congress is a political institution because that is where committee and subcommittee chairmen fight over the distribution of federal resources. On the other hand, the judiciary is obviously not the locus of wealth, power, and patronage, and therefore politics does not intrude.

However, we must remember that politics is a conflict over the rules that shape human action in ordered communities (see Chapter 1). Judges do have a rule-making function, a very important one as we shall see; and insofar as judges make rules (and they do), rather than merely find or declare them (as they sometimes pretend to be doing), they are as much involved in the political process as any other actor on the political scene. One can even say that they are probably more involved in politics than most of the figures, the president included, we read about in the newspapers.

Politics is intertwined with the distribution of resources, which underlies the ability of parties to mount contests over the rules and even to win them. Even so, all such conflicts are decided by reference to the existing rules, which gives the judiciary an important role. For example, when the Nixon administration overreached itself in a thrust to consolidate power, a series of judicial determinations—most important that "national security" and "executive privilege" were not sufficient justification for breaking laws—brought the executive branch to heel.[1] If the distribution of political resources alone had decided this contest, the outcome, though not an impossibility, would be so remote as to be dismissed from consideration.

To illustrate the role of the judiciary in shaping the rules that order the American political community, let us look at a few examples drawn from recent years:

In *Furman* v. *Georgia,* 408 U.S. 238 (1972), the Supreme Court withdrew the right of a state to execute prisoners if its criminal statutes provided no clear standards for the imposition of this penalty. The Court said that where the relevant statutes failed to provide standards to enable the jury to evaluate the punishment in relation to the character of the defendant, the seriousness of the offense, and the circumstances in which it was committed, the taking of a person's life was not "execution" but a "cruel and unusual punishment," prohibited by the Eighth Amendment. The effect of the Court's ruling, prompted by the fact that 53.3 percent of those executed between 1930 and 1975 were black,[2] was to modify the right of the state to take human life. The Court did not declare capital punishment unconstitutional; rather the states were urged to tighten the criteria that warranted it. Nevertheless, the ruling was an important change in the balance of social forces between those favoring a tough and those a deliberative sentencing policy.

Formerly, blacks who sat at lunch counters in drugstores or dime stores, along with the few whites brave enough to sit with them, could be successfully prosecuted in many Southern states for criminal trespass. Blacks who disobeyed a police order to move on were arrested and later tried on charges of trespass and disturbing the peace.[3] In a chain of cases beginning in the early 1960s [*Peterson* v. *Greenville* S.C., 373 U.S. 244 (1963); *Shuttleworth* v. *Birmingham Ala.,* 373 U.S. 262 (1963)], the Supreme Court reversed the state courts that upheld a judgment of criminal trespass against black defendants. The Court said that use of police power to enforce segregated facilities was a denial of the "equal protection of the laws" guaranteed by the Fourteenth Amendment.

Elaborating its views, the Court stated that the rights of private property had to be balanced against the interests of the community. The community had an overriding right to maintain facilities which did not arbitrarily exclude some of its members, the blacks, from the full use of such services as were provided. Having invited the business of all, the store had to conduct its business in a uniform, fair, and nonexclusionary way. These rulings greatly changed the relationships between the races in Southern settings, racial barriers were lowered, and property rights were made more responsive to human rights.

Until very recently, it was a crime in most states to perform an abortion except under conditions of incest or rape, to save the life of the mother, or if the fetus had been injured by disease. All these conditions establish a presumption against abortion except in the most extreme cases. Against this presumption, many women have asserted a right to have an abortion as a simple element of their plans, expectations, and desires, rather than as dire extremity.[4] The Court has sought to reconcile these conflicting views, in general ruling that removal of the fetus before term under certain conditions is an "abortion," protected by the rights of "privacy" of the Fourteenth Amendment, not "infanticide," punishable by criminal prosecution. In the cases of *Roe* v. *Wade,* 410 U.S. 113 (1973), and *Doe* v. *Bolton,* 410 U.S. 179 (1973), the Court stated conditions under which an abortion was constitutionally protected. (1) During the first three months of pregnancy the state must leave the decision of whether to have an abortion and how to carry it out to a woman and her doctor. The mother's right not to carry an unwanted pregnancy to term is protected by the Fourteenth Amendment, which safeguards the privacy of the individual under due process of law. (2) During the second three months of pregnancy the state may not forbid the abortion but it may regulate the procedure. At this point the right of the state to protect the health of the mother and of the child supersedes the right of privacy. (3) The state may prohibit an abortion after six months except under the conditions of dire extremity previously mentioned. A recent decision of the Court holds that although the states do not have a right to prevent abortion in most cases, they are not under an obligation to subsidize it. (Roughly one-third of the 1.1 million abortions performed annually are subsidized by medicaid.)[5] Thus, whereas all women have a right to an abortion, the state is not under a compulsion to ensure that all have an equal right to avail themselves of it.

A lower court in New Jersey has extended the right of privacy protected by the Fourteenth Amendment to the refusal of medical services and support for individuals who have relapsed into a vegetative, nonsapient condition. Medical science has reached the stage where it can sustain life even when brain activity can no longer be recorded. This capability presents a human dilemma. The life-sustaining devices are obviously meant to enhance human life; yet they also represent an intrusion into the individual's right of decision concerning the circumstances of his life and death.[6] The court expressed a sense of obligation to answer the challenge presented by medical science to the community. "The law, equity, and justice must not themselves quail and be helpless in the face of modern technological marvels presenting questions hitherto unthought of."[7] The court found that respect for the individual's right of privacy included a right to terminate further treatment. Since this right could not be exercised by the individual, it was available to the next of kin in consultation with a doctor. If the exercise of the right to privacy led to withdrawal of treatment and, in turn, to death, neither relatives nor medical staff could be charged with a homicide. Rather, death was an act of privacy safeguarded by the Fourteenth Amendment.

These examples are meant to illustrate the role of the Court in making the rules that order the community. The examples should not obscure the truth that the Court also makes decisions about the allocation of resources. Although this is a lesser function of the judiciary, in comparison to the legislature and the executive, this is not to say that the judiciary is not involved at all. A student of judicial politics notes the following examples of allocative decisions made in recent years:

> Courts have struck down laws requiring a period of in-state residence as a condition of eligibility for welfare. They have invalidated presumptions of child support arising from the presence in the home of a "substitute" father. Federal district courts have laid down elaborate standards for food handling, hospital operations, recreation facilities, inmate employment and education, sanitation and laundry, painting, lighting, plumbing, and renovation in some prisons; they have ordered other prisons closed. Courts have established equally comprehensive programs of care and treatment for the mentally ill confined in hospitals. They have ordered the equalization of school expenditures on teachers' salaries and said that bilingual studies must be provided for Mexican-American children. They have enjoined the construction of roads and bridges on environmental grounds and suspended performance requirements for automobile tires and air bags. They have told the Farmer's Home Administration to restore a disaster loan program, the Forest Service to stop the clear-cutting of timber, and the Corps of Engineers to maintain the nation's non-navigable waterways.[8]

SOURCE, NATURE, EXTENT OF JUDICIAL AUTHORITY

SOURCE

Why should other parties to the social conflict obey the judgments of the Court regarding the rules and resources of the community? What gives the Court the right to decide when a woman may lawfully terminate a pregnancy, whom a property owner must admit to his place of business, under what circumstances the state can lawfully take a person's life, under what conditions death may be chosen?

We might suppose in some vague way that the authority of the Court to make these decisions is derived from the Constitution. The Constitution, it is frequently supposed, is the source both of judicial authority and of the rules that the Court applies. But this impression is not true in the form just stated. There is nothing in the Constitution that gives the Supreme Court a power to review the actions of the coordinate branches of government and of the states with the intention of bringing these actions into conformity with its own interpretation of the Constitution. The wording of the Constitution is consistent with an independent finding by the states and the coordinate branches of its meaning. All that the Constitution has to say on the scope of judicial authority is "The judicial power of the United States, shall be vested in one Supreme Court, and in such inferior courts as the Congress may from time to time ordain and establish." This is followed by the unenlightening comment "The judicial power shall extend to all cases in law and equity arising under this Constitution." Moreover, there is little in the Constitution to back up the Court's determination, say in the abortion cases, that the right to privacy includes the right to terminate an unwanted pregnancy. Many rulings of the Court, of which this is a single example, are not obviously based on the wording of the Constitution or the intention of the framers.

The Court is also a most unrepresentative institution, and this makes the issue of its authority all the more puzzling. The pool of lawyers considered for appointment to the Supreme Court is a tiny fraction of an already highly elitist group. The hallmarks of judicial appointment in the period between 1789 and 1962 were social prominence, political influence, and upper-class family background. Over 90 percent of the ninety-four appointments fell into this category.[9] No blacks served on the Court until the appointment of Thurgood Marshall in 1967, and the first female justice was appointed in 1981. The social characteristics of the typical justice underline these elitist attributes: "White, generally Protestant . . . ; fifty to fifty-five years of age at the time of his appointment; Anglo-Saxon ethnic stock . . . ; high social status; reared in urban environment; member of a civic minded, politically active, economically comfortable family; legal training; some type of public office; generally well educated."[10]

Thus, because the Supreme Court has no clear charter of authority from the Constitution and is one of the least representative of our political institutions, we are faced with the problem of explaining its rule-making powers. Unlike the members of the executive and the legislature, the judiciary is not directly accountable for its actions to the electorate. Members of the Court are appointed by the president by and with the advice and consent of the Senate. Once they are appointed they hold office for life during good behavior, which means long after the elected representatives who installed them have faded from the scene. There is no way to hold a justice accountable for his actions short of impeachment, an unsuitable instrument in any case. The authority of the Supreme Court outweighs any other institution; yet the basis of that authority is a mystery.

The first case testing the rule-making powers of the Supreme Court is the famed *Marbury* v. *Madison,* 1 Cranch 137 (1803). Marbury was a justice of the peace appointed to office at the end of John Adams's administration in 1800. The commission appointing him to office was signed by the president and was to be delivered to Marbury by Madison himself, then serving as secretary of state. Nevertheless, in the rush of final business Madison left the commissions undelivered on his desk. Marbury brought suit, asking the Supreme Court to exercise its powers of original jurisdiction pursuant to the Judiciary Act (1801). Specifically, Marbury requested the Court to issue a *writ of mandamus* against Madison, ordering the delivery of the signed commissions pursuant to its powers in the Judiciary Act. (A writ of mandamus is an order addressed to a public official to perform a nondiscretionary duty.) Marshall instructed Madison to show cause why such a writ should not be issued, an instruction Madison ignored.

Marshall found that Marbury had a real grievance to which the provisions of the Judicary Act provided an appropriate remedy. He was prevented from executing the power conferred on the judiciary by the act, however, because it had been conferred by ordinary legislation. That is, the power to issue the writ of mandamus enlarged the original jurisdiction of the Court contrary to the provisions of the Constitution. Declaring that "the Constitution controls any legislative Act repugnant to it," Marshall said that Congress had exceeded its authority in passing the Judiciary Act. He rested his opinion on (1) the supremacy of the Constitution, which is a "superior paramount law, unchangeable by ordinary means"; (2) the functions of the judiciary: "It is emphatically the province and duty of the judicial department to say what the law is"; (3) the logic of the system: "If two laws conflict with each other [the Constitution and ordinary law], the courts must decide . . . which of these conflicting rules governs the case."

In the controversies of the day, the significance of Marshall's assertion of judicial authority was largely overlooked. The Jefferson administration was angered by the finding that Marbury was entitled to his commission and that the government had been derelict in its duty by not delivering it. The assertion of an authority to declare null and void an action of one of the coordinate branches did not receive as much attention. Had Marshall's opinion succeeded in establishing this authority on an unquestionable basis?

Marshall solved the problem of the Constitution's silence by an act of political creation. He cast the Supreme Court in the role of an umpire, and to some extent participant, in a political conflict waged over the entire social and institutional landscape. In doing so Marshall went beyond the intention of the framers, yet in a manner consistent with their basic purposes. He showed that the logic of the constitutional system required a final political will somewhere to say, with some degree of finality, "what the law is." The constitutional system was built on the principle of managing conflict between the national government and state and local governments and among the coordinate branches of government. Yet the framers had neglected to identify an institution, probably because of their paranoiac concerns, which would have the responsibility of arbitrating among the parties to this conflict. Marshall stepped in to answer a need the framers had created but which they had not made provision for. The logic of his opinion in *Marbury* rests heavily on the logical need for a final authority created by the constitutional system, not on any express grant of power from the written Constitution or the special qualifications of the judiciary.[11] Members of the legislature and the executive, many of them qualified lawyers, have pointed out that they too are competent to make a determination of the constitutionality of their actions. They have not been able to answer the force of Marshall's logic, however, which places stress on *whose* interpretation is to prevail. To this day, the power of judicial review rests on the need for a party of the last resort in a system based on the principle of conflict management.

NATURE

The nature of judicial power, as Marshall pointed out in his opinion, is to decide which among two or more conflicting rules shall govern a case. Marshall pretended that this was a very straightforward thing to do, requiring little of the Court in the way of reflection or choice. The Constitution, he implied, could always be unambiguously interpreted to favor one of the competing rules against other possibilities. This opinion closely resembles the outlook of Justice Roberts (encountered in Chapter 2), who expounded a very literal idea of the Constitution. Roberts said that the essence of the judicial task consisted in laying a contested statute beside the relevant article of the Constitution and deciding "whether the latter squares with the former." Along with Marshall, Roberts implies that the written Constitution embodies a rule which governs every case and that there is no problem in applying it.

Actually, as we have seen, the American Constitution exists in other forms than the written memorandum which the justices like to talk about. It also exists as the historical enthusiasm of a people, for example. Justice Douglas stated in *Gray* v. *Sanders,* 372 U.S. 368, 381 (1963), that the "conception of political equality from the Declaration of Independence, to Lincoln's Gettysburg Address, to the Fifteenth, Seventeenth, and Nineteenth Amendments can mean only one thing—one person one vote." Note that Lincoln's Gettysburg Address and the Declaration of Independence, documents that highlight the historical enthusiasms of the American people, are put alongside the written Constitution. The quotation strongly suggests that a historical commitment to liberalism, especially the principle of the choice-making individual, compelled the Court to undertake the difficult and tricky business of reapportioning congressional districts. Thus a ruling cluster of ideas informs the thinking of the Court, enlivening its interpretation of particular clauses of the Constitution.

In terms of practical political arrangements, the constitutional system also requires that the rulings of the Supreme Court be accommodated over time to the coalition of groups which has captured the White House and one or both houses of Congress. One reason for this is that the executive can expect to appoint about two new justices during one term of office. A judiciary scholar writes that "Over the whole history of the Court, on the average one new justice has been appointed every twenty-two months."[12] Hoover had three appointments; Roosevelt, nine; Truman, four; Eisenhower, five; Nixon, four; Carter, none. Of course, presidents appoint justices who reflect their own views on public policy insofar as these are known. At the same time a president can anticipate that an appointment in conflict with the dominant opinion in the Senate will fail to be confirmed. Through a change in personnel on the Court, the president can tip policy in the direction that he favors. Additionally, legislative majorities with major policy objectives in mind usually have an opportunity of overcoming the Court's veto. Congress and the president do generally succeed over

time in triumphing over a hostile Court on major policy issues.[13] Therefore, the system of separate institutions sharing power forces on the
Court a pattern of accommodation and compromise in a manner similar
to the negotiating style of congressmen, bureaucrats, and presidents.
Particular clauses of the written Constitution are not looked at in isolation but in relation to the dominant opinion in the White House and
on Capitol Hill. The operative realities of American politics dictate a role
for the Court as one power group among others which must find a basis
for conciliation and compromise.

Thus the criteria of judicial policymaking are more complex than
the statements of Marshall and Roberts would lead one to suspect. The
ideas of the liberal democratic heritage and the distribution of power in
government enter into these criteria, affecting in important ways the
interpretation of particular clauses of the Constitution. Justice Oliver
Wendell Holmes, one of the giants of court history, has summed it all
up by suggesting that the life of the law is not logic, a deduction from
particular clauses of the Constitution, but experience, placing the
clauses of the Constitution into their ideological, institutional, cultural,
and historical setting. Such an exercise enables us to see that the boundaries of the Constitution are wider than the view of Roberts will allow
but that they are not nonexistent. A powerful opponent of the tendency
to abstract law from its political context, Holmes says:

> The life of the law has not been logic: it has been experience. The felt
> necessities of the time, the prevalent moral and political theories, intuitions
> of public policy, avowed or unconscious, even the prejudices which judges
> share with their fellow-men, have a great deal more to do than the syllo-
> gism in determining the rules by which men should be governed. The law
> embodies the story of a nation's development through many centuries, and
> it cannot be dealt with as if it contained only the axioms and corollaries of
> a book of mathematics.[14]

EXTENT

To say that the Court has extensive policymaking authority is not the
same as saying that it makes policy at will. The Court is limited in its
policymaking role to the extent that it must wait until an actual "case
or controversy" arises under the Constitution before it can intervene.
That is, there must be an actual contest between adversary parties, one
of whom claims that a right has been infringed by the government,
either federal or state, and he relies on the Constitution to support his
contention. Generally, the Court intervenes when a lower court has
declared unconstitutional some provision of national law or upheld

the validity of some provision of state law against a claim that it is contrary to the Constitution. These limitations surrounding judicial intervention mean that the Court is essentially a passive instrument: "Courts are like defective clocks; they have to be shaken to get them going."[15]

Another limitation on the policymaking functions of the Court also flows from the case method. The Court makes policy as an incident of deciding cases, not the other way around. Its rulings are couched in the form of a decision concerning a particular controversy, which binds only the parties to the dispute. Parties who oppose the decision are at liberty to interpret its effect narrowly, to ignore it, to evade it through marginal change, and even to find political gain, as Wallace did in relation to civil rights rulings, in outright opposition.[16] The Court must rely to a great extent on the voluntary compliance of national, state, and local officials in widening the scope of its judicial decisions. This voluntary cooperation may not be forthcoming. Alternative social policies get short shrift in judicial opinions because the judges decide only actual contests between adversary parties. If judges were free to decide between competing social policies, their role would closely resemble a legislator's. But as we have been stressing, judges do not have *carte blanche:* Their range of policy choice is narrowed in advance by the case method; they must decide between the competing rights advanced in the particular case before them; and they may not alter the boundaries into which the contest is set.

A third limitation on judicial review is that the Court relies solely on its authority to obtain compliance with its rulings; it lacks the power to enforce them. Authority arises from a consensually recognized right to make decisions; power is the ability to control the behavior of others.[17] From the beginning, Hamilton recognized that the power of the Court would be puny in relation to the other branches and that this alone would be sufficient to keep the judiciary in check. The executive and the legislature possess the power of the purse and sword, he points out, which gives them the capacity to enforce compliance with their decisions. On the other hand, the judiciary must rely on the authority of its judgments, a weak factor:

> The judiciary . . . has no influence over either the sword or the purse; no direction either of the strength or the wealth of the society; and can take no active resolution whatever. It may truly be said to have neither FORCE nor WILL, but merely judgment. . . . [This] proves incontestably, that the judiciary is beyond comparison the weakest of the three departments of power; that it can never attack with success either of the other two; and

that all possible care is requisite to enable it to defend itself against their attacks.[18]

Hamilton's views are underscored by the massive resources of coercion and wealth at the disposition of the coordinate branches of government in the modern day. Yet the authority of the Supreme Court to "declare what the law is" provides the coloration of legitimacy to actions of the government, and this is a function of indispensable value to elective officials in obtaining compliance with government policy-making.[19] Despite their superior resources, neither the executive nor the legislature is likely to flout the decisions of the Court. It is probably some consideration such as this that led Richard Nixon, despite the overwhelming power of the chief executive, to comply with a Court order requiring the surrender of incriminating tape recordings of conversations between himself and his aides in the weeks immediately following the Watergate break-in. Not to comply with the ruling of the Court would have deprived executive actions of all cover of legitimacy. Unless the president was prepared to conduct a shoot-out on the White House lawn over the possession of the tapes, a consideration which may have crossed his mind, release of the tapes was necessary.

Within the general limits of judicial authority just described, the Court has some room for maneuver in terms of those cases over which it accepts jurisdiction. The Court has two kinds of jurisdiction, original and appellate. Of these two, the appellate jurisdiction is by far the most important.

The Supreme Court has original jurisdiction over cases concerning ambassadors, ministers, and consuls and cases in which a state is a party. An illustration of original jurisdiction is the water dispute between California and Arizona [*Arizona* v. *California,* 373 U.S. 546 (1963)] and an attempt by the state of Delaware, unsuccessful as it turned out, to have the Court declare the electoral college system unconstitutional [*Delaware et al.* v. *New York et al.,* 385 U.S. 895 (1966)]. The Court exercises its powers of original jurisdiction rarely, partly because of the scarcity of that type of case and partly because of its own and Congress's desire to share its power with the lower federal judiciary. Consequently, the Supreme Court exercises its original jurisdiction *exclusively* in instances involving two or more states.

By far the primary task of the Court is in appellate jurisdiction. Here it serves as the final arbiter on the construction of the Constitution, providing an authoritative interpretation of the law of the land. Cases come to the Supreme Court on appeal (1) from the U.S. courts of appeal (of which there are eleven); (2) from the state courts of last resort, which normally, but not always, are the state supreme courts; and (3) in selected cases directly from the district courts (of which there are ninety-one). The two most common instances of appeal are when a state court of the last resort has declared unconstitutional some provision of national law, or upheld the validity of some provision of state law, against a claim that it is contrary to the Constitution; or when a district court has granted or denied an injunction against a federal or state statute on the grounds of unconstitutionality. (An injunction is a court order prohibiting an individual, organization, or official from performing an action.) Over 4,000 cases on appeal are filed before the Court, in each term of which it agrees to hear approximately 175.

There are two main avenues, called writs, by which matters of appellate jurisdiction reach the Court: (1) on what lawyers call *appeal*, that is, a writ issued as a matter of right when the petitioner has succeeded in raising a constitutional issue of major importance in the lower court; (2) on *certiorari*, that is, a writ issued by the Court solely at its discretion calling up the record of the lower court to determine whether a substantial federal question has been raised. Although the Court is obliged to consider cases brought by writ of appeal, it is not obliged to hear the cases on their merits. By the same token, petitions for a writ of certiorari are granted solely at the pleasure of the Court. A petition for review by the Supreme Court, brought either by writ of appeal or certiorari, is granted when in the opinion of four justices the case raises an issue of some importance to the constitutional system. Fully 50 to 60 percent of the writs of appeal fail to meet this test and are denied review; certiorari is denied in over 97 percent of the cases.[20] The acceptance of writs of appeal is greater because by definition, a constitutional issue has been introduced into the record of the lower court.

The discretionary powers of the Court in exercising appellate jurisdiction enhances its political significance. In the words of a former chief justice, the Court grants review only to "those cases which present questions whose resolution will have immediate importance far beyond the particular facts and parties involved."[21] In short, the Court grants jurisdiction in many cases because the dispute is laden with importance for public policy. Thus, in the normal course of voting on the cases it receives on appeal, the Supreme Court can actively shape public policy, and is called by judicial scholars an "activist" Court; or it can defer to the policies of the institutions with whom it shares power, a role commonly referred to as judicial "self-restraint."[22] For example, the Warren Court won a reputation for judicial activism because it made frequent use of the judicial process to oppose policies of malapportionment and racial segregation approved of by state and local majorities. The chief justice often sets the tone for the Court, whether of activism or restraint.

THE BAKKE CASE

The functions and limitations of judical review will stand out more clearly if we place them in the setting of an actual "case or controversy" arising under the Constitution. The Bakke case, argued before the Supreme Court on October 12, 1977, is already compared with the landmark case of *Brown* v. *Board of Education of Topeka,* 347 U.S. 483 (1954), in raising constitutional issues of great magnitude.

The facts of the case are that Allan Bakke, a white applicant for admission to the medical school of the University of California at Davis, was turned down on two successive occasions, first in 1973 and then again in 1974. Ordinarily, there is nothing uncommon about an applicant for medical school being turned down. Each year about two-thirds of the 45,000 men and women who apply for admission to the nation's medical schools are turned away.[23] Thus Bakke's fate was more the norm than the exception, except for two facts.

First, Bakke, even by the rarefied criteria used by the nation's medical schools, was an exceptional, if not a distinguished, student. He held a 3.5 grade average (out of a possible 4.0) from the University of Minnesota as an undergraduate; he ranked in the 97th percentile of all applicants nationally who had taken the Medical College Admissions Test; he had worked after hours as a hospital volunteer, a "candy striper," from his job as a research engineer with the National Aeuronautics and Space Administration; and he had been granted a personal interview, accorded to only one out of six applicants, indicating keen interest in his application by the medical school.[24]

Second, the medical college at Davis reserved sixteen spaces in its entering freshman class for minority applicants (blacks, Asians, and Mexican-Americans). Under the special admissions program which had been created by the faculty at the beginning of the college in 1968, an applicant was considered under a separate set of criteria if he or she marked line 22 of the application form as "disadvantaged." In that case, a 2.5 grade average under the special admissions program did not necessarily disqualify the applicant, and scores on the MCAT considerably below the minimum for regular applicants were acceptable. In 1973, the year in which Bakke was denied admission, the sixteen applicants selected under this program had undergraduate averages of 2.88 compared with 3.49 for students admitted through the regular channels; in scientific knowledge ratings on the MCAT regular premeds ranked in the

83rd percentile, whereas special students ranked in the 35th. No whites had ever been admitted under the special admissions program, even though several hundred had applied for consideration. In four years of operation at Davis the program had admitted thirty-five Mexican-Americans, twenty-six blacks, and one American Indian. The program was similar to those set up at more than one hundred medical schools across the country.[25]

Bakke contended that the special admissions program infringed on his right to an "equal protection of the laws" under the Fourteenth Amendment because it advanced, as a matter of set policy, the interests of unqualified minority applicants against those of qualified applicants who happen to be members of the white majority. He asserted that he had good standing to pose this issue in the courts since denial of admission by the medical college had injured his constitutional rights. Thus the issue presented in the case is whether affirmative-action programs such as the one instituted at Davis are consistent with the law of the land as spelled out in the Fourteenth Amendment.

The Bakke case is often cited as an instance of "reverse discrimination" and contrasted with the historic ruling of the Court in *Brown* v. *Topeka Board of Education*. The ruling in the Brown case sought to end some of the effects of a century and more of racial discrimination against members of the black race by the dominant white majority. It established, contrary to the ruling of the post–Civil War Court in *Plessy* v. *Ferguson*, 163 U.S. 537 (1896), that separate school facilities for black elementary school children were "inherently unequal" because they imposed a stigma on the members of the black race which could not be erased by equality in resources, physical facilities, and staff. This ruling stimulated congressional legislation (the Civil Rights Acts of 1960 and 1964) and administrative efforts to reduce discrimination in a range of other areas, such as public accommodations, voting, and employment.

The advances made by blacks and other minorities under these programs have brought the countercharge that the government now discriminates in behalf of minority groups against the dominant white majority. The Bakke case formulates this political issue in terms of the U.S. Constitution. The affirmative-action program at Davis, except for the use of specific quotas instead of guidelines, resembles many of those administered at the national level. For example, the Equal Employment Opportunity Commission, an independent executive agency created to enforce Title VII of the Civil Rights Act of 1964, can bring suit against employers who reveal a pattern of discrimination in their employment practices. An office in the Department of Labor requires employers awarded government contracts to show the affirmative steps they are taking to increase the employment of disadvantaged groups. Personnel standards set by the Civil Service Commission require affirmative action from state and local governments administering federal programs in health, welfare, employment, security, and civil defense.[26] In all these cases, specific guidelines are set up as a matter of policy to advance the interests of minorities in an effort to compensate for the nation's past history of prejudice.

The suit of the *Regents of the University of California* v. *Allan Bakke* was first brought in the Yolo County Courthouse in California in late 1973. Bakke's lawyer, Reynold H. Colvin, had once persuaded a federal district court to overturn a San Francisco Board of Education proposal barring whites from certain school administrative jobs. Colvin insisted that the sole reason for Bakke's rejection was his race, and that he had therefore been deprived of the Fourteenth Amendment provision of equal protection under the law. Judge F. Leslie Manker came out of retirement to hear the case. Quoting from the majority opinion of Chief Justice Warren in *Brown* v. *Topeka Board of Education*—"where the state has undertaken to provide it [an education] it must be made available to all on equal terms"[27]—Manker declared that Bakke had indeed been denied equal protection. To justify a special admissions program, such as the one at Davis, on a constitutional basis, a pattern of past discrimination against minorities at the school must be shown. But he declared that Bakke was still ineligible for admission because he had not established that he deserved admission, in competition with the regular students, even if the special admission programs had not existed. Neither Bakke nor the Board of Regents was satisfied with this ruling, and the case was appealed to the next higher court.

Normally, the case would have gone to a state appellate court, but the state supreme court decided to take it directly because of the substantial federal question which it raised. In a six-to-one decision on September 26, 1976, the court upheld Manker's decision that the two-track admissions policy was unconstitutional but overturned his ruling that Bakke was not entitled to admission. The decision of the state supreme court contained three main themes: (1) No evidence was presented that the medical college had discriminated against minorities in the past; (2) the sixteen admission spots assigned to disadvantaged students were, in fact, a quota based on race; (3) although it is not unconstitutional to classify persons on the basis of race, it must be shown that the state has a compelling interest in doing so, and every reasonable alternative to achieve these goals without discrimination must be pursued before fundamental rights are abridged. The court took the unusual step of pointing out alternative policies, not pursued by the medical college at Davis, which might have alleviated past patterns of discrimination without injury to white applicants. Among the suggestions were to increase the number of groups qualifying under "minority" guidelines, to build more medical schools with more admission spots, and to recruit more aggressively among minority groups.[28]

A strong dissent was entered by one lone justice, Justice Matthew Tobriner: "Two centuries of slavery and racial discrimination have left our nation an awful legacy, a largely separated society in which wealth, educational resources—indeed all society's benefits—remain largely the preserve of the white Anglo-Saxon majority."[29] It was inconsistent, he argued, to say that the Fourteenth Amendment which "served as the basis for the requirement that the elementary schools and secondary schools be required to integrate should now be turned around to forbid graduate schools from voluntarily seeking that very objective."[30] To this opinion Justice Stanley Moss made the reply for the majority: "Originating as a means of exclusion of racial and religious minorities from higher education, a quota becomes no less offensive when it serves to exclude a racial majority."[31]

The Bakke case reached the Supreme Court on a writ of appeal on February 22, 1977, and the Court agreed to hear it in October. The case was argued before the Court by Reynold Colvin, Bakke's attorney throughout the appeal process, and representing the University of California, was Archibald Cox, former solicitor general, Watergate special prosecutor, and professor of law at Harvard. The two attorneys were joined in oral argument by Solicitor General Wade H. McCree, Jr., third-ranking official in the Justice Department, who represents the United States in all cases to which it is a litigant and who may, at the pleasure of the Court, intervene in cases freighted with large policy significance through an *amicus curiae* (friend of the court) brief. Over sixty *amici curiae* briefs were presented in the Bakke case, more than in any other case brought before the Court, an indication of the great amount of public interest in the issues involved. The oral arguments of the attorneys lasted for two hours, no more than is customarily allowed. Cox argued for a flat-out reversal of the lower court ruling, and Colvin urged unqualified affirmation.

The conflicts swirling about the Bakke case are illuminated in the vicissitudes of the solicitor general's brief, circulated among interested parties in the Carter administration in the weeks immediately preceding oral argument. In his initial brief, routinely circulated on September 1, 1977, McCree concluded that the special admissions program at the Davis medical college was unconstitutional because it reserved a specific number of slots in each class for disadvantaged minorities, and further, that Bakke's claim for admission to the medical college was well founded.[32] The brief aroused a storm of protest in the Carter administration among department heads and officials responsible for affirmative-action programs. At a cabinet meeting on September 12, Joseph A. Califano, secretary of Health, Education, and Welfare; Patricia Harris, secretary of Housing and Urban Development; and Andrew Young, ambassador to the United Nations, demanded that the brief be redrafted showing support for the university and strongly encouraging affirmative action. These groups were joined by Eleanor Holmes Norton, chairman of the Equal Employment Opportunity Council (EEOC). In addition, word of the contents of the brief leaked out to Capitol Hill. Parren Mitchell (Democrat, Maryland), chairman of the Black Caucus in the House of Representatives, called for a change in line with the views of the dissident administration members, a request also echoed by Joseph Rauh, chairman of the American Civil Liberties Union.[33]

McCree, a black, succumbed to these pressures and redrafted the brief to support affirmative-action programs without taking sides in the dispute between Bakke and the University of California. The brief filed with the Supreme Court by the solicitor general walked a tightrope between the university and Allan Bakke in its four main tenets. These were summarized by an observer as follows:

> (1) strongly supported affirmative action programs to help disadvantaged minorities and urged the Supreme Court to reverse the California Supreme Court ruling that race may not be considered in such programs; (2) believed that rigid racial quotas in favor of minorities that bar others from participating in programs solely because of race are unconstitutional; (3) believed that the Bakke case is not a good vehicle for determining the limits of affirmative action because the record of the case is sparse and the university did not contest it adequately; (4) felt compelled, nevertheless, to set out its position favoring vigorous affirmative action and opposing rigid quotas because issues are raised that vitally concern the interests of the government.[34]

A decision in the Bakke case was handed down on June 28, 1978, by a divided Court. Rulings are decided in a secret conference among the nine justices of the Court at which no records are kept except for the handwritten notes of the chief justice recording the outcome of particular votes. When he is in the majority, the chief justice assigns the writing of the opinion of the Court; and when he is on the losing side, assignment is made by the senior justice voting with the majority. If a justice agrees with the ruling of the majority opinion but thinks it ought to rest on a different basis, he or she may write a separate concurring opinion. If a justice agrees with neither the ruling nor the basis of reasoning, he or she writes a dissenting opinion.

Five members of the Court (Burger, Stewart, Rehnquist, Stevens, and Powell) affirmed the judgment of the Supreme Court of California that Bakke "is entitled to an order that he be admitted to the University." Four of the justices, excluding Powell, based this finding on Title VI of the Civil Rights Act of 1964, a narrower basis for decision than the constitutional issue of equal protection of the laws. Title VI says, "No person in the United States shall on the grounds of race, color, or national origin, be excluded from participation in, be denied the benefits of, or be subjected to discrimination under any program receiving federal financial assistance." Justice Stevens, writing for Burger, Rehnquist, and Stewart, found that Title VI prohibited the medical college from apportioning funds on the basis of racial quotas. Yet Stevens stated that government may take race into account when it acts not to demean or insult a racial group but to remedy disadvantages cast on minorities by past racial prejudice. Stevens's ruling adhered to the canons of judicial restraint which require that cases be decided on grounds other than the Constitution whenever possible.

Powell concurred in the decision of these justices but touched on the constitutional issue before the Court. He said that the use of racial quotas by the admissions committee at Davis denied Bakke the "equal protection of the laws." "It is far too late to argue that the guarantee of equal protection to *all* persons permits the recognition of special wards entitled to a degree of protection greater than that accorded others." Nevertheless, Powell stated that the affirmance of the ruling of the Supreme Court of California should not be construed to put an end to racially conscious admissions policies. Although schools cannot use quotas, race can be used as one factor in admissions decisions, especially when there has been a past history of discrimination by the relevant institution.

A dissenting opinion was entered by Justices Brennan, Marshall, and Blackmun. Speaking for the members of this group, Brennan stated that the affirmative admissions program at Davis is constitutional and that the judgment of the California State Supreme Court should be reversed. Brennan said, "[A] state government may adopt race-conscious programs if the purpose of such programs is to remove the disparate racial impact its actions might otherwise have and if there is reason to believe that the disparate impact is itself the product of past discrimination, whether its own, or that of society at large." In a separate dissenting opinion, Marshall, who argued the landmark Brown case before the Court more than two decades before, sharply reminded his colleagues and the nation of the peculiar history of blacks in this country. "The dream of America as the great melting pot has not been realized for the Negro; because of his skin color he never even made it into the pot."

The decision of the Court in the Bakke case provides qualified support for affirmative-action programs. The Court left intact the fundamental basis for affirmative action by ruling that race-conscious remedies may be used. But it disapproved—for educational institutions only—a remedy that was especially strong, reserving places for disadvantaged minorities.[35]

This case gives us some insight into the judicial process and into the constraints imposed on the judiciary by features of the constitutional system. Most important among these constraints is that the judiciary cannot resolve disputes by engendering new resources; it can only afford relative parity among groups in the distribution of existing resources. The interpretation of the "equal protection" clause in the Bakke case required scaling down the resources made available to the white majority, represented by Bakke, or scaling down the resources made available to minority groups. Neither of these forms of resolution seems fair, given that there is a great deal of justice to the claims of each group.

The Association of American Medical Colleges concedes that three-quarters of the 45,000 applicants turned away from medical schools each year are fully qualified to receive medical training.[36] These parsimonious gate-keeping policies seem very curious when placed alongside the considerable use of foreign medical graduates in the public hospitals, the high incidence of fatigue and coronary attack among overworked physicians, the scarce supply of medical staff in rural and urban ghettos, and the still very high salaries of physicians in comparison to other professions.[37] There would seem to be justice in the claims of both white and black medical applicants who are turned away in droves, yet the courts are prevented from dealing with this larger issue.

Medically underserved elements of the population are disproportionately injured by a trend toward closure or suburban relocation of large, inner city, public hospitals. This trend, which became apparent in the latter part of the 1970s, is expected to continue.[38] Since many of these hospitals are federally funded, as is the medical school at Davis, it has been possible in some instances to invoke successfully Title VI of the Civil Rights Act of 1964 against a projected closure or relocation.[39] However, district courts confronted with this issue have difficulty addressing the root problem, which lies in the distribution of medical resources. The courts lack authority, the key word, to deal with this aspect of the dispute.

Another "reverse discrimination" case which illustrates the limited authority of the court is *Weber* v. *Kaiser Aluminum and Chemical Corporation* (1979). Weber, a lab technician in Kaiser's Gramercy, Louisiana, plant, contended that his constitutional rights were violated by a voluntary agreement between the U.S. Steelworkers and the Kaiser management.

The agreement called for special training programs to correct the imbalance between whites and blacks in skilled positions. Openings in training programs would be provided to whites and blacks on an equal basis until the number of blacks in skilled positions was in proportion to the number of blacks in the labor force from which the plants were recruiting. The work force in the Gramercy plant was more than 39 percent black; yet blacks held only 2 percent of the 273 skilled jobs.[40] There were thirteen new openings in the training program. Weber had insufficient seniority to obtain one of the six places reserved for whites, but he had more seniority than two of the blacks selected for the program. Weber brought suit on the grounds of the "equal protection of the laws" clause of the Fourteenth Amendment and Title VII of the Civil Rights Act of 1964, which prohibits discriminatory employment practices. He was upheld in district court and in the Fifth Circuit Court of Appeals; the case came to the Supreme Court on appeal.

Justice Brennan, who wrote a dissenting opinion in the Bakke case, this time spoke for the majority. He did not touch the constitutional issue, deciding the case instead on the basis of his interpretation of Title VII. He said that the object of Title VII was to break down old patterns of racial segregation and hierarchy and that race-conscious employment practices which furthered this end without unduly interfering with the rights of white workers were not barred by the statute. Since the agreement between the Steelworkers and Kaiser was a temporary expedient, did not require the discharge of white workers nor indefinitely bar their advancement, the agreement passed the appropriate test. Brennan then ordered the judgment of the Fifth Circuit Court of Appeals reversed.[41] The decision was hailed by black political leadership and the EEOC for putting affirmative-action programs back on the right track.[42]

UMPIRE AND PARTICIPANT IN SOCIAL CONFLICT

The limitations on judicial authority lay behind the remarks of Chief Justice Warren Burger at the time of his appointment to the Supreme Court. In an interview which coincided with the Senate hearings on his nomination, Burger pointedly rejected the idea that it was the function of judicial review to introduce progressive social change through judicial opinion: "It was never contemplated in our system that judges would make dramatic changes by judicial decision. That is what the legislative function and the rule-making function is all about." He added that young people entering the legal profession "on the theory that they can change the world by litigation in courts," were bound to be disappointed. They were entering the profession for the wrong reasons because the law "is not the route by which basic changes in a country like ours should be made. That is a legislative and policy process, part of the political process. And there is a very limited role for the courts in that respect." He summed up his judicial philosophy by saying that it was the function of the Court to settle cases expeditiously, and thus to reinforce the public's faith in the judicial process, not to advance social causes and thereby add to social unrest. "Inherently the Supreme Court function is one in which nothing ought to happen very rapidly except the disposition of specific cases."[43]

A substantial body of opinion would agree that the Court has limited authority to allocate resources. Nevertheless, when an opportunity to exercise a redistributive function has presented itself, the Court has frequently tipped social policy in a direction favorable to privileged groups at the expense of the disadvantaged. The evidence for this position is drawn mainly, though not exclusively, from the record of Supreme Court actions in the late nineteenth and early twentieth centuries. A full examination of the record, it is argued, will show that the Court is not neutral among the parties to the social conflict, as the views of Burger suggest, but is allied with property and privilege.[44] Some of the cases frequently cited in support of this view follow:

1. *Dred Scott* v. *Sanford,* 19 How. 393 (1857). For the first time since the Marbury decision the Court struck down an act of Congress, the Missouri Compromise, declaring that Congress may not prohibit slavery from the territories. It stated that the slave was not a citizen of the United States and, therefore, could not be a citizen of a state. Since slavery was constitutionally protected, Congress lacked power to exclude it from the new territories.
2. *Pollock* v. *Farmer's Loan and Trust Co.,* 158 U.S. 601 (1895). The Court declared that Congress lacked authority to enact a progressive income tax. The burden of taxation would have shifted to more affluent groups under the proposed legislation.
3. *United States.* v. *E. C. Knight Co.,* 156 U.S. 1 (1895). The Court misconstrued the Sherman Antitrust Act (1887), whose provisions outlawing "conspiracies in restraint of trade" were aimed at monopolistic practices. Instead, the Court applied these provisions to the struggling labor movement and by doing so greatly slowed its rate of growth.
4. *Lochner* v. *New York,* 198 U.S. 45 (1905). The Court interpreted constitutional prohibitions against denial of "due process of law" (Fifth and Fourteenth Amendments) and laws impairing the "obligation of

contracts" (Article I, sec. 10) to strike down state legislation that regulated the hours and conditions of work. This decision drew from Holmes the pained comment, "The Fourteenth Amendment does not enact Mr. Herbert Spencer's Social Statics." Holmes was bringing to view the hidden Social Darwinist view behind the majority opinion.

5. *Hammer* v. *Dagenhart,* 247 U.S. 251 (1918); *Bailey* v. *Drexel Furniture Co.,* 259 U.S. 20 (1922). In these two cases the Supreme Court struck down congressional legislation that attempted to curtail the use of child labor through the exercise of its power to "regulate commerce" and to "lay taxes [for] . . . the general welfare." By inquiring into the object of regulation and taxation, the Court found that Congress had exceeded its authority under the Constitution.

6. *Schecter Poultry Corp.* v. *United States,* 295 U.S. 495 (1935). Basing its ruling on a restrictive interpretation of the power to regulate commerce and an improper delegation of power to the executive, the Supreme Court struck down New Deal legislation attempting to create "codes of fair competition" among employers, unions, and middlemen.

Although the Supreme Court has abandoned an obstructionist role in all these areas, the memory of a Court which has sided with monopolists, slaveholders, and the privileged has not been erased. On the whole, the Court is seen as the bastion of elite interests, the select composition of the justices and the intention of the framers of the Constitution lending additional support to this view.[45]

In contrast, an equally strong opinion sees the Court as the champion of the rights of minority groups and the guardian of civil liberties, pointing out that time and again the Court has come to the rescue of those whose rights have been trampled on by the dominant majority. Within this general outlook there are two views: One, often associated with the opinion of Justice Cardozo, holds that the freedoms of the Bill of Rights are provisional and need to be balanced against the powers conferred on the government elsewhere by the Constitution. It also holds that the Bill of Rights is only selectively, not entirely, incorporated into the "due process" clause of the Fourteenth Amendment. That is, the Court will intervene to protect "fundamental freedoms," such as speech, religion, press, and assembly, against encroachment by the states, but will not interfere with the impairment of liberties considered to be less vital to the political process.[46] The other view most often linked with the name of Justice Black, holds just the opposite, asserting that all the freedoms of the Bill of Rights are incorporated into the Fourteenth Amendment and that these rights are absolute.[47] Taking note of the unconditional language of the First Amendment, it states that government lacks authority to impair any of the freedoms of the Bill of Rights in any degree.

Over the course of the last quarter century, the latter view has come to prevail, thereby adding strength to the view that the Supreme Court is a progressive institution which zealously defends the rights of submerged groups. Some of the cases on which this view of the Court is based follow:

1. *The New York Times* v. *United States,* 403 U.S. 713 (1971). The Supreme Court held that the government could not enjoin further publication of the Pentagon Papers by *The New York Times.* The Court said that the prohibition of the First Amendment against prior censorship of the press outweighed the claim of the government that publication hurt the national interest. In upholding the right of the *Times* to publish the story of U.S. involvement in Vietnam, the Court was following a precedent set in *Near* v. *Minnesota,* 283 U.S. 697 (1931). In the case of *Burstyn* v. *Wilson,* 303 U.S. 495 (1952), the Court extended to the motion picture industry the protection of First Amendment freedoms.[48]

2. *Engle* v. *Vitale,* 370 U.S. 421 (1962). Justice Black wrote the majority opinion in a case that struck down a directive of the Board of Education in New Hyde Park, New York, to read a prayer aloud in class at the beginning of each school day. Black said that the prayer violated the unequivocal prohibition of the First Amendment against the "establishment of religion" by the government.

3. *Brown* v. *the Board of Education of Topeka,* 347 U.S. 483 (1954). As we have seen from the earlier discussion, this case upheld the rights of a racial minority against state and local majorities which condoned segregation in the public schools. In no other area has the Court had so much trouble obtaining compliance as that affected by this ruling.

4. *Baker* v. *Carr,* 369 U.S. 186 (1962); *Reynolds* v. *Sims,* 377 U.S. 533 (1964). In these cases the Supreme Court held that legislative districts must be drawn to reflect the principle of "one person, one vote." The Court indicated a willingness to scrutinize all districting for offices at the state and local levels to determine whether it was in conformity with Fourteenth Amendment safeguards for "equal protection of the laws."

5. The Court has incorporated procedural safeguards set out in the Bill of Rights into the meaning of the "due process" clause of the Fourteenth Amendment. The procedural rights so protected are these: *Mapp* v. *Ohio,* 367 U.S. 643 (1961), barred the use of illegally seized evidence in criminal cases by applying the Fourth Amendment guarantee against unreasonable search and seizures. Even if the evidence

seized proves the guilt of the accused, the accused goes free because the police committed a procedural error.

Gideon v. *Wainwright,* 372 U.S. 355 (1963). The Court ruled that the Fourteenth Amendment absorbs the Sixth Amendment right to have the "assistance of counsel" in the preparation for trial of all felony cases. The ruling effectively required the states to provide free legal counsel in all criminal cases involving indigents.

Escobeda v. *United States,* 378 U.S. 478 (1964), established that a suspect is entitled to have the assistance of counsel as soon as police investigation is focused on him or her, or once the process shifts from "investigatory to accusatory."

Miranda v. *Arizona,* 384 U.S. 436 (1966), required that police, before questioning a suspect, must inform him or her of all constitutional rights, including the right to counsel, appointed free, if necessary, and the right to remain silent. Although the suspect may knowingly waive these rights, the police cannot question anyone who at any point asks for a lawyer or indicates "in any manner" that he or she does not wish to be questioned. If the police commit an error in these procedures, the accused goes free, regardless of the evidence of guilt.

The two conflicting views of the Court, as protector of minority rights and as a bastion of privileged groups, will appear less curious if we remember that historically liberalism is committed to the expanding rights both of conscience and of property. The Court has been zealous to protect religious and racial minorities from oppression because it requires little alteration in social and economic priorities. Similarly, it is relatively inexpensive, so to speak, to protect the rights of free speech and press in relation to the prevailing distribution of power. Tacitly, the Court has accepted a situation in the last thirty years in which human freedom as a function of economic arrangements is protected, if at all, by the legislative and executive institutions.[49] If we put the structural biases of Madisonian politics alongside the reluctance of the Court to intervene in the allocation of resources, we can see why poor minorities, as distinguished from religious minorities, have a difficult time in America.

The rationale for letting the executive and legislature decide on matters of economic policy is sometimes expressed in terms of a constitutional division of labor. It is said that the executive and legislature have greater expertise in managing conflicts over the distribution of resources. By the same token, the judiciary is said to be better qualified to safeguard cultural freedoms through guardianship of the Constitution and the Bill of Rights.[50] The difficulty with this view, as the Bakke case shows, is that the issue of resource allocation is often inseparable from that of human freedoms. One of the things we can learn from the Bakke case and from the history of the Supreme Court is that justice in America is blind in one eye. It can protect human freedoms only insofar as they are distinct from the economic sphere. Thus it is true, as Chief Justice Burger tells us, that the Court is not an appropriate instrument for social change. But it is not the case that such a stance is nonpolitical. Rather it reflects the historical commitment of a liberal democracy to cultural freedom and experimentation and to the expanding rights of propertied interests.

NOTES

1. Philippa Strum, "Watergate and the Federal Judiciary: Authoritarianism or Judicial Discretion?" Prepared for Delivery at the 1974 Annual Meeting of the American Political Science Association, Chicago, Ill., August 29-September 2, 1974.
2. Abe Fortas, "The Case against Capital Punishment," *The New York Times Magazine,* January 23, 1977, p. 26.
3. Robert L. Cord, *Protest, Dissent, and the Supreme Court* (Cambridge, Mass.: Winthrop Publishers, 1971); Harrell R. Rodgers, Jr., and Charles S. Bullock, *Law and Social Change* (New York: McGraw-Hill, 1972).
4. See the discussion by Richard Flathman, "The Theory of Rights and Practice of Abortion," Prepared for Delivery at the 1977 Meeting of the American Political Science Association, Washington, D.C., September 1–4, 1977.
5. "Court Clears Hill Curb on U.S. Abortion Aid," *Washington Post,* June 30, 1977, A1, 20.
6. See the discussion by Mary Cornelia Porter, "State Supreme Courts and the Legacy of the Warren Court: Some Old Inquiries for a new Situation," Prepared for Delivery at the 1977 Annual Meeting of the American Political Science Association, Washington, D.C., September 1–4, 1977, pp. 41–46.
7. *Ibid.,* p. 42.
8. Donald L. Horowitz, *The Courts and Social Policy* (Washington, D.C.: The Brookings Institution, 1977), pp. 4–5.
9. John R. Schmidhauser, *The Supreme Court* (New York: Holt, Rinehart & Winston, 1960).
10. Henry Abraham, *The Judicial Process* (New York: Oxford University Press, 1962), p. 58; Henry Abraham, *The Judiciary,* 3rd ed. (Boston: Allyn & Bacon, 1973), p. 125.
11. See the discussions of judicial review by Robert H. Jackson, *The Supreme Court in the American System of Government* (New York: Harper & Row, 1955); Paul A. Freund, *On Understanding the Supreme Court* (Boston: Little, Brown, 1949); Archibald Cox, *The Role of the Supreme Court in American Government* (New York: Oxford University Press, 1976).

12. Robert A. Dahl, "Decision Making in a Democracy," *Journal of Public Law*, vol. 6 (1958), pp. 279–95.

13. *Ibid.*

14. Max Lerner, ed., *The Mind and Faith of Justice Holmes* (New York: The Modern Library, 1943), pp. 51–52.

15. Horowitz, *Courts and Public Policy*, p. 38.

16. Theodore L. Becker and Malcolm M. Feeley, 2nd. ed., *The Impact of Supreme Court Decisions* (New York: Oxford University Press, 1973).

17. Glendon Schubert, *Judicial Policy-Making* (Glenview, Ill.: Scott, Foresman, 1965), p. 1.

18. *Federalist* No. 78.

19. Walter F. Murphy, "The Framework of Judicial Power," in *Elements of Judicial Strategy* (Chicago: University of Chicago Press, 1964), pp. 12–29.

20. Schubert, *Judicial Policy-Making*, p. 57; Abraham, *The Judiciary*, p. 23.

21. Fred Vinson, "Work of the Federal Courts," *Supreme Court Reporter*, 1949, cited in Emmette S. Redford *et al.*, Politics and Government in the United States (New York: Harcourt Brace Jovanovich, 1968).

22. Schubert, *Judicial Policy-Making*, pp. 153–57.

23. Richard J. Margolis, "Why 117 Medical Schools Can't Be Right," in *Change*, vol 9, no. 10 (October 1977), p. 28.

24. Robert Lindsey, "White Caucasian—And Rejected," *The New York Times Magazine*, April 3, 1977, pp. 42–47, 95.

25. *Ibid.*

26. James W. Singer, "Reverse Discrimination—Will Bakke Decide the Issue?" in *National Journal*, September 17, 1977, pp. 1,436–41.

27. Quoted in Lindsey, "White Caucasian."

28. *Ibid.*

29. *Ibid.*

30. *Ibid.*

31. *Ibid.*

32. Singer, "Reverse Discrimination."

33. *Ibid.*

34. *Ibid.*

35. Morton Mintz, "Bakke Decision May Rely on Civil Rights Law," *Washington Post*, October 18, 1977, A1, 4.

36. Margolis, "Why 117 Medical Schools Can't Be Right," pp. 26–33, 64.

37. *The New York Times*, July 4, 1971, pp. 1, 24.

38. Dorothy McNeil and Robert Williams, "Wide Range of Causes Found for Hospital Closures," *Hospitals*, December 1, 1978, pp. 76–81; Emily Friedman, "Hospital Closings," *Hospitals*, December 1, 1978, pp. 69–75; "The Closing of Philadelphia General Hospital," *Urban Health*, November 1978, pp. 40–47.

39. *Berenice Terry et al.* v. *Methodist Hospital of Gary, Indiana*, June 10, 1977, U.S. District Court for the Northern Division of Indiana (Hammond Division).

40. *The New York Times*, July 28, 1979, A1, B12.

41. *Ibid.*

42. *Ibid.*

43. *The New York Times,* July 4, 1971, pp. 1, 24.

44. Dahl, "Decision Making in a Democracy"; Thomas Dye and L. Harmon Zeigler, *The Irony of Democracy* (Belmont, Cal.: Wadsworth, 1970).

45. Charles A. Beard, *The Supreme Court and the Constitution* (New York: Macmillan, 1912).

46. *Palko* v. *Connecticut,* 302 U.S. 319 (1937).

47. *Adamson* v. *California,* 332 U.S. 46 (1947).

48. See Richard S. Randall, *Censorship of the Movies* (Madison: University of Wisconsin Press, 1970).

49. Freund, *Understanding the Supreme Court,* pp. 15–20.

50. Abraham, *The Judiciary,* pp. 47–53.

CHAPTER 12

City Politics

The Constitution of 1787 was written in an era when most of the population lived in rural areas, villages, and townships. Washington, D.C., the present national capital, existed only in the planner's imagination. Philadelphia, the national capital at the turn of the eighteenth century, boasted a population of no more than 40,000, about the size of a large town. Boston, at the signing of the Declaration of Independence, had a population of 20,000.[1] Many of the features of modern urban life, shaped by the I-beam, the elevator, the skyscraper, the arrival of immigrant groups from foreign shores, and the automobile, were unknown to the men who drafted the Constitution. What, then, can be the relationship between the properties of the constitutional system and the characteristics of modern urban life?

THE POLITICS OF DESIGN

An important idea embedded in the constitutional system that has lastingly influenced the nature of American cities is that land is a commodity. As a commodity, land has a value and use assigned by possessive individuals confronting each other in a market. The right of individuals to acquire and dispose of property unmolested by the government is placed by Madison and the framers at the heart of the constitutional system. Madison asserts that the basic function of government is to protect the property spheres of possessive individuals. "[The] first object of government," he writes, is to afford protection to the "diversity in the faculties of men from which the rights of property originate."[2]

The notion that land is solely a commodity has decisive aesthetic and political consequences for American cities. Politically, it transfers power in urban settings to the power broker. Owners, not voters, are

288

the most important voices in deciding how urban space is to be allocated. Aesthetically, this idea inspires a universal preference for the "gridiron plan," which converts land into standard units, rectangular building lots, and thereby facilitates buying and selling.[3]

The speculative ground plan, or gridiron plan, used almost everywhere in the design of American cities, originated in the market economy and liberal democratic institutions introduced by the commercial Protestant middle class in seventeenth-century England. The new merchant class wished to engage in land development and sale for speculative purposes, and the gridiron plan emphasized the values important to entrepreneurial individuals—the lawyer, realtor, banker, builder, developer, speculator, and surveyor—all negotiating with each other in the market. Additionally, the plan had the merit in their eyes of relegating to a position of secondary importance other values which a society might assign to the use of urban space: play, recreation, ceremony, parade, conservation.

The design of urban Philadelphia, a site of immense historical significance for the new republic, illustrates the application of the gridiron plan. Its adoption in Philadelphia led to its imitation on Manhattan Island in 1811 and its acceptance by the new towns of the West and Midwest, St. Louis, Chicago, Detroit, Los Angeles, and Houston. Thus, in a sense, to know one American city is to know them all. Speaking of the design of urban Philadelphia in the eighteenth century, a historian writes:

> The rectangular survey of open farm land, the laying out of city streets and blocks into even rectangles, the subdivision of blocks into narrow house lots, this was the simplest, cheapest, and clearest way of dividing land for rapid development. It was an ideal method, since it treated all land similarly, for a real estate market composed of hundreds of speculators and home builders, and thousands of petty landlords and small home buyers.[4]

The same historian notes that the grid concept has an enduring influence on the setting of urban life in Philadelphia lasting into the present day. Basically, the grid emphasizes the private and commercial values at the great expense of the public functions of the city:

> The genius of Philadelphia in the 1920s lay not in its public institutions but in the containment of people in thousands of private settings. The single generation family, the private company's work group, and the income segregated neighborhood were the metropolis' basic units.[5]

In contrast to the commercial values embedded in the gridiron plan, consider L'Enfant's axial plan for the city of Washington. This plan, emphasizing the public and monumental values of French baroque civilization, was submitted to Congress, then holding sessions in Philadelphia, in 1791. Its governing idea, still visible in the location of public buildings and city streets to this day, is the axial location of the major federal buildings. *Axial* refers to lines that converge and pass through a body or system around which the parts are symmetrically arranged. The White House and the Capitol, the centerpieces of the new federal republic, are connected by Pennsylvania Avenue, which runs through the center of each building (in an imaginary line). The avenues emerge on the other side of the White House and the Capitol, resuming their majestic processional movement. The Capitol is set off by parallel boulevards to the Mall in the direction of the Lincoln Memorial and Washington Monument. The White House, looked at from above, is sliced into pie shapes by the intersection of Pennsylvania, Connecticut, Vermont, and New York avenues. The plan tends to emphasize the dignity and power of institutions in the public domain. They are placed at the hub of affairs, with spokes extending into the life of the city.[6]

I shall define a city as a settlement containing differentiated spaces for residence, business, assembly, and movement.[7] L'Enfant's plan does not provide sufficient recognition to the private functions of city life, business and residence. Whereas his plan is admirably suited to visual conversation among the principal buildings in the public sphere, he forgot that we sometimes wish to have conversations in private settings. On the other hand, the gridiron plan succeeds in emphasizing the private and commercial values of city life, but at the expense of public functions, such as assembly, spectacle, recreation, and ceremony, which have much to do with making the city an attractive human community.

A comprehensive, balanced plan for urban design would include values from both the axial and gridiron plans combined in a very different pattern. The reduction of urban space to undifferentiated, standardized units produces monotony and lack of focus.[8] Gertrude Stein summed it up well when speaking of Los Angeles, but she could have been remarking on almost any other American city: "There is no there there."

ROLE OF THE POWER BROKER

We have often noted the tendency of the constitutional system to create independent, self-sustaining centers of power, requiring the services of intermediaries or power brokers in order to get anything done. This tendency applies with particular force to the characteristics of urban politics, where the role of the power broker is shaped by the features of both the constitutional system and gridiron plan. Affecting the functions of the power broker are the subordinate legal and political status of the city, the influence of the private sector, and patterns of ethnic group conflict.

SUBORDINATE POLITICAL STATUS

The services of the power broker are required to make adjustments between the city and the state and federal units of government. The superior constitutional and political status of the state and federal units enables them to originate programs which vitally affect the welfare of the city. The power broker seeks to adjust the concerns of elites at the level of municipal politics to the higher levels of government.

City politicians tend to prefer programs, such as urban renewal and block grants, that link them to influential groups and allow them maximum autonomy in the disposition of funds. They are less comfortable with programs that portend state and federal influence in city affairs and which may intensify cleavages among religious, racial, and ethnic groups.[9] Examples of the latter are categorical grants-in-aid for public housing, community action, and model cities. The power broker in municipal politics seeks to negotiate conflicting priorities with elites in the federal system who are activated by different political constituencies. He or she intercedes in a bargaining relationship with managers of federal programs to advance the priorities of the city politicians.

To a greater extent than supposed, the states are heavily involved in the politics of city life. According to judicial doctrine, the city is a mere "creature" of the state, and the legal power exercised by states affects the workings of city politics. Thus the power broker must intervene in the city's behalf at the state capitol no less than in Washington. The ways in which the state government influences city politics are outlined in the following analysis.

First, "the state may determine, limit or manipulate the structure of local government. The state constitution or acts of the legislature may grant the cities 'home rule' (the right to organize their own charter commissions and adopt their own charters, electoral forms, and administrative organization), or they may prescribe various options in government structure for different categories of cities, or they may spell out governmental structure in detail."[10]

Second, "state constitutions and laws set conditions for municipal incorporation, consolidation, and annexation."[11] These laws impose a major constraint on a city's power to deal by political and legal means with the movement of population and business. One of the more important and influential factors in city politics is suburbia. Although suburbs do not act in city politics at all, save by withholding resources, they can check city efforts to consolidate, annex, or incorporate through influence on the state legislature.

Third, "states may and do restrict a city's fiscal options by limiting both the types of taxes which the cities may impose and the amounts of tax revenue which they may raise."[12] They may forbid cities to tax revenue sources tapped by the state itself (sales, income, or commuter taxes); they may place limits on the maximum rate of taxation, on the amount of tax imposed per capita, or on the actual dollar amounts to be levied. Also, they may limit the city's ability to borrow money.

Fourth, "states limit local administrative organization in many ways. They may reorganize local agencies (in all cities, certain cities, or individual cities) by statute, may require that local administrative reorganizations be submitted to them for approval, and may even retain the power to appoint local personnel."[13]

The involvement of state governments in the ordinary operations of city politics requires constant negotiation and adjustments between the two centers of power. Power brokers are an intermediary, deriving their own power and influence by virtue of their indispensable role in maintaining communications and getting things done.

DISTRIBUTION OF POWER IN THE URBAN SYSTEM

In the urban political arena, as in the political system generally, the influence conferred by the authority of office does not compare well with that possessed by actors in the private sector. The influence of the latter over such matters as sanitation, urban renewal, law enforcement, fiscal management, and patterns of growth is at least equal to those who occupy political office, and frequently is more. Unions, bankers, contractors, lawyers, and insurance companies often have as much to say about urban policy as the mayor and the city council, even though none of the former holds elective office.[14] This is not to say that influence conferred by the authority of office is negligible or unimportant. The actors in whom the lines of formal authority converge, the mayor and the city council in most urban governments, do have an important role in sanctioning, or legitimating, policy, which private influentials have played a major role in shaping.[15] Yet to a considerable extent the real government of the city does not show up on the organization chart.

Mayors and city councils are dependent not only on units placed higher above them in the federal system but also on influential people in the private sector to mobilize resources and produce results. The role of the power broker is created by the parcelling out of power in the federal system and by the weakness of municipal political institutions. This role is illustrated in the case of Robert Moses, chairman of the New York City Triborough Bridge and Tunnel Authority, whose ouster was unsuccessfully sought by both President Franklin D. Roosevelt and Mayor Fiorello La Guardia (see Chapter 7). Moses was able to withstand the enormous pressures mobilized against him because he was supported by a private coalition of businessmen, bankers, lawyers, contractors, builders, department store owners, bond underwriters, restaurant managers, developers, and so on, who wished to sustain the kind of progress Moses brought to the city. Not only Roosevelt and LaGuardia but also Mayors Lindsay, Wagner, and O'Dwyer were unsuccessful in removing Moses or diminishing his power; his private power base proved to be more compelling than the legal authority of political figures placed higher above him by formal governmental schemes.[16]

POLITICAL CLEAVAGES

Cleavages among sociocategoric groups (that is, racial, ethnic, and religious groups) tend to be more visible and intense in the urban political arena than at other governmental levels. These groups tend to be more concentrated in the metropolis than in small cities and towns, imparting an edge to big city politics not found in communities of smaller scale.[17] For example, in 1970, 57.8 percent of the black population lived in central cities of metropolitan areas compared to only 27.5 percent of the white population. More than 80 percent of American Catholic ethnic groups (with the exception of the French) and 95 percent of American Jews live in metropolitan areas.[18]

In many cities ethnic groups have captured one of the political parties, using it among other things for the advancement of their own interests. Italians have been a central force in the Republican party in New Haven, Connecticut and the Democratic party in Philadelphia; in recent years they have made an effort to control the Conservative party in New York City. Eastern European ethnics controlled the Democratic party in Cleveland and Gary before they had to share it with the blacks. The Irish have been the chief proprietors of Democratic party organizations in Boston and Chicago.[19]

Political cleavages in the urban arena have created a role for the sociocategoric power broker, an ethnic group entrepreneur. Such entrepreneurs find their opportunity in the needs of a particular ethnic group, become its authorized spokesman, and then proceed to exploit needs elsewhere in the urban political system in order to serve their clientele. For years the Democratic party candidates for the mayoral office of

Chicago, New York, and Boston have been chosen through an informal process of negotiation among the leaders of ethnic groups. Balancing political tickets among ethnic groups, formerly a concern of national politics, has now been relegated largely to the urban political arena. The power base of ethnic group brokers, however, has been weakened by the growing role of the federal government in administering welfare and relief services.[20]

The patterns of political dialogue encouraged by the constitutional system, negotiations between private influentials dealing in the coin of mutual interest, conform to the patterns encouraged by the gridiron plan, negotiations between buyer and seller concerning the disposition of city lots. The tendency for city politics to be conducted as a private matter among influential figures is further accentuated by the subordinate constitutional status of the city in the federal system, political cleavages at the urban level, and the weakness of municipal government.

THE POWER BROKER AND CONURBATION

An example of the role of the power broker in city politics can be seen in Robert Moses, a key figure in shaping New York City's response to the phenomenon of *conurbation*. Another word for urban sprawl, it is the consequence of a movement of people and jobs which has occurred in every major city in the northeast. The movement is initiated by the inflow of low-income (often black) groups into the central city and continued by the flow of white and second generation immigrant groups to the dormitory neighborhoods and to the suburbs. The result in every case is a sprawling mass with a great blighted core.

Several forces cooperate to produce conurbation. One is the in-migration of black low-income groups displaced by the mechanization of farm labor and attracted by the prospect of jobs in the industrial centers of the northeast. One analyst notes, "in 1910, 91 percent of the nation's black population lived in the south, predominantly in the rural south. By 1940, one-half of all blacks lived in urban areas; this figure reached 80 percent by 1965. Some 4 million blacks moved from the rural south to the central cities of the north between 1940 and 1970, concentrating in such cities as New York, Chicago, Detroit, Philadelphia, Washington, Cleveland, Baltimore, and St. Louis."[21]

A matching out-migration of middle- and upper-income groups (mostly white) has occurred from the central cities to the suburbs, where population has surged both absolutely and relatively. In the view of an observer, this was partly caused by "the magnetic pull of the American ideal, a low density environment characterized by a de-centralization of life and entertainment, the privacy of the single-family detached unit, the mobility of privately owned autos."[22] Not to be minimized is white flight from low-income black neighborhoods. A useful source documents the extent of out-migration: "At the end of World War II, the suburban proportion of SMSA population [standard metropolitan statistical area] was about 40%. By 1960, suburbs and central cities each accounted for 50% of SMSA population. In the decade from 1960 to 1970, the suburbs added 16 million while the central cities were adding only 3.1 million. That latest surge pushed the suburban proportion of the SMSA population up to 57%."[23]

To sum up, while the suburbs have grown, the central cities have actually lost population; the central cities have a high proportion of low-income black population, whereas the suburbs are predominantly white and middle or upper income. This result is statistically expressed in the following analysis: "The central cities in eight of the ten largest SMSAs (Chicago, Philadelphia, Detroit, San Francisco-Oakland, Washington, Boston, Pittsburgh, St. Louis) declined in population in the 1960–70 decade. . . . By 1970, 31 percent of the nation's population was located in central cities, whereas the suburban proportion had risen to 38 percent. The remaining 31 percent of the population lived outside metropolitan areas in rural settings."[24] New York City's population declined about 10,000 in the decade between 1960 and 1970. The 1970s saw further declines in central city population as the trend toward conurbation continues unabated.

Conurbation has had a differential impact on the population of metropolitan areas, segmenting it into a variety of groups with disparate ages, income, education, and type of labor force. Much has been made, and properly so, of the effects of conurbation on the central city resident, but there is reason to believe that it has many negative effects on the suburban population as well.

Those who remain in the central city, to put matters simply, are those with little choice or those with flexibility who choose an urban milieu. The former live in or near the oldest and densest neighborhoods; they are the poor, the ethnic minorities, and the old, all unable to afford the flight to the suburbs. Young professionals take the better housing in new condominium and apartment projects such as the Watergate apartments in Washington, D.C. Frequently, they are business executives, retailers, salesmen, lawyers, accountants, clerks, or professionals in service industries.[25]

The central city has suffered the multiple and accumulated impact of loss of jobs, population, and tax base, combined with the deterioration of capital infrastructure (bridges, roads, sewers, tunnels, sidewalks), reduction of municipal services and amenities (sanitation, libraries, parks, public concerts), and rising municipal expenses. Logically, the expense of municipal services should decline with the decline in population. However, "once a city's road, sewer, and water networks have been constructed to serve a given population, the cost of maintaining these networks does not decline significantly when population shrinks. On the contrary, as capital infrastructure ages, it becomes more costly to keep in repair. Cities that are losing population actually spend more, per capita, in capital investment than cities that are gaining in population, due largely to the necessity (and difficulty) of replacing their antiquated capital stock."[26] The ultimate expression of capital stock deterioration may be the collapse of the elevated portions of New York City's West Side Highway and its sealing off from further use. Similarly, "when households abandon the central city, the need for police and fire protection does not diminish in proportion to population. Instead, abandoned homes become the focus for vandalism and crime, pose fire hazards, and ultimately must be razed at city expense."

A further point is that job losses in the private sector impose pressure on city officials to expand employment in the public sector. This pressure is applied at an inopportune time. The net out-migration of the more affluent portion of the population reduces the tax base of the city government. City officials are placed in a double bind. They can neither reduce the level of employment in the public sector commensurate with population loss, nor can they expand the number of jobs needed to offset decline from the private sector.[27]

Compounding the fiscal dilemma is the circumstance that low-income groups moving into the city require an expansion of city welfare and relief services at the same time that more prosperous groups, with the capacity to offset fiscal burdens, are moving to the suburbs. The property tax base is highly inflexible; state and federal institutions of government have largely preempted the more progressive and elastic forms of taxation. The typical big-city mayor is faced with a variety of approaches in the attempt to bring expenditures and revenues into balance. A partial listing of painful measures includes the following: "He may increase taxes, impose new taxes, borrow money (at high interest rates and contingent upon state approval), forward budget items from one year to the next, sneak operating expenses into the capital budget, refuse to fill jobs that become vacant, cut municipal services (close a hospital here and a library branch there, pick up the garbage less often); he may postpone ordinary maintenance on the city's bridges, roads, tunnels, sewers, and commuter railroads."[28] He may also sue for state and federal aid to help meet city needs, and finally, he may

adopt "planned shrinkage" in dealing with areas of the city overcome
by the accumulated impact of decline.

Although the adverse impact of conurbation on central city populations is stark and dramatic, suburban groups have not escaped negative
effects. Suburbanites, judging from the real estate ads, are lured by the
fantasy of life on an estate in the countryside of England or Scotland,
a coastline romance with the billowing main, or a home in the deep
forest. Names such as Balmoral, Gleneagle, Ocean View Estates, Bay-
shore, Bayberry Woods, Ridge Lea Hills, Cedarbrook, Rollingwood, and
Springfield promise such a life; and the amenities of twentieth-century
home technology, electronic carports, central heating and air-condition-
ing, microwave ovens, and so forth, are thrown in with little regard for
the symmetry of escapist romance. As the population has spread out in
a largely unplanned way across the countryside, the distinction between
city and country and one metropolitan area and another becomes
blurred. Suburbanites moved to live in the country but the country
continues to recede. Contiguous metropolitan areas swallow up the
proud identity of exclusive suburban communities, transforming Balmoral, Gleneagle, and the like into Chickpitts (Chicago to Pittsburgh),
Sansan (San Francisco to San Diego), Bowash (Boston to Washington),
Newmo (New Orleans to Mobile), and Laudiam (Fort Lauderdale to
Miami). "Slurbs" and "strip cities" may replace suburbs as the dominant residential form of American life.[29]

The quality of design in suburban communities is not high. The
National Association of Home Builders, which represents a cluster of
business interests engaged in suburban development, states that less
than 34 percent of its members require the services of an architect.[30] Site
planning as well as home construction tends to be performed by businessmen, contractors, developers, lawyers, and bankers, who are not
visually trained and who take few precautions to preserve aesthetic
values. Suburban tract developments range from those constructed for
the factory operative and clerk (Levittown) to those designed for the
junior executive (Park Forest, Reston) and up.

Older suburbs and dormitory neighborhoods (Bronx, Brooklyn, and
Queens; Gary, Indiana; Newark, New Jersey) exist in a twilight zone
between the central city and the suburbs, belonging to neither camp.
The effect of conurbation on these populations is severe. As the population moves further out it leaves behind a debris of expressways, liquor
stores, car lots, cleaners, and hamburger stands; these facilities are
chiefly intended for those who live further out, yet their effect is to
choke traffic, destroy greenery, and depress land values. Federal programs may be planned to help central city areas—model cities, urban
renewal, grants-in-aid—and suburban communities—subsidized mort-

gage loans by the Federal Housing Authority and Veterans' Administration —but there is no identifiable program to offset deterioration in the older suburbs.

Related to conurbation is the recent migration from the cities and suburbs of the North and Midwest to the cities and suburbs of the South and Southwest. Among the elements contributing to this trend are climate, reliable sources of energy, access to cheap labor, attractive tax incentives and fringe benefits, and a history of spending on public works by Sunbelt legislators.[31]

ROBERT MOSES, POWER BROKER

The conventional model of urban politics departs significantly from the working arrangements described in this section. According to the conventional wisdom, the urban electorate is the single most important source of influence on the policies of the mayor, the city council, and the administration. Diverse means—elections, ethnic pressure groups, and neighborhood influences—are used by the electorate to transmit signals to city hall respecting their wishes. It is the business of the political leadership, mainly the city council and the mayor, to interpret these signals and to transform them into visible policy issues. After a course of policy has been agreed on by the political organs of urban government, the administration seeks to implement the result. At periodic intervals, the electorate passes judgment on the outcome of this process by retaining or ousting the existing political leadership. Thus, the top leadership of urban government is kept continuously abreast of the wishes of the people.[32]

In actual practice the arrangements of the constitutional system and the weakness of municipal authority, coupled with political cleavages in the urban arena, tip the power of initiative in urban affairs to the power broker rather than to the elements identified by the traditional model: the people, elected officials, and administrative hierarchy. Power brokers may occupy office as a mayor, member of the city council, or bureaucrat; but the influence they exercise is not a function of the office they hold. Rather it stems from placing themselves at the center of complex negotiations between the public and private sphere, among federal, state and local political actors, concerning the substance of urban policy. In these negotiations power brokers are more attentive to signals emanating from those with whom they share power than to signals from the public or elected officials higher than them in the political hierarchy. They are prone, as have been power brokers from the beginning of the republic, to deal relationally with those with whom power is shared and manipulatively with all others.

Robert Moses is a leading, probably the foremost, example of the influence the power broker can deploy in the urban arena. Although he never held an elective office, he exerted more influence on the physical and social fabric of New York City than any of its mayors in this century.[33] No enumeration of the beaches, parks, apartment houses, housing projects, bridges, stadia, swimming pools, and golf courses Moses built in the city does more than suggest the immensity of his influence. According to one authoritative estimate, "Robert Moses built public works costing, in 1968 dollars, twenty-seven billion dollars."[34] No other public official in the history of the United States has built public works costing an equivalent amount. Above all, Moses accelerated the pace of conurbation in New York City by building a vast network of thruways and expressways leading to the Bronx, Westchester and Nassau Counties, and Staten Island. These expressways, combined with federal policies favoring home ownership, are estimated to have expanded the land area of New York City and other major cities by as much as 17 percent.[35] Moses also built each of the seven major bridges which link the island boroughs of the metropolis to each other and to the giant expressway system.

The means Moses used to accumulate and exercise power involved a combination of elements. No one of these elements was decisive but in concert they gave him preponderant influence. Critical to his success was mayoral appointment to the head of independent public authorities created by the state to construct and maintain special projects—a bridge, a tunnel, an expressway, a beach, and the like. Moses used his position as head of special purpose authorities further to promote and extend his influence over city projects. Most important, he perceived and exploited the possibilities of using the revenues collected from a successful project to capitalize further projects. Ordinarily, revenues accumulated from tolls and fees are used to retire the bonds sold for financing construction; the facility is returned to city control and the authority dissolved after its purpose is exhausted. However, Moses used projected revenues from facilities such as the Triborough Bridge as a basis for floating bonds to construct additional projects.[36] He made himself virtually irremovable as the head of these authorities by proposing public works projects and, with the cooperation of the banks, supplying the funds through which they would be financed. Mayors, governors, and even heads of state basked in the visibility provided by the dedication of a Moses project, further cementing his control over the direction of policy.

Another way Moses could direct policy was to acquire multiple and overlapping offices. At one time or another, and often in combination, he was chairman of the Triborough Bridge and Tunnel Authority

(TBTA), the city parks commissioner, the city construction coordinator, a member of the City Planning Commission, and a director of the Long Island State Parks Commission. As a member of the City Planning Commission, he was able to participate in decisions on the merits of a policy he proposed in a different capacity.[37] When mayors threatened him with the loss of his accumulated influence by proposing to reduce the offices he held, he would threaten to resign from them all. Such a risk was too great for a mayor to take. The publicity and jobs provided by Moses's projects were too beneficial to lose by contesting a single office. Moses blackmailed a succession of city mayors to retain him in five to seven posts by threatening to resign at strategic moments.[38]

The revenues from independent authorities and multiple and overlapping offices helped place Moses at the center of negotiations with multiple actors—federal, state, and local and public and private—which constituted a third means of acquiring influence over the course of urban policy. As his biographer suggests, Moses radically changed the role of power broker in city politics from "the tribal, ethnic leader who passes out turkey at Thanksgiving" and provides an occasional job at city hall to one who systematically provided benefits for influential economic interests who supported his urban projects.[39] Behind public works projects he improvised a political and economic coalition consisting of labor unions who wanted work, bond underwriters who needed commissions, insurance firms which benefited from new policies, governors and mayors who liked to shine in the reflected glow of public construction, retail stores who desired new locations, lawyers who sought fees, developers who were in search of schemes for enhancing land values, consultants who needed contracts, architects who needed commissions, and on and on.[40] This coalition proved virtually irresistible, as Franklin D. Roosevelt found out when he tried to remove Moses as chairman of the TBTA.

A final element of Moses's power was his cultivation of relationships with the big presses of New York City and his willingness to let figures in the public domain take the credit for his projects. He was content to let mayors and governors have the reputation of power provided they entrusted its actual use to him. He took pains to invite the press to ribbon-cutting ceremonies, giving the politicians what they wanted. In turn, they were glad to confer on him the substance of power, giving him what he wanted.[41]

During Moses's reign over public works in New York—a thirty-four-year reign occurring at a crucial time in the city's history when conurbation was in progress and vast open spaces were filling up and being shaped on a significant scale—it was not the shouts of the people but the muted voices of bank officials, labor organizers, insurance company executives, big construction combines, and of course, the "retainer regiment" (of bond underwriters, lawyers, consultants) that determined what public works would be built. Moses centralized in his person and in his projects all those forces which have little to do with city politics, according to traditional models of urban political behavior, and by doing so made the system work for those for whom it was intended to work. One might reply that Moses was simply giving shape to the expressed desire of many people "voting by van" to leave the city. But it was Moses and a limited number of influential people who made the key decision concerning the pace, costs, and shape of suburbanization and who principally benefited from the plans adopted. If a public review of these decisions had been aired through public hearings and elections, the course of development might have been different in important ways.

For example, Moses refused to provide space for mass transit facilities on any of the major expressways leading out of the city. He would not allow a bus lane on the side of the road or along the center strip; he lowered the bridge clearances on the Long Island expressways from the standard twelve feet to nine feet to keep buses from the system.[42] He refused to provide space for rail transit along the center strip of the Long Island projects despite vigorous objections. His opposition to mass transit services along the expressways seems particularly short-sighted in view of the swelling volume of automobile traffic and deterioration of the old commuter railroads which serviced the city. Ultimately, this hostility to mass transit defeated the purpose the expressway system was intended to serve, the movement of large numbers of people into and out of the city during peak periods with minimum congestion and pollution. Robert Caro, whose biography of Moses is as monumental as the man himself, writes, "The Long Island Expressway's designed daily capacity was 80,000 vehicles; by 1963, it was carrying 132,000 vehicles per day, a load that jammed the expressway even at 'off' hours. During rush hours, the expressway was solid with cars, congealed with them, chaos solidified. One man's dream became a nightmare—an enduring, year-after-year nightmare—for tens of thousands of other men. Drivers trapped on the Long Island Expressway nicknamed it 'the world's longest parking lot.' "[43]

Another area of decision making by Moses that required public scrutiny—but never received it—was the removal of over one-half million people from their homes in the name of urban renewal and slum clearance. A statistical report concludes that a remarkably high percentage of these people were low income groups, black, and Puerto Rican. "Although the 1950 census found that only 12 percent of the city's population was nonwhite, above 37 percent of the evictees were nonwhite. . . . In 1951, the Federal Bureau of Labor Statistics found that

$4,083 was needed for a family of four to maintain a minimum standard of living for a year. Only one out of every four of the evicted families earned $4,083 per year; 20 percent earned less than $2,000 per year."[44] Although the areas Moses cleared were unsightly, studies show that slums contained low-cost, spacious housing and were regarded by its residents as "home" and "neighborhood." The public housing projects Moses built were sterile and anonymous and contained a higher density of low-income groups in a more restricted space. A black writer says that they were "hated almost as much as the police and that is saying a great deal."[45] Often, evictees were moved into temporary quarters until public housing was constructed, keeping "one jump ahead of the federal bulldozer" through a succession of moves.

One cannot say that the expressway system or slum clearance would have been different with the involvement of the public, or how they would have been different. One can only observe that the public was not involved, although they were permanently and irremediably affected for generations and generations to come.

FEDERAL RESPONSE TO THE CITIES

The federal response to the cities is often described as an attempt to balance programs that benefit the suburbs with those that aid the central cities.[46] Insofar as the major problem of the central city is conurbation, the main consequence of federal programs is to accentuate the problem, benefiting the suburbs at the expense of the central cities. A look at major federal programs suggests that they have made the problems of the city worse.

TRANSPORTATION

The federal contribution for urban highway construction was approximately $2 billion per year in the 1970s, twice the amount of the allocation for the year 1960.[47] The greater part of these funds is spent on the construction of urban expressways, demanded for the convenience of suburbanites. Certain worthy objects appear to be served by this undertaking: Junior executives and businessmen have a desirable route to work; new shopping malls and residential areas are encouraged; suburban housewives who might have shopped in the neighborhood are lured downtown. In the context of the conurbation problem, however, the urban expressways have a baleful influence. They subsidize the very forces that are undermining the fiscal health of the city. Schools and community facilities become more segregated; jobs are reduced by the out-migration of commerce and industry; blight occurs in the neighbor-hoods through which the expressways pass; the tax base of the city is weakened by the migration of the wealthier members of the popula-tion.[48] Very few of the poor are able to reverse the effects of this out-migration by commuting to jobs in the suburbs.

The expenditure now being made for mass transit—about $2 billion per year—may at least hold the line against deterioration of capital stock, and new facilities such as Bay Area Transit (Bart) in San Francisco and Metro in Washington, D.C. make the city more attractive, inte-grated, and commercially competitive.[49] However, the funds being in-vested in urban mass transit cannot possibly offset the massive subsidy of suburban sprawl over twenty years and more. Serious problems associated with conurbation will remain even with the installation of good mass transit systems.

HOUSING

For the last thirty years, the federal government's biggest housing pro-gram has been run through the tax system. In 1978 deductions for home mortgage interest and property taxes provided home owners with a subsidy of $10.2 billion, and the deferral of capital gains on home sales provided a subsidy of another $0.9 billion. By comparison, the entire budget for all programs of the Department of Housing and Urban De-velopment in 1978 is estimated at $8.9 billion.[50]

Another way the government has subsidized private home con-struction is through mortgage guarantees and insurance. Both the FHA and the VA administer mortgage programs whose principal beneficiaries are suburbanites. The FHA pioneered the development of a model cove-nant of racial restriction and instructed its appraisers to make low rat-ings of properties where there existed "inharmonious racial and nation-ality groups."[51] The operating guidelines of the FHA through the late 1960s were tilted significantly toward suburban neighborhoods. These guidelines emphasized newness, tract development on vacant land, and financial security of the mortgagee. The all-white suburban develop-ment is not an accident of the urban milieu but a deliberate matter of federal policy sustained over a lengthy period of time.[52]

In effect, then, FHA and VA programs, in combination with deduc-tions for home mortgage interest and property taxes, have subsidized the movement of the white middle class out of the central cities and older suburbs while at the same time penalizing investment in the rehabilitation of the run-down neighborhoods of the older cities. The poor—especially the black and Puerto Rican poor—have not received any direct benefit from these programs. Among the inalienable rights talked about by Locke and Jefferson, one may now probably rank property tax and mortgage interest deductions, and of course, an urban expressway to work. The federal government has been reluctant to question these rights, lest they be placed in the role of George III. But it is worthwhile noting whom the rights considered by the American people to be important, then and now, serve.

URBAN RENEWAL

Federal urban renewal programs have been accurately described as an "expensive game of musical chairs"[53] in which the city attempts to exchange the poor of one tax jurisdiction for the rich and the well-off of another. This is far from the intention of the program declared by Congress to be "the realization as soon as feasible of the goal of a decent home and a suitable living environment for every American family."[54] The gap between legislative intent and practical operation is explained by the fractioning of the metropolitan area into different tax units and by the decision-making power of power brokers in urban politics.

Under renewal programs the federal government makes available to city government two-thirds of the cost of land purchased. The city pays the other third. The initiation of a renewal program will seem like a desirable course to many city officials. By exercising powers of eminent domain to buy up unsightly slums in the vicinity of central city shopping areas, they can set in motion forces for job creation, development, reform, and modernization. The land purchased under eminent domain is resold to developers and investors, who in turn prepare the way for a complex of hotels, convention centers, and high-rise apartment projects designed for the wealthy middle class.[55] No one can afford to build on expensive central city land without the intention of obtaining a high return on investment. By attracting the rich into downtown areas through renewal, the city can succeed in exchanging its poor for the well-off of another tax jurisdiction.

Neglected in these arrangements are the poor. They are divested of their homes and livelihoods under the auspices of renewal with little or no compensating benefits. For the most part, city officials look on their departure with no regrets. It is a fact that the poor are a heavy expense, costing the city much more than other groups for police, fire protection, welfare, and schools.[56] To the extent that the condition of the poor is given thought, it is hoped that they have gone to another tax jurisdiction more nearly able to afford the additional expense. Thus, although the city may take satisfaction in the gleaming new buildings brought by the renewal program, it is doubtful that there has been a net gain for the metropolitan area in which the program occurred.[57]

The injury inflicted on the poor by urban renewal is not offset by the benefits of public housing. On this point opinion appears to be unanimous. A critical report asserts that urban renewal "destroyed more homes than were built; primarily destroyed low-rent homes; built predominantly high-rent homes; made housing conditions worse for those whose housing conditions were least good; and improved housing conditions for those whose housing conditions were best."[58] A sociologist wrote during the high-water mark of renewal projects that at "a cost of $3 billion the Urban Renewal Agency has succeeded in materially reducing the supply of low-cost housing in American cities."[59] An urban affairs expert adds to this indictment: "Hundreds of thousands of low-income people, most of them black and Puerto Ricans, have been forced out of low-cost housing, by no means all of it substandard, in order to make way for luxury apartments, hotels, civic centers, industrial parks, office buildings and the like."[60] The overall result, he summarizes, is to compress the poor into "high density slums."

MODEL CITIES AND URBANK

Model Cities and Urbank are federal programs directed to the problems of the inner city. Although they were advanced by different presidents in different times, the former by Lyndon Johnson in 1965 and the latter by Jimmy Carter in 1978, they are sufficiently alike to offer a basis for comparative analysis. The most important similarity is that they are both aimed at the inner city, and the second most important feature in common is that they depend on strong presidential backing. Both programs were meant to be a signature of presidential concern about the inner city.

The Model Cities Program, in contrast to Urbank, was generated by a period of great political unrest. The leadership of the black community had turned attention from the infringement of civil rights in Southern towns to the much thornier issue of blacks living and working in the cities of the North. The concrete penitentiaries built under the auspices of renewal led the black leadership to seek a voice in the formulation of policies affecting neighborhoods and housing. With the change in the direction of attention, conflict shifted in the mid-1960s from sites such as Birmingham to Northern cities. In 1964 there were riots and disorders in New York, Rochester, Jersey City, Paterson, Chicago, Cleveland, and Philadelphia. A riot in the Watts area of Los Angeles in August 1965 compared with the Detroit riots of 1943 in severity, damage, and loss of life. The National Guard was called in to provide reinforcement to the police, and the toll at the end of several days of fighting was 34 people dead, hundreds injured, and 4,000 arrested.[61]

These events were a potent force in stimulating presidential action, and a task force was appointed to make recommendations concerning the unsolved problems of poverty and race in the cities. The recommendation of the task force, later embodied in a presidential address to Congress, was to establish the Model Cities program targeted on the needs of the inner city population of sixty-six cities. Among the cities selected for the program, six had populations over 500,000, ten had populations from 250,000 to 500,000, and fifty had populations below 250,000. This breakdown represented the judgment of the task force about a balanced distribution of aid among regions and city sizes, tempered by a sense of what would be a reasonable cost for the program. The task force advised the president that the program for sixty-six cities would cost $2.3 billion over five years, of which the federal share would be $1.9 billion.[62] The Model Cities program required the Department of Housing and Urban Development (HUD) to set forward the criteria for favorable grant proposal. Conception and planning, however, were to originate at the local level, subject to final review and approval by HUD.[63]

By comparison with the turbulent 1960s, the urban political climate of the 1970s was subdued. An occasional signal of distress was visible, as when thousands from the South Bronx pillaged and looted the streets of New York City during a power failure in the summer of 1977. Then the smoldering and unsolved problems of the inner city surfaced once again and there was a flurry of federal activity. In keeping with the more restrained atmosphere of the times, the proposal set forth for the inner cities by the Carter administration was modest. Working through the Department of Commerce and HUD, Urbank would guarantee up to $11 billion worth of loans at low interest rates and with a long repayment period to businesses wanting to build plants in troubled areas. The Urbank proposal would work in combination with a $2,000 tax credit for each unemployed young person hired in the first year and $1,500 for each hired in the second year. Additionally, a 15 percent investment tax credit would be given to businesses that built or expanded in financially troubled inner city areas.[64]

The Urbank proposal is plainly a more modest conception than Model Cities since it did not actually involve an expenditure of federal resources except in the case of a defaulted loan. Also, it did not involve the comprehensive assessment of needs and planning originating from the local community of the sort that characterized the Model Cities. Instead, Urbank sought to stimulate revival of inner city areas by offering financial incentives to venture capital. One advantage of working through financial intermediaries such as Urbank is that the federal government can take the credit for responding to central city needs while incurring little political or financial risk.

Although the Model Cities program received vigorous presidential backing in the Johnson administration and at least adequate backing in the succeeding administration of Richard Nixon, it did not fulfill its ambitious objectives. The price of support for the program by intergovernmental lobbies—the National Conference of Mayors, the National League of Cities, and the National Governor's conference—and by Congress was a considerable dilution of the original objectives. Congress doubled the number of cities eligible for the program and made plans to increase the number still further in the future. This dilution of assistance weakened the prospects of achieving stated goals.[65] The Model Cities program is now defunct; its demise is attributed to failure to acquire a constituency of support in Congress, the executive branch, or the intergovernmental lobbies.

The impact of the Urbank proposal on the problems of the inner cities will be close to neglible. Studies show that the type of industries locating in inner city neighborhoods are not of the size to change the employment picture of the community.[66] Additionally, it is doubtful that tax incentives to employ unskilled youths are sufficient to offset the costs of training and absenteeism. The narrowing of federal assistance to the provision of financial stimulus overlooks problems of much greater magnitude that a relocating industry would have to face—the declining physical infrastructure of the city, tunnels, roads, bridges, sewage lines, water mains, and docks and harbors.

THE FUTURE AND THE PAST

American cities are criticized from a variety of perspectives, all of them telling and important. From an aesthetic viewpoint, critics stress a general decline into "standardized chaos."[67] Inefficiency was emphasized by President Carter in presenting the first National Energy Plan to Congress (April 1977). He asserted that government-subsidized highway construction promoted "energy-inefficient truck and air transportation" drawing "people, businesses, and industry out of central cities into suburbia."[68] The National Commission on the Causes and Prevention of Violence stressed the multiple inequalities which distinguished life-styles in the affluent suburb and the central city. To drive home the political consequence of these inequalities, the commission portrayed a harrowing vision of the American city of the future:

> Central business districts in the heart of the city, surrounded by mixed areas of accelerating deterioration, will be partially protected by large numbers of people shopping or working in commercial buildings during day-

time hours, plus a substantial police presence, and will be largely deserted
except for police patrols during nightime hours. . . .

High speed patrolled expressways will be sanitized corridors connect-
ing safe areas, and private automobiles, taxicabs, and commercial vehicles
will be routinely equipped with unbreakable glass, light armor, and other
security features. . . . Armed guards will ride "shotgun" on all forms of
public transportation . . . the ghetto slum neighborhoods will be places of
terror with widespread crime, perhaps entirely out of control during night-
time hours. . . .

Between the unsafe, deteriorating central city on the one hand and the
network of safe, prosperous areas and sanitized corridors on the other, there
will be, not unnaturally, intensifying hatred and deepening division. Violence will increase further, and the defensive response of the affluent will
become still more elaborate.[69]

This appalling vision of the future is born from forces in existence
in the distant past. Specifically, the constitutional system tips power in
American urban settings toward inequalities and sprawl by enshrining
the rights of possessive individualism and vesting political power in
power brokers rather than in voters. As one looks at the balance of
federal programs allocated to urban areas (urban renewal, model cities,
and Urbank) as compared to the road construction, tax deductions, and
mortgage loans and guaranties directed to the suburbs, it becomes apparent that the suburbs are the main beneficiaries of federal support.
Thus, the federal government helps promote the conflict between city
and suburb portrayed in the commission's report.

In contrast, it is useful to consider a different view. At the same time
that the framers of the American Constitution were stressing the rights
of possessive individualism, Edmund Burke, an English political thinker
and pamphleteer, was invoking England's feudal past against the tendency of liberals everywhere, on both sides of the Atlantic, to elevate
abstract rights above social welfare. He argued that society had certain
prescriptive rights which superseded those asserted by possessive individuals and which controlled their exercise. Burke was among the first
to perceive self-destructive tendencies embedded in liberal democratic
ideology and to register his alarm in terms which still have current
meaning. He said, replying especially to Locke, that society was indeed
a contract. But:

. . . the state ought not to be considered as nothing better than a
partnership agreement in a trade of pepper and coffee, calico, or tobacco,
or some other such low concern, to be taken up for a little temporary
interest, and to be dissolved by the fancy of the parties. . . . It is a partner-

ship in all science; a partnership in all art; a partnership in every virtue and in all perfection. As the ends of such a partnership cannot be obtained in many generations, it becomes a partnership not only between those who are living, but between those who are living, those who are dead, and those who are to be born.[70]

Burke provides the philosophical basis on which England, specifically the London metropolitan region, has been able to save itself from the ravages of conurbation in the post–World War II period. The Town and Country Planning Act (1947), in combination with powers vested in the Greater London Council, enabled planning authority to check sprawl by requiring future growth to be grafted onto existing village communities and by preserving the separate identities of the village communities and the city of London by creating green belts encircling the city.[71] Such exodus as has occurred in England in the 1950s and 1960s has been moderated by the relative desirability of neighborhoods and living accommodations in both city and country; additionally, the population movement has not been characterized by class and ethnic differences of comparable intensity. The Greater London Council, through which the planned dispersion was drafted and implemented, included on its board (no less than bankers, lawyers, and realtors) architects and city planners. Thus the speculative interests of the wealthy were adjusted to a plan which embraced the interests of the London metropolitan area. Whether America, crippled by its historical constitutional enthusiasms, can profit from this example remains to be seen.

NOTES

1. Sam Bass Warner, *The Private City* (Philadelphia: University of Pennsylvania Press, 1968), p. 225.
2. *Federalist* No. 10.
3. Arnold Heidenheimer *et al.*, *Comparative Public Policy* (New York: St. Martin's Press, 1975), pp. 104–09; Lewis Mumford, *The City in History* (New York: Harcourt, Brace & World, 1961), pp. 421–26.
4. Warner, *The Private City,* p. 50.
5. Ibid., p. 52.
6. Mumford, *City in History,* pp. 403–09.
7. John Russell Passoneau, "The Emergence of City Form," in *Urban Life and Form,* ed. Werner Z. Hirsch (New York: Holt, Rinehart, & Winston), p. 12.
8. Mumford, *City in History,* graphic 46.
9. Lawrence D. Brown, *Mayors and Models* (Washington, D.C.: Brookings Reprint No. 348, 1979).
10. *Ibid.*

11. *Ibid.*
12. *Ibid.*
13. *Ibid.*
14. See Floyd Hunter, *Community Power Structure* (New York: Anchor Books, 1963); Peter Bachrach and Morton S. Baratz, *Power and Poverty* (New York: Oxford University Press, 1970); Karen Orren, *Corporate Power and Social Change* (Baltimore, Md.: Johns Hopkins University Press, 1974).
15. Robert A. Dahl, *Who Governs?* (New Haven, Conn.: Yale University Press, 1961), chap. 22.
16. Robert A. Caro, *The Power Broker* (New York: Vintage Books, 1975).
17. Peter K. Eisinger, "Understanding Urban Politics," *Polity,* Fall 1976.
18. *Ibid.*
19. *Ibid.*
20. Seymour Mandelbaum, *Boss Tweed's New York City* (New York: John Wiley, 1965).
21. Clarence N. Stone *et al., Urban Policy and Politics* (Englewood Cliffs, N.J.: Prentice-Hall, 1979), pp. 7–10.
22. Christopher Tunnard and Boris Pushkarev, *Man-Made America* (New Haven, Conn.: Yale University Press, 1974), pp. 57–72.
23. Stone *et al., Urban Policy and Politics,* pp. 7–10.
24. *Ibid.*
25. Paul and Percival Goodman, *Communitas* (New York: Vintage Books, 1960), chap. 2.
26. This quotation and the following from George E. Peterson, "Finance," in *The Urban Predicament,* ed. William Gorham and Nathan Glazer (Washington, D.C.: The Urban Institute, 1976), pp. 44–45.
27. *Ibid.*
28. Brown, *Mayors and Models.*
29. Tunnard and Pushkarev, *Man-Made America,* pp. 57–72; David J. Rose *et al.,* "Energy for Urbia," in *Energy and the City,* Hearings Before the Subcommittee on the City of the Committee on Banking, Finance, and Urban Affairs (Washington, D.C.: U.S. Government Printing Office, 1977) pp. 374–90.
30. Tunnard and Pushkarev, *Man-Made America,* p. 67.
31. Stone, *et al., Urban Policy and Politics,* pp. 7–10.
32. Brown, *Mayors and Models.*
33. Caro, *Power Broker,* p. 753.
34. *Ibid.,* p. 9.
35. Edward C. Banfield, *The Unheavenly City Revisited* (Boston: Little, Brown, 1974), p. 18.
36. Caro, *Power Broker,* pp. 715–16, 729–35.
37. *Ibid.,* pp. 750–51.
38. *Ibid.,* chap. 34.
39. *Ibid.,* pp. 743–54.
40. *Ibid.*
41. *Ibid.,* pp. 16–17, 238–39, 716.
42. *Ibid.,* pp. 951–53.

43. *Ibid.*, pp. 949.

44. *Ibid.*, p. 968.

45. *Ibid.*, p. 20.

46. Brown, *Mayors and Models.*

47. Banfield, *Unheavenly City Revisited,* pp. 14–15.

48. *Ibid.*

49. *Ibid.*

50. Committee on Banking, Finance, and Urban Affairs, Subcommittee on the City, *Federal Tax Policy and Urban Development* (Washington, D.C.: U.S. Government Printing Office, 1977), pp. 2–3.

51. Banfield, *Unheavenly City Revisited,* p. 15.

52. *Ibid.*

53. William Alonso, "Cities, Planners, and Urban Renewal," in *Urban Renewal: The Record and the Controversy,* ed. James Q. Wilson (Cambridge, Mass.: MIT Press, 1968), p. 447.

54. Quoted in Banfield, *Unheavenly City Revisited,* p. 16.

55. Alonso, "Cities, Planners, and Urban Renewal," p. 447.

56. *Ibid.*

57. *Ibid.*

58. Martin Anderson, "The Federal Bulldozer," in *Urban Renewal: The Record and the Controversy,* p. 495.

59. Scott Greer, *Urban Renewal and American Cities* (Indianapolis, Ind.: Bobbs-Merrill, 1965), p. 3.

60. Banfield, *Unheavenly City Revisited,* p. 16.

61. Bernard J. Frieden and Marshall Kaplan, *The Politics of Neglect* (Cambridge, Mass.: MIT Press, 1977), pp. 33–34.

62. *Ibid.*, p. 215.

63. Lawrence D. Brown and Bernard J. Frieden, *Guidelines and Goals in the Model Cities Program* (Washington, D.C.: Brookings Reprint No. 332, 1978).

64. "President Unveils $8.3 Billion Plan to Aid U.S. Cities," *Washington Post,* March 28, 1978, A1, 4.

65. Frieden and Kaplan, *Politics of Neglect,* p. 231.

66. William K. Tabb, *The Political Economy of the Black Ghetto* (New York: W. W. Norton, 1970), pp. 65–79.

67. Mumford, *City in History,* graphic 46.

68. *The National Energy Plan* (Washington, D.C.: U.S. Government Printing Office, 1977), p. 4.

69. *Final Report of the National Commission on the Causes and Prevention of Violence* (Washington, D.C.: U.S. Government Printing Office), pp. 44–45.

70. Edmund Burke, *Reflections on the Revolution in France* (New York: The Liberal Arts Press, 1955), p. 110.

71. See Frank Smallwood, *Greater London: The Politics of Metropolitan Reform* (New York: Bobbs-Merrill, 1965); and Heidenheimer *et al., Comparative Public Policy,* pp. 84–86, 116–18.

CHAPTER 13

The Terms of
Political Conflict

This chapter deals with America's most celebrated political value, independence. It traces the idea of independence to its origins in colonial times and English constitutional conflicts, uncovers the relationship between the goals of independence and constitutional underpinnings, shows the significance of independence movements in American political history, and discusses the limitations imposed on American politics by the single-mindedness with which independence has been pursued.

Everyone knows that the Declaration of Independence was struck off in 1776 and that Thomas Jefferson is chiefly credited with its stirring prose style and leading ideas. Less often appreciated is that passages read as though they were taken directly from Locke's *Second Treatise of Civil Government.* Jefferson's famous lines, "But when a long train of abuses and usurpations, pursuing invariably the same Object evinces a design to reduce them under absolute Despotism," may be found almost verbatim in Locke.[1] Jefferson's notion that governments are instituted among men to secure the rights of "Life, Liberty, and the pursuit of Happiness" is only a slight change from Locke's view that government is meant to insure "Life, Liberty, and Estate."[2] These relationships show that the idea of independence celebrated by the Declaration is allied with Locke's notion of man as an acquisitive, choice-making, idiosyncratic individual. By *independence,* Americans sometimes seem to mean many things; but they have never strayed very far from the idea that the primary form in which the rights of independence are asserted is possessive individualism. To underscore the point, remember that Madison, the father of the constitutional system, placed "protection of the

312

diversity in the faculties of [individual] men," from which the rights of property originate, as the "first object of government."

The idea of independence has been a seminal influence on American political movements throughout the course of national history. Americans did not stop fighting for independence following the successful termination of their struggles with Great Britain. The idea of independence has offered fertile grounds for clashes with public authority on many subsequent occasions. Out-groups in America have fought for a form of independence in line with national traditions; in-groups are prepared to fight for their independence in the event that the results of public policy threaten to change substantially. There is basically no difference between the *manifest* violence of the out-groups who are attempting to change the status quo and the *latent* violence of in-groups who are prepared to fight to restore it.

The violence to which independence movements are prone is best characterized as *rebellion,* the attempt to extract short-term gains from presently constituted authority. *Revolution,* a change in the principles on which authority in society is constituted, has never been sought by any American independence movement.[3] By trying to obtain a form of independence in line with national traditions, independence movements have the paradoxical effect of undergirding the stability of institutions even while causing a high incidence of social turmoil. Comparative studies reveal that *turmoil,* that is, spontaneous, unorganized strife (strikes, clashes, demonstrations, riots, rebellions), is much higher in America than in other western democracies and that there is a marked tendency to channel violence into politics.[4]

Independence movements in America are fundamentally inspired by the notion of Hobbes and Locke, the first liberals, that the "natural" condition of individuals and groups is to be isolate and hostile. The various forms in which Americans have sought and continue to seek independence reflect a search for this natural condition. Among these forms are job security and stable local organization; untrammeled pursuit of the profit motive; separationist claims of racial and ethnic groups; right to receive government assistance without the onus of government regulation; religious and intellectual freedoms; sacredness of private property; right to carry a handgun; and the unrestricted exploitation of natural resources. Although each of these forms has a different emphasis, there is sufficient family resemblance to group them together as a type of social and political behavior. As in Jefferson's borrowing from Locke's *Second Treatise,* the idea of independence has so permeated the thought and language of Americans that its expression is often unconscious.

Joint cooperation among social groups to distribute the burdens of public policy is not fostered by the drive for independence. The lesson inferred by in-groups who have obtained a position of relative autonomy, such as WASPs, organized labor, corporate capital, and political incumbents, is that the worst effects of public policy can be passed on to those groups least able to resist them. To the out-groups, the Indians, blacks, migrant labor, immigrants, and women, the object lesson is that the route to social progress involves the use of violence to win marginal change. Nevertheless, whether an in-group or an out-group, independence movements do not constitute a grave threat to the stability of the political system. On the contrary, these movements may be understood to be affirming the principles on which authority in a liberal democratic society has traditionally been constituted. To repeat, even though these groups push, jostle, and struggle with each other to the point of outright bloodshed, there is little difference in principle among them.

To illustrate the force and conventionality of the idea of independence in our own time, we need look no further than the 1980 presidential elections. The speeches of Ronald Reagan invariably referred to the ancestral impulse of the American people to recover a form of independence which appeared threatened by loss. Casting Washington, D.C., in the role of an oppressive British colonial power; his opponent, Jimmy Carter, in the garb of a grasping, arbitrary despot like George III; and the federal bureaucracy in the lineaments of Whitehall (which administered the colonies), Reagan promised that our liberation would follow his election. Specifically, liberation would hinge on the selective abolition of major federal agencies and regulatory programs and, of course, a reduction in taxes. For example, the environmental controls imposed by the EPA on industry, the social welfare functions jointly administered by HUD and HEW, the overseeing responsibilities of OSHA and the FTC for occupational safety and consumer protection, and the oil and gas pricing policies administered by the Energy Department would be overhauled or scrapped.[5]

The group chiefly responsive to this version of a struggle for independence is business, both small (competitive) capital and big (corporate enterprise) capital. Phrases that flatter their outlook, for example, "the genius of industry, the imagination of management," spring easily to Reagan's lips. He has been leading this particular sort of independence movement since the 1950s, when he hosted a television show sponsored by General Electric that dealt with the virtues of free enterprise and the evils of government regulation. He returned to this theme again in the 1960s, supporting Barry Goldwater for the Republican party nomination and the presidency in 1964. Nomination by the

Republican party in 1980 afforded Reagan an opportunity to present his cause to a national political audience. He is an outstanding example of the hegemony of Lockean liberal ideas and of the continued inspiration these ideas provide to American independence movements.

AMERICAN REVOLUTION

The American "revolution" originated as an independence-seeking movement to restore the status quo ante, a condition of personal autonomy secured by free trade, local government, and private property. The overthrow of the government at Whitehall (the seat of British administration) and its replacement by a regime on these shores was a consequence of the independence thrust, not its source of inspiration. As long as the colonists were secure in the traditional "rights of Englishmen," they were fully content to remain loyal British subjects. British efforts following the Peace of Paris to impose detailed supervision of colonial affairs inadvertently signaled a desire to abridge these freedoms. The colonists fought to restore a cluster of basic freedoms which appeared to be threatened with further loss.[6]

For a century before the outbreak of hostilities, the colonists had been more or less let alone by the mother country. Britain was sufficiently preoccupied by its struggles with France to be unable to devote itself to the internal management of American affairs. The Peace of Paris changed all that. It enabled Britain to try to impose its authority at the local level of government, interfering to an unaccustomed extent in the daily administration of colonial life. A series of measures, ill considered, obnoxious, and onerous, persuaded the colonists that their basic freedoms were in jeopardy. These measures were the Quartering Act, appointments to office by the colonial governors, and the tax on imports. Rather than back down, retaining the support of moderate opinion in the colonies, Parliament played into the hands of the radicals. Hostilities broke out because the colonists were unwilling to sustain further loss of their independent status.

It follows that the American "revolution" was not over innovative questions of social policy as, for example, the distribution of property, the class divisions of colonial society, the status of blacks and women, or the form of government. The war was not fought over these questions and contributed nothing to their solution. Rather the war was deeply conservative in nature, seeking to restore a condition altered by an overly aggressive, imperial policy. Consistent with the objectives of later independence movements, the colonists sought modest changes in social and economic arrangements, a restoration of the status quo ante, and a marginal change in the distribution and location of power (Whitehall to Washington).[7]

CIVIL WAR

Independence was the cause for which the South fought in the Civil War. In this case the metaphor was stretched to cover culture, property, and regional autonomy. In the pre-Civil War period the South used the theme of independence to block an enlightened policy on miscegenation, manumission, and civil rights for the blacks.[8] Generally, the North was prepared to tolerate these assertions, but the Southern assertion of juridical independence was inconsistent with the existence of a legally unified nation.[9] Lincoln went to war to preserve "the Union," upholding the doctrine conceded even by Calhoun that local autonomy should not infringe the legal unity of the governmental system.

Again, it is worth noting that the war was over independence, not social policy. A gradualist social policy transforming the black from the status of a slave to a citizen neither provoked the war nor constituted its logical outcome. The status of the black was not materially affected by the war and really did not improve for the better for almost a full century after the struggle. The white Southerners failed to obtain their maximum demand, juridical independence, yet they obtained its equivalent in the post-Civil War period. Southern klansmen ran carpetbaggers and scalawags out of the South and reasserted by force white control over political institutions, customs, and economic opportunities.[10]

In the modern political scene, black secessionism and white backlash evoke the static and violent character of American politics. Blacks and whites alike have demanded local control over schools, businesses, social services, and police. George Wallace and Malcolm X were united in threatening violence against institutions that interfered with the independence of local groups.

RACIAL AND ETHNIC GROUP CONFLICT

The form of independence sought in ethnic group conflict, a staple of American politics, has been freedom from domination, territorial integrity, and advancement in the political and economic sphere. During the 1840s and throughout the latter part of the nineteenth century, ethnic group conflict was a regular feature of life in the city. The cities were divided up into different "turfs," dominated by rival ethnic groups. Newly arrived immigrant groups learned to defend themselves by organizing paramilitary street gangs which engaged in continuous, limited wars in defense of shifting group territory. Municipal government arose largely as a response to the need for a police authority to maintain a modicum of stability.[11]

WASPs and other groups who occupy a secure base of influence disapprove of the violent propensities of newcomers, forgetting that this is the route by which their own group rose to power. Violence in behalf of a form of independence in line with national traditions is a logical step for an insurgent ethnic or racial group to make. In effect, the claim is for a redistribution of economic burdens and political opportunities, a claim backed by historic precedent (the American Revolution) and ideological inheritance (the Declaration of Independence and the *Second Treatise*). In-groups have shown that they are unwilling to surrender power without a political struggle. Out-groups have responded by mounting independence drives and by deploying violence as a route to political influence.

The aim of black insurrection in American cities in the late 1960s was not to overturn the system but to win for blacks a degree of "independence" in the pursuit of education, life-style, and employment opportunities in line with national traditions. The Kerner Commission established that the typical rioter was not a criminal or migrant or social misfit but a self-respecting, competitive black male with above-average education, employment prospects, and political education in relation to members of his peer group.[12] The commission interpreted the needs of this rioter in keeping with the outlook of moderate reform. It urged the federal administration to reduce the multiple inequalities between the central city and the suburban periphery through increased educational and job opportunities, fair housing, bigger welfare checks, and public and private investment.[13]

These recommendations, acted on in more or less good faith by successive administrations, illustrate the advantages and shortcomings of independence movements. Insofar as these reforms improved the lot of many members of a marginal group, they were an undoubted advance over the past. However, by providing individualistic remedies for a collective predicament and overlooking the general deterioration of city life, they illustrate the narrow interpretation to which the goals of independence are susceptible. Urban change, in a broad sense, did not spark the black insurrection of the 1960s, and urban needs were still unmet in American cities more than a decade after the convulsions and turmoil.

LABOR UNIONS

A historian makes the comparison that as "the constitution of the Ku Klux Klan begins with a declaration of allegiance to the United States," and as rioting, "urban ethnic groups never dreamed of establishing a Paris commune," so militant labor unionists in America have not encouraged (or wished to encourage) a socialist revolution.[14] American labor's fight for independence has focused on job security, working conditions, and income, which differentiates it from the more comprehensive aims sought by unions in the European political scene. Victor Gotbaum, president of District Council 37 of the AFSCME (American Federation of State, County, and Municipal Employees), chief spokesman for the civil service unions in New York City, encapsulates the history and objectives of the labor movement in these words: "The labor union movement in this country was built by the hope, the courage, and the strength and the ideals of the outs who wanted in."[15] In the pursuit of this objective, Gotbaum once ordered a shutdown of all bridge traffic leading into New York City for a twenty-four hour period, cutting off the city from the outside world.

For labor, the economic equivalent of territorial independence and cultural particularity has been jobs and stable local organization. To obtain these goals, unionists have resorted to violence against local enemies and symbols of oppression, like scabs, Pinkerton men, and company property. They have refrained from attacking employers in person, federal troops, or institutions appointed to the tasks of government.[16] Labor violence in America is sometimes labeled as "nonideological" in contrast with the disposition of European labor unions to employ violence in the pursuit of more comprehensive, ideological goals, such as political overthrow, party organization, and socioeconomic change. The American labor union movement is not really less ideological than the European; it is merely ideological in a different way. The focus of American labor on "independence" tends to restrict the spheres in which it is willing to exert influence. A European social scientist states that the chief question raised by American labor is "the non-existence . . . of a large Socialist party, and it seems to be connected with the absence of class consciousness in the American worker, and with his deep individualism."[17] Asked this way the question answers itself. It is the focus on independence that has atrophied labor's interest in a separate party organization reflecting a socialist perspective.

The distinguishing features of the American labor movement are its emphasis on local union organization and bargaining on a plant-by-plant basis to improve wages, working conditions, and security.[18] The union movement has remained markedly decentralized in the sense that the central federation has relatively little authority over its member unions. In part, this is the result of a lack of class sentiment strong enough to transcend the attachment of workers to their own separate crafts and occupations; in part, it reflects the emphasis on bargaining rather than political action. George Meany, former president of the seventeen-million-member AFL-CIO, stressed the fact that he headed a "federation of autonomous unions. Each takes care of its own business, makes its own decisions, and in a sense no individual worker belongs to the AFL-CIO."[19] This union has little or no authority over the bargaining or strike policies of its members, nor is it able to control their membership requirements or political activities.

The Wagner Act (1935) summed up the narrow objectives for which labor had been fighting since the 1880s. The act created stable local organization and job security by recognizing the right to strike and to organize free of employer harassment. Also, the act prevented employers from engaging in unfair labor practices. The AFL–CIO established a strong bargaining position with monopoly capital on the foundations provided by the Wagner Act. That segment of the labor community that is employed in the skilled trades required by capital-intensive production enjoys an extraordinarily high standard of compensation in comparison with the remainder of the work force.

At the same time, organized labor has failed to expand appreciably in terms of union membership or its general goals. At the time of the AFL-CIO merger in 1955, there were 17.4 million union members out of a total work force of 67 million. Today, the work force has grown to 95 million, but union membership has inched forward only to 20 million. This failure of expansion is related to the limited aims of the movement. Having obtained lucrative contracts in negotiations with monopoly capital, labor is now unwilling to mount an organizational drive to unionize the competitive sector of the economy where major problems—race and sex discrimination and low wages—truly abound. As out-groups who captured power in the nineteenth century treated newcomers with the same disdain accorded to them by prominent WASPs, so organized labor offers slender means of support to fringe movements led by blacks, women, migrants, and youth, who might upset the advantages of present arrangements.

BUSINESS

American business is also seeking independence. Although its goals are roughly similar to other independence movements, it has been differently positioned in relation to its ability to achieve them. First, the history of American business, at least until the New Deal era, is one of complete freedom from social and governmental restrictions. When the New Deal controls were formulated, they did not alter the nature of the relationship between the public and private sector but imposed limits on the scope of that freedom necessary to the survival of capitalism as an institution. To put the matter pointedly, the relevant meaning of freedom for the capitalist, whether a technocrat, financier, entrepreneur, engineer, or whatever, remains unchanged. The capitalist after the New Deal has the same decision-making power over the appropriation and allocation of resources, without interference from labor unions, consumer groups, or government officials, as he or she did before the New Deal. Indeed, the evidence points to the view that independence over investment decisions is increased by the ability of corporate capital to furnish investment funds from its own internal sources in the post-New Deal era.[20] Second, the business sector has far more resources at its disposal to pursue and maintain independence than do other groups. The organization, money, and communications ability of corporate capital are put to the task of fortifying the autonomy of the private sector.

Business is the group whose independence is most assured by the arrangements of the Constitution. Property interests of all descriptions —personalty, realty, and slaveholding—benefited from its provisions. Additionally, as I have repeatedly emphasized, the practical arrangements of American politics set forward by Madison in *Federalist* Nos. 10 and 51 tip outcomes of the political struggle toward privileged groups, thus reflecting the attitudes and principles of Hobbes and Locke. Locke's solicitude toward the commercial class has been sufficiently emphasized not to require further treatment.

In the nineteenth century the liberal state shielded the activities of business entrepreneurs by suppressing labor strikes and enacting tariff legislation which discriminated against foreign manufacturers. The state heavily subsidized the construction of the railroads in the 1870s and 1880s, providing land at minimal expense and financial assistance. All the ingredients of the future are embodied in the arrangements between the state and the railroad industry which developed at this time. The industry was successful in deflecting state resources to underwrite the expenses of capitalist enterprise, while at the same time skillfully eluding the efforts of the state to exert a corresponding degree of regulatory authority. The Supreme Court narrowly interpreted the provisions of the Interstate Commerce Act (1887), depriving the state of any important role in supervising the vast, integrated system of transportation, communication, and manufacture, which some of its own funds had helped to set in motion. Efforts by the federal and state legislatures to regulate the hours and conditions of work and to prohibit the employment of women and children in dangerous situations were struck down in the early twentieth century by a Court that consistently reflected probusiness attitudes.[21]

We are accustomed to associating the term *bureaucracy* with the federal administration that has grown up in the post–New Deal era. In fact, the first nationally integrated bureaucracies in America occurred in the private sector. They were created by American industry in the late nineteenth century, and they preceded the development of a federal governmental bureaucracy by a full half century. Under the umbrella of protection and assistance provided by the liberal state, a proficient business organization organized along bureaucratic lines was visible in America at least by the early twentieth century. Many of the present Fortune 500 companies appeared at this time, among them American Tobacco, Singer, U.S. Steel, Westinghouse, Dupont, United Rubber, American Can, United Fruit, Standard Oil, and General Electric.[22]

It is commonly believed that a new page was written in the history of American capitalism with the New Deal: Laissez-faire was ended, and the independence formerly enjoyed by business enterprise was taken away by a powerful state bureaucracy. However, this is not the case, and it would be very, very surprising if it were. The hegemony of Lockian liberal ideas, the arrangements of the Constitution, and the powerful institutional position built up by business in the nineteenth century assured that the New Deal would be a conservative political effort—and indeed it was. American capitalism was saved from its own excesses by a liberal state which agreeably assumed many of its administrative burdens and social expenses.[23] The state provided work relief and unemployment compensation to those injured by the deficiencies of a market economy. It provided social security in the absence of a pension benefits scheme administered by the private sector. Compensatory countercyclical fiscal and monetary policy was commenced in the New Deal to counteract inflation and recession. Regulatory agencies such as the Securities Exchange Commission (1934) and the Federal Communications Commission (1934) sought to provide a framework for the competition of business interests.

In none of these activities did the liberal state intrude on the sacred principle that investment decisions were the sole authority of the private sector. To this day, business rhetoric to the contrary, the American state has the weakest control over corporate investment decisions of any nation in the world. We are and remain the world's "freest" economy.

From the perspective of history and present political arrangements, independence is a slogan whose value accrues mainly to the interest of the business community, particularly corporate capital. As a slogan it appears to link business in a broad alliance, rich with historical association, to the many groups—regional, racial, ethnic, labor—who have sought independence in the American political community. Yet when used by the business community, the slogan diverts attention from nongovernmental exercises of power by corporations; it justifies a use of the state as an instrument of capital accumulation and resistance to extensions of state authority over the productive enterprise; it enables business to withhold resources from the community while claiming to be outside the arena of political àction. In addition, it obscures perception of social and economic class cleavages and focuses attention on those of race, ethnic groups, and other social categories.

DÉJÀ VU

America's independence movements, among them the election of Ronald Reagan, engender the experience of déjà vu, a term more frequently encountered in literary, rather than political, analysis. It means that we are witnesses to a replay of events brought to pass by inexorable, uncanny forces, far beyond the conscious intentions of the actors who may be involved. Déjà vu operates in a time frame different from, say, the videotaped transmission of a football game played that afternoon. Sustained, hidden, powerful elements collaborate to produce the same result, over and over. Given the tendency of American political partisans to repeat themselves and the power of the independence theme in American history, déjà vu, the sense that we have heard it all, seen it all before, seems particularly appropriate and descriptive of the patterns of American politics.

We might suppose that the politics of déjà vu are harmless enough. After all, what is the consequence of this repetition except boredom? However, there is a nightmarish sensation that accompanies it, the feeling that America cannot escape from its past. Karl Marx, a genius in distinguishing cosmetic from genuine political change, once said, "The tradition of all the dead generations weighs like a nightmare on the brain of the living. And just when men seem engaged in revolutionizing themselves and things . . . precisely in such epochs of revolutionary crisis, they anxiously conjure up the spirits of the past to their service."[24] This observation applies with particular force to American independence movements. They promise to introduce change but they only deliver repetition.

Despite the fact that *independence* is a word favored by many political groups, it is important to notice who is principally served by it. It is used, both in the past and currently, to invest private accumulation with a patriotic halo and to mask the power business groups exercise over others. Taking cover in the slogan of independence enables business groups to escape scrutiny over the power which they directly exercise over other groups in the political arena and indirectly through the intervention of the government. Further, social and economic class cleavages are dampened down or aborted by the splintering effect of many groups waging independence struggles. Corporate capital is happy to take its place alongside Indians, the poor, competitive capitalists, blacks, and women, struggling for a form of independence in line with national traditions.

NOTES

1. *Second Treatise,* sec. 225.

2. *Ibid.,* sec. 123.

3. Richard Rubenstein, *Rebels in Eden* (Boston: Little Brown, 1970); Chalmers Johnson, *Revolutionary Change* (Boston: Little Brown, 1966), chap. 7.

4. Hugh Davis Graham and Ted Robert Gurr, *A Report to the National Commission on the Causes and Prevention of Violence* (New York: Bantam Books, 1970), chap. 17.

5. *The New York Times,* February 29, 1980, B4; *Washington Post,* July 11, 1980, A1, 3.

6. Rubenstein, *Rebels in Eden,* pp. 26, 48–55.

7. *Ibid.*

8. Frank Tannenbaum, *Slave and Citizen* (New York: Vintage Books, 1946).

9. Rubenstein, *Rebels in Eden,* pp. 56–64.

10. *Ibid.*

11. Sam Bass Warner, Jr., *The Private City* (Philadelphia: University of Pennsylvania Press, 1968), chap. 7.

12. *Report of the National Advisory Commission on Civil Disorders* (New York: Bantam Books, 1968), pp. 128–29; Jerome H. Skolnick, *The Politics of Protest* (New York: Simon & Schuster, Clarion Books, 1969), chap. 4.

13. *Report of the National Advisory Commission,* chap. 17.

14. Rubenstein, *Rebels in Eden,* p. 36.

15. Victor Gotbaum, "The Philosophy of a Unionist," *The New York Times,* June 8, 1971, p. 37.

16. Rubenstein, *Rebels in Eden,* p. 36.

17. Maurice Duverger, *Political Parties* (New York: John Wiley, 1963), pp. 22–23.

18. Derek C. Bok and John T. Dunlop, *Labor and the American Community* (New York: Simon & Schuster, 1970), chap. 2.

19. Quoted in Nick Kotz, "Can Labor's Tired Leaders Deal with a Troubled Movement?" *The New York Times Magazine,* September 4, 1977, p. 44.

20. John Kenneth Galbraith, *The New Industrial State* (New York: Signet, 1967), chap. 4.

21. David Vogel, "Why Businessmen Mistrust Their State: The Political Consciousness of American Corporate Executives," Prepared for Delivery at the American Political Science Association Convention, Chicago, September 2–5, 1976.

CHAPTER 14

The Constitutional System: In Dreams, Equilibrium, and Crisis

This book has stressed a sound approach to political inquiry. Caution is suggested by the fact that the interpretation of American politics is surrounded by controversy. "Popular sovereignty," "rule of law," "pluralism," "class domination," and "power elitism" are the names rival persuasions apply to their viewpoints. When we are in the presence of conflicting claims to the truth, it is best to proceed in as prudent a manner as possible, reserving judgment until all sides have been heard.

To attend fairly to rival views, we must avoid "tabloid" versions of political reality and, conversely, pay more attention to the theories that shape perceptions of factual experience. A tabloid version of reality confines itself to the surface of events by pretending that facts exist in the world independently of their observers and that the task of inquiry is satisfied by their collection. Examples of such an outlook are commonly found in newspaper journalism, television coverage, and criminal investigation, and they have a surprising vogue among political scientists. Sergeant Friday, whom we talked about before, typifies this outlook of naive empiricism well.

However, this approach is unsound because the nature of events and facts, within certain limits, depends on the professional and personal standards of judgment brought to their observation. Thus, the best procedure is to make the biases that influence outlook as explicit as possible. A tabloid version of political events is biased against critical interpretation because it tends to treat the world as independent of human agency. By excising consciousness from experience, naive empiricism is able to present the world as "normal" and to excuse itself from explaining how it came to be or might be changed.

A contextual approach has been put forward as a basis for evaluating the conflicting interpretations of American politics. This approach focuses on the origin, idea, operation, and predicament of the American constitutional system. The origin of American constitutionalism is traced back to seventeenth-century English constitutional conflicts; the leading ideas of the founding fathers are derived by way of Locke from the one true ancestor of American liberalism, Thomas Hobbes; the operative realities of American politics are shown to be the product of Madisonian arrangements; and the current predicament of American constitutionalism is the overthrow of Madisonian politics by modern oligopoly.

Now that we have adopted an approach and collected evidence, it is time to assess the several interpretations of American politics. Before offering a view, it is worth remembering that American politics is a shared enterprise, a common set of understandings, transmitted over many generations, which contemporary figures seek to shape and direct. One of the ways contemporary politics is shaped is precisely through interpretations and investigations of the sort that we are making. That is to say, interpretations of politics are themselves a part of politics. The reader is encouraged, therefore, to regard all interpretation as provisional, including the one offered here, and to keep alive the possibilities of an independent view.

THE CONSTITUTIONAL SYSTEM: IN DREAMS

Reform means, literally, to re-form the life of the nation to certain original principles from which recent experience constitutes an unfortunate departure. Although the interpretations that follow differ to some extent on who or what is the final authority, the people or the rule of law, the area in which they agree—that there is a crying need to reform the life of the nation—is of far greater importance. Accordingly, these interpretations shall be considered and discussed together, while allowing for necessary differences among them.

POPULAR SOVEREIGNTY

One of the most attractive and widely believed notions of American politics is that the people are sovereign. *Sovereign* means "no higher ruler than," and in this view there is no higher ruler in political affairs than the people.[1] Who the people are that do the ruling is an elusive matter.

Often the view is presented that the people rule by expressing their preferences of candidates and issues at election time. A related idea is that opinion polls are an important influence in shaping public policy. Sometimes we encounter the view that the people rule through a political party, certain "right thinking people" within a political party, or even the titular leader of the party. The people are viewed as an independently acting, ruling authority alive in the course of American history.

The popular sovereignty interpretation has its roots in Thomas Jefferson's idea of majority democracy. He hinted at his inauguration in 1801 that the party and president-elect were the appropriate means for the expression of majority rule. But he softened the implications of his position with the reminder that the majority must be respectful of the rights of the minority. "All, too, will bear in mind this sacred principle, that though the will of the majority is in all cases to prevail, that will to be rightful must be reasonable; that the minority possess their equal rights, which equal law must protect, and to violate would be oppression. . . ." Today, it is often emphasized that in a large and diverse nation such as ours, the majority must provide a moderate course of political rule.

Over time the concept of majority rule through presidential and party leadership has been further developed and invigorated, but at no time has it received more forceful expression than in the writings of Woodrow Wilson. In an essay written before his own election to the presidency, Wilson asserted that the president was "at once the choice of the party and the nation" and that he therefore had an obligation "in law and in conscience to be as big a man as he can."[2] The echoes of Wilson's views are unmistakable in the public addresses of Kennedy— the "Chief Executive is the vital center of action in our whole scheme of government"—and Carter—"I think the Founding Fathers expected the President to be the leader of our country"—prior to their election to presidential office (Chapter 9). Wilson argued that the president ought to prevail over rival claimants to power because only the president represents the will of the whole people. This interpretation of American politics, as this line of reasoning shows, easily resolves itself into rule by one man, or a small collection of men, who claim to represent the popular will.[3]

The popular sovereignty interpretation is flattering to the electorate and to the presidential candidate. For a candidate skilled in the rhetoric of summoning the public, it is a powerful political weapon. As we saw in Chapter 4, Kennedy used the rhetoric of popular leadership in the 1960 presidential race against Nixon even though, as president, Kennedy turned out to resemble his predecessor in many ways.

Kennedy's wit, style, and sense of history enabled him to associate himself in the public mind with the great men of America's past, whereas Nixon was linked to presidential failures. Similarly, Carter was generally successful in stirring public expectations concerning his capacities as a presidential leader. After a year in office and repeated setbacks in his efforts to fashion an energy policy, Carter recanted his earlier views, as did Kennedy also: "I would say the problems are more difficult than I imagined them to be" (see Chapter 9).

The popular sovereignty interpretation takes a progressive, partisan, and simplistic view of American political history as a succession of problems which are produced by the "bad guys." Just in the nick of time, the "good guys" are elected by an enlightened majority and matters are tidied up until such time as the scoundrels, oligarchs, and party bosses resume power once again. One has the impression that such problems as come along are mentioned to augment interest in the always-certain rescue. Thus, while pretending to take a straight look at difficulties, history is staged to provide a reassuring outcome. Whenever a critical situation arises, we know the rescue party will get there in time. This interpretation is fond of a journalistic and dramatic treatment of events. American political history tends to become the record of the actions of great men and progressive parties.

Despite the recantations of Carter and Kennedy, the myth of presidential leadership and popular sovereignty lives on. Its basis in fact and popular fancy is strengthened by the occasional drives to abolish the electoral college, by the renewed interest in presidential debates, by the proliferation of public opinion polls on every conceivable subject, and by the push toward a widened use of presidential primaries in the states.

RULE OF LAW

A slightly different but allied view holds that the final authority in American politics is a pattern of law, the law of the Constitution. The supremacy of the Constitution is said to derive from the people who have, finally and irrevocably, committed themselves to obey its provisions. The reason the people have made such a commitment, according to this view, is that the Constitution embodies unchanging principles of right and justice.[4]

The ideal purposes of the written Constitution are interpreted and applied for successive generations through the offices of the Supreme Court. This view sharply emphasizes the role of the Court, just as the popular sovereignty interpretation exaggerates the importance of the presidency. Also, the supremacy of the written Constitution easily resolves itself into the supremacy of the justices of the Supreme Court, a pattern similar but opposed to the view that the president should have the decisive voice. Chief Justice Charles Evan Hughes once bluntly asserted, "the Constitution is what the Judges say it is." Felix Frankfurter, a Harvard law professor and later a Supreme Court justice, used to tell his law classes, "the Supreme Court is the Constitution."

A review of Court history over the last fifty years is used to support this interpretation of American politics. On national policy issues, such as racial equality, due process of law for criminal defendants, religious tolerance, free speech and press, right to privacy, legislative reapportionment, and the rights of women, it is pointed out that the Court has been more progressive than the legislature or the presidency and that the people have done well to repose faith in the Court's interpretation. The Supreme Court, an admittedly elitist group, is nevertheless said to be a truly progressive voice in national affairs.[5]

A CRITICAL VIEW OF REFORM

The popular sovereignty and rule of law interpretations of American politics differ in their view of where final authority is vested. At times this difference has seemed important. Presidential leaders claiming to represent the will of the people have sought to bypass constitutional provisions. In the case of *Youngstown Sheet and Tube Co.* v. *Sawyer*, 343 U.S. 579 (1952), the Court held that the president exceeded his authority under the Constitution in seizing the property of Youngstown Sheet and Tube Co. The supremacy of the Constitution, as interpreted by the Court, was upheld against a broad interpretation of the powers of presidential office. At the same time, the Court has bowed to the will of the people as expressed by a coalition of forces which has captured the presidency and both houses of Congress. The case of *National Labor Relations Board* v. *Jones and Laughlin Steel Corp.*, 301 U.S. 1 (1937), is referred to as the "switch in time that saved nine," because here, for the first time, the Court indicated that it would terminate its obstructionist role over the great spate of New Deal legislation. In the light of these controversies the differences between the popular sovereignty and rule of law interpretation—one vesting supremacy in the Constitution as interpreted by the Court, and the other vesting final authority in a president backed by a coalition of political forces—has seemed to be significant.

All in all, however, the area of agreement between these views is more important than the area of opposition. Both interpretations agree that American political institutions are socially progressive. They view problems the nation confronts as *epiphenomenal;* the problems lie upon the surface of things and are susceptible to improvement by pragmatic political action, a heroic presidential leader, or an enlightened judiciary.

Consequently, it is not especially disturbing to find that America is confronted with a host of pervasive and serious issues—racial injustice, fiscal crisis, energy shortages, urban deterioration, and so on—because no matter what their extent, they can always be resolved through existing institutions. *Reform* means, as noted before, to re-form the life of the nation to certain enduring principles from which present experience is an unfortunate departure.

However, reform interpretations of American politics have a flawed and misleading idea of how the Constitution exists in national society, which leads to a gross misinterpretation of political experience. To a major degree this idea of the Constitution is the familiar *literal* outlook which we discussed in Chapter 2. The Constitution is seen as an abstraction existing in isolation from the world of political practice. Reformers are free to invest politics with a rich fantasy life because they fail to recognize the constraining features of a Constitution existing in multiple form, as a tradition of ideas, method of doing politics, and written memorandum. A straight look at the constraining features of the Constitution raises the possibility that the problems I have mentioned are not epiphenomenal but arise out of the constituent principles of political association, that is, out of the Constitution itself.

To be more specific, the popular sovereignty view of American politics is not borne out by the properties of the constitutional system. Political institutions were not designed to transmit popular enthusiasms through the organs of party government and presidential leadership, as is seen by such features of the constitutional system as separation of powers, federalism, and the electoral college. The object of this institutional design, as the framers of the Constitution never tired of explaining, is to blunt popular government and to make it incapable of action. Madison was not satisfied with the checks imposed by a two-party system but sought to build antidemocratic features into the permanent structure of American political institutions. To a remarkable degree, he succeeded. America's decentralized cadre parties, in which state and local party notables co-opt other influentials and deal manipulatively with the electorate, are a perfect reflection of Madison's eighteenth-century Constitution at work in the daily politics of modern America (Chapter 4).

The rhetoric of popular sovereignty is often used by presidential candidates to divert attention from the process by which power in America is grasped and held, the brokerage arrangements which truly govern the actions of all political participants. Politics in America, as Madison saw it, and as present experience confirms, is a private matter among influential parties, dealing with one another on a one-to-one basis in terms of their mutual interests. Others enter into the picture only as they prove useful to one or another of these power barons in building up their base of personal influence. The role of the president as power broker is imposed by constitutional arrangements and the patterns of American politics (Chapter 9). Many presidents have found reason to regret the rhetorical excesses of the electoral campaign as they went about the necessary business of bargaining and negotiation, adjusting their public positions to the influential groups with whom they share power on Capitol Hill and in the executive branch. All this is common knowledge among practitioners of American politics. If we do not make the mistake of severing politics from constitutional arrangements, we shall not be misled by the popular sovereignty outlook.

The rule of law interpretation is similarly inattentive to the constraining features of the Constitution. This interpretation takes a very exalted view of the function of the Supreme Court and of the document it interprets, but such a view is most often rejected by men who are themselves important jurists. Chief Justice Warren Burger dismissed the notion that the courts were an appropriate instrument of social reform, emphasizing instead their role in safeguarding public order (Chapter 11). In giving priority to stability over social justice, Burger was providing a contemporary application of views which link him to the framers of the Constitution. Learned Hand, a justice of the United States Circuit Court, repeatedly warned his colleagues against elevating their judgments over the legislature on the presumption that judges were smarter and better than other men and therefore qualified to chart a course of social reform. In a democracy, Hand kept saying, judges ought to defer to the judgment of popularly elected representatives. Asked by his colleagues if this wasn't a sheeplike attitude to take toward the views of the people, Hand said that he replied with Saint Francis, "My brother, the sheep."[6]

There is much about the rule of law interpretation that is plainly irreconcilable with the spirit of American democracy and the working arrangements of American politics. The notion that the American people fled European aristocracy to reconstitute an "aristocracy of the robe" on these shores does not pay attention to constitutional prohibitions against building inequalities of status into the government (Art. I, sec. 9). Americans have been tolerant of inequalities based on wealth but not of those arising from claims of status. Such a prejudice militates against elevating the members of the Supreme Court into a bevy of platonic guardians. Further, the working arrangements of American politics require the Court to reach an accommodation with the dominant coalition of interests in Congress and the White House thus imposing major obstacles to an independent course of social reform. Finally, as we have seen, judicial review has certain inherent limitations which greatly limit the sphere of human freedom to which protection is offered. Insofar as human freedom is a function of economic arrangements, it is afforded precious little protection by the written Constitution or the Supreme Court. There is no constitutional prohibition against poverty. Also, as the Bakke case shows, although the Court may redistribute existing resources, it cannot create new resources to meet an area of pressing social need.

The rule of law interpretation places great stress on the ideal purposes embedded in the written document; but looking at the provisions of the written Constitution, it is difficult to find any of the positive and developmental forces it is said to promote. The preamble to the Constitution asserts that the document is enacted "to form a more perfect union, establish justice . . . promote the general welfare, and secure the blessings of liberty to ourselves and our posterity. . . ." Only the "general welfare" is given effect in the main text, and that is in connection with the power of Congress to levy taxes. On the matter of establishing justice, it is plain that the minds of the framers were elsewhere. Their minds were on business. The business of the nation is business, and the text reflects this attitude more than any other. If we mean by "justice" the enforcement of contracts and the collection of debts, then there is something to the view that the framers meant to establish it. The Constitution established a prohibition against the impairment of contracts and coinage of money by the states, and it created a federal system of courts so that creditors did not have to resort to state and lower courts in pursuit of debtors.[7]

Given this bias toward property, it is not surprising to find that the Court has frequently sided with privileged groups over the course of national history. It is a fair-weather philosophy of constitutionalism which finds that the Court has been the guardian of the rights of the weak, the unfortunate, and the unprotected. One must avert one's gaze from periods in which the Court has ruled in behalf of monopolists, segregationists, slaveowners, western land speculators, and public utility companies, and done its utmost to obstruct social reform initiated by the coordinate branches.[8]

The rulings of the Court reflect the insensitivity of the Constitution to submerged groups and the bias toward property. For example, in a recent case, the Supreme Court ruled that trial courts could not award attorney fees for those involved in public interest law suits unless specifically empowered by law. For those bringing suits in behalf of mental patients, racial and ethnic groups, environmental and consumer interests, and the poor, such compensation is often the only available source of funds. Many groups who are poorly represented in the judicial process will be harmed by the Court's decision. Whereas formerly they were inadequately defended, now it is uncertain whether they will be defended at all.[9] As noted earlier (Chapter 11), the Court has found that although the Constitution protects a woman's right to have an abortion, it does not obligate the state to provide funding to enable the right to be exercised. In short, the right to have an abortion is only protected for women who can afford the medical expense. Additionally, in the *First National Bank* v. *Bellotti* (April 26, 1978), the Court extended to corporations the same rights of free speech as those possessed by individuals or the press. The Court did not seem to notice that the resources of corporations in propagating their views far exceed those of ordinary individuals or even the facilities of a major daily newspaper.

To sum up, if we look at the properties of the constitutional system, considered as a written memorandum of association, a tradition of ideas, and a set of working arrangements, we know, allowing for a reasonable margin of doubt, that it cannot be what reform interpretations of American constitutionalism say it is. We are now ready to press our inquiry to a higher level.

THE CONSTITUTIONAL SYSTEM: IN EQUILIBRIUM

An optimistic faith in reform is not shared by either of the two other major theories we now want to consider, equilibrium and crisis. The former holds that American political institutions maintain a fragile purchase on social order through their capacity for managing political conflict; the latter advances the notion that political institutions are likely to be overwhelmed by conflicts they are incapable of managing.

Equilibrium theory believes that balance and stability are the product of the working arrangements of the Madisonian constitutional system. There are two variants of this theory, an early version which we shall simply call Madisonian politics, and a later version which is referred to as pluralism. The similarities between the two variants are more important than their differences.

Madisonian theory, to refresh our memory, holds that political stability is the product of institutional arrangements—in this case federalism and separation of powers—which withhold opportunities for domination by a particular group. Federalism divided power among parties acting in the national sphere of government from those exercising power in the state and local spheres. Similarly, the separation of executive, legislative, and judicial power among several departments gave each department the means to resist transfers of power away from itself to one of the others. As Madison put it, one should contrive ". . . the interior structure of government as that its several constituent parts may, by their mutual relations be the means of keeping each other in their proper places."[10]

The later version of equilibrium theory, pluralism, is heavily indebted to Madison for its basic outlook. With the help of like-minded men, Madison designed a set of institutions which would impose a pattern of bargaining and negotiation and conflict management on the working arrangements of American politics, that is, entrepreneurial group leaders dealing with other entrepreneurial group leaders in the coin of self-interest. However, pluralism asserts that it is the composition of social forces that produces the equilibrium desired by Madison, rather than the institutional design upon which he placed his major stress.[11] It argues that political resources such as money, organizational skills, education, office, numbers, access, and cohesion are distributed noncumulatively within society so that no one group can pyramid them. As a consequence, no one group can dominate the others, and all groups have an opportunity to enter into the negotiation process by which public goods are distributed at some point in the political process. Moreover, it is sometimes asserted that the historical evolution of America is toward an increasingly even distribution of status, skill, and wealth.[12] Thus the goal of stability and balance flowing from the self-interested activities of individuals and groups, so much desired by Madison, will be more perfectly realized in our own day than in the beginning of the republic.

The idea that political equality is growing apace has been widely attacked, forcing a retreat to the more defensible position that stability, at least, is the product of social and political arrangements. This emphasis on stability derived from conflict management distinguishes equilibrium theory from reform interpretations. For the equilibrists, American politics is not the march of progressive majorities behind heroic presidential leaders. Nor is it the imposition of an ideal pattern on human existence by an aristocracy of the robe. The two versions of equilibrium theory differ on whether stability is the product of institutional design or the distribution of political resources or some combination of the two. But governmental stability is their highest political value, and this is achieved through the working arrangements of the constitutional system.

Pluralism is an advance over reform interpretations because the idea that American politics involves group conflict seems to fit the facts better than the notion of the steady march of progressive majorities or rule by an aristocracy of the robe. In the pluralist view the decisions made by an electoral majority (of candidates, issues, and parties) are set within a framework of alternatives in which active and influential groups have a critical, though not decisive, role. The electoral majority has the power of decision. But to an extent that would have pleased Madison enormously, American politics is a system of "minorities rule."[13] The majority reigns but does not rule because the process of group politics governs the framework within which its decisions are made.

Pluralism insists, correctly, that the Supreme Court is also embedded in the patterns of group politics. Although the Court speaks last in the ordinary process of making law, still it must reach an accommodation with any coalition of groups that has captured the presidency and one or both chambers of Congress (Chapter 11) because they share in the judicial power through appointment and confirmation of new justices. Therefore, the judicial process limits the access of groups to the Court, but judicial policymaking is not removed from the patterns of group conflict and compromise.[14]

Despite its clear advance over reform interpretations of American constitutionalism, there is much that is unreal about the pluralist outlook. It does not take into account the favored position of corporate capital in the state (Chapters 5, 6, 9) nor the intentional structure of the ruthless, possessive individualists who power the political process (Chapters 3 and 4). The favored position of both corporate capital and ruthless individualism points to destabilizing features inherent in the working arrangements of American politics. Pluralism cannot absorb these elements into its analysis without impairing its image of the political process as a self-correcting, equilibriating mechanism. Pluralism believes that social process is an all-competent, self-adjusting machine which overcomes destabilizing elements such as individual rapacity or cumulative social inequalities, all independent of human agency. In short, it encourages a complacent image of social process which is at considerable variance with reality.

Although the ruthless individualism of Madison's politics is apparently elided by the pluralist emphasis on "group" conflict, one learns that the goals and conduct of politics remain highly private. For example, each individual in the political process, whether cabinet officials, committee chairmen, party whips, mayors, governors, or the chief executive, is isolated by unique constellations of interests. This field of interests, swirling about each individual in a diverse pattern, variably affects *his* "frame of reference," *his* tenure in office, and the pursuit of *his* immediate aims.[15] Thus, it is clear that each interest group is really composed of the intersection of interests of independently situated actors, each of whom has an overriding loyalty, in the end, only to himself. In short, the "groups" that the pluralists talk about are really individuals aggregated behind political entrepreneurs; and thus the dominant pattern of American politics is not group conflict and compromise, as the pluralists would have us believe, but the politicized battle of each against every other, as visualized by Hobbes, Locke, and Madison.

This politicized battle is clearly displayed in several of the major trends identified in this book: the tendency to form independent candidate organizations at every level; the devolution of power in Congress from committee chairmen to subcommittee chairmen; and the adversary relationships among a president, his cabinet staff, and nominal party allies in the Senate and House. Above all, Watergate revealed the presence of an intense, interpersonal struggle beneath the bland and tranquil patterns of pluralist politics. Various theories have been propounded to show Watergate as an aberration. These theories focus on the enormous sums accumulated by CREEP, the augmented powers of the modern presidency, the political inexperience of the president's White House staff, and the unusual effort to politicize sensitive governmental units (IRS and CIA).

However, Watergate is the norm and not the exceptional case, and the wonder is why it does not happen more often. It was precisely for ruthless, possessive individuals such as the former president, whom Madison anticipated would be coming, that drastically negative features were built into our institutions. Madison clearly assumed that each individual would use the power of the state to support his individual interests and those of supporting clienteles. He used "ambition . . . to counter-act ambition" and the opposition of interests to "remedy the defect of better motives."[16] Madison set the wolves to guard each other, and institutions of the sort that he designed engender the atmosphere of secrecy and suspicion that characterized the Nixon years in office.

The paranoiac vision which controlled the mind of the president and his aides is hinted at by John Dean, the president's personal attorney, in testimony before the Senate Investigating Committee on June 25, 1973:

> The Watergate matter was an inevitable outgrowth of an excessive concern over the political impact of demonstrators, excessive concern over leaks, an insatiable appetite for political intelligence, all coupled with a do-it-yourself White House staff, regardless of the law.[17]

Dean might have added that the president believed that his enemies, both without and within the executive branch, were led in some vague and imponderable way by the "Eastern liberal press," a term that refers more to a state of mind than a region of the country. It includes not only CBS News, the *Washington Post,* and *The New York Times* but also the *St. Louis Post Dispatch,* the *Boston Globe,* and the *Chicago Sun Times.* [18] Confronted with these adversaries in the politicized war of each against every other, why not launch a preemptive strike and "regain the offensive," as the president was fond of saying?

As the story of the invasion of the Democratic national party headquarters began to be pieced together, the politicized battle against those outside the precinct of the White House turned inward. The members of Nixon's White House staff, Ehrlichman, Haldeman, Dean, Mitchell, Colson, and so on, competed among themselves to "stonewall" or "sell out" to the attorney general's office or to the Senate Investigating Committee, depending on where their fortunes lay at the moment. Leading the pack was the president himself who, in the final months, conjured up the vision of a shoot-out on the White House lawn over the release of the incriminating tapes.

The destabilizing effects of Watergate show up in a poll taken in late 1973. The public was asked whether it had more or less confidence in the three levels of government than it had in the previous five years. Confidence in all three levels of government declined more than it rose, but the proportion of the population which reported a decline in confidence in the federal government (57 percent) was higher than those for state (26 percent) or local (30 percent) government. Corroborating these judgments, only 11 percent and 14 percent, respectively, thought that state and local governments had made their lives worse in the past few years; 27 percent and 28 percent thought it had improved their lives. In contrast, only 23 percent of the population thought the federal government had improved their lives, whereas a whopping 37 percent thought it made their lives worse. [19]

Although the effect of Watergate on the political system was destabilizing, it did not present a challenge to principles on which authority has traditionally been constituted. Senator Hugh Scott, as we pointed out in Chapter 9, wrote a letter to James Madison in which he acknowledged the efficacy of the system in correcting its own worst tendencies. "It worked," he stated simply. Others have argued that Nixon was the "last liberal," and that far from seeking to overturn the political system, he was fanatically committed to its central beliefs. [20] On the whole, Watergate provides evidence of the self-correcting features of the Madisonian constitutional system. The same reflections may not hold good for corporate capital, which has broken loose from the restrictions Madison placed on the capture of state power. Its new position in relation to the state may be destabilizing and also contain the seeds of political crisis. Unlike the ruthless individuals involved in the Watergate caper, corporate capital may present a challenge to the principles on which authority in a liberal democratic society has traditionally been constituted.

Pluralists assert that it is difficult to muster evidence proving the existence of a determinate group, such as corporate capital, which regularly prevails throughout a range of public issues. They affirm that a thorough investigation tends to show that in all cases where there is an observable conflict of issues, the prevailing group varies with the issue under study. Thus, no one determinate group prevails throughout public policy, but rather a plurality of groups prevails on selected issues.

To offer an illustration of this view, the groups sustaining Kennedy and the New Frontier in power varied with the political arena in which the candidate and his programs were being tested. Kennedy obtained one coalition of support, the regular party leadership of the Democratic party, to prevail over his rivals for the nomination; he obtained the assistance of another coalition, the legendary "fat cats" of the Democratic party, to obtain the financial support needed for the general election; and he needed the assistance of a third coalition, the Washington establishment, to help him in running the country (Chapter 4). The group or coalition of groups which prevailed in each case varied with the contest, thus tending to disprove the existence of a determinate group that pyramids social, economic, and political resources and regularly prevails in many issues.

In contrast, we should remember that privileged groups, even though seemingly unrelated, have shown a remarkable capacity for moving in a uniform direction against the modest claims of submerged groups. A well-known study of the politics of Newark, for example, employs the same model of analysis as the pluralists—that is, group conflict over a number of observable issues—but finds that a substantial low-income black population is routinely dealt with on a manipulative basis by a plurality of political actors.[21] Realty investors, the mayor, the members of the City Council, the transit authority, the courts, the police, and the political machines showed an extraordinary degree of unity in resisting modest claims voiced by black spokesmen for inspection of rental units and a new traffic light. Looked at from the bottom, pluralism may well resemble a single determinate group which regularly prevails.

Second, by narrowly defining the exercise of power, pluralists eliminate from consideration events that tend to disprove their interpretation of American politics. They insist that the only occasion in which power is exercised is when there is an observable conflict on the issues, A wanting policy X and B wanting policy Y, with A or B prevailing to the extent that the other party accepts a preferred alternative. But *A* may prevail, unresisted by *B,* by so arranging the structure of public preferences that *B* can always be assured of wanting policy *X.* In this case, an observable conflict is eliminated, but I do not believe that any one would say that *A* has not exercised power over *B.* It is a far more significant exercise of power to shape the criteria of interest than to prevail in an observable conflict.[22] Therefore, pluralism defines the exercise of power in a narrow and misleading way.

To offer an illustration of this exercise of power, remember that the triumvirate of General Motors, Firestone, and Standard Oil deflected the entire course of urban mass transit by convincing local officials that "progress" was allied with conversion from trolley cars to diesel buses. Only in retrospect has this conversion been called into question as the cities, fouled by exhaust fumes, faced with the mounting expense of oil products, and beset by the problems of traffic congestion, have tried to restore a failing rail transit system or to undertake the costly expense of building a new one (Chapter 5). Although it is now too late to fight the policy covertly pursued—after all it is now some thirty to forty years after the fact, and the conversion to diesel buses would cost millions to reverse—I do not believe that anyone would say that the corporate triumvirate failed to exercise power.

Parallel to this success of the automobile-oil-tire combine in the local arena is that of nearly identical groups in influencing the national energy policy. The law of anticipated reactions offers a probable and partial explanation of why funding for mass transit was not included among the conservationist measures of the National Energy Plan (Chapter 5). In an observable conflict of issues the president did not want to confront two sets of oligopolistic interests, the automobile-highway-tire complex and the oil and gas producers, refiners, and shippers, at one and the same time. Another part of the explanation for the president's reluctance is that he did not want to confront the well-known structure of preferences of the American public concerning transportation. Jefferson's and Locke's language about the "pursuit of happiness" has been transmuted over time, with the assistance of the automobile and advertising industries, into an inalienable right to two cars in the suburbs and an expressway to one's place of work (Chapter 6). No president, even one who would rather "be right than be president," could hope to prevail in this situation. Thus although there is no record of an observable conflict on funding for mass transit in the passage of the National Energy Plan, one cannot say that significant power has not been exercised.

Another way in which corporate power can triumph, without the fuss of a public conflict over issues, is simply by withholding resources.

A leading case in point, although many other examples could be cited, is U.S. Steel in Gary, Indiana. By "doing nothing," U.S. Steel was able to evade responsibility for adverse events—pollution, suburban flight, urban deterioration—which were the product of a single-minded devotion to higher profits (Chapter 5). The costs of its policies were passed on to the community, and efforts to get the company to recognize and respond to the adverse effects did not bear fruit. In a similar fashion, banks and insurance companies have been able to chart the course of residential development for whole cities simply by withholding funds from neighborhoods considered to be in decline and deflecting resources elsewhere, primarily to suburban and condominium housing. Even though there is little public debate over these policies, and hence no observable conflict on the issues, one would not say that power has not been exercised.

If we put these elements together—the manner in which a plurality of actors can move in a uniform direction, the exercise of power by shaping the structure of public preferences, and the exercise of power by withholding resources—we can see that corporate capital generally, and oligopoly in particular, exerts an enormous influence on public policy and has a destabilizing effect on the distribution of resources within the political system. The automobile-highway-tire–oil complex is one of the better examples of a plurality of actors who have moved in a uniform direction over a period of time to shape public policy, covertly by influencing the criteria of interest and withholding resources and overtly by prevailing over other groups on contested issues. This dominance has been as characteristic in state and local arenas of political action as in the national arena. When we look at the activity of particular departments of the federal executive branch, for example, transportation, defense, and energy, we do see something like a pyramid of political and economic resources (Chapter 10). Additionally, corporate capital has had great success in using the state as an instrument for the accumulation of capital resources. A fiscal crisis of the state may arise from its conflicting requirement to underwrite the capital expenses of corporate enterprise at the same time that it legitimizes itself to state and local communities and to social and welfare groups through a proper allocation of federal resources.[23]

Pluralism is an advance on reform interpretations of American politics in that it points to the conflict-management and bargaining aspect of our political arrangements. But it fails to consider that a determinate group, corporate capital, may be the chief beneficiary of these arrangements, and it is blind to the intentional structure of the actors who sustain them. Pluralism's incapacity to deal with these elements of the real world suggests that we press this inquiry into the nature of the constitutional system to still another level of analysis by taking up, finally, crisis theories of American politics.

THE CONSTITUTIONAL SYSTEM: IN CRISIS

To sum up the discussion to the present stage, let us review the major conclusions of the reform and equilibrium theories. The reform, progressive view of American politics teaches us to regard constitutional constraints as *desirable*. Ideal purposes, such as an ideal pattern of law drafted by the judiciary or the onward march of progressive majorities, are ascribed to the constitutional system; and the written Constitution is seen as a broadly enabling document which shapes the patterns of politics in a desirable manner. When problems arise in the political system, they can be resolved by reforming the party system, the internal structure of power in Congress, or the judicial process, so that the ideal purposes which inspired the nation at its founding can resume their effective operation.

Equilibrist theory maintains an ambiguous attitude toward problems that arise. Inequities are granted. Strategically located groups have more of an impact on the decision-making process than the electorate. But these minorities are indirectly influenced by mass preferences at the same time that they compete to shape them. Power is distributed non-cumulatively among these minorities so that no one group can exclude a rival from the competition for votes and political resources. The stability of the American political system is taken as evidence that it mirrors the enthusiasms of the people and a fair distribution of power. Since the working arrangements of American politics reflect an acceptable balance of social forces, any constraints that may accompany them are viewed as *necessary*. By definition, the political system is a self-equilibriating mechanism beyond the wit of human agency to improve. What should be done about such problems as the nation confronts, therefore, is to scale down our expectations regarding their solution.

These leading and widely accepted interpretations of American politics remove the possibility and desirability of significant political change. Crisis theory, however, presents a view that is just the reverse. Arising out of a dissatisfaction with political arrangements, it argues for the desirability and necessity of significant political change. Contrasting squarely with the equilibrists, the two variants of crisis theory, power elitism[24] and class domination,[25] assert that the liberal democratic state is unable to maintain a position of neutrality in the management of social conflict. This assertion rests on the judgment that countervailing power cannot assure relative parity of political resources or an observable conflict on the issues. A plurality of influential actors may move in a uniform direction to exclude significant items from the political agenda; countervailing power often does not exist in local political arenas; through advertising and technology, the public structure of preferences may be determined in advance of an observable conflict; and even where there is an observable conflict, oligopoly may prevail through superior resources and organization.

Power elite theory is primarily concerned with the manner in which the agenda of democratic discussion is visibly, and more often invisibly, constrained by specific actors in the political system. Believing that the boundaries of political conflict are much more tightly drawn than is commonly realized, it hypothesizes that the political issues which lie outside the normal scope of conflict and decision making are more significant, politically, than those which lie within it.[26] At the bottom of such a working hypothesis lies, of course, a belief that a determinate group or groups, a power elite, reach a tacit understanding on a political agenda which will preserve their own secure place within the prevailing distribution of power.

This theory urges widening the scope of political conflict to include issues and groups normally excluded from the political process, even at the risk of destabilizing the system. Indeed, its assertion that those issues that lie outside the normal scope of discussion and decision making are more significant, politically, strongly implies that the political system needs destabilizing. The governing concern of power elite theory is that issues of critical importance to the public are systematically shunted aside by the working arrangements of American politics.

Seeds of power elitism may be found in the biases of the Madisonian constitutional system. Madison sought to narrow the boundaries of political conflict, excluding issues of representation, status of the blacks, and property redistribution from the political agenda, and he sought to maintain the superiority of privileged groups in the outcome of social conflict. The constitutional system preserves a bias against democratic participation which is maintained to this day by the arrangements of decentralized cadre parties and by the role of power brokers in city politics (Chapters 4 and 12). The cadre leadership of the political parties fulfills the role of power brokers created by Madison's arrangements. It ensures that difficult issues do not gain entry to the political agenda, a function which serves to keep the electorate apathetic and uninformed. Power brokers in urban politics make critical decisions concerning the course of development and renewal with modest public input. In the eighteenth century, Madison and his peers showed that a plurality of influential actors could move in a uniform direction against submerged groups. Similar tendencies are observable among elites at every governmental level in the twentieth century.

The theory of class domination differs from that of power elitism in focusing primarily on the distribution of economic resources rather than elite restriction of the political agenda. The former holds that social inequality arises out of the relationships of production of capitalism. This inequality is extremely harmful not only because of deprivation but also because it frustrates the development of human potential. Embittered individuals such as Mike Lefevre, the steelworker from Cicero, Illinois, remind us that capitalism fails to nurture human growth (Chapter 6). Both variants of crisis theory point out that the uneven distribution of wealth limits the capacity of groups and individuals to mount a contest over the issues.

A leading critical thrust of this outlook concerns the modern roles of the state and corporate industry. Class domination theory shows that the main function of the modern state is to underwrite the capital expenses (physical, human, and financial) and to defray the social costs (in terms of environmental damage, employee security, health, and safety) of modern corporate capital. The favored position of corporate capital in the state upsets the relative equality among social groups, also dependent on the services and resources of the state, and creates a deficit in legitimacy among the groups who are disadvantaged. The use of the state as an instrument of capital accumulation dries up resources which might otherwise be available to state and local communities, welfare services, and competitive capital. Fiscal crisis is pleaded as the reason for phasing out or reducing grants-in-aid directed to health, nutrition, transportation, and educational programs. The contribution corporate capital makes to the current fiscal crisis is unnoticed because the benefits are less visible. Thus, the practice of socialized productive activity continues unabated even though the taxpayer must foot the bill for it too.[27]

Liberalism helps class interests disguise the new situation, enabling political elites to prescribe capitalism for competitive capital, to socialize the costs of the rich through subsidies and tax write-offs, and to give the poor short shrift. The period of fiscal crisis into which the nation has entered has much to do with the popularity of liberal themes in the Reagan administration. The solvency of corporate capital is made to appear a matter of holy reform. Competitive capital, the supposed beneficiary of the policies of the Reagan administration, is as much disadvantaged in the new situation as any other group. Unlike corporate capital, it lacks the capacity to control its prices and costs, to manipulate the tastes of its consumers through advertising, to supply itself with capital from its earnings, or to prevail in the political arena. None of these handicapping conditions is altered by the policies of the current administration. Insofar as interest rates continue at record levels, competitive capital is no better off than before, and probably worse.

Another negative function performed by liberal ideology is to block a solution to the predicament of capitalism. Since the modern corporation destroys the arrangements that make capitalism possible, socialism becomes a reasonable alternative for the near future. Socializing the uses of capital would help to resolve the contradiction between private appropriation of profits and state subsidies. Let us take, for example, the situation of Chrysler Corporation. Since the state already participates in the capital structure of Chrysler by providing loans to meet operating expenses, it might as well use its influence to induce the firm to market a better product at cheaper cost. Since the United Auto Workers contribute human capital to this enterprise, it, too, deserves a seat in the board room. State and labor participation in the management of private industry would extend democracy to a hitherto neglected area of public concern. Unquestionably, it would start America on the path toward socialist democracy, but it would have the virtue of saving the capitalist system from its own excesses. The liberal ideology prohibits constructive solutions such as these, removing them to a never-never land where they linger and die out of sight and out of mind.

Looking at the past, we find that the class domination view, like that of power elitism, has its roots in constitutional underpinnings. In both Madison's and Hamilton's writings the survival of the state is linked to the survival of a propertied class, which is prepared to use coercion to sustain its favored position. Madison preferred manipulative relationships and Hamilton outright coercion, but that is the only difference between them. Madison thought that institutions managing social conflicts over property would safeguard "the permanent and aggregate [property] interests of the community." Hamilton said that a "vigorous Executive" would provide for the "protection of property . . . against the enterprises and assaults of ambition, of faction, and of anarchy." In the twentieth century, as the inequalities among social groups have grown apace and as the state has fallen under the influence of corporate capital, Hamilton's attitudes have acquired new life among the political elite. President Nixon more or less openly threatened the use of coercion against groups consigned to permanent defeat by Madison's arrangements.

National energy policy illuminates the critical insight of the power elite and class domination theories. Elements of the latter are borne out not only by the profits and public influence of the oil industry but also by the tendency of public officials to pass off the burdens of conserving energy on low-income groups while leaving undisturbed the energy-intensive consumption habits of high-income groups. The Reagan administration immediately lifted price controls on all categories of crude oil, despite the shock exerted on small, independent refiners, and seeks to deregulate the price of natural gas shipped in interstate commerce before the expiration of controls in 1985. At the same time the administration wants to terminate programs designed to encourage equitable patterns of energy conservation, including energy performance standards, residential energy conservation, performance standards for household appliances, and public transit. Additionally, the abolition of low-income energy assistance programs to defray the rising cost of utility bills is urged by the administration.[28]

A considerable body of literature suggests that these policies may have a catastrophic effect on low-income groups, who allocate on the average as much as 30 percent of disposable income for household energy expenses. In some regions of the country it is more. In contrast, high-income groups allocate as little as 7 percent.[29] It follows that the consumption habits of upper-income groups will be little affected by the pricing policies of the Reagan administration, whereas the poor will be lucky to have the resources to heat their homes. Conservation programs to help close the gap would serve a logical function in this situation, but the Reagan policies help upper-income groups maintain a privileged life-style.

Lending support to the power elite outlook are the narrow boundaries within which the debate on national energy policy has been conducted. Among the proposals that have never obtained a place on the political agenda are horizontal and vertical divestiture of the oil majors, a substantial investment in mass transit funding, a decentralization of decision-making power over energy utilization and resources, a conversion to small-scale energy technologies, and an appropriately funded energy conservation program directed to all income groups. These topics are not favored by political elites because they confront a mobilization of bias in favor of production, producer interests, and a luxurious life-style.

That is not all. To divert attention from the partnership between modern oligopoly and the liberal state, the political elite provides daily assurances that we live in an eighteenth-century world of Whig gentlemen, or sometimes in a more democratic mood, a nineteenth-century world of cowboys, or still implausibly, an early twentieth-century world of venture capitalists, captains of industry, entrepreneurs, and the like. The suspicion arises that these nostalgic images are provided to disguise the partnership between modern oligopoly and the liberal state. If the public is ensnared by dreams, the subversion of arrangements intended to safeguard the liberties of independently situated actors can be accelerated. Formerly in the nation's history, the Whig liberal ideology played a creative role in social and political reality. Now, its role exhausted and superseded by different conditions, liberalism is used to manipulate public attitudes.

The burden of sustaining the credibility of political institutions in these interesting times falls to public figures. Presidents and presidential candidates have shown themselves adept in the evangelical style which is now required for the highest office in the land. As we have noted before, presidents are selected from a narrow strata of the population, representative in many ways of the Whig elites who founded America's constitutional arrangements. The physical circumstances of these candidates, Nixon on his estates in California and Florida, Carter on his peanut farm, Reagan and Johnson on their ranches in California and Texas, provide the Whig version of the independently situated political actor with many touches of verisimilitude. By contrast, the American voter, for the most part, participates in this Whig version of politics only vicariously by casting his or her ballot on election day. Such vicarious participation, as for the cigarette smoker who fantasizes that he is a cowpoke, a deep-sea diver, a lumberjack, or a mountain climber, may be diverting but not satisfying. The absence of genuine satisfaction is indicated by the droves who stay home on election day. For voters and candidates the words of a tune by the rock group the Rolling Stones seem to apply, "Baby, baby, baby, you're out of time."

NOTES

1. See James MacGregor Burns, *The Deadlock of Democracy* (Englewood Cliffs, N.J.: Prentice-Hall, 1963), and *Uncommon Sense* (New York: Harper & Row, 1972); J. Allen Smith, *The Spirit of American Government* (New York: Macmillan, 1907); Woodrow Wilson, *Congressional Government* (New York: Meridian Books, 1956); William H. Riker, *Democracy in the United States,* 2nd ed. (New York: Macmillan, 1965); Committee on Political Parties of the APSA, *Toward a More Responsible Two-Party System* (New York: Rinehart, 1950).
2. Woodrow Wilson, *Constitutional Government in the United States* (New York: Columbia University Press, 1961), pp. 60, 70.
3. Burns, *Deadlock of Democracy,* pp. 306, 307.
4. See E. S. Corwin, *The 'Higher Law' Background of American Constitutional Law* (Ithaca, N.Y.: Cornell University Press, 1955); Carl J. Friedrich, *Constitutional Government and Democracy,* 4th ed. (Waltham, Mass.: Blaisdell Publishing Co., 1968); Charles Howard McIlwain, *Constitutionalism: Ancient and Modern,* rev. ed. (Ithaca, N.Y.: Cornell University Press, 1947); Andrew C. McLaughlin, *The Foundations of American Constitutionalism* (Greenwich, Conn.: Fawcett Publications, 1961); David G. Smith, *The Convention and the Constitution* (New York: St. Martin's Press, 1965).

5. For example, see Richard E. Johnston, "Supreme Court Voting Behavior," in Robert L. Peabody, *Cases in American Politics* (New York: Praeger, 1976), pp. 71–110.

6. Learned Hand, *The Bill of Rights* (Cambridge, Mass.: Harvard University Press, 1958).

7. Kenneth M. Dolbeare and Murray J. Edelman, *American Politics: Politics, Power, and Change* (Lexington, Mass.: Heath, 1974), p. 252; H. Mark Roelofs, *Ideology and Myth in American Politics* (Boston: Little, Brown, 1976), pp. 84–92.

8. Robert A. Dahl, "Decision Making in a Democracy," *Journal of Public Law,* vol. 6 (1958), 279–95.

9. Nathan Lewin, "Avoiding the Supreme Court," *The New York Times Magazine* October 17, 1976, pp. 31, 90–100.

10. *Federalist* No. 51.

11. Robert A. Dahl, *A Preface to Democratic Theory* (Chicago: Phoenix Books; University of Chicago Press, 1963), p. 137. See also Robert A. Dahl, *Democracy in the United States,* 2nd ed. (Chicago: Rand McNally, 1973); *Who Governs?* (New Haven, Conn.: Yale University Press, 1961); George Von der Muhll, "Robert A. Dahl and the Study of Contemporary Democracy," *American Political Science Review,* vol. LXXI (September 1977), 1,070–96.

12. Dahl, *Democracy in the United States,* chap. 9.

13. Dahl, *Preface to Democratic Theory,* p. 132.

14. Dahl, "Decision Making in a Democracy."

15. David Truman, *The Governmental Process* (New York: Knopf, 1951), chap. 13.

16. *Federalist* No. 51.

17. *The New York Times,* June 25, 1973, pp. 30–35.

18. Theodore White, *The Making of the President: 1972* (New York: Bantam Books, 1973), chap. 10.

19. Louis Harris and Associates, *Confidence and Concern: Citizens View American Government* (Washington, D.C.: U.S. Senate, Committee on Government Operations, Subcommittee on Intergovernmental Relations, 93rd Congress, 1st Sess., December 3, 1973), pp. 42–43, 299.

20. Garry Wills, *Nixon Agonistes* (New York: New American Library, 1970), part 5, chap. 5.

21. Michael Parenti, "Power and Pluralism: A View from the Bottom," *Journal of Politics,* vol. 32 (August 1970).

22. Steven Lukes, *Power: A Radical View* (New York: Macmillan, 1976).

23. James O'Connor, *The Fiscal Crisis of the State* (New York: St. Martin's Press, 1973).

24. Peter Bachrach, *The Theory of Democratic Elitism* (Boston: Little, Brown, 1967); Peter Bachrach and Morton S. Baratz, "Two Faces of Power," *American Political Science Review,* vol. 56 (December 1962), 947–52; Decisions and Non-Decisions: An Analytical Framework," *American Political Science Review,* vol. 57 (September 1963), 632–42; *Power and Poverty* (New York: Oxford University Press, 1970); Michael Parenti, *Democracy for the Few* (New York: St. Martin's Press, 1977); G. William Domhoff and Hoyt B. Ballard, eds., *C. Wright Mills and the Power Elite* (Boston: Beacon Press, 1969).

25. O'Connor, *Fiscal Crisis of the State;* Douglas F. Dowd, *The Twisted Dream* (Cambridge, Mass.: Winthrop Publishers, 1974); Ralph Milliband, *The State in Capitalist Society* (New York: Basic Books, 1969); Paul M. Sweezy, *Modern Capitalism and Other Essays* (New York: Monthly Review Press, 1972); William K. Tabb, *The Political Economy of the Black Ghetto* (New York: W. W. Norton, 1970); Phillip Brenner, Robert Borosage, Bethany Weidner, eds., *Exploring Contradictions* (New York: David McKay, 1974); Ira Katznelson and Mark Kesselman, *The Politics of Power* (New York: Harcourt Brace Jovanovich, 1975).

26. Bachrach and Baratz, *Power and Poverty,* chap. 3.

27. O'Connor, *Fiscal Crisis.*

28. *The New York Times,* November 26, 1980, D6; *The New York Times,* February 20, 1981, A12; *The New York Times,* February 23, 1981, D3.

29. John L. Palmer *et al.,* "The Distributional Impact of Rising Energy Prices" (Washington, D.C.: Brookings Reprint No. 331, 1978); Task Force on the Distributive Impacts of Budget and Economic Policies (Washington, D.C.: U.S. Government Printing Office, 1977); Fuel Oil Marketing Advisory Committee of the Department of Energy, *Low-Income Energy Assistance Programs,* July 1980.

Index